THE BIRDS OF TEXAS

THE

BIRDS OF TEXAS

by John L. Tveten

SHEARER PUBLISHING
FREDERICKSBURG, TEXAS

To Gloria, for whom the birds sing

Western meadowlark (page 1). Vesper sparrow (pages 2-3). Male bobolink (above).

Library of Congress Cataloging-in-Publication Data

Tveten, John L., 1934–
The birds of Texas / John L. Tveten
p.   cm.
Includes bibliographical references (p. 384) and index.
ISBN 0-940672-62-6—ISBN 0-940672-63-4 (pbk.)
1. Birds—Texas.   2. Birds—Texas—Identification.
3. Birds—Texas—Pictorial works.   I. Title
QL684.T4T93 1993
598.29764—dc20   93-17445
                                        CIP

Published in 1993 by
Shearer Publishing
406 Post Oak Road
Fredericksburg, Texas 78624

Printed in Hong Kong

CONTENTS

Snowy egret near its nest in a willow tree.

PHOTOGRAPHIC CREDITS

Photographs appearing in this book other than those taken by the author include the following:

John Baird 10, 297; **R. A. Behrstock/VIREO** 13, 68, 121, 270; **Steve Bentsen** 131 (lower), 151, 155, 158, 162 (upper), 163, 164, 189, 195, 203, 207, 210, 211 (right), 220, 232, 236, 238, 245 (lower), 246, 248, 272, 327 (lower), 346, 355 (lower); **Larry R. Ditto** 4, 17, 37, 43, 46 (lower), 47, 50-51, 54, 56, 69, 82, 83, 89 (lower), 91 (lower), 105 (upper), 109 (upper), 145, 146, 159, 183, 202, 235, 259, 287, 319, 326, 331; **Ted L. Eubanks** 126, 128, 137; **Barbara P. Grove** 181; **Vernon Eugene Grove Jr.** 12, 35, 62, 64, 144 (lower), 153, 336, 353; **Greg W. Lasley** 53, 65, 91 (upper), 135 (lower), 138 (upper), 193, 233, 260, 279, 286, 305, 306; **Gail Diane Luckner** 157; **Maslowski Photo** 25, 27, 70, 129 (lower), 149 (upper), 161, 227, 254, 258, 269, 273, 274, 276, 280, 282, 283, 288, 289, 290, 307, 315, 317, 321, 322, 328, 337, 347, 350 (lower), 356, 360, 361, 362, 368; **Wyman Meinzer** 180 (lower), 186, 188, 264, 293, 298; **Jim Morgan** 247 (upper), 277 (lower); **Natural PhoTex** 223; **David J. Sams** 49, 86, 99, 138 (lower), 147, 178-79, 196 (lower), 199, 243, 265; **Jeffrey G. Schultz** 165; **Tom J. Ulrich** 28-29, 142-43, 149 (lower), 212-13, 215, 216, 241, 301, 309, 320, 324, 348, 369 (lower); **Luke Wade** 34 (upper), 72, 184, 204-5, 209, 211 (left); **Tom C. Winn** 74-75; **Barry R. Zimmer** 26.

PREFACE

I no longer consider the study of nature and its creatures a pleasant pastime; through the years it has become an all-consuming passion. To keep me occupied for hours when I was a very young child, my parents had only to give me a jar and send me off to collect insects. To their credit, they indulged and even encouraged these pursuits, showing interest in every spider, snake or turtle that I discovered and invariably hauled home.

Birds were less accessible and more difficult to observe, but a fascination with them was inevitable. Their myriad colors, their power of flight, their sheer vitality make them the envy of any small boy trying his own fledgling wings. To watch an osprey drop from the sky and catch a fish in its flashing talons, to meet an owl face to face in the night woods—those are the experiences that shape a lifetime of outdoor interests.

I did not become a dedicated bird watcher, however, until I moved to Texas more than 30 years ago. I was interested, and I carried binoculars and a bird book on vacation trips, but there was not yet the lure of the list. All of the sparrows were simply "sparrows," and all of the shorebirds were generic "sandpipers." They all looked discouragingly alike.

The incubation period ended, and the birding disease really hit, during a hot week in August in the Rio Grande Valley. My wife, Gloria, and I were visiting South Padre Island for the first time and happened to pick up a brochure on Santa Ana National Wildlife Refuge. We drove over to take a look and, completely enthralled, returned again the following day, in spite of the 107-degree heat. Next we found nearby Laguna Atascosa National Wildlife Refuge, where I lay in the back of our station wagon and tried to identify shorebirds with an old-fashioned telescope propped on the window. We were stricken forever and have become lifelong carriers of birding fever.

It was easy to become enamored of such strange and colorful birds as the green jay and the chachalaca. We watched an Altamira oriole (then called Lichtenstein's oriole) on its hanging nest of Spanish moss. We must certainly be among the very few North American birders who put groove-billed anis and kiskadees on their life lists before blue jays and robins.

After that fateful week, our vacations revolved around finding new birds, and birding side trips made business travel more palatable. We returned to the Rio Grande Valley many times to seek out the region's exotic wildlife, and we covered Texas from the coastal beaches to the Guadalupe Mountains and from the northern Panhandle to Big Bend in search of the state's avian bounty.

As our life lists grew longer, and finding new species became less likely, I began photographing birds, a challenging hobby to which there is no end. Later, I acquired the federal and state permits necessary to band birds and to rehabilitate injured and orphaned ones. These pursuits gave me a chance to work more closely with wildlife and to get to know birds as individuals.

Ultimately, I left a career as a research organic chemist to concentrate on a new life with nature. I photograph and write about wildlife not because I particularly like the disciplines of photography or writing, but because I love the subjects.

Modern bird watchers now like to call themselves "birders." There is a competitive aspect to their pursuit, and they travel widely to add new species to their ever-expanding lists. I, however, remain a "bird watcher" in the literal sense of the term. I am just as excited as the next birder if I come across a rare and unusual bird; but I also enjoy seeing common birds doing uncommon things, or just going about the business of being birds uncommonly well. That is the essence of this book.

ACKNOWLEDGMENTS

This book is the result of many years of living with and loving birds. It could not have been written alone, for family and friends have shared the experiences and the joys of discovering each and every species.

I am particularly indebted to the contributing photographers, who made their work available for publication. Each has spent long hours in the field to capture our wild birds at their best, and their efforts and talents are greatly appreciated.

Members of the Ornithology Group of the Houston Outdoor Nature Club began the incubation of this fledgling birder more than thirty years ago, and their unfailing enthusiasm and knowledge remain an inspiration today. My thanks to Randy Beavers and Carl Aiken, with whom I have shared so many birding trips and discussions, and to Jim Morgan and Ted Eubanks, to whom I turn with ornithological questions.

I must acknowledge the personnel of the state and federal parks and wildlife refuges, where many of my photographs were taken. They have been of enormous help during years of birding and photography across the state of Texas.

Finally, I will always be indebted to William Shearer, who conceived this project and made it possible; to editor Jean Hardy, who understood what I wanted to say and helped me say it better; and to Barbara Jezek for her sensitive layout and design. I have enjoyed my experiences with the birds, but these people helped turn those experiences into this book.

This book is dedicated to the appreciation, understanding and enjoyment of Texas birds. I hope it will also serve the reader in identifying most of the birds seen in Texas and elsewhere across the country. It is not encyclopedic in its coverage, however, nor is it intended to replace the standard field guides. The latter attempt to include all species, no matter how rare or difficult to find, sacrificing to some extent the "personality" of birds for completeness. This book portrays, in color photos and a more detailed text, the beauty and vitality of birds that the average Texas resident or traveler is most likely to encounter.

The book treats about half of all the state's bird species in detail, and mentions many others briefly. I have given preference to the most abundant and widespread, as well as to those that are large, colorful or easily seen. The casual observer is more likely to notice a large heron or pelican than some of the shy little sparrows, even though the sparrows may actually occur in greater numbers. Likewise, a brilliant tanager or oriole attracts more attention than a wandering sandpiper.

The reader will find representatives of most bird families, and individual accounts illustrate the wide variety of Texas birdlife and the dramatic differences in their habits. Introductory sections summarize the distinctive features of each family and the number and status of its members. Special attention is given to threatened species and to the relationships of birds to their overall environment.

TEXAS BIRDLIFE

Diversity

Texas can boast of having more bird species—nearly 600—than any other state or province in North America, according to the American Birding Association. California runs a close second, and both states add new vagrants to their lists yearly. Arizona, Florida and New Mexico round out the top five, well behind the two leaders.

Some birds sighted in Texas occur nowhere else in the nation, and bird watchers from around the world flock to see them. The Rio Grande Valley is home to colorful green jays, Altamira orioles and raucous, pheasant-sized chachalacas. Visitors to the Hill Country search for the endangered golden-cheeked warbler and black-capped vireo, while others comb the East Texas Piney Woods for the red-cockaded woodpecker and brown-headed nuthatch.

The Texas Gulf Coast harbors roseate spoonbills, with their bizarre spatulate beaks, and reddish egrets that prance about in the surf in search of small fish and

Greater roadrunner.

crustaceans. Magnificent frigatebirds sail over the bays and beaches on seven-foot wings, while dapper black skimmers fly along just above the waves, cutting the water with razor-edged beaks. Aransas National Wildlife Refuge on the central coast is the winter home of the endangered whooping cranes, the tallest birds in North America.

So popular is Texas among birders that coastal "hot spots" and little communities along the Rio Grande have become world-famous. High Island, Rockport, Salineno and San Ygnacio are household names, at least among the field-glass fraternity.

The Christmas Bird Count, the annual winter census sponsored by the National Audubon Society, also reflects the enormous number of Texas birds. Freeport boasts the all-time count record of 226 species, all seen in a single day within a 15-mile-diameter circle. That record was set in 1971 and equaled in 1989. During the intervening years, Freeport ranked no lower than second in North America. And all that in competition with 1,500 other bird counts by up to 42,000 observers across the continent.

The sheer size of Texas, 275,416 square miles, contributes to the biological diversity. Size alone, however, does not explain it. Alaska, although larger, has 150 fewer species, even though it is the only state to record many of the Asian strays. In general, biological diversity increases as one moves toward the tropics; the five leading bird states all lie along the southern edge of the country.

Not only do many warm-weather species nest in Texas, but northern ones also pass through on their long migration flights. Many, like their human counterparts, remain for the winter. Thus, when autumn approaches and some birds leave for Central and South America, others arrive to take their places. Even the hardiest birds from the far North turn up occasionally when ice and snow make food impossible to find at higher latitudes. Texas birds change with the seasons, but they are always plentiful at any time of year.

Canada geese.

Habitats

Every Texan knows the feisty mockingbird, the flamboyant cardinal and the unassuming mourning dove. They, and many others, occur virtually throughout the state at every season of the year. Other birds, however, seek out areas that fit their special needs.

Biologically speaking, East meets West along a broad front running down the middle of Texas— through Dallas and Fort Worth, Waco, Austin, San Antonio and the lower Rio Grande Valley. East of that line, you find birds typical of the southeastern U.S. and northward to Minnesota and Maine. They are adapted to life in forests, rich blackland prairies and the coastal plain. West of the line, the birds are more characteristic of Mexico, New Mexico and Arizona, and the migrants may be Rocky Mountain species. They, in turn, are at home in a more arid climate and in the limestone hills and rugged mountain ranges.

The blue jay, for example, resides in woodlands and parks and along tree-lined city streets in the eastern half of Texas. In West Texas, it gives way to others like the scrub, gray-breasted and Steller's jays. Eastern and western kingbirds are similarly limited in their ranges, as are the brown thrasher, which nests in the thickets of East Texas, and the curve-billed thrasher of the brush country and deserts. The brilliant scarlet tanager and the equally lovely western tanager take separate migration routes through the state, and the list goes on and on.

Overlap occurs, of course, and strays often turn up to delight the ardent birder. Western species wander to the coast, and eastern birds are frequently spotted in the West. As birders are fond of saying, "Birds have wings, and they don't read the books."

Other influences further complicate this east/west dichotomy. Mexican birds inhabit the Rio Grande Valley, while Great Plains species are perfectly at home in the grasslands of the Panhandle. Severe winter storms drive down birds from the Arctic, and West Indian species are sometimes caught up in hurricanes over the Caribbean and deposited on Texas shores. The search for the new and unexpected gives the sport of birding an endless and lifelong appeal.

Even within their broad ranges, some birds occupy very specific habitats. As Roger Tory Peterson so nicely phrases it in his *Field Guide to the Birds of Texas*, "One looks for meadowlarks in meadows, wood thrushes in woods." Grassland birds may even select homes in grass of a particular species and height, to the exclusion of others. Mountain birds prefer rocky slopes and cliffs at specific elevations. Learning these preferences can greatly aid both the novice and the experienced birder in finding and identifying new species.

The Changing Scene

While some birds are declining seriously in number, others are increasing or expanding their ranges across Texas. Bird populations change dramatically in response to habitat alterations. Interactions among the various species and predator-prey relationships also lead to fluctuations in the relative abundance of birds and other wildlife.

A red-tailed hawk surveys West Texas from a sotol stalk.

The friendly little Inca dove, for example, gradually worked its way northward from deep South Texas and Mexico as settlers and ranchers cleared the land. The birds first moved up through the Hill Country, then continued farther east to reach the coast. They are now abundant in Houston, where they were virtually unknown 25 years ago.

The familiar American robin is primarily a winter resident in Texas and formerly nested only in the wooded eastern quarter of the state. As an increase in tree planting and lawn sprinkling in Texas communities provided sites

Shorebirds, gulls, terns and skimmers at Bolivar Flats on the Texas coast.

and mud for nest construction, breeding increased in North Texas and spread as far south as Corpus Christi.

Cliff swallows, which historically built their mud-jug nests in rocky crevices and under overhanging ledges, now use bridges and culverts as well, enabling them to spread across the prairies. Purple martins, too, have profited from artificial nesting sites. They formerly used hollow trees. Now bird lovers provide them with fancy store-bought apartments and condominiums, and no self-respecting martin would choose to live in an old tree.

Some birds have been introduced to Texas from other countries, either deliberately or accidentally. Ringed turtle-doves and monk parakeets have established colonies in various parts of the state after escaping from captivity. Ring-necked pheasants, originally native to Asia, have been released repeatedly on coastal prairies and in the Panhandle to provide hunters with another game bird.

Among the most notorious introduced species are the European starling, house sparrow and rock dove (the domestic pigeon). Brought to the East Coast from Europe, all three have spread uncontrollably across the land, becoming nuisance species in the cities and competing with native birds for food and nesting space.

Another successful colonizer of Texas, the cattle egret, apparently reached the New World from Africa on the wings of the wind. First establishing colonies in South America, it was discovered in the

Tricolored heron chick and eggs.

United States in 1952 and in Texas about 1955. Now, large flocks can be seen in pastures and along our roadways, where they feed on insects chased up by cattle and by mowers, much as they forage behind wild game herds in their native Africa.

Balancing these success stories is the serious decline of other species. A few have vanished forever in the face of human advancement and the resulting environmental change. In the mid-19th century, passenger pigeons migrated through Texas in enormous flocks. One such flock in Washington County in 1853 was described as requiring three days to pass overhead. Roosting trees toppled from the weight of the masses, and hunters camped near those roosts to kill thousands of the tasty birds with guns and clubs. By the turn of the century, the passenger pigeon had vanished from Texas. Soon after that, it was extinct.

The huge ivory-billed woodpecker, once common in the bottomland swamps of the Big Thicket, has apparently joined the passenger pigeon. Unlike the slightly smaller pileated woodpecker with its more cosmopolitan feeding habits, the ivory-bill could not adjust to the loss of large timbered tracts.

Attwater's prairie-chicken is severely endangered, in large part because of the loss of virgin coastal prairie. The tiny piping plover found on our state's beaches is likewise threatened. Such stories have no taxonomic or geographic bounds. The interior least tern found along the Red River, the red-cockaded woodpecker of the Piney Woods, the black-capped vireo and the golden-cheeked warbler of the Edwards Plateau—all are threatened, primarily because their native habitats are being destroyed.

The picture is not entirely bleak, however. The whooping crane flock that returns to Texas every winter numbered more than 130 birds at the beginning of this decade, a remarkable increase from a mere 15 in 1941. The future is by no means secure for this great white bird, but the outcome looks a little brighter. With the banning of the pesticide DDT in the early 1970s, populations of bald eagles, ospreys, peregrine falcons and brown pelicans have also begun to increase.

Habitat loss and pollution of our environment remain serious threats to birdlife around the world. Texas is fortunate in having large tracts of wildlife habitat remaining, and that fact is mirrored in the variety and numbers of our birds. Yet many of those special habitats—mixed woodlands and bottomlands, brackish marshes, coastal prairies, subtropical scrub forests—are declining rapidly. As they disappear, the richest birdlife in North America is also at risk.

CLASSIFICATION AND NAMES

Families

Ornithologists, the scientists who study birds, organize the various bird species into families that share certain anatomical characteristics. Some of those families contain many members and are nearly worldwide in their range. Others contain but a single unique species that appears to have no close relatives. Learning the characteristics and being able to recognize a bird's familial relationships aids greatly in identification. Recognizing that a bird is a flycatcher or a thrush, for example, simplifies the task of trying to find it in a book.

Most field guides are arranged in phylogenetic order, with the most primitive birds first and the most advanced last. For North America, this means starting with the loons and grebes and ending with the finches. Not all ornithologists, however, agree on the exact progression, and new data frequently lead to a restructuring of a bird's family tree. As more careful genetic work is done, it appears likely that the families will be reordered dramatically, and we will discover relationships that were not suspected from outward appearance or internal anatomy.

In their work with molecules that encode the genetic information of different birds, Charles Sibley and Jon Ahlquist have discovered a great deal about such relationships. In their new scheme, for example, the vireos are more closely related to the shrikes and to the crows and jays than to the wood warblers. The mockingbirds and thrashers, in turn, occupy a single family with the starlings.

In their review of this DNA work, Ehrlich, Dobkin and Wheye note in *The Birder's Handbook* that they believe the Sibley-Ahlquist classification to be much closer to biological reality than that recognized in the 1983 *Check-list of North American Birds* published by the American Ornithologists' Union. Since the Sibley-Ahlquist proposal remains somewhat controversial and is unfamiliar to most bird watchers, however, most current bird books and checklists still follow the standard AOU treatment. But the day may come when we will see a drastic revision of bird taxonomy and the way in which we regard avian relationships.

This book takes a somewhat different approach in its organization. Birds within a family will generally be

A great blue heron fishes in a coastal bay.

found together, but those families are not in strict phylogenetic order. Instead, they are placed in larger groups with others they most resemble, thus making it easier for the beginning birder to find the appropriate information. Loons and grebes are not closely related to ducks, but that is the family with which they are most likely to be confused by the novice. Thus they are all placed in the section of "Ducklike Water Birds." The checklist for the state at the back of this book is included so that the reader will have a complete record of Texas birds in their currently accepted taxonomic order.

Common and Scientific Names

Most common names are imprecise at best. Ornithologists and birders know our slate-gray coot as the American coot, to distinguish it from closely related species elsewhere. To natives of the North, however, it has always been the "mud-hen," and to those from Louisiana and East Texas, it is the *poule d'eau.* Similarly, the common nighthawk is widely called the "bull-bat," and the shrikes are "butcher-birds." The same confusion reigns for a great number of our plants and animals. A "gopher" can be a ground squirrel, a pocket gopher or a tortoise, depending on the region of the country.

Scientific names are more precise. In a system devised by 18th-century Swedish botanist Linnaeus, every species has a two-part Latin name. Current usage places that name in italics for publication. The first part is always capitalized and indicates the genus, a group of very closely related organisms. The second is not capitalized and describes the individual species. There can be only one pair of names for any life-form, and no two plants or animals share the same scientific name.

The word "robin" represents a very different bird in North America than it does in England. The American robin, a member of the thrush family, is *Turdus migratorius*; the European robin is *Erithacus rubecula*. The two are not closely related, and each is clearly designated by the scientific binomial.

Actually, the common names of North American birds are standardized to a much greater degree than the common names used in most other biological disciplines. The American Ornithologists' Union has a Committee on Classification and Nomenclature to decide such matters, and other organizations generally accept its decisions. Thus, virtually all bird publications and checklists follow the same nomenclature. There is one set of "correct" bird names for North America. This book, too, follows the dictates of the AOU 1983 checklist and its subsequent supplements.

Name Changes

Unfortunately, no such list is inviolable, and even bird names change from time to time. The AOU in recent years has made many changes as a result of new scientific facts and in a concentrated effort to standardize names throughout the world. These changes have the unhappy effect of making all of the older books and checklists out-of-date.

The cardinal, the robin, the mockingbird and the roadrunner have long been familiar birds to Texans. Now, however, they are officially the northern cardinal, the American robin, the northern mockingbird and the greater roadrunner. Related birds live in other countries, and the new names are less provincial. They apply everywhere and identify the species exactly. The complete names are seldom used in everyday conversation, for there is little chance of confusing our common species with the Bahama mockingbird or Mexico's clay-colored or rufous-backed robins, although the latter do stray across U.S. borders on occasion.

We now call the old sparrow hawk the American kestrel; the marsh hawk, the northern harrier. The common gallinule has become the common moorhen, although moors are few and far between in

A northern harrier drops feet-first on its prey. This common raptor was formerly called the marsh hawk.

Female northern cardinal.

Texas. The birds have been renamed to be consistent with earlier British names for related species.

New taxonomy lumps some species together and splits others. Autumn winds formerly brought both snow geese and blue geese to Texas. Now experts consider the two to be merely color morphs, or phases, of the snow goose. Biologists have found that the two freely interbreed and that both forms emerge from a single clutch of eggs, somewhat like blond and brunette children in a family. There are clear genetic tendencies but no barriers to breeding, one of the tests for species separation.

The Baltimore oriole no longer exists, although the baseball team reportedly has no plans to change its name. The old Baltimore oriole of the eastern states and Bullock's oriole of the West have been found to interbreed freely where their ranges join, with no loss of vitality in the resulting young. The two are now collectively called the northern oriole.

The little screech-owl, on the other hand, has recently been separated into two species, eastern and western, that meet in Texas near the Pecos River. Several other such cases of both "splitting" and "lumping" affect present-day bird names.

Scientific names, too, must be added or deleted when these taxonomic revisions are made. They may also change as ornithologists clarify relationships or discover that earlier names claim precedence. Because the common names of birds are so well standardized, the scientific ones are used less frequently than in such disciplines as botany or entomology, even by specialists working in the field. They do, however, serve to define particular birds without equivocation and indicate their places in bird classification.

For the ornithologists, the sweeping changes have necessitated publishing new articles and books, perhaps progressing closer to the truth. To dedicated birders, they mean a review of precious life lists, removing species lost and rushing to add those newly named. To the birds, it all must seem irrelevant. They pay no attention to scientific decisions of that kind. They apparently knew what they were doing all along.

PLUMAGE VARIATION

If all birds were as clearly marked as the common blue jay, identification would be much easier. Males and females look alike, and little variation occurs with age or season. Even a fledgling fresh from the nest displays its family colors and the beginnings of a crest. It leaves no doubt as to its ancestry. To borrow Gertrude Stein's line about the rose: Jay is a jay is a jay is a jay.

Not so with many other species. The two sexes may differ in their plumage, and some young birds resemble neither parent until they are adults. There are geographic races that vary dramatically within a species, and there are color phases possible even within a single brood. The seasons, too, cause plumage changes, further complicating identification.

Most people recognize the male cardinal and his consort. He sports flaming red, while she wears a drabber buffy-brown with only a hint of red on wings and tail. Far more dramatic is the sexual dimorphism of the red-winged blackbird. The boisterous black male displays from his perch by flaring red shoulder patches bordered with yellow. With loud, gurgling song and flashing epaulettes, he proclaims his domain within the marsh. His ladies—for there is often more than one—are somewhat smaller and more secretive. Dressed in somber brown above, light underparts heavily streaked, they might be mistaken for sparrows but for their size and slimmer bills.

Young bald eagles take from three to five years to reach adulthood. Until then, they appear mainly dark, with only hints of white on the underwings and without the trademark white head and tail. Gulls, too, take several years to gain full plumage, and many of the drab and strangely mottled young look distressingly alike. They change markedly every season until they become adults.

Smaller birds mature more quickly, yet they still may take a year or more to acquire adult plumage. For species in which the sexes differ, young males frequently resemble adult females.

The season of the year may also dictate the plumage that birds wear. Most species undergo a complete molt after the summer breeding season, replacing worn feathers with new. Those that were brightly colored for spring courtship may then be much less colorful. A breeding male scarlet tanager is a gleaming, fluorescent red, with contrasting black wings and tail. After the fall molt, he dons a more dingy olive color, a better camouflage perhaps when there is no need for formal dress. As spring approaches, he molts again to red.

Male ducks adopt a post-breeding "eclipse" plumage resembling the females. Shorebirds shed many of the individual marks that make them more readily identifiable in spring, and spend autumn and winter in camouflage brown and gray. These seasonal plumages, and the transitional stages between them, multiply the problems of beginning birders.

Various subspecies, or geographic races of a single species, may also look like very different birds. Baltimore and Bullock's orioles, yellow-shafted and red-shafted flickers, black-crested and tufted titmice, and the slate-colored, Oregon and gray-headed juncos were all considered separate species until recently. All occur in Texas. Now the forms have been recognized as subspecies of their respective species, and redesignated the northern oriole, northern flicker, tufted titmouse and dark-eyed junco.

Color morphs, or color phases, also occur within a bird population. They need not be separated geographically. Snow and blue geese are avian blonds and brunettes; red-phase and gray-phase eastern screech-owls may hatch from the same clutch of eggs. Field guides portray light-phase and dark-phase examples of many

American wigeon in eclipse plumage.

of the larger hawks. In the field, a birder may encounter intermediates between the two extremes. There is a great deal of individual variation, and some of the more distinctive individuals can be puzzling indeed.

Actually, that should not seem so strange. One can imagine those same birds perched on a limb, watching us as we go by. They would see humans that were short and tall, fat and thin. Some would be light plumaged; some, dark. Some of us would obviously be molting and would be topped by very little plumage at all. "How can they all be one species?" a bird might ask. "They don't even look and act alike."

The appearance of a bird can vary with its sex and age and with the season of the year. Residents of different regions may wear different garb, and there are nonconformists in almost every flock. Confusing? Yes, but therein lies the challenge. Even the experts will be puzzled now and then.

IDENTIFICATION

Experienced birders know what to look for when they encounter a new or unexpected bird. They place it quickly in its appropriate family by noting such characteristics as size and shape of the body, beak shape, and even its behavior. They then note the various "field marks" that are necessary to identify it by ruling out all other possibilities. Some of those field marks can be subtle ones that a beginner might not notice. The only path to expertise is experience in the field, but study at home provides a good foundation.

The size of a bird is obviously important, yet it can be very hard to judge. A sandpiper or gull on a fog-shrouded beach might loom enormous through the mists, while a hawk in the top of a distant tree may seem far smaller than it really is. Distance is difficult to estimate, and it helps to have a frame of reference. Try to compare the bird to one you know. Is it the size of a house sparrow, a robin, a pigeon or a goose? Such comparisons are much more helpful than noting, "It was big," or "It was small."

A long-billed curlew stalks the surf.

Body proportions and postures are also useful. Greater and lesser yellowlegs look very much alike, differing primarily in size. That, however, is hard to judge for a single bird. The lesser has a proportionately shorter bill, with a length equal to the depth of the head. The greater's bill is longer. Imagine folding back that bill at the base, projecting backward through the eye. The tip of the lesser yellowlegs' bill would reach the back of the head; that of the greater would project well beyond. It is a simple but helpful test.

The slender sandpipers have longer legs and bills than the chunky plovers with which they might associate. Flycatchers perch upright on a limb or wire and seem "big headed" for their size. Some birds have long tails; some, short. Wrens often cock their tails upward, while several species wag their tails up and down.

Bill shape provides a useful key to familial relationships. Finches and sparrows have short, heavy, conical bills typical of seed-eating birds. Warblers' bills are thin and pointed, for gleaning insects from the leaves or prying them from cracks in the bark. Vireos resemble warblers in size and shape, but their bills are thicker, sturdier, and slightly hooked. The spatulate beak of a duck, the spearlike beak of a

A Forster's tern hovers before diving for a fish.

heron, and the massive, fiercely hooked beak of an eagle reveal much about their owners' feeding habits and hence their places in the avian family tree.

Subtle markings distinguish many birds from their close relatives. An identification may hinge on the color of a bird's legs or on whether or not it has light rings around its eyes. Warblers can be divided into those with light wing-bars and those without. Sparrows fall into groups with streaked breasts and unstreaked breasts, and some are best identified by white outer tail feathers revealed as they take flight.

Behavior, too, provides a key. The black-and-white warbler creeps along the branches of a tree, much in the manner of a nuthatch or brown creeper, something few other warblers do. Terns dive headlong into the water to capture fish, while gulls pick their meal from the surface or sit down to float beside it while they dine. In flight, a turkey vulture sails on long, narrow wings, while the short-winged black vulture must flap more frequently.

Flight patterns offer many clues to bird identities. Woodpeckers display an undulating, roller-coaster flight as they move from tree to tree. Swifts dart across the sky on flickering, swept-back wings, beating them more rapidly than do the somewhat similar, but unrelated, swallows. Waterfowl also have different wingbeat rates. Ducks flap more rapidly than larger, more ponderous geese. Such distinctions can be used when birds are still too far away to estimate size or detect color patterns.

Some of the best birders rely as much on their ears as on their eyes. They know virtually every bird's song and recognize each one instantly. Not only does this help enormously in finding a desired bird, but it saves time that would otherwise be spent in tracking down species previously seen.

The song of a bird, in some cases, is even more diagnostic than its appearance. The little *Empidonax* flycatchers, for example, all look very much alike. Only the most experienced birders attempt to sort them out on sight, and then only after careful study. Yet each has its own characteristic song that distinguishes the species from all others. Because birds use songs in claiming territories and

A week-old least bittern explores the marsh near its nest.

initiating courtship, the different vocalizations serve as barriers to interbreeding as effectively as differences in habitat or plumage.

Range, habitat and season all contribute to the data bank a birder processes mentally in identifying an unknown bird. A blue jay is highly unlikely in the Davis Mountains, and a scrub jay would be unprecedented on the upper Texas coast. By the same token, Texas birders do not expect to see a Canada warbler in the summer, when members of that species should all be on their breeding grounds much farther north.

Birds do stray far from their normal routes at times, and those unexpected sightings provide the highlights of a birder's list. Individuals also digress from their seasonal routines, perhaps because of illness or injury, perhaps as forerunners of a population trend. Most, however, follow their instinctive pathways with remarkable precision. The most probable alternatives are usually the proper ones, and only when they have been eliminated does the practiced birder identify his subject as an unexpected rarity.

Bird identification is like putting together a jigsaw puzzle. Size, shape, color, posture, behavior, song, habitat, range, season—all are pieces of that puzzle. When they all fit, the picture is complete.

TOOLS OF THE TRADE

Binoculars are essential for bird watching, even at a backyard feeder. Seldom can one approach birds closely enough to discern small details that may be needed for identification. The enlarged view makes it possible to study birds and observe their behavior without disturbing them.

Binocular prices range from the inexpensive to the astronomical. Those who spend a great deal of time in the field often pay several hundred dollars for optical equipment, and a good binocular is worth the price. Generally, the image will be brighter and sharper, and an expensive binocular is usually sealed better against moisture and dust. Price should not be a deterrent, however. Birding can be fun for everyone, and an inexpensive binocular provides a good start down the road to discovery.

A moderately priced 7x35 binocular is one of the most popular choices and can be used at sporting events and for other activities. The first number is the magnification or "power"; it means that a bird will appear seven times closer in the field of view. The second number is the diameter of the front lens expressed in millimeters. It determines the amount of light admitted and the brightness of the image. Ideally, the second number should be about five times the first; hence, 7x35. Compact and pocket-sized binoculars are admittedly convenient, but they are not as useful for birding because of their lower magnification, lack of brightness and smaller field of view. Many serious birders choose 10x40 binoculars for their increased power. Although the ratio of these numbers is less than five, the better brands make up for it with high-quality lenses and lens coatings.

Birders may also carry spotting scopes ranging in power from about 20 to 60 or more. Some have "zoom" capabilities to vary the magnification. Scopes, too, come in a wide variety of models and price ranges. They prove most useful for examining shorebirds or gulls on mud flats and beaches, hawks in distant trees, and ducks on the open water. A spotting scope usually requires a tripod for stability, and such a system allows several people in turn to examine the same bird. Window mounts are available to attach the scope to the side window of a vehicle, and many birders mount scopes on gun stocks or shoulder braces for use in the field. Remember, however, that any increase in magnification also magnifies your involuntary movements and atmospheric haze or air currents.

Tape recorders have become common birding tools in recent years, and a large number of birdsong tapes have been published. Some serve as companions to the field guides and are keyed to each page of the books, enabling the user to learn specific songs for each species. Others contain birdsongs of a particular region or of an individual group of birds.

In its simplest form, this encourages the birder to learn the distinctive songs that prove so useful in finding and identifying birds in the field. In practice, birders also use tapes to attract certain birds by playing their characteristic songs. The most ardent actually carry recording equipment to tape a bird's song and then play it back, attracting the bird within closer viewing or camera range.

The latter methods are often misused, and the concerned birder should be very careful with them. They are most useful where birds are difficult to locate and observe, as in the dense forests of tropical America. When birders visit such a spot, there is probably little harm in calling birds with a tape, studying them for a few moments, and moving on. The birds can then return to their normal routines with a minimum of disturbance. Repeating the process time after time, however, is harassment of the birds. They must interrupt their activities to meet each new "challenger." There have been instances where rare birds were pursued and called so frequently by persistent birders that they were driven from their territories. The welfare of the birds is paramount, and no ethical birder or bird photographer pursues his subject so vigorously as to cause it harm.

Books

This book is intended as an introduction to Texas birdlife and is a personal look at many of the more common and distinctive species. Countless other books deal with particular types of birds, with their biology, or with their myriad habits and personalities. The birder will also want to carry a pocket-sized field guide that illustrates all of the species found in a particular country or area. There are several good field guides for North America, and the buyer should study the merits of each. For Texas, a one-volume guide that covers the entire continent proves

A female purple martin feeds her hungry fledglings.

most useful, since our state draws both eastern and western birds. In addition to the illustrations and brief text, most field guides contain range maps showing where each species normally occurs. Birders commonly refer to more than one book when faced with difficult identification problems.

Bird-finding guides have proliferated in recent years, to the benefit of new birders and to the delight of travelers in unfamiliar regions. Many countries, states and local areas have books which describe the best birding spots and list the species to be found in them. They are well worth the usually small investment and can be of enormous help in planning a simple one-day trip or an extended vacation. The birding locations listed will often be scenic ones and should provide excellent chances to view other wildlife as well.

Texas abounds with excellent birding locations. Some spots along the coast like High Island, Galveston and Rockport have earned fame as "hot spots" during spring migration, while the refuges and remnant woodlands along the Rio Grande provide chances to see Mexican species found nowhere else. The Big Thicket, the Texas Hill Country, the Panhandle, the Big Bend region and the Guadalupe Mountains all have their specialties. Almost every state park and national wildlife refuge offers good birding opportunities. No matter where you live in Texas, you are certain to be near some choice location visited by birders from across the continent.

The bibliography in this book lists several good field guides and bird-finding books. Local book stores, libraries and nature clubs can also provide information on those available for your area.

Checklists

The best buys for the birding dollar are checklists for specific areas. These frequently take the form of simple folded or accordion-pleated cards that cost only a few cents and fit easily into a pocket. They contain a list of all the birds reported from the checklist region, and many also indicate the abundance of each bird during the various seasons of the year. The most useful, in fact, use bar graphs to illustrate the likelihood of seeing a specific bird in any given month.

There are continent-wide checklists as well as ones for individual countries of the world. Many state and local birding groups compile such lists for their areas, and there are checklists for most of the national parks and wildlife refuges and for the state parks in Texas and throughout the nation. Remember that the smaller the scope, the more precise the information can be. A good checklist for a particular park or county within the state provides the best summary of that area's birdlife.

Birders use the pocket lists for recording their daily sightings as well as for permanent records from specific locations. A checklist is much more than a convenient way to keep a bird tally, however. It can be an invaluable guide to planning a birding trip and determining which species might be seen. It is the region's ornithological history wrapped up in a convenient and inexpensive package.

Life Lists

Birders play a variety of games and keep lists as a measure of their success. Most common is the "life list," simply a list of all the species seen in the person's birding lifetime. These can be world lists, or they might be for specific countries or regions. The American Birding Association, the ABA, defines precisely the limits of its North American region for purposes of record-keeping and competitive lists. There are state lists, county lists, year lists and "my backyard" lists. Each can be a rewarding game to play. A simple printed checklist as described in the section above will serve for record keeping, but some choose to keep more detailed notebooks or card files. There are even home-computer programs for keeping track of life lists and sorting them to fit the game.

ATTRACTING BIRDS TO YOUR YARD

According to a recent survey by the U.S. Fish and Wildlife Service, Americans spend more than half a billion dollars every year on birdseed to stock backyard feeders. At least one family in four feeds the birds, enjoying their colorful plumage and constant activity at closer range than is normally possible in the field. Birds have three major needs that you can supply: food, water, and shelter from predators and the weather.

Northern cardinals, blue jays, white-throated sparrows and rufous-sided towhees flock to a well-stocked winter feeder.

Many publications and programs emphasize planting for wildlife, and only a little effort is required to make your yard a miniature wildlife sanctuary. Trees and shrubs of several kinds, some of them evergreen, provide birds with shelter throughout the year. Summer residents choose nesting sites among the branches or in tangles of climbing vines, while winter visitors find protection from chilling winds, rain and snow.

Fruiting trees and shrubs attract a wide variety of birds. A mulberry tree hosts grosbeaks, tanagers, buntings, orioles, thrushes and jays. Rare is the bird that can resist a ripe mulberry. Yaupon berries and the fruits of other hollies disappear in a swirl of wings as wintering robins and waxwings descend from the skies. Goldfinches and siskins are irresistibly drawn to sunflowers and other composites left standing as they go to seed. Whatever your section of the state, whether along the coast or in the more arid West, there are native plants that will thrive to provide both flowered and feathered beauty throughout the year.

Male rufous hummingbird.

Birdbaths increase greatly the attractiveness of your yard to birds, especially during the hot, dry summer months. Some birds like a raised bath, well away from stalking cats and other threats. Others prefer a more natural one on the ground. Either should be cleaned regularly to prevent the spread of avian diseases.

The sound of running or dripping water pulls birds like a magnet. Some people use a small recirculating pump to create a miniature waterfall, trickling over a series of rocks and into a basin. Others simply suspend a piece of thin tubing above the bath to provide the dripping water. The tubing can be connected to a hose or outdoor faucet, or it can drain an overhead container that is filled periodically.

Commercial bird feeders come in a host of sizes and designs. Choose ones that best fit the residents of your area; they need not be too fancy or expensive. In winter, when insects and wild fruits are scarce, birds flock to the abundance of the feeders. Year-round feeding, however, provides an opportunity to watch as parent birds raise their young. Nestlings are fed primarily on high-protein insects, but fledglings often join adults at feeders. There is no evidence to suggest such supplemental feeding harms the birds.

Many of our most popular feeder birds favor sunflower seeds above all others. Chickadees, titmice, cardinals, jays and winter finches will eat little else as long as sunflower feeders are well stocked. Small finches also like imported niger, or "thistle" seed, served in special tubes with tiny openings.

Many species feed on white proso millet, which is easily eaten because of its thin hull. Small songbirds take less readily to milo, wheat, oats and corn, but those grains prove popular with doves, grackles and blackbirds. Commercial mixes contain most of the varieties, although you may prefer to blend your own. Scatter scratch grains or inexpensive seed mixtures on the ground for the larger birds, then use specialized, higher-priced seed in hanging feeders for finches, chickadees and titmice.

Bread crumbs and bakery goods appeal to many species, including insect eaters, and the high visibility provides a good way of attracting the first customers to a new feeder. Birds also relish nuts, raisins, pieces of apple, grapes and other fruit. Halved oranges impaled on nails or twigs bring in jays, woodpeckers, grosbeaks, tanagers, orioles and others, some of which will not come for seeds. The bigger the menu, the broader the clientele.

Suet, peanut butter and other high-fat foods are often recommended as winter feeder rations. They are excellent in the North, where they remain frozen, but they should be used cautiously in Texas and throughout the warmer South. Small amounts can be mixed with grains to form popular and nutritious cakes. Such fatty foods must never be allowed to get rancid, however. Clean feeders and fresh food are essential to the customers' welfare.

A tufted titmouse adopts a backyard birdhouse.

Hummingbird feeders offer many delights, for few birds are as active or as widely admired as are these tiny feathered gems. The recommended mixture for hummingbirds is one part white sugar to four parts boiled water. Boiling the water first inhibits the growth of bacteria and fungi. Honey is not recommended because of a potentially lethal fungal disease, and artificial sugar substitutes offer no nutritional value. Most commercial feeders have red containers or accents, so it is not necessary to add red food coloring to the solution. Feeders should be checked and refilled often and kept scrupulously clean. Scrub them at least once a week with a solution of one tablespoon of chlorine bleach in a bucket of soapy water. Then rinse thoroughly with fresh water to remove all traces of soap and bleach.

Planting for hummingbirds brings rapid and rich rewards. Attracted to your yard by flowers, hummers then stay to utilize the feeders too. Residents along the coast and through East Texas attract the little ruby-throated hummingbird; those in Central and West Texas, the black-chinned hummingbird. In the southern tip of the state, the pretty buff-bellied hummer visits feeders and flowers, while several other species occupy western mountain regions and wander eastward in the fall.

They show a marked preference for orange or red tubular flowers but patronize almost any rich nectar source. The various salvias, shrimp-plant, trumpet-creeper, native honeysuckles, Turk's cap, coralbean, hummingbird bush (hamelia), anisacanthus, scarlet bouvardia, ocotillo and many others all produce remarkable results, depending on the region of the state. Consult garden or landscaping books or your local nursery for the plants best suited to your area and soil. Many nature centers and arboretums have native plant sales of local or adaptable species and can recommend others. The same flowers also attract butterflies, so the lucky gardener is doubly blessed.

Many birds have a sweet tooth. The sugar-water used in hummingbird feeders also draws orioles, tanagers, warblers, grosbeaks and woodpeckers. They can best reach the treat if it is placed in open, suspended cups or small bottles. The containers, however, will also attract ants, bees and wasps and must be washed and refilled frequently.

Each part of Texas has its own characteristic feeder species, sometimes different ones in each season of the year, and everyone who feeds birds develops favorite foods and special techniques. With shelter, food and water, you can create a small and simple refuge in your own backyard. It will provide countless hours of pleasure, both for you and for the birds.

LONG-LEGGED WADING BIRDS

The herons, egrets, ibises, spoonbills, storks and cranes are all long-necked, long-legged birds that at first glance seem quite similar in appearance and habits. They frequent marshes and wet fields, or stalk our shorelines and riverbanks, feeding heavily on various forms of aquatic life. The similarities, however, are superficial, and those families are not necessarily related. The cranes are more closely linked to the coots and rails than to the herons, and the storks are of a different lineage entirely.

The shape of the beak is very useful in determining familial relationships, just as it determines how the various species feed and how they partition the food resources to decrease competition. Flight profiles are also distinctive: cranes, storks, ibises and spoonbills fly with their necks outstretched; herons and egrets fly with heads drawn back onto their shoulders and necks in a graceful S-curve.

Roseate spoonbills.

HERONS (Family Ardeidae)

Heron colonies often contain several species.

The herons are among the most conspicuous of the birds along the Texas coast and on inland lakes and marshes. There are a dozen species, including the egrets and bitterns, that regularly occur in North America, and all are fairly common within our state. They range in size from the four-foot-tall great blue heron to the 13-inch least bittern. Several of the species nest in large mixed colonies together with the ibises and spoonbill.

During the breeding season the herons are at their best: their legs, beaks and faces become brilliantly colored as the hormones flow, and extravagant plumes adorn their heads and backs. The lovely plumage nearly proved the downfall of these graceful birds during the latter half of the 19th century, when they were killed by the hundreds of thousands and shipped to the East Coast for the millinery trade. It was then fashionable for women to wear large hats decorated with feathers or whole birds. Ornithologist Frank Chapman, of the American Museum of Natural History, reported that on the streets of Manhattan in 1886, three-quarters of the women's hats were so adorned. He spotted 40 native species in a brief fashion survey, including terns, woodpeckers, bluebirds, cedar waxwings, warblers, orioles and tanagers.

Most popular of all were the herons and especially the snowy and great egrets. Sprays of their white nuptial plumes, "aigrettes," became so valuable that the birds faced extinction. Plume hunters earned $32 an ounce for their bounty, twice the price of gold. One London auction house sold 1,608 packages of heron plumes in a single year, a total of 48,240 ounces of feathers representing nearly 200,000 birds killed at the nest. The toll in untended eggs and young was undoubtedly higher.

Preservationists were incensed at the slaughter. Bird-conservation societies sprang up, and thousands quickly joined. The Massachusetts Audubon Society was formed in 1896; the Pennsylvania Audubon Society, a few months later. By 1899, 15 states had formed similar groups that shared a common goal: "To discourage the buying and wearing for ornamental purposes of the feathers of any wild birds except ducks and game birds, and to otherwise further the protection of native birds."

Frank Chapman began publishing *Bird-Lore* magazine in 1899, and it became a unifying national forum for the first Audubon clubs. In 1901, some of them formed a loose alliance, and four years later they incorporated under the rather formidable name of National Association of Audubon Societies for the Protection of Wild Birds and Animals. The association continued to grow and in 1935 bought *Bird-Lore* as a means of keeping members united and informed. The name was changed to *Audubon Magazine* in 1940, and the group became the National Audubon Society.

Legislation spurred by those pioneering conservationists and the new environmental ethic undoubtedly saved many of our birds from following the passenger pigeon and the Carolina parakeet into extinction. There are still numerous threats from land-use changes and habitat destruction, but the public is much more aware of the value of natural resources. At least for now, the stately herons remain as prominent residents of Texas beaches and marshes.

GREAT BLUE HERON
Ardea herodias

Standing four feet tall, and with a wingspread of six feet, the great blue heron ranks as the largest of the North American herons and egrets. It is also one of the most widely distributed, breeding from southeastern Alaska to Nova Scotia and southward across the continent to Mexico and the West Indies.

In Texas it is most common along the coast, but it can also be seen beside streams, ponds and lakes throughout the state. It is often erroneously called a "crane," but the herons and cranes are quite different in their anatomy and habits and are not closely related.

During the breeding season, ornate plumes decorate the head, neck and back of the blue-gray adults and are shown to good advantage as the large birds preen and posture in their courtship routine. The nest is a crude platform of sticks in a bush or tree, usually in a colony with other herons. Along the coast nests are also found on gas wells and duck blinds in the shallow bays. The three to five large blue eggs hatch in 28 days, and it is another two months before the gangly young are ready to fly.

Standing quietly among the marsh grasses, seeking shelter from wind or rain, the great blue heron draws its head down on its shoulders and looks much smaller than when it stalks the shore or shallows with its long neck extended. In flight, its neck is drawn back in a graceful S-curve, and the long legs trail out behind. The wide, powerful wings beat only twice each second.

On a warm, windy day in March, I watched as a great blue heron paced the shallows along the Rockport waterfront, leaning into the brisk sea breeze for balance. Turning its head to focus one eye on the choppy water just ahead, it slowed its pace to a careful stalk. Then, in a motion almost too fast to follow, it drove its head beneath the surface, emerging

The largest of the heron family, a great blue heron surveys its domain from a coastal dune.

with a foot-long mullet impaled on its rapier beak. The amazing force of the blow had driven the heron's upper mandible completely through the writhing fish. The giant bird then walked deliberately to the shore and shook its catch onto the sandy beach. Drawing back its head, it stabbed the fish twice more until it lay quiet on the sand, then picked it up and swallowed it headfirst in one eye-popping gulp. Looking around as if for approval, the heron then fluffed its long neck plumes in the wind, walked a few strides into the surf, and launched into ponderous flight.

GREAT EGRET
Casmerodius albus

The great egret is the largest of the white herons in Texas and is distinguished by its yellow bill and blackish legs and feet. Formerly called the common egret and the American egret, it ranges from the United States through Central and South America to the Strait of Magellan and also occurs in portions of the Old World. With its wide distribution, it is the most cosmopolitan of the heron family.

In Texas it is resident primarily along the coast, where it feeds in both saline and freshwater marshes, mud flats, rice fields, ponds and streams. Nests are crude platforms of sticks, usually in large colonies. The three to five light blue eggs hatch in 23 to 26 days, and the young clamber out of the nest about three weeks after hatching, although they do not fly for another three or four weeks. Wanderers in summer reach northern Texas and the Panhandle and occasionally as far west as El Paso.

The great egret was called "long white" by the plume hunters, who treasured its long, delicate back plumes at the turn of the century. Near the brink of extinction, it recovered during the 1920s and 1930s to nearly historic numbers, with thousands of the tall, handsome birds in Texas. Land development, however, has more recently crowded out many of the nesting colonies, particularly inland from the coast.

Yellow beak and black legs distinguish the tall, stately great egret.

SNOWY EGRET
Egretta thula

A slender black bill and black legs with bright yellow feet separate the slim, dainty snowy egret from the other white herons. "The bird with the golden slippers," it is sometimes called. Much smaller than the great egret, it feeds more actively and flies with a more rapid wingbeat. Rather than stalking slowly for its prey, it moves briskly through the shallow water, shuffling its feet to stir up the bottom and stabbing repeatedly for the aquatic life that darts from cover. It may also feed in pastures and fields to supplement a varied diet that includes small fish, shrimp, crayfish, frogs, worms, snails, insects and occasional rodents.

The snowy egret is particularly striking during the breeding season, when the bare facial skin around its yellow eyes turns red and the yellow slippers blush with orange. Long nuptial plumes curve gracefully upward from the head, neck and back and are erected repeatedly in greeting to its mate or in territorial posturing to other birds.

Like the great egret, the snowy was hunted for those filmy aigrettes, and by 1910 most of the colonies in Texas had been decimated. Because only the breeding birds sported plumes that were "worth their weight in gold," the practice killed two generations at once. Abandoned eggs and helpless chicks could only perish in the Texas sun.

Once the birds were granted protection by law and public pressure, however, they staged a rapid comeback. As the population recovered, the range also expanded northward. The snowy egret now ranges into the northern states as well as southward to Argentina and Chile. It is partially migratory and withdraws from the North in winter. In Texas, it breeds primarily along the coast and in scattered marshes and swamps to the north and east. After the nesting season, it wanders widely, returning in winter to the coast.

A snowy egret shows its "golden slippers" as it fishes in a quiet pool.

LITTLE BLUE HERON   ## Egretta caerulea

The adult little blue heron is entirely dark slate-blue, with a more reddish purple head and neck in breeding plumage. The bill is blue with a darker tip; the legs are bluish green. The somewhat similar reddish egret is much larger and paler in color, while the tricolored heron has white underparts.

The immature little blue heron causes the most confusion in identification, for it is entirely white. In size and color, it resembles a snowy egret, but it has a thicker, two-toned grayish bill and greenish legs and feet. The snowy egret has a slim black bill and black legs with yellow feet.

Not until the spring after its hatching year does the little blue heron begin to acquire dark adult plumage. During a gradual molt it appears blotchy blue and white, sometimes called the "calico heron." I remember with embarrassment my first encounter with such a molting bird nearly 30 years ago. Thinking I had found a partially albino heron, I followed it for half a mile through knee-deep marsh, trying to photograph my rare discovery.

The little blue heron breeds in the Atlantic and Gulf states and wanders widely after the nesting season, appearing across much of the eastern two-thirds of the country and as far north as Canada. It migrates from that inland range in winter, however, remaining only along the coast. Nesting in the eastern half of Texas, it wanders in late summer to other sections of the state. Here, too, it winters chiefly near the coast.

Little blue herons are colonial nesters, but if the colony contains other species, they tend to keep to themselves on the fringes of the noisy tenement. The nests, as with most other herons, are flimsy platforms of

twigs, barely sufficient to keep the three to five light blue eggs from rolling out.

Little blue herons are more common in fresh water than in salt water. Slow, deliberate hunters along ponds, lakes and marshes, they feed on an array of small fish and other aquatic life. So fond are they of crayfish that they are frequently seen stalking along the dikes of rice fields, giving them the name "levee walker" in East Texas and Louisiana.

TRICOLORED HERON
Egretta tricolor

Until recently called the Louisiana heron, this colorful species is primarily a bird of the coast. Only the reddish egret is more tied to the saltwater environment. The tricolored heron inhabits saline marshes and mangrove swamps of the eastern and Gulf coasts southward to northern South America. It also occurs on the Pacific coast from Baja California south. Some birds tend to wander inland in late summer and may then be seen occasionally in ponds and marshes across Texas.

The tricolored heron is a slender bird with a long bill and what one field guide describes as a "snaky neck." The upperparts are dark blue, contrasting with a white belly and foreneck. The long, filmy nuptial plumes on the back are cinnamon in color, while young birds exhibit chestnut markings on the neck and wings.

The breeding season begins in late March in Texas, and young have been found in the nests into late August. The crude nests of twigs are built in low shrubs or trees in large colonies, usually with other heron species. Both sexes share in the incubation of the three or four light bluish eggs and in feeding the young on regurgitated fish, aquatic invertebrates and insects.

The tricolored heron escaped the guns of the plume hunters because its tawny plumes were not as desirable

A little blue heron (above) examines its eggs in a crude nest of twigs. A tricolored heron (right) stalks the edge of a coastal marsh.

for the millinery trade as the snowy white feathers of the egrets. It continues to be one of the most abundant herons in the South, but its habitat is rapidly giving way to coastal development. The future is by no means assured for this active, pretty heron that Audubon called "the lady of the waters."

REDDISH EGRET
Egretta rufescens

Few bird acts appear more comical than a reddish egret in search of food. Shaggy head and neck plumes blowing in the wind, it dashes about in the water on long, spindly legs, leaping in the air, whirling around, stabbing repeatedly with its beak after fleeing fish. Wings raised to cut the glare from the surface, a trick called "canopy feeding," it pauses for a moment to watch the shoals. Then it is off again at a trot with long, lurching strides, looking for all the world like it has been drinking something much stronger than water.

The reddish egret is an uncommon resident of coastal Texas and Florida, and thence southward through Mexico and the West Indies. It seldom forsakes the saltwater beaches and bays and is rarely seen inland. This is one of the real specialties of the Texas coast from Bolivar to Boca Chica, attracting birders from across the country who seek to add it to their lists.

The typical plumage of this large heron is gray, with a rusty red head and neck. The bill is pink with a black tip, the legs cobalt blue. However, a white form of the reddish egret also makes up a small percentage of the Texas population. Unlike the immature little blue heron, which is white only in its youth, it remains white throughout life. Although it might easily be mistaken for a great egret, the white-phase reddish egret can be recognized by its flesh-colored bill.

Like its white cousins, the reddish

Nuptial plumes blowing in the wind, a reddish egret adds a twig to its nest.

egret was nearly wiped out by plume hunters at the turn of the century. It disappeared completely from Florida, but has since been reestablished. One Texas colony was apparently overlooked by the hunters, and the reddish egret survived to become one of the avian jewels of the coastal strand.

CATTLE EGRET *Bubulcus ibis*

The saga of the cattle egret is one of the most amazing success stories in the world of birds. Native to Africa, Asia and southern Europe, the stocky little white herons first appeared in Surinam in the late 1870s. Nothing is known about their arrival, but ornithologists speculate that a flock may have been caught up in a tropical storm that moved across the Atlantic. Whatever the initial impetus, the adventurers were in the New World to stay. Within a decade they were advancing across the South American continent.

The first documented record for North America was a specimen collected in Massachusetts in 1952, perhaps again arriving on the wings of a storm. In 1953, cattle egrets were found nesting with other herons in Florida; by 1971 they had reached Minnesota. They have now colonized more than half of the United States and parts of Canada.

The Texas coast proved an inviting beachhead for the invasion. The first confirmed sighting was on Mustang Island in November 1955, and young egrets were seen near Galveston in 1958. A survey of heron rookeries in 1959 found 11 nesting pairs of cattle egrets; another in 1965 found an astonishing 20,379 breeding pairs.

The birds feed with herds of cattle, catching insects chased up by the grazing animals, and even defend their little territories around individual cows. Huge flocks follow farm tractors to grab exposed insects and earthworms, and others stalk along behind the mowers on highway shoulders and city esplanades. They have adopted these modern-day beasts of burden just as they adopted the herds of animals on their native African plains.

The cattle egret is roughly the size of the snowy egret, but it has a shorter, thicker neck and shorter legs, giving it a much stockier appearance. Bill and legs are yellow, but become flushed with red during the breeding season, when buff-colored plumes also ornament the head, shoulders and breast.

Because cattle egrets feed mainly in fields and pastures, they are much less dependent on water than other herons. They moved into an ecological niche that no other large birds occupied, and they have taken full advantage of it. A major concern is that they might be displacing native species from the communal nesting colonies, especially as available habitat decreases in the face of industrial and urban development. They have certainly proved, however, that America is the land of opportunity for immigrants.

GREEN-BACKED HERON
Butorides striatus

Formerly called the green heron, this is the smallest of all the North American herons with the exception of the least bittern. It prefers a solitary life, shunning the mixed colonies of larger herons and building its nest in a sheltering bush or tree far from the maddening crowd.

A patient hunter, it perches unmoving along the bank of a quiet stream or pond to wait for small fish, frogs, crustaceans or insects to happen by. It is easily overlooked as it blends with the vegetation, but if its patience goes unrewarded, it may resort to stirring and raking the bottom sediment with its feet, forcing its prey to flee and darting off in hot pursuit. It prefers a more wooded environment than most other herons and is at home in dense swamps and marshes with heavy growth around the edge. It frequently perches in trees and walks nimbly along the branches.

If alarmed, the green-backed heron raises its greenish black crown feathers into a shaggy crest and utters a loud, sharp *kyowk*. Standing only 18 inches tall, it has a shorter neck and legs than most other herons. The upperparts are bluish green; the neck is deep chestnut with white below. Immature birds are browner and more

Cattle egrets catch insects chased up by grazing animals.

streaked, looking somewhat like bitterns.

The green-backed heron is widespread and generally common from eastern Canada to northern South America, although it is less abundant in the West. It summers throughout Texas but occurs most frequently in the eastern half. This handsome heron migrates from the northern portion of its range and usually spends the winters south of the Rio Grande.

The nest is a flimsy platform of sticks in a tree or bush, usually near or over water. Two to four light greenish blue eggs form the normal clutch, but up to seven have been found in a single nest. Both parents incubate those eggs for 21 to 25 days, and it takes an additional five weeks after hatching before the young are ready to fly.

AMERICAN BITTERN
Botaurus lentiginosus

The tuft of brown reeds looks like all the others in the Texas coastal marsh as it sways gently in the winter wind. On closer examination, however, a round yellow eye peers back intently, and there is the outline of a massive yellowish beak pointing skyward. This particular clump of reeds is really a large brown bird, mottled with a delicate camouflage pattern and with dark-edged rusty stripes beneath, an inscrutable American bittern in its very best bittern pose. A more careful examination reveals a broad black "mustache" streak on the side of the neck. Take your eyes from the bird for a moment and it vanishes once more into the background. Only if pressed will it take flight, its dark wing feathers confirming that it is indeed a bittern.

This shy denizen of the freshwater and brackish marshes occurs from Canada south to the Gulf of Mexico, migrating southward as far as Central America for the winter. In Texas it is a migrant (March–May and September–November) through most sections of the state. It winters along the coast and sparingly inland and breeds very locally in the northern counties.

The nest is a platform of dead reeds hidden away in the recesses of the marsh. The female alone incubates the four to seven olive or buffy eggs and feeds the young by regurgitating her prey. A bittern will eat almost anything it can catch, adding small mammals, snakes and insects to the basic aquatic fare of fish, frogs and crustaceans.

The spring love song of the male American bittern is a strange, resonant *oong-ka-choonk, oong-ka-choonk.* Thoreau, on hearing the booming notes, wrote, "The Bittern pumps in the fen." The call is suggestive of an old pump and gives rise to such other regional names as "thunder pumper" and "slough pumper." Others call it the "stake driver," because at a distance the middle note sounds like a mallet pounding a stake. While hardly musical, this unique song serves both to warn away rivals and to entice a mate.

The bittern was included on the Blue List in 1976. Published by the National Audubon Society, the list

A green-backed heron waits quietly beside a pond.

At sunset, an American bittern leaves the safety of the reeds and grasses to prowl the marsh.

serves warning of the bird species that are undergoing population or range reductions. They may remain locally common, but they appear to be in trouble in at least part of their range and should be watched more closely. In this case, the continued loss of marsh habitat is probably the reason for the decline of the American bittern, one of our most unusual and fascinating birds.

LEAST BITTERN
Ixobrychus exilis

I cannot be objective about this smallest of all our herons. In my introduction to bird photography many years ago, I watched from a blind for five weeks as a pair incubated their eggs and raised their young in a Texas coastal marsh. I have never forgotten that experience, and the least bittern will always be one of my favorite birds.

Only 13 inches long, and appearing even smaller with its slender neck pulled in, the least bittern is dwarfed by the better known American bittern and by the other herons and egrets that share its marshy environs. Large buffy wing-patches show in flight as it flushes from dense cover, flies a short distance with outstretched neck and dangling legs, and then pitches back into the marsh. Neither the rails nor the green-backed heron, with which the bittern could be confused, have light patches on their wings.

The least bittern occurs from southern Canada to the Gulf Coast and southward through Central and South America. It is quite common in the eastern half of the United States, rarer and more local in the West. During the colder months, it withdraws from Texas to winter south of the border. It is widespread in the freshwater and brackish marshes of the eastern half of the state and is occasionally observed farther west.

Even where fairly common, the shy least bittern is usually overlooked.

It flies only when pressed and prefers to remain motionless in the face of danger, beak pointed skyward, imitating the reeds among which it lives. It may even sway gently in the breeze.

The nest is a flimsy platform of cattails or sedges, often over the water, with a few small twigs as a token lining. On that crude pallet the female lays four or five bluish white eggs, and both sexes share the incubation chores.

Hatchlings are covered with sparse, light-colored down and are fed on regurgitated fish, frogs, tadpoles, leeches, crayfish, aquatic insects and other tasty gourmet morsels. Within two or three days the young instinctively assume the motionless alarm position at the first sign of an intruder, beaks in the air, large eyes peering out beneath fright wigs of unruly feathers. In a few more days, they are clambering through the reeds around the nest, practicing the sly and sneaky subterfuge necessary to be least bitterns.

BLACK-CROWNED NIGHT-HERON
Nycticorax nycticorax

While most herons are tall and rangy, the night-herons are cast in a somewhat different mold. Bulky, heavy-bodied birds, they have relatively short legs and stouter necks and beaks than most of the heron clan. Their large, light-sensitive eyes enable them to forage mainly at night, except when feeding their perpetually hungry young.

The black-crowned night-heron is easily recognized in adult plumage by its black crown and back, gray wings and white underparts. During the breeding season, a pair of long, slender white head-plumes extends down the back.

The immature night-heron looks very different in dull gray-brown, streaked and spotted with lighter

Male (front) and female least bitterns (above) tend their young among the sedges of the marsh. Stockier than most other herons, the black-crowned night-heron (right) has a massive beak.

markings. It is similar to the young yellow-crowned night-heron, and the distinction is not an easy one. Most evident are the black-crown's shorter legs, which do not extend beyond the tail in flight. Both immatures might also be confused with the American bittern by beginning birders.

The black-crowned night-heron occurs across the United States and southward through Central and South America, as well as on the Old World continents of Europe, Asia and Africa. It migrates from the northern portion of its U.S. range and spends the winter along the southern coast. Fairly common on the Texas Gulf Coast, the black-crown can be found roosting quietly, sometimes in large groups, in marshes or clumps of salt-cedars during the day. It also perches on piers and boats along the water's edge. In summer it disperses throughout the state, nesting in colonies near water, often with other herons.

At dusk the large birds leave their daytime roosts to hunt, taking wing with loud cries variously described as *kwawk* and *quock*. The scientific name, *Nycticorax*, means "night raven" and refers to the croaking, ravenlike call.

Yellow-crowned night-heron.

YELLOW-CROWNED NIGHT-HERON
Nyctanassa violacea

The yellow-crowned night-heron is a handsome bird, with its pewter-gray body and black head contrasting sharply with white cap and cheek patch. The yellow tinge to the crown, for which it is named, is not easily seen. Long head plumes trail down the back during the breeding season. Adult plumage is not achieved until the third year, and immatures look very much like black-crowns. They are slightly grayer with less conspicuous spotting and have stouter beaks and longer legs.

Less common than its black-crowned cousin, the yellow-crown is also less social in its habits. It is a denizen of the wooded swamps and marshes, but I also see it frequently in the ditches beside Houston roadways, stalking along quietly in search of crayfish, cars whizzing past in all directions. The bulky stick nests may also be built in tall trees within city parks and residential areas.

The yellow-crowned night-heron is resident in the southeastern states and thence southward to Peru and Brazil. Like many other birds, it tends to wander northward after the breeding season, reaching most of the eastern U.S. but returning to the deep South in autumn. In Texas it winters very locally along the coast and can be difficult to find, but during the breeding season it spreads out across the eastern portions of the state.

Less nocturnal than the black-crown, it forages during the day as well as at dusk. It is particularly fond of crabs and crayfish, and to that end has an unusually heavy bill for cracking its hard-shelled catch. It seems infinitely patient, remaining rigid for hours beside a pond. The stalk is agonizingly slow, but the strike is lightning fast. If surprised, the two-foot-tall bird may freeze rather than fly, giving the lucky bird watcher a close-up look at a very striking heron.

IBISES AND SPOONBILLS (Family Threskiornithidae)

These long-legged, heronlike waders are notable for their strangely shaped bills. The bills of the ibises are slender and curved sharply downward; those of the spoonbills, flattened and spatulate. About 30 species occur around the world.

The family has received a broad spectrum of treatment from various human cultures. The sacred ibis was deified as the god Toth by the ancient Egyptians, and the very rare Japanese ibis was declared a national treasure by that government. Ibises have been popular subjects for Japanese and Chinese artists through the ages. In the United States, on the other hand, hundreds of thousands of white ibises and roseate spoonbills were slaughtered in the late 19th century because their feathers were prized for ladies' hats.

White ibises probe the marsh with long, downcurved bills.

WHITE IBIS *Eudocimus albus*

They come in streamers and ragged V-formations, stark white against the blue Texas sky. At a distance they might be mistaken for geese, but they look too long and lean, slender necks outstretched in front, legs behind. The flight is different too, an alternate flapping and gliding as the skeins swing in over the marsh. There is no noisy clamor as from geese, only the sound of the wind in the reeds. At closer range the black wing-tips are visible, and the long, downcurved pink bills. Then stiltlike pink legs come down and the flock of white ibises settles lightly and gracefully into the shallow water. Immediately they begin to feed.

They move in unison, as if following a choreographed routine, beaks probing the mud ahead. Stride, probe. Stride, probe. Occasionally an ibis raises its head to swallow a tasty morsel, then, as if afraid of losing ground, hurries to regain its place in the advancing line. It is one of nature's great ballets.

The ibis uses its long, probing bill to search for crabs, crayfish, snails, insects and other tidbits in the marshes, swamps and flooded rice fields. As the nesting season nears and the hormones flow, that bill and the bare facial skin and legs turn brilliant, shiny scarlet, as if freshly enameled for the nuptial event. Few birds are more striking in a bizarre yet elegant way.

The white ibis is a bird of the southeastern coastal marshes, from the Carolinas to Florida and around the Gulf, then southward into Central and South America. In Texas it lives primarily along the coast but wanders occasionally inland. It nests frequently in colonies on the coastal islands, building a stick platform to contain the two to four light greenish eggs blotched with brown.

At the nest the usually silent birds talk to each other in nasal grunts, *urnk, urnk,* a poor attempt at birdsong but somehow appropriate coming from the strangely primordial ibis.

Immatures are brownish with white underparts and rumps. They gradually molt into the immaculate white of the adults by their second fall. Although these strangely mottled young may be confusing to the beginning birder, they are easily recognized as ibises by the drooping bills, and are distinguished from the all-dark white-faced ibises by their two-toned plumage.

WHITE-FACED IBIS *Plegadis chihi*

The long-legged birds striding through the marsh grass appear at first to be entirely a dark and dingy brown. Their long, decurved bills, with which they constantly probe the mud, mark them unquestionably as ibises. Occasionally some flutter up and move on ahead; the others then scurry forward to catch up, eating on the run.

They stop and begin to preen, sickle bills smoothing and arranging each errant feather. Sunlight strikes the lanky birds and turns their plumage to a richer chestnut hue, bathing them in a rainbow iridescence of bronze and green and violet. The bills and legs are red; the red facial skin is bordered by a white, feathered line that extends around behind the eyes and under the chin. At close range and in good light, they are unexpectedly beautiful birds.

The white facial border gives this ibis its common name. A bird of the Great Plains and western marshes, it ranges along the Texas coast and has bred as far inland as San Antonio. It also appears as a transient in the Panhandle and West Texas.

Highly social birds, white-faced ibises nest in colonies, sometimes with several other species of water

White-faced ibis.

birds and waders. They build shallow cuplike nests of reeds or sticks in the marsh grass or low bushes, lining them with finer plant materials. Both parents care for the three or four pale bluish or blue-green eggs, the female incubating through the night, the male during the day. They both feed the young on crustaceans, frogs, insects and worms.

Populations have been declining throughout their North American range, at least partially because of the draining of wetlands. Heavy use of pesticides and herbicides in the rice fields of Texas and Louisiana presents another threat. Analysis of nest failures along the Texas coast has revealed lethal concentrations of dieldrin and other persistent insecticides in the bodies of the nestlings.

A close relative of the white-faced ibis, the glossy ibis *(Plegadis falcinellus),* ranges along the Atlantic and eastern Gulf coasts. Birders are now reporting this eastern species more frequently along the upper Texas coast, although it is not clear whether this marks a real range expansion or simply an increase in observant birders. The distinction is not an easy one, especially when the white-face loses its white facial border after the breeding season. The glossy ibis has gray rather than pink facial skin, and the legs are gray-green with red only at the joints. Only a few glossy ibises are detected in Texas each year, however, and most dark ibises in our region can safely be assumed to be white-faced.

ROSEATE SPOONBILL
Ajaia ajaja

There is no mistaking the roseate spoonbill, with its gorgeous pink plumage and uniquely shaped bill. Many Texans call it the "pink flamingo," but the true flamingo is a very different bird, taller and lankier and with a heavy, sharply bent bill. No truly wild flamingos breed in the United States; the closest colonies are

Roseate spoonbill in flight.

in the West Indies and the Yucatán. A few stragglers have been reported from southern Texas and from Florida, but most appear to be escapees from captivity.

From about 1890 to 1919, the roseate spoonbill population was severely depleted by plume hunters. An extensive survey in 1920 found only 179 birds along the lower Texas coast. With protective legislation, the species has made a significant recovery, although biologists still worry about the long-term effects of pollution and habitat loss.

The roseate spoonbill breeds from southern Florida, southwestern Louisiana and the Texas coast through Central America and the Greater Antilles to Argentina and Chile. Many leave Texas in the winter, but a few can usually be found in coastal bays and ponds. There they feed in the shallow water, immersing their spatulate bills and swinging their heads in wide arcs from side to side, grasping small fish, shrimp, water beetles, and any other aquatic creatures they might encounter.

Spoonbills breed in colonies scattered along the Texas coast, some-

times as far inland as Eagle Lake and Bay City. Stragglers have been reported near Dallas and even in Pecos and the Panhandle, but such sightings are rare.

The nest is a crude platform of sticks in a bush or tree, often in a mixed colony of herons and other wading birds. Both sexes assist with the nest and take turns incubating the two or three chalky white eggs mottled with brown. As the pair exchange places at the nest, they bow and croak to each other. The low grunting croak, *huh huh huh,* is the only "song" of the usually silent spoonbill.

During their first year, immature birds are pale pink with feathered heads, but they become bald as they reach adulthood. The pink coloration deepens with age, enhanced by the shellfish on which they feed, and the red splashes on the wings and the flashing orange tails become especially brilliant during breeding season. The combination of bare head and flattened beak gives the spoonbill a slightly ridiculous, almost reptilian look that seems strangely at odds with the beautiful plumage.

STORKS (Family Ciconiidae)

The storks are big, long-legged, heronlike birds that fly with their necks outstretched rather than pulled back in a graceful S-curve like the herons. About 18 species occur throughout the world, but only one, the wood stork, is found regularly in North America. Another, the even larger jabiru (*Jabiru mycteria),* is an extremely rare straggler to southern Texas from Central and South America.

WOOD STORK *Mycteria americana*

Named for its penchant for nesting and roosting in trees, the wood stork is a summer visitor to Texas, wandering northward in family groups or small flocks after the breeding season in the tropics. It occurs mainly along the coast, where it stalks slowly and deliberately through the marshes and shallow ponds, feeding on almost anything it can catch. Fish, crabs, crayfish, small snakes, turtles, frogs and large insects are all grabbed in the half-open beak, which is swung from side to side in the water.

One of the largest of the wading birds, the wood stork stands three-and-one-half feet tall and has a wingspread of more than five feet. The black trailing edges of the wings and the black tail contrast sharply with the white plumage. The massive beak is nearly ten inches long, thick and slightly downcurved. It is this remarkable appendage that gives our stork its scientific name: *mykter* is the Greek word for "snout."

Immature birds have feathered heads, but they become progressively more bald as they near adulthood. The dark gray, naked head and neck are responsible for the stork's popular nickname, "flinthead." Close-up, it is definitely not just another pretty face, but what it lacks in facial beauty, it makes up for in grace on the wing. It flies with long neck and legs extended, huge wings flapping slowly and rhythmically. Catching the thermals on a hot summer afternoon, a flock may soar upward in sweeping spirals until lost from sight among the clouds.

In older bird books the wood stork was called the wood ibis. It was more recently determined to be a true stork, not an ibis, and was renamed. Once fairly common in the southeastern U.S. and around the Gulf Coast, where it nested in the treetops of cypress swamps, the wood stork has declined drastically in the last few decades and is seriously threatened. The logging and draining of swamps, the channelization of rivers and bayous, pollution and pesticides have all taken their toll. Our only North American stork faces an uncertain future.

The wood stork (above and opposite) has declined seriously in recent decades.

CRANES (Family Gruidae)

Sandhill crane.

Fifteen species of cranes occur throughout the world, inhabiting every continent except South America and Antarctica. They are tall, stately birds, more robust than herons, and often with red patches of bare facial skin. The long tertial feathers of the wings drape over the rump as a "bustle," further distinguishing them from the large herons, which many people erroneously call "cranes." Two species, the whooping crane and the sandhill crane, occur in North America.

Cranes that breed in the northern latitudes around the globe make long migration flights, soaring high into the sky on the thermals and flying in lines or V-formations like geese. Their necks are outstretched in flight, and their resonant, trumpeting calls can be heard for miles. Elaborate courtship displays involve leaping and prancing in wild dances, accompanied by the sonorous notes made possible by an extraordinarily long windpipe coiled within the breastbone.

Many of the world's cranes face serious threats from destruction of their environments. It is an ancient lineage, dating back at least to the Eocene, some 40 to 60 million years ago, and the birds cannot readily alter their long-established habits. Captive breeding offers hope for several species, for most have produced young in zoos and research centers. Tomb drawings in Egypt indicate young cranes were reared in captivity thousands of years ago. A major problem with such breeding programs, however, lies in maintaining behavior patterns necessary for survival after releasing captive-raised birds in the wild.

Whooping crane calling.

A whooping crane comes in for a landing at Texas' Aransas National Wildlife Refuge.

WHOOPING CRANE *Grus americana*

The tall, stately birds stride across the coastal marsh, stopping occasionally to pluck a tasty morsel from the shallow water. The two adults are plumaged in immaculate white, their elongated tertial feathers forming the "bustle" that gives cranes their distinctive shape. Their slightly smaller youngster is still washed and mottled with rusty brown.

One of the parents catches a blue crab and drops it on the muddy bank, where the juvenile grabs it and wolfs it down. They wander a little farther and then launch themselves into the air, seven-foot wings beating ponderously, revealing for the first time the black wing-tips that are hidden except in flight. Long necks are outstretched; legs trail far out behind. Across the marsh comes the trumpeting call, *ker-loo ker-lee-loo*, an echo from the Pleistocene, resonating within the five-foot windpipe of this tallest of all North American birds.

The story of the whooping crane has been called "a love affair of two nations with a great white bird." One of the most famous birds in the world, the whooper once ranged across the continent. Widespread, but probably never abundant, the species gave way to the advancing human settlers of the land. Many were shot for food or trophies; others vanished as their marsh-lands were drained and cleared. When President Franklin D. Roosevelt signed the executive order creating the new federal Aransas Migratory Waterfowl Refuge on December 31, 1937, only two small flocks of whooping cranes remained. One flock migrated south from Canada to winter at Aransas. The other remained year-round in Louisiana.

The latter flock, containing a dozen cranes, was halved by a tropical storm in 1940, and the remaining birds disappeared one by one within the next few years. The new Texas refuge, now known as the Aransas National Wildlife Refuge, provided a haven for all that were left. The fate of the whooping crane rested on a tiny remnant of 15 birds.

The nesting ground of these migratory cranes was not known until 1954. After several searches had failed, a forester and helicopter pilot flying to a wildfire spotted adults with young along the Sass River in Wood Buffalo National Park in the Northwest Territories. Since then, Canadian and U.S. biologists have been able to study the whooping cranes on the breeding grounds and to follow them on their annual migration of some 2,400 miles between northern Canada and the Texas coast.

Whooping cranes lay two eggs, but only one chick normally survives. Thus, at little risk to the wild population, the biologists began in 1967 to remove one egg from some of the nests in order to raise a captive flock at the Patuxent Research Center of the U.S. Fish and Wildlife Service in Laurel, Maryland.

In 1975, another experiment began in which whooping crane eggs were placed in the nests of sandhill cranes at Idaho's Grays Lake Refuge. This practice continued for several years and seemed at first to have great potential. The fledgling whoopers migrated with their foster-parent sandhill cranes from Idaho to refuges in New Mexico; however, they showed no interest in mating with others of their kind as they reached adulthood and gradually succumbed to accidents

and predators. The experiment was recently terminated, and captive flocks are now being maintained at the Patuxent site and at the International Crane Foundation in Baraboo, Wisconsin.

The migratory flock wintering in Texas, meanwhile, began to increase slowly with added protection and concern. From a low of 15 in 1941, the population passed 100 in 1986. In the fall of 1990, a record 146 whooping cranes arrived on the Texas coast from Canada, but only 134 survived to make the return journey. At least one was shot; others apparently died or were killed by predators. Several mated pairs failed to nest in 1991 because of a severe drought, and breeding success was poor. Although 21 chicks were sighted early in the summer, only nine survived the season. By the time the flock reached Aransas for the winter, it numbered 131 birds, 123 adults and eight young.

The future is much brighter than it was a half century ago, but the fate of the whooping crane is by no means assured. Loss of habitat to coastal erosion, dredging, poisonous contaminants in the soil and water, and possible oil or chemical spills in the Intracoastal Canal all threaten the only wild flock of the great white birds.

The cranes begin arriving at Aransas Refuge in late October and remain into April. Migrating as family groups, they set up territories of nearly a square mile in the coastal marsh and stalk through the shallows to feed on blue crabs, clams and occasional small fish. Acorns, berries, roots and grains supplement the varied diet. The long-legged cranes roost standing in shallow water, where it is difficult for predators to approach.

Cranes can sometimes be seen from the observation tower at Aransas, and a number of boats docked in the Rockport-Fulton area offer crane-watching trips. The boats guarantee seeing a number of cranes, and close-up views are frequent. Few experiences in Texas birding equal a personal encounter with the majestic whooping cranes.

SANDHILL CRANE
Grus canadensis

High overhead they fly, a ragged line of giant birds silhouetted against the stormy sky. Powerful wings beat slowly and rhythmically with little apparent effort. Long necks are outstretched; legs trail far out behind. Over the sound of the prairie wind comes the rolling, trumpeting cry, gar-oo-oo gar-oo-oo, echoing back and forth within the flock. There is no more thrilling sound in wild America than the call of the sandhill cranes.

If the whooping cranes are the aristocrats of Texas birds, then the sandhills are Everyman's birds. They come in large flocks from the North to spend the winter on the Panhandle plains and in the South Texas brush country. They settle into the rice fields west of Houston and on the prairies along the coast. They stalk majestically through open marshes and grasslands, feeding on a cosmopolitan diet of small animals and aquatic life, insects, grain, green shoots and berries. Ever alert, the wary birds scan the horizon from their four-foot height, ready to take to the air if danger threatens, sounding the alarm with a bugle call.

The gray plumage of the sandhill crane may be stained with rusty red from the iron-rich mud of northern marshes. The bare red skin on the crown and the "bustle" of fluffy feathers distinguish it from the great blue heron. The latter is frequently called a "blue crane," but the two are very different in posture and behavior as well as in their lineage.

Sandhills breed on the tundra of Canada and Alaska and in the marshes and grasslands of the northern states. Nests are bulky piles of sticks, reeds or moss and usually contain two eggs. Incubation lasts 28 to 32 days, and it is nearly ten weeks before the young can fly. In the fall the families band together and head southward to spend the winter in the southwestern states and on into Mexico. A nonmigratory subspecies of the sandhill that nests in Florida and along the eastern Gulf Coast is severely endangered.

The greatest threat to the future of the sandhill crane exists neither on its nesting grounds nor in its winter territory, but rather at a major stopping point on its migratory path. In the spring the cranes assemble by the tens of thousands along the Platte River in Nebraska, feeding on worms and snails in the meadows and on waste corn in the fields. At night they return to the Platte to roost, standing in the shallow water where predators can less readily surprise them.

The gathering of the sandhill cranes is one of the world's premier wildlife spectacles, and people come from across the country to watch the flights. A half million birds make the journey every spring, "the largest concentration of any species of crane anywhere in the world," writes famed bird expert Roger Tory Peterson.

Yet the Platte itself is in danger. Water is channeled away for a variety of human uses, and the flow decreases annually. The fate of the sandhills may well depend on the fate of the river, for the habits of the ages are difficult to change.

Huge flocks of stately sandhill cranes spend the winter at the Muleshoe National Wildlife Refuge in the Texas Panhandle.

DUCKLIKE WATER BIRDS

lmost everyone, whether a birder or not, recognizes many of the common species of ducks and geese. Some of the other families included here, however, are less well known. Loons, grebes and gallinules might easily be mistaken for ducks, while the secretive rails seldom venture far from sheltering reeds and marsh grasses and thus are easily overlooked.

This organization implies no taxonomic relationship, but is merely one of convenience in grouping birds of somewhat similar appearance and habitat. The families are not closely related, and further examination shows that their beaks and feet vary greatly in form and function. These dictate the feeding habits of the various species and their specialized niches in the environment.

Although ducks, loons, grebes, coots, gallinules and cormorants may all be seen swimming together on large bodies of water, they apportion the available food according to their own anatomical adaptations and abilities and do not compete as much as it might first appear. Some feed on small fish and aquatic creatures; some are primarily vegetarian. And while some are deep-diving birds of prey, others usually remain in shallow water or wade among the aquatic plants. A careful look at the beak shape of water birds will reveal a great deal about familial relationships.

Tundra swans and American wigeon.

LOONS (Family Gaviidae)

Loons inhabit the far North, with some breeding in the Arctic almost to the northern limits of land. Because they are exclusively aquatic, however, they must migrate southward in winter to find open water. It is then that loons make their appearance in Texas.

The family consists of only five species that range across the Northern Hemisphere: the common loon, which is the one most frequently seen in Texas; the yellow-billed loon; the red-throated loon; and the Pacific and Arctic loons. The latter two were only recently determined to be separate species. Loons are collectively called "divers" by European ornithologists and birders.

Loons are considered the most primitive of North American birds, tracing their ancestry far back into avian antiquity. Such determinations are highly subjective, of course, but for this reason the loons are generally placed at the beginning of our current field guides, which attempt to arrange the families from the most primitive to the most highly evolved.

In spite of their seemingly archaic lineage, loons are perfectly adapted for life in the water. They are, quite literally, swimming and diving machines, streamlined and with their webbed feet located far back on their bodies, the original stern-wheeler paddleboats. Canadian bird artist Terence Shortt calls their legs "the perfect swimming devices—the most efficient paddles ever developed." The feet are laterally compressed and flare into long, webbed toes. These paddles give a vigorous thrust, while on the return stroke the toes fold along the knife-edge feet to give a minimum of resistance.

With all their skill in the water, loons are virtually helpless on land. Because they cannot bring their feet forward under their bodies, they waddle awkwardly along, pushing themselves on their bellies. They build their nests at the water's edge, where they can readily slide on and off. They are strong fliers, but their bones are solid rather than pneumatic as in most other birds, another adaptation for diving. Thus loons have difficulty getting airborne and take off with a long, flapping run across the surface.

COMMON LOON *Gavia immer*

More than any other bird, the common loon has become a symbol of the northern wilderness. Its haunting cries echo through the boreal forests from Alaska to Iceland and southward through Canada to the upper regions of the United States. Scores of wildlife artists have painted its image, which also adorns souvenirs of every description from the resort areas of the great North Woods. European ornithologists give it the far more romantic name "great northern diver."

In breeding plumage, the common loon is glossy black above and white below. White spots checker the black back; a collar of white streaks encircles the neck. In the sunlight, the head and neck shimmer with a greenish iridescence. Swimming on the blue surface of a deep glacial lake surrounded by dark spruce trees and white-trunked birches, it seems the epitome of avian elegance.

Unfortunately for Texas birders, this is not the bird that migrates on powerful wings across our state to spend the winter along the coast. In its postnuptial molt, the common loon loses its dapper plumage and becomes a more uniform dark gray on the head, neck and back. Stilled, too, is the beautiful, melancholy call described by various authors as a cry, a yodel or an eerie laugh. The loon seldom calls on its wintering grounds, for it uses the wild song to proclaim a nesting territory, and it usually departs Texas before molting again to courtship plumage in the spring.

Despite its drabber plumage and its silence, Texas' version of the common loon is no less fascinating a bird. A magnificent swimmer and diver, it is fairly common along the upper and central coast from late October into April. It occurs less frequently south of Corpus Christi and on large inland lakes. A bird the size of a small goose, the loon swims low in the water, diving repeatedly in pursuit of fish. When approached, it disappears instantly and can remain submerged for a minute or more, reappearing well out of danger. It seldom flies when threatened, for its heavy body and solid bones make the take-off a frantic, scrambling run across the surface. Safety lies in its natural element below the waves.

The common loon is by far the most abundant loon in Texas. The smaller red-throated (*Gavia stellata*) and Pacific (*G. pacifica*) loons occasionally turn up along the coast or on inland lakes, but it requires an experienced and sharp-eyed birder to sort them out in winter plumage. Cormorants also share their habitat with loons and are often mistaken for them. One of the easiest distinctions at a distance is that the loon holds its head level, with its massive, daggerlike bill parallel to the water's surface. Cormorants tend to hold their heads tilted while swimming, with their hook-tipped bills pointing slightly upward.

For all its elegance and beauty, and in spite of it ancient lineage, the common loon faces an uncertain future. Pollution and acid rain in once-pure northern lakes have depleted small fish and aquatic invertebrates on which loons feed. An increasing number of lakeside homes and cabins, with their attendant boat traffic, makes it difficult to find the solitude they demand. Oil spills, too, take their toll as loons spend the winter season along the coasts. The common loon warrants immediate public concern, for there is no more elegant nor poetic symbol of the North American wilderness.

A common loon begins to molt from its drab gray winter plumage.

GREBES (Family Podicipedidae)

The grebes compose a worldwide family, seven of which occur in North America. All can be seen occasionally in Texas; however, the horned grebe, the red-necked grebe, and the recently separated Clark's and western grebes are rare or irregular transients. The pied-billed and eared grebes are more abundant throughout the state, while the tiny least grebe inhabits deep South Texas. The last three are considered here.

The Podicipedidae take their name from the Latin *podiceps,* for "rump-footed." Like the loons, grebes have their legs contained largely within the body skin, and the feet emerge far to the rear, serving as efficient paddles. The toes are widely lobed, rather than webbed, and the flaps spread out in the propulsion stroke and fold around the toes on the recovery stroke while swimming and diving. The position of the feet makes grebes extremely awkward out of water, and they seldom venture onto land.

They might be confused with ducks, but they sit higher in the water and have pointed beaks and longer, more slender necks. The feathers of the breast are dense and sleek, perfectly waterproofed for an aquatic life. During the era of the plume hunters, grebes were shot by the thousands and shipped to eastern markets to make women's hats, muffs and handbags from the rich "grebe fur."

Some of the species are noted for their elaborate courtship displays in which both partners bow and bob and race upright across the water in a synchronized love dance.

An eared grebe carries its young on its back.

PIED-BILLED GREBE *Podilymbus podiceps*

The marshy pond is quiet under the hot Texas sun. An occasional dragonfly skims the surface hawking insects, but there is little other movement. Suddenly a head appears like a periscope among the reeds, its beady brown eyes ringed with white. The head remains motionless for several minutes and then sinks slowly, only to reappear beside a floating pile of moldering vegetation. Finally, deciding the coast is clear, the bird rises to the surface like a miniature foot-long submarine and clambers onto the pile. It picks aside a covering of damp reeds with its white, black-ringed bill to reveal a half-dozen eggs. Droplets glistening on its waterproof gray-brown plumage, the pied-billed grebe settles down to incubate.

The whitish eggs are stained brown by the sodden, decaying vegetation of the nest. In a few days they will hatch into bizarrely striped black-and-white chicks. As soon as their downy feathers dry, the precocial young will slide from the nest and paddle off to join their parents, frequently riding on their backs and peering out from beneath a sheltering wing. The strange, resonant calls of the grebes break the summer silence, *cow-cow-cow-cow-cow-cowm-cowm.*

The pied-billed grebe occurs across most of North, Central and South America, from Canada to Argentina, migrating from the coldest regions to seek open water. It ranges through virtually all of Texas where appropriate marshy ponds, lakes and sloughs can be found but is more abundant in the eastern half. More solitary than other grebes, which nest in loose colonies, the pied-bill breeds in fresh water but also moves into the coastal bays for the winter.

Food items include small fish, insects, crustaceans and snails. Like most grebes, the pied-bill also eats quantities of its own feathers for reasons that are not well understood. Balls of feathers have been found in its stomach, and even small chicks consume feathers taken from the parents. It may be that the feathers pad the stomach and protect it from sharp fish bones, slowing down digestion so the bones have more time to dissolve.

A pied-billed grebe might be mistaken for a small duck, but the beak is like that of a chicken. In winter the white beak turns dusky, and the black ring, for which the species is named, disappears. Locally called "water witch," "dabchick" or "helldiver," the pied-billed grebe may be encountered on almost any body of water in Texas, swimming buoyantly along, diving repeatedly for food, or sinking slowly out of sight at your approach.

LEAST GREBE
Tachybaptus dominicus

The least grebe is a secretive resident of the freshwater ponds and resacas of South Texas, one of the checklist prizes for which birders come from across the continent to visit the lower Rio Grande Valley. A tropical species, it ranges from Mexico southward to Argentina and into the West Indies. However, in the United States it occurs only in Texas and very rarely in southern Arizona.

Nine to ten inches long and less than half the bulk of the more abundant and widespread pied-billed grebe, this tiny bird is brownish gray with a black crown and throat in breeding plumage. Because size can be hard to judge without proper reference, the slender little beak and the gleaming yellow eyes constitute the best field marks. White wing-patches are also characteristic but seldom seen, since least grebes rarely fly.

The normally shy grebes nest up to four times a year on semi-floating rafts anchored to the vegetation of sheltered ponds. The four to six pale eggs are stained by the wet nest, and the precocial young take to the water upon hatching to swim with their parents. In defense of their young or their territories, least grebes can be surprisingly aggressive. Heads lowered, and uttering a series of high-pitched cries, they charge an unwary

Young pied-billed grebes (top) ride on the backs of their parents. A least grebe (above) fiercely defends its South Texas pond.

intruder, chasing off pied-billed grebes and ducks far larger than themselves.

Their food consists largely of aquatic insects such as diving beetles, water bugs and dragonfly nymphs. Other insects are plucked from the emergent vegetation, and a quick snap of the slender beak may even nab a careless dragonfly intent on its own next meal. Small fish, crustaceans, tadpoles and some algae add variety to the diet.

Although the least grebe occurs mainly in the Rio Grande Valley and northward occasionally to San Antonio and Rockport, it may wander in winter to the upper Texas coast. It has even been spotted in the Big Bend region and the Panhandle. Never common, it can usually be found in the ponds at Santa Ana and Laguna Atascosa National Wildlife Refuges or in the waterholes along Highway 281 between Brownsville and McAllen. It is well worth the search to get to know this charming, bright-eyed little "Mexican grebe."

EARED GREBE
Podiceps nigricollis

The small, slender birds bob buoyantly on the waves as the surf rolls onto the Texas beach. They ride high in the water, then dive cleanly and smoothly with forward leaps that propel them far beneath the surface. Swimming powerfully with their broad-lobed toes, they reappear and then dive again in concert. Seldom do eared grebes remain still for long.

In the winter plumage most often seen in Texas, the eared grebe is dark, sooty gray above and white below, with a slim neck and long, thin, pointed bill. Only in breeding plumage does it sport the fanlike golden plumes on the sides of its head from which it takes its name. Then, too, the entire head, neck and back are blackish, giving rise to the European name of "black-necked grebe."

Eared grebes nest across the western half of North America, from southern Canada to the lower tier of states. They also occur in Europe, Asia and Africa. Breeding takes place in large colonies on shallow, reed-bordered freshwater lakes and prairie sloughs. The nests are sloppy piles of vegetation, anchored among the reeds and half awash. When disturbed, the attendant adults slip silently over the edge and swim away underwater. The precocious young ride on their parents' backs and are fed on aquatic insects as well as on occasional small fish, crustaceans and snails. As they grow, they assemble in creches watched over by a few adults, the avian day-care centers of the marsh.

Only rarely do eared grebes nest in Texas, but records do exist from the Panhandle through the central portions of the state. In migration, however, they may be found almost anywhere there is water, and they spend the winter both inland and along the coast.

Eared grebe in breeding plumage.

CORMORANTS (Family Phalacrocoracidae)

The scene is a familiar one from countless paintings and photographs. Tethered birds dive beneath the waves to reappear with small fish clasped securely in their hook-tipped beaks. Prevented from swallowing their catch by rings around their necks, they give up the fish to their handlers in little boats. Thus have fishermen in the Orient utilized for centuries the aquatic skills of Asian cormorants.

Other species inhabit the seacoasts and larger lakes of most regions of the world. Two occur in Texas—the double-crested and neotropic cormorants—while others occupy the Atlantic and Pacific coasts. They are generally dark-plumaged birds with long necks, hooked bills, wedge-shaped tails and bare facial skin and throat pouches. With their legs set far back on their bodies, they perch up-right and waddle clumsily on land. In the water, however, they are truly masters of their realm. On emerging, they often extend their wings to dry, for their outer feathers are not waterproof. While this may seem a surprising adaptation, the wettable feathers decrease buoyancy and help the birds in their underwater pursuit of fish.

Neotropic cormorants.

The word cormorant comes from the Romance languages and means "sea crow." The scientific family name Phalacrocoracidae is from the Greek for "bald raven." The allusions are apparently to the birds' dark plumage and their bare facial skin, for cormorants are not bald.

Cormorants frequently nest in huge colonies, the environments of which are anything but savory. The guano collected from such colonies along the coasts of Chile and Peru has been of enormous value as fertilizer because of its high nitrogen content, leading American ornithologist Robert Cushman Murphy to call the guanay cormorant (*Phalacrocorax bougainvillii*) "the world's most valuable wild bird."

DOUBLE-CRESTED CORMORANT *Phalacrocorax auritus*

It is a common scene along the waterfronts of Galveston, Rockport, Port Isabel and other Texas coastal towns in winter. Large, dark birds sit perched on the piers and pilings, some with their wings outstretched to dry in the brisk sea breeze. Others swim nearby, low in the water and with long necks erect, beaks angled slightly skyward. Occasionally one dives and resurfaces with a small fish in its hook-tipped beak, gulping it down whole as the gulls sweep in to steal the prize away.

Other double-crested cormorants fly overhead in long, ragged lines and V-formations. Nearly three feet long, and with wingspans of more than four feet, they might at first be mistaken for flights of geese. These birds are silent, however, with none of the clamor heard from flocks of geese.

The double-crested cormorant is the larger of Texas' two cormorant species and is the more common one

in winter. It breeds across much of North America, from Alaska to Newfoundland and south to Baja California, Florida and the West Indies. It withdraws from the icebound inland lakes and winters as far south as Central America. During migration, cormorants are found across the state, and many remain until heading north again in spring. They are most numerous along the Gulf Coast, but also inhabit freshwater lakes, ponds and rivers. The few breeding records for Texas are scattered and rare.

Double-crested cormorants normally nest in large colonies wherever there are adequate fishing grounds nearby. The untidy, bulky nests of sticks and debris might be located in towering trees beside a northern lake, on rocky sea cliffs, or among the bushes fringing a southern swamp. Biologists have determined that the race wintering in Texas breeds on the lakes of the central and northern Great Plains and the prairie provinces of Canada.

Adult birds in breeding plumage are black, glossed with bronze and green. The throat pouch is orange. Two small tufts of feathers curve backward from behind the eyes, giving the species its name. The crests are white on western birds, darker and less conspicuous on eastern populations, but they are not usually present while the birds are in Texas. Immature birds have brownish upperparts and paler underparts, particularly on the upper breast and neck. Thus a flock might display a great deal of variety in plumage.

The double-crested cormorant was the subject of great concern during the 1970s and early 1980s as some populations dwindled. Now, however, the species appears to be increasing once again and is a common sight along the Texas coast.

A wintering double-crested cormorant perches with webbed feet on a piling and dries a wing in the warm Texas sun.

Neotropic Cormorant *Phalacrocorax brasilianus*

This smaller of the two Texas cormorants has traveled under several names over the years. It has been known by various authors as the Mexican, Brazilian, bigua, neotropic and olivaceous cormorant. Olivaceous cormorant *(Phalacrocorax olivaceus)* has been the official name for several years, and the species is thus described in most of the field guides presently in use. However, in the 38th supplement to the American Ornithologists' Union *Check-list of North American Birds,* published in July 1991 in *The Auk,* the name was changed again. The AOU, the governing board of bird nomenclature, decided that *P. brasilianus* took scientific precedence over *P. olivaceus.* In addition, the supplement noted, "The English name is changed herein to conform to widespread use among ornithologists working with Neotropical birds and to remove the misleading connotation that the species is 'olivaceous.' "

In truth, adult birds are black, with only a slight olive gloss to the back and wings. The small throat-pouch is dull yellow and, in breeding plumage, has a white border. During the breeding season, adults also have short white plumes on the sides of the neck. Immatures are browner, especially on the underparts.

As the present name implies, the neotropic cormorant is primarily a southern species. It breeds along the Gulf Coast of Louisiana and Texas and thence south through Central and South America. In Texas it inhabits the coastal counties, ranging infrequently inland as far as Dallas, Austin and San Antonio. It appears to be less common in the winter, when it shares its domain with large flocks of double-crested cormorants.

Colonial nesters, as are most related species, neotropic cormorants build in bushes and trees over water or on the ground on islands in the bays. Their stick nests hold four or five pale blue, chalky eggs. Young are fed an unappetizing but nutritious diet of regurgitated fish, frogs and aquatic insects.

The neotropic cormorant can be distinguished from the double-crested by its smaller size and slimmer bill, by the proportionately longer tail, and by the white border on the throat-pouch of breeding adults. Without a direct comparison, the task is not always an easy one. Roger Tory Peterson writes in his field guide to Texas birds, "Distinguishing Olivaceous [now neotropic] from Double-crested Cormorant when the two are not together is one of the *real problems* of Texas field ornithology."

In breeding plumage the neotropic cormorant sports a white border on its throat pouch.

ANHINGAS (Family Anhingidae)

Texas "water-turkey."

The anhingas, also called "darters," are oddly shaped birds that Canadian ornithologist and bird artist Terence Shortt aptly describes as, "Like a slender cormorant with the neck and head of a heron." Most authors recognize four species—one each in Africa, Asia, Australia and the Americas—while some lobby for lumping them together in a single worldwide species. They occupy tropical and warm temperate zones and prefer freshwater habitats.

Excellent swimmers and divers, anhingas often perch with outstretched wings in the manner of the cormorants. While cormorants adopt the posture to dry their poorly waterproofed wings, however, anhingas apparently use it as a means of thermoregulation. They have unusually high rates of heat loss from their bodies and low metabolic rates. Thus they spread their wings and turn their backs to the warming sun to absorb solar energy and supplement their own low heat production.

Anhingas also have strangely structured neck vertebrae that result in a pronounced crook in the long neck, similar to that of the herons. This gives the birds the ability to thrust forward quickly and powerfully, driving their sharp fish-spear bills into their prey.

ANHINGA *Anhinga anhinga*

Rays of sunlight filter through draperies of Spanish moss, illuminating the dark waters of a cypress swamp. A large bird swims smoothly along with scarcely a ripple, little more than its head and neck above the surface. It sinks slowly from sight and soon reappears with a fish impaled on its rapier bill. With a quick flip of its head, the bird tosses the fish into the air and swallows it whole, a bulge marking the progress of the fish down the long and sinuous neck. Swimming to the bank, the anhinga clambers awkwardly up onto a fallen tree, its sharply clawed, webbed feet scrabbling for a hold on the slippery wood. It perches on a branch and spreads its wings in a patch of sun. Epaulettes of silvery white spots and streaks ornament its glossy black plumage.

The anhinga is unique in American ornithology in having its common name and both parts of its scientific name the same. It is the name given to this handsome bird by the Tupi Indians of Brazil. Also called "snakebird" for its habit of swimming with only its neck and head exposed, the anhinga is frequently confused with the cormorants. However, it can easily be distinguished by its sharply pointed bill, much longer tail, and the light patches on the wings and upper back. Males are otherwise entirely black; females have buffy necks and breasts.

While cormorants inhabit both freshwater lakes and saline coastal bays and beaches, anhingas prefer freshwater swamps, ponds and rivers. They build their nests of sticks in trees and bushes along the water, usually in small groups or among colonies of herons and egrets. The one to five light bluish white eggs require nearly a month to hatch, and the naked, helpless altricial chicks must be brooded constantly until they gain their first thick coats of buffy down. Immature birds resemble females, but are browner overall.

Anhingas range across the Southeast, from North Carolina to Texas, and southward to Argentina. They are partially migratory, presumably because their low metabolic rate makes it difficult for them to keep warm in colder water. In Texas, they are fairly common in the eastern portions and along the coast, wandering occasionally inland as far as the edge of the Edwards Plateau. They winter in the southern tip of the state and sparingly near the coast.

While anhingas are adapted for a life in the water, they are marvelously graceful on the wing. Small flocks can frequently be seen soaring high overhead, spiraling like hawks for hours on end. Their long necks are outstretched in front, long tails fanned wide behind. It is this large tail that presumably led to another colloquial name for the anhinga, the "water-turkey."

Perched in a Texas swamp, this anhinga is growing new feathers to replace those molted from its long tail.

RAILS, GALLINULES AND COOTS (Family Rallidae)

Common moorhen.

The Rallidae are primarily marsh birds with stubby, soft, upturned tails and short, rounded wings. Some 130 species occur around the world in habitats ranging from dense jungle swamps to remote oceanic islands. Most species fly only under duress, wings beating frantically and long legs dangling. Seeing a rail flush from cover, it is difficult to believe that many of them migrate considerable distances.

Coots and gallinules swim like ducks, frequently pumping their heads back and forth as they glide through the water. They have chickenlike bills that extend in horny frontal shields up their foreheads. Coots are equipped with lobed toes for paddling; gallinules have extremely long, slender toes suited for walking across the lily pads and emergent vegetation. Two gallinules and a single coot species are common U.S. and Texas residents.

The chicken-shaped rails spend much of their time among the dense grasses and reeds. Surprised while feeding on the fringes of the marsh, they melt away into the vegetation without the slightest movement of the leaves to mark their passage. Their laterally compressed bodies give rise to the common saying "thin as a rail." Six species occur regularly in Texas. The large clapper and king rails and the somewhat smaller Virginia rail have moderately long, slightly downcurved bills. The sora and the tiny black and yellow rails have short, stout bills. The latter two are extremely secretive and difficult to find.

The various rails are prizes absent from many birders' lists, yet several are common enough to be hunted as game birds. Because of their secretive nature and cryptic coloration, they usually go unnoticed by the casual observer. More often heard than seen, this family provides what authors have called "the mysterious voices of the swamp."

Many of the worldwide Rallidae are seriously threatened. Some have adapted to isolated islands and other specialized niches and now lack the ability to react to the introduction of domestic animals and such imported pests as rats and mice. Pesticides, pollution, and habitat destruction as wetlands are drained and filled have also taken a heavy toll.

AMERICAN COOT *Fulica americana*

The ubiquitous coot can be found on almost any lake, pond, marsh or bay in Texas, especially along the coast. It breeds locally throughout the state but is especially abundant during migration and in the winter, when it withdraws from the icebound northern portions of its range. It occurs from the Atlantic to the Pacific and from Canada to Ecuador.

Many sections of the country have their own colloquial names for this strange bird with the body and habits of a duck, the bill of a chicken, the lobed toes of a grebe, and the family lineage of the rails and gallinules. The coot is called the "mud hen" in the Midwest. In Louisiana and East Texas, it is the *"poule d'eau."* The word coot can be traced back to 14th-century English, but its origins are not known. In present usage it has also come to signify a foolish or silly person, a not inappropriate simile, one might think, on watching a flock of coots in action.

The American coot is dark slate-gray, with a black head and neck and white undertail coverts. The white bill, encircled by a dark ring, extends up onto the forehead in a small, brownish shield. Related species occur in other portions of the world.

Coots prefer to nest in weedy freshwater marshes and wetlands but assemble in large flocks on both fresh and salt water in winter. Their omnivorous diet includes marsh plants, algae, seeds, roots, snails, worms, aquatic insects and small fish. They frequently feed with ducks, picking up water plants and animals stirred up by the ducks' feet. This "commensal feeding" benefits the coots at no material cost to their hosts. They feed from the surface like the dabbling ducks but are also capable of diving deep in search of tasty morsels. Coots may be encountered, too, on waterfront lawns and roadsides, where they wander about like chickens, eating seeds and insects.

Coots are conspicuous and noisy birds, aggressively defending their territories. They "splatter" across the water with flapping wings to confront intruders, uttering a vocal barrage of what Texas ornithologist Harry Oberholser wonderfully describes as "croaks, squawks, grunts, cackles, and other raucous notes, whistles, and toots."

The flapping, scrambling run across the surface is usually used to move from one feeding location to another. Coots fly when necessary, and are capable of long migrations, but getting airborne presents a problem. Nature writer Guy Murchie, Jr., once noted that the coot "takes off like a 1915 scout plane missing on three cylinders."

The nest is a saucer of reeds concealed among the marsh grasses or on a raft of dead vegetation. Incubation of the 6 to 15 buffy eggs speckled with brown and black begins after only a portion of the clutch is laid. Thus, the downy chicks do not all hatch at the same time. The new hatchlings join one parent to feed and to be brooded in a series of nestlike platforms built nearby while the other adult continues incubation. Over much of their range, coots breed but once, but an early start may allow a second, overlapping brood.

The dumpy, dusky, somewhat comical coot is one of Texas' most common water birds. It is also one of the most adaptable. In places where bird populations are in decline, the American coot serves as an indicator species of the health and future of our vital wetlands.

American coots nibble at water plants picked beneath the surface of a Texas pond.

Common moorhens.

COMMON MOORHEN *Gallinula chloropus*

Until recent years this cosmopolitan bird was named the common gallinule throughout its extensive range in the Americas. In the Old World, however, where the same species occurs on the European, Asian and African continents, it was called the moorhen. American ornithologists, in an effort to standardize bird names, finally bowed to international usage, and we now have the common moorhen, although there is not a moor in sight.

The moorhen, née gallinule, is equally at home swimming with the ducks or wading through the marsh grasses and reeds with its rail cousins. Bolder than many of the Rallidae, it also wanders along the banks to feed on weed seeds and berries. It prefers freshwater marshes, ponds and resacas with emergent vegetation and grassy edges and is less common in saline and brackish environments.

The common moorhen ranges across the U.S. east of the Great Plains, as well as through portions of southern California, Arizona and New Mexico. In Texas, it spends the summer in the eastern half of the state, from the Red River to the Rio Grande. Most abundant near the coast, it ranges sporadically inland, with nesting records even for El Paso. It moves southward for the winter, but can usually be found along the coast and in the lower Rio Grande Valley.

Slate gray, with black head and neck and dark brown back, the moorhen displays a white line of feathers along its flanks. The chickenlike bill is red with a yellow tip and ascends in a red shield up the forehead. The legs and feet are greenish yellow, leading to the specific name *chloropus*. Winter adults have brownish bills and frontal shields but can always be distinguished from coots by their more slender shape and white blaze on the flanks.

The nest is a shallow saucer of reeds, either floating or anchored in the vegetation, often with a ramp of reeds leading down to the water. The 8 to 14 buffy eggs spotted with brown hatch in about three weeks, but, since incubation begins when the first egg is laid, the young emerge over a period of as much as two weeks. They are covered with black down that is sparser about the head, allowing patches of pink and blue skin to shine through. The asynchronous hatching presents no problem, for the babies soon follow one of their parents into the water and are brooded on nearby nestlike platforms.

Within a month the female may leave her brood to nest again. The family remains together, however, and the brownish juveniles from the first brood later aid in the care of the next. Occasionally, other females lay their eggs in the same nest. By midsummer, the Texas coastal marsh sees common moorhens of all ages swimming about and wandering across the lily pads and water hyacinths, supported by their unusually large feet, eating tender aquatic vegetation and tidbits of snails, worms and insects. Their loud, complaining cries break the summer stillness, *kr-r-ruk kek kek kek.*

PURPLE GALLINULE *Porphyrula martinica*

Few people, given the opportunity to design a bird, would have the audacity to invent the purple gallinule. The head, neck and underparts of this foot-long, feathered rainbow are bright bluish purple, flashing a variety of hues in the summer sun. The back is glossy, bronzy green, with shades of blue in the wings. The bright red bill is tipped with yellow and extends up into a forehead shield of pale sky-blue. Below this crazy-quilt assemblage of brilliant colors is a pair of long, bright yellow legs and feet, terminating in absurdly long yellow toes.

The gallinule stalks the overgrown marshes and swamps, using the long toes to walk lightly across the lily pads and floating reeds, constantly bobbing and nodding its head and twitching its short, upturned tail with gleaming white undercoverts. It normally chooses to swim across patches of open water but, if startled, takes off in labored flight, long legs dangling awkwardly.

It is little wonder that this bizarre and gorgeous bird represents one of the highlights for birders first visiting the southeastern states. The myriad bright colors hint at tropical origins, and the species ranges from South Carolina around the Gulf of Mexico to Texas and southward through Central and South America. In spite of its seeming awkwardness in flight, it migrates from most of North America in winter. It also wanders far north of its normal range on occasion, turning up in the northern states and Canada.

The purple gallinule breeds in the eastern half of Texas, westward sparingly to Dallas, Austin and San Antonio, and is most frequent in coastal marshes. It usually winters well south of our state but may be seen in deep South Texas and along the lower coast.

The nest is a crude saucer of grasses, cattails or rushes partly concealed by an arched canopy of vegetation and constructed just above the water. A ramp of reeds frequently serves as an approach. The six to ten cinnamon-pink eggs are speckled with brown. Both parents incubate for 22 to 25 days, and the downy, precocial hatchlings soon leave the nest to wander through the grass and paddle in the shallows. Some reports indicate the young may be brooded in a second nest nearby.

Purple gallinules sometimes live in small family groups, with the nonbreeders helping to defend the territory and feed the young. They are surprisingly noisy, especially in defense of the nest, uttering raucous, laughing cries of *hiddy-hiddy-hiddy, hit-up, hit-up, hit-up.* Their omnivorous diet includes seeds, fruits, leaves, snails, aquatic insects and frogs, and they have also been found to prey occasionally on the eggs and young of other small marsh birds.

The word gallinule is derived from the diminutive of the Latin *gallina* and means "little hen." This little hen, with its huge feet and brilliant colors, is one of the most striking inhabitants of Texas' coastal marshes.

A purple gallinule dines on a tender young cattail.

The clapper rail is duller in color than the similar king rail, with grayish edges on the feathers of its back.

CLAPPER RAIL
Rallus longirostris

The setting sun hangs low over the hot, humid coastal salt marsh, and the birds begin to feed again as night approaches. Out of the spartina grass stalks a long-legged, gray-brown bird with a short, upturned tail. Behind her tumble a half-dozen tiny chicks covered with black down. The clapper rail wades slowly along in the shallows, probing for small crabs, snails, worms and insects with her long, slightly downcurved bill. When she finds a tasty morsel, she retreats to the edge and feeds it to one of the babies keeping pace with her along the bank. They move on slowly, cautiously, never far from cover.

Sensing our presence, the rail suddenly turns and blends into the grass, her thin body slipping through the vegetation without a trace. Her clapper call, *kek kek kek,* is loud and commanding, and the downy chicks scurry for cover. In a few seconds they are gone. We pose no threat to these "saltwater marsh hens," but they can afford to take no chances. In spite of their reclusiveness, few of the baby rails will survive the summer. A host of furred, feathered and scaled predators relish just such a tender meal.

The clapper rail inhabits salt marshes and coastal mangrove swamps from New England to Texas and on into South America. Another population in southern California and the lower Colorado River basin of Arizona is severely endangered. It is not uncommon along Texas' tidal bays and estuaries, but its secretive ways make it hard to find. Only when surprised at close range does it take wing, legs dangling awkwardly, to pitch back into the marsh a short distance away.

The nest is a bowl of grass, often hidden away beneath a shrub above high tide and covered with a partial dome of arching grasses. The clutch of buffy eggs spotted with brown varies in size from as few as six or seven to as many as 14. Incubation starts midway through laying, so the downy chicks hatch at different times. They are precocial and follow one of the parents almost immediately. Their coal-black down and small size may at times give rise to erroneous reports of the much rarer six-inch black rail *(Laterallus jamaicensis)*.

The clapper rail of the salt marsh looks very much like the king rail of freshwater habitats. In fact, where those habitats overlap, the species may hybridize. The clapper is a grayish brown; the king, a richer rusty brown with brighter barring on the flanks. Both, at 14 to 15 inches long, are larger than the similarly marked 9-to 10-inch Virginia rail *(Rallus limicola)*. Both king and clapper inhabit Texas throughout the year, while the Virginia rail moves farther north to breed. All of the rail species are threatened by pesticide use and habitat loss as wetlands vanish.

KING RAIL
Rallus elegans

At about 15 inches in length, the hen-size king rail is the largest of the North American rails. It inhabits freshwater and brackish marshes across most of the eastern half of the U.S. The slightly smaller clapper rail is limited to coastal salt marshes, but the two sometimes hybridize when their habitats overlap. Some authorities, in fact, consider them subspecies or races of a single species.

In Texas the king rail can be found locally throughout the eastern portions of the state, west as far as Fort Worth and San Antonio and south to Corpus Christi. In winter, when rails migrate from the colder regions, they occur primarily along the coast, sometimes as far south as Brownsville.

King and clapper rails look much alike and can be hard to separate. The best distinction is one of habitat, for the clapper seldom strays from the salt marshes, while the king does not tolerate high salinity. The king rail is a richer brown color than the gray-brown clapper, with tawny edges on the back feathers, bright cinnamon brown underparts, and brighter barring on the flanks. Immatures are paler and grayer. The Virginia rail *(Rallus limicola)*, which has similar proportions and coloring, is much smaller at nine to ten inches long.

The two larger rails share many of the same calls and are more often heard than seen. Even when common, they are easily overlooked. Midwestern farmers once likened the *kek kek kek* of the king rail to the sound of a teamster clucking to his horses, hence the old regional name "stage driver."

King rails feed primarily on aquatic invertebrates, particularly crustaceans. They also consume grain and other seeds, however, and this led to a severe decline of Texas populations. According to Harry C. Oberholser, in his monumental *The Bird Life of Texas*, the rice fields around Eagle Lake and Houston once swarmed with king rails, white-faced ibises and fulvous whistling-ducks. Then, in 1959, rice farmers began treating their seeds liberally with mercury fungicides and chlorinated-hydrocarbon pesticides. "In one year," wrote Oberholser, "the duck plunged from very common to almost zero, ibis numbers were reduced, and the rail almost wiped out."

The rail was on the National Audubon Society's Blue List during the 1970s and 1980s as being a species warranting special concern. Numbers remain low but have apparently stabilized. Nevertheless, pesticides and loss of wetlands hold the king rail in peril.

SORA
Porzana carolina

This chunky, charming little rail is one of the delightful surprises one encounters in our nation's wetlands. Only nine inches long, it is gray-brown with barred flanks and a black mask extending from the face down onto the throat and breast. The bill is short, stout and bright yellow. The short, cocked tail flicks up and down as the sora walks slowly and deliberately through the marsh vegetation, pecking like a tiny chicken at seeds, snails and aquatic invertebrates. Occasionally it wanders out into plain view along roadsides and trails to pick up weed seeds and insects, scurrying back to cover only if approached too closely.

Quite unlike the larger king, clapper and Virginia rails—which have proportionately longer necks, legs and bills—the sora is a member of the short-billed group of rails called "crakes" in many portions of the world, a name that mimics some of their calls. The origin of the name sora is unknown, although some have suggested it may have an American Indian derivation.

The sora nests across much of Canada, from British Columbia to Prince Edward Island, and south through the midsection of the United

States. It is a migrant throughout Texas on its way to and from Central and South America. Some remain in winter along the coast, but summer records for the state are rare.

A king rail (top) defends its nearby nest with an aggressive display. A little sora (above) feeds at dusk along a roadside through the marsh.

DUCKS, GEESE AND SWANS (Family Anatidae)

Male redhead in breeding plumage.

The Anatidae comprises one of the best known groups of birds in the world. Its members occur virtually everywhere there is water, from the tip of Tierra del Fuego to the edge of the Arctic ice. Their portraits ornament temple walls of ancient Egypt, and they have inspired epic works of poetry and music. Probably no other birds have been as relentlessly counted, studied and managed as the waterfowl. This is due in no small degree to their favor as table birds, for waterfowl have been hunted for food and sport down through the ages.

Their place as prized game birds, however, has also helped to secure the future of the various ducks and geese. Revenue from duck stamps and money raised by such organizations as Ducks Unlimited have been invaluable in securing breeding and wintering habitats for waterfowl in Texas and across the continent. At a time when prairie potholes are drying up and coastal wetlands are being drained and filled, it is essential to protect these vital habitats, and several new refuges have recently been acquired along the Texas coast. Although the conservation efforts owe their impetus to the hunters' interest in waterfowl, those same refuges harbor a wealth of other nongame birds and wildlife.

Some 145 species of Anatidae occur around the world, nearly half of them in North America. The Texas list contains 42, but nine of those species appear only as accidental visitors. Waterfowl range in size from the giant trumpeter swan, which may weigh 30 pounds or more, to tiny teal and buffleheads. For the most part, they are aquatic, web-footed and gregarious, flying in long lines and V-formations and feeding on the water. The geese and some ducks may also graze in fields on green shoots and seeds.

The reason for V-formation flight remains a mystery. It has long been suggested that it enables all but the lead bird to obtain additional lift from the wing-tip vortices of the birds ahead. Extensive study of flight films and mathematical calculations have shown, however, that the birds would have to be much closer together to obtain significant lift. Some biologists suggest the formations are merely ways of remaining in visual contact and avoiding collisions.

The ducks may be divided into two general groups, the dabblers and the diving ducks. The dabblers, or "puddle ducks," have smaller feet and legs mounted well forward on their bodies. Thus they walk well on land. Their wings are larger relative to body weight, and they are able to fly slowly and under greater control, dropping down onto small ponds and springing up again in flight directly from the surface. Dabblers occur throughout Texas, making use of small marshy areas and ephemeral ponds, even in the more arid western portions of the state.

The diving ducks have larger feet on short legs, a more efficient paddle mechanism. The legs are mounted well back on the body for swimming but are less adapted to land. Divers walk with a distinctive waddling gait. They fly faster and normally prefer open bodies of water, for they must run pattering across the surface in order to take off.

The two types partition the food supply with their different habitat preferences and feeding behaviors. Dabblers skim the surface with their spatulate, strainer bills or feed by tipping to reach below the surface, with their tails sticking skyward. They prefer to feed in shallow water where they can reach the underwater vegetation with extended necks. The diving ducks, on the other hand, may dive to 40 feet or more in search of food. They are more likely to be encountered in the surf along the coast or on the larger bays and lakes in Texas.

Most male ducks are distinctively patterned and easy to identify in breeding plumage. They use their bright colors for elaborate courtship displays in competition for mates. Ornithologist Terence Shortt says it wonderfully: "Even among the hot-blooded, amorous class *Aves,* waterfowl are salacious to a remarkable degree."

Shortly after breeding, most male ducks in the Northern Hemisphere shed their bright nuptial garb for a dull, cryptic pattern known as the "eclipse plumage." Some remain in eclipse for only a month or two; others retain that plumage until the following spring before molting again. They look much like the drabber, protectively colored females and are more difficult to separate. Duck identification becomes much simpler in late winter and early spring in Texas than it is in late summer or fall, for by that time courtship has begun again, and drakes have regained their distinctive plumages. Because birds of a species tend to flock together, females can usually be told by the company they keep.

A tundra swan stretches its wings.

Eclipse plumage helps protect the birds when they have no need for courtship colors. Waterfowl, along with grebes, pelicans and auks, are synchronous molters. That is, they change all of their flight feathers over a brief period of two to four weeks after breeding. During that time they cannot fly, so they hide away in the marshes. It would be a poor time to be bright and gaudy. Because these birds have heavy bodies relative to the amount of wing surface, the loss of even a few wing feathers is a serious hindrance to their flying ability. Rather than molt a feather or two at a time, as do most other birds, it is better for waterfowl to undergo a "quick overhaul."

The use of lead shot by hunters has caused the death by poisoning of countless waterfowl. Decades after being used, the expended shot still lies on the bottom of ponds and bays and is picked up by feeding birds. Even endangered trumpeter swans, which are being carefully managed and restocked, have succumbed to accidental lead poisoning. Conversion to steel shot has been a slow process, but it will save the lives of thousands of birds. Loss of habitat, however, is a problem that is less easily solved.

Huge tundra swans take flight with labored wingbeats.

TUNDRA SWAN *Cygnus columbianus*

The huge, white tundra swan is a rare winter visitor to Texas from the high Arctic. It nests on the tundra and in sheltered marshes of northern Alaska and Canada and migrates in winter primarily to the Atlantic and Pacific coasts of the United States. Some also turn up on scattered inland lakes and ponds across the country, however, and swans have been recorded from virtually every corner of our state.

Although it does not occur frequently in Texas, its presence is not likely to go unnoticed. At 52 inches long, and with a wingspread of nearly seven feet, it is far larger than any goose. Word of wintering swans spreads quickly among the birding fraternity, and the handsome visitors usually remain long enough to be seen by many.

The adult is immaculate white with a long neck and black bill. It does not have the black flight feathers displayed by most other large white water birds. Immatures are dingier with dull pinkish bills.

Older field guides call this the whistling swan, which is the North American subspecies. It was subsequently merged with Bewick's swan, the subspecies from Eurasia, and given the new and appropriate name. The similar trumpeter swan (*Cygnus buccinator*) once ranged across Texas as well, but it was extirpated in the state by about 1900 and is unlikely to be seen. Both of these native species hold their necks erect rather than in the graceful curve of the mute swan often pictured in books and art. The mute swan (*C. olor*) is an Old World species that has been introduced on the East Coast and in numerous city parks. The eastern population appears to be increasing.

CANADA GOOSE *Branta canadensis*

Canada geese migrate throughout Texas but spend the winter mainly in the eastern half of the state and in the Panhandle. They are particularly abundant on the prairies along the coast. They fly in large V-formations across the sky, their wild music delighting everyone along their path. Flights of this most popular of geese provide one of the highlights of the Texas winter season.

The "Canadian honker" is the best known of the geese in North America. Actually, the species is composed of a dozen subspecies that breed in different portions of the continent, from the northern coast of Alaska and the Arctic islands of Canada down through the upper portions of the United States. They range in size from the giant Canada goose that is nearly four feet long and may weigh 18 pounds or more to the tiny "cackling goose." The latter is just two feet long and weighs about three pounds; it is little bigger than a mallard. The larger forms utter the deep, musical honking calls, *ka-ronk, ka-ronk, ka-ronk*. The smaller ones have a rapid, high-pitched cackle.

Fortunately for birders, all of the forms look much the same. The gray-brown birds are lighter beneath and have the characteristic black head and neck marked with a distinctive white "chin strap" stretching up onto the sides of the head. In flight, the Canada goose has dark wings, white undertail coverts and a white crescent on the rump.

Canada geese form lasting pair bonds and show remarkable fidelity to their mates and to their nesting territory, returning to the same site year after year. They are relatively long-lived, and captives have lived as much as 33 years, although no more than half the fledglings are likely to survive the many threats of their first dangerous year.

Nests are large, bulky piles of dried grasses, moss, sticks and feathers and are lined with down as the incubation of the four to seven white eggs begins. The female incubates the eggs alone, while the male guards the nest. Fiercely protective of his family, he charges intruders that come too close. The eggs hatch in 25 to 30 days, with both parents shepherding the downy, yellowish goslings on their rounds. The young can fly after about two months and may remain with the parents through the winter, until they return to the nesting grounds the following spring.

Canada geese form long-term pair bonds and head northward to their nesting territories as spring arrives in Texas.

GREATER WHITE-FRONTED GOOSE *Anser albifrons*

This medium-size goose is the "specklebelly" of the hunters, so named for the irregular black barring across the grayish underparts of the adult. That barring serves as a more obvious field mark than the white band at the base of the pink bill, from which the common and scientific names are derived. The "front" of a bird in ornithological terminology is the area just above the bill and does not refer to the breast or belly. It stems from the Latin *frons,* or "forehead." A lesser white-fronted goose also exists, but it is largely Asian in its range.

The greater white-front breeds on the Arctic tundra of Alaska and Canada as well as through northern Eurasia. North American populations migrate southward west of the Mississippi Valley and winter locally in freshwater wetlands, grassy fields and grainfields. In Texas, they migrate through much of the state but rarely occur in the Trans-Pecos. Some flights continue into Mexico, while others remain in fields along the Texas coast from October through March or April.

White-fronted geese fly high in the sky in wedge-shaped flocks, usually led by older male birds. The flights are much like those of Canada geese, but white-fronts are faster and more agile, and their music is a series of chuckling calls, *kah-lah-aluk* and *wah-wah-wah,* that gives rise to the regional name of "laughing geese." In flight they display a white crescent on the rump as well as the dark belly markings.

White-fronts usually form long-lasting pair bonds, mating for life and remaining together throughout the year. The young migrate with their parents and stay in the family group until the following spring. They do not gain the dark barring on their bellies until the second fall and begin breeding at about three years of age.

Greater white-fronted geese graze at the edge of an open woodlot.

SNOW GOOSE   *Chen caerulescens*

Few wildlife spectacles equal the sight of thousands of snow geese spread out to feed across a Texas coastal prairie, resembling giant snowflakes drifted by the wind. Groups of the large white birds flutter up from the ground on black-tipped wings and settle back into the vanguard of the advancing front. Other flocks come streaming in, flying in ragged, interlacing lines and U-shaped formations rather than the precise Vs employed by the larger Canada geese. The calls of the newcomers overhead are strangely musical, a high-pitched *whouk* or *kaahk*, but the massed voices on the ground become a constant, ringing clamor.

With the white birds are smaller numbers of darker geese—their backs and chests dark grayish brown; their heads, necks and bellies white. These are the "blue geese," formerly considered a separate species. Biologists now recognize the two as simply color phases—avian blondes and brunettes—and both the white phase and blue phase are called snow geese. However, the scientific name *Chen caerulescens* literally means "blue goose." Chosen because of scientific precedent, it replaced *Chen hyperborea*, the original name of the more abundant white phase. The latter seems a far more romantic name, meaning "goose from beyond the north wind."

These abundant birds do, indeed, breed beyond the north wind on the high Arctic tundra, and they migrate southward after the nesting season to spend the winter in scattered locations throughout the interior of the U.S. and Mexico. The populations that contain most of the "blue geese" winter primarily along the Gulf Coast of Louisiana and Texas. That color phase is rare elsewhere. Immature birds are dusky gray, much darker in the blue phase than in the white one, but easily recognizable as snow geese. Intermediate color combinations

sometimes occur as well, and many birds exhibit rusty heads stained by iron-rich soils of regions to the North.

Snow geese migrate across most of Texas and inhabit the eastern half of the state and the Panhandle during the winter months. They are most abundant along the coast and rare in far West Texas.

Texas birds, both white and blue, are members of a subspecies sometimes called the "lesser snow goose." The larger "greater snow goose" breeds around Baffin Bay and winters only along the mid-Atlantic coast. The

blue phase of the latter subspecies is virtually unknown.

Ross' goose (*C. rossii*) resembles the white-phase snow goose but is considerably smaller, about the size of a mallard. It also lacks the black "grinning patch" on its short, stubby bill. Ross' goose normally winters in central California; however, individuals are sometimes seen in flocks of snow geese. Texas reports have been more frequent in recent years, probably because birders have just begun to watch for them.

Snow geese set their wings and drop in to feed on the prairie west of Houston.

BLACK-BELLIED WHISTLING-DUCK
Dendrocygna autumnalis

The handsome black-bellied whistling-duck (formerly called the black-bellied tree duck) is one of the prizes that birders seek when they visit South Texas for its many rarities. A largely tropical species, it occurs southward through Mexico and Central America into the South American lowlands. Its U.S. range is centered in the Rio Grande Valley, north locally to Corpus Christi. In recent years it appears to be wandering more widely, and flocks are seen frequently in the Houston area and on the upper Texas coast. It is also sporadic westward into Arizona and California and eastward to Louisiana.

The sexes look alike, with a rusty body and black belly, rump and tail. The gray face has a white eye-ring; the bill and legs are red or coral-pink. A white wing-patch shows as a broad stripe in flight. The call, a high-pitched whistle, *pe-che-che-ne*, gives rise to the name whistling-duck.

Black-bellied whistling-ducks prefer to nest in tree cavities but may build on the ground amidst marsh vegetation. They also utilize nest boxes that have been constructed for them on several South Texas refuges and ranches. Both sexes incubate the 12 to 16 whitish eggs. A day after hatching, the precocial ducklings answer the mother's call and jump one-by-one from the nest to follow their parents to water. The adults form long-term pair bonds and frequently return to the same nesting area. In spite of this fidelity, females sometimes lay their eggs in other nests. "Dump nests" containing up to 100 eggs have been found, the product of several females' thwarted instincts.

Black-bellied whistling-ducks bathe and squabble over some real or imagined affront to their avian dignity.

FULVOUS WHISTLING-DUCK *Dendrocygna bicolor*

They don't walk like ducks or fly like ducks. They certainly don't quack like ducks. They look more like strange little geese with their long, erect necks and long legs, and their scientific name, *Dendrocygna,* means "tree swan." In spite of these anomalies, the whistling-ducks do have webbed feet and spatulate, ducklike bills, and they are therefore classified that way. They are called tree ducks in the older literature.

The fulvous whistling-duck has an extensive, disjointed range that includes India, eastern Africa, South America and the southern fringes of the United States and Mexico. The U.S. population is most common along the southern Texas coast and the tip of the Florida peninsula, but wanderers reach all of the southern states from California to the Atlantic Coast and occasionally much farther north.

Named for its tawny color, the fulvous whistling-duck has a darker back with tawny feather edgings and a creamy stripe along the flanks. The bill and legs are gray. A white rump band is conspicuous in flight. Its distinctive call, a squealing *pe-chee,* gives rise to the term "whistling-duck" and to the local name "Mexican squealer."

Whistling-ducks walk upright without a waddle and fly with drooping necks and long, trailing legs. The wingbeat is slower than that of other ducks and sometimes alternates with short glides, more in the fashion of an ibis. These taxonomic mavericks also feed primarily at night on seeds and grain.

The nest is a grass-lined saucer in long grass or marsh vegetation. The fulvous whistling-duck rarely nests in a tree cavity, the preferred site of several others of its genus. The normal clutch is about a dozen buffy eggs, but nests with 30 or more have been found. These are likely "dump nests," with more than one female contributing her eggs, for whistling-ducks are known brood parasites that often lay in each other's nests. The dump nests sometimes go untended.

Fulvous whistling-ducks breed along the Texas coast and wander inland in the winter. Once abundant in the state, they suffered greatly when rice farmers began treating their seeds with heavy doses of pesticides in 1959. Surveys showed a 90 percent reduction in the breeding population within a year. The effects have lessened in the last decade, and these strange and attractive ducks are reappearing. But they probably will never reach the levels they once enjoyed.

WOOD DUCK
Aix sponsa

In a recent poll conducted by *American Birds* magazine, ten outstanding wildlife artists were asked to name their candidates for the ten most beautiful birds in the world. The wood duck tied for third place with the blue bird of paradise. Only the American swallow-tailed kite and the resplendent quetzal of Central America garnered more votes. Many of the world's birds exhibit remarkable beauty, but few can equal the iridescent rainbow splendor of this most colorful of ducks.

The male in breeding plumage, with his shimmering colors and sleek crest, can be mistaken for no other. Duller in eclipse, he still retains the unique head pattern. The female has a short crest and a distinctive light teardrop-shaped patch around the eye. Even the scientific name testifies to the glamour of the species. A hybrid of Greek and Latin, *Aix sponsa* translates loosely as "waterfowl in wedding raiment."

This wedding raiment nearly led to the demise of the species in the era of the plume hunters. The wood duck was shot in large numbers and the feathers used for everything from women's hats to artificial trout flies. In the early 20th century, few remained. A 1918 law placed the wood duck under total protection, and today the gorgeous birds are again relatively common.

Wood ducks inhabit bottomland

Fulvous whistling-ducks.

swamps and open woodlands near ponds and rivers, ranging across much of North America from Canada to California and Florida. They nest locally in eastern Texas and are casual visitors to other portions of the state, particularly when they withdraw from the frozen North in winter. They often perch in trees and feed primarily on a vegetarian diet of seeds, acorns, berries and grain, with a few insects and other invertebrates for variety.

Courtship and pair formation begin in autumn and continue into spring. Groups of several birds gather and display, each male trying to attract a receptive female. Once mated, a pair frequently returns to the site where the female has nested before. The nest is a bed of wood chips and downy feathers in a tree cavity, sometimes as much as 50 feet in the air. The female alone incubates the 10 to 15 whitish eggs that hatch in four or five weeks. Shortly after hatching, the precocious ducklings clamber up to the entrance hole in response to their mother's calls and drop to the ground, bouncing unharmed like little balls of fluff. The hen then leads her brood to water for their first swim, watching over them with little or no help from her preening consort.

The wood duck has made a remarkable recovery, thanks to carefully controlled hunting limits and to nest boxes erected in many parts of the country to replace hollow trees lost on timbered tracts. Today it is again possible to watch a pair of the beautiful ducks swimming amidst the floating lily pads and basking turtles of a Big Thicket pond, lit by rays of sunlight filtered through moss-draped cypress trees. Leaping into flight, they zigzag through the forest, distinctive with their large heads and long, squared-off tails. The female's squealing call— a loud, rising *whoo-eek*—is truly a welcome cry out of the past.

A pair of wood ducks greets the dawn on a quiet woodland pond.

MALLARD *Anas platyrhynchos*

The male mallard is undoubtedly the best known of all the ducks. With his metallic green head and neck, white collar, chestnut breast and gleaming yellow bill, he sets the example for sartorial splendor. His swaggering gait is accentuated by a cocky curl of black feathers above the whitish tail. The female wears more subdued plumage in shades of mottled camouflage brown; her orange bill is marked with black. Both share the iridescent violet-blue wing-patch, the speculum, bordered on both sides by white. Although the hen lacks the elegant plumage of the drake, she is equally famous for her voice. Her loud *quack* represents the family as universally as does the male's shiny green head. His voice is limited to a low, conversational *kwek*.

Mallards range throughout the northern hemisphere. Birds breeding in northern Europe and Asia migrate southward as far as Africa and India. In North America, they nest across most of Canada and the U.S. and winter on into Mexico. The mallard is the ancestor of many domestic breeds. Some still resemble the wild stock; others have been bred almost beyond recognition. The lineage has been an important food source among peoples of the world for thousands of years.

The mallard migrates and winters throughout Texas. It is most abundant in the Panhandle, more scattered and local elsewhere. Nesting records are likewise scattered across the state, but the mallard is not one of the more common breeding ducks. Some of the records may be of birds diluted by domestic stock.

Seasonally monogamous, mallards choose mates each year. Groups of males pursue a single female in courtship until she selects one and flies off with him. The drake defends the territory around his mate, while she forms a shallow depression well hidden in the vegetation and lines it with grasses and down as she lays her 8 to 15 greenish buff eggs. When she begins to incubate, however, he deserts, leaving her to hatch and rear the young alone. He then molts into eclipse plumage.

Mallard pair in breeding plumage.

MOTTLED DUCK
Anas fulvigula

Because of its limited range, the mottled duck is one of the rarest of North American ducks. However, it can be seen quite easily at any season of the year in the marshes along the Texas coast.

It is a nonmigratory resident of freshwater and brackish coastal wetlands, ranging from southern Florida around the Gulf to northeastern Mexico. Occasionally, Texas bird watchers might find it as far inland as San Antonio, Waco and Dallas. Local names include "black mallard" and "summer mallard."

Both sexes resemble the female mallard but are slightly darker. The iridescent wing-patch, the speculum, is more bluish green and has a narrow white border only on the trailing edge. The mottled duck also lacks the white in the tail. Some authorities consider the mottled duck a sedentary subspecies of the wide-ranging mallard, but that view has not been accepted in the current taxonomy.

The still darker American black duck *(Anas rubripes)* is similar, but it is a species of the Northeast and ranges only rarely into Texas. There has been a great deal of confusion between the two in the field, and most local birders lack the temerity to report a black duck on their counts.

The diet of the mottled duck contains more animal protein than that of any other dabbling duck, at least 40 percent according to one study. This includes snails and other mollusks, crustaceans, small fish and insects, as well as the more typical aquatic vegetation, grasses and grain.

Mottled ducks begin pairing early in the winter and remain together through the season. The nest of grasses and reeds is lined with down and hidden away in dense vegetation, usually in or near a marsh but sometimes surprisingly far from water. The female incubates the 6 to 11 buffy eggs that hatch in 25 to 27 days and rears the downy, precocial young alone.

Predators take a heavy toll of eggs

and young. Raccoons, opossums, skunks, snakes and grackles all relish a meal of duck eggs, while alligators and large fish also prey on ducklings. Females frequently desert their nests if disturbed. They may nest again if the first effort fails, but only one brood is raised each year.

The encroachment of residential development and agriculture on the wetlands and the heavy use of pesticides pose the major threats to the mottled duck. The problem has been alleviated somewhat by the creation of several large coastal wildlife refuges that protect a wealth of plant and animal species.

Unlike most other ducks, the nonmigratory mottled duck is a year-round resident of the Texas coastal marsh.

NORTHERN PINTAIL
Anas acuta

The name pintail describes the male of the species perfectly, as does the scientific name *acuta*. An old hunter's term is "sprig." All denote the black central tail feathers that extend well beyond the rest of the wedge-shaped tail. One bird book called the pintail the "greyhound of waterfowl," an appropriate appellation for this trim, fast-flying, graceful bird. Widely published bird artists Cindy House and Lars Jonsson both listed it among the ten most beautiful birds in the world in a recent *American Birds* survey.

The male pintail has a white neck and breast, with the white extending upward in narrow bands onto the sides of the chocolate brown head. The female is mottled in drab camouflage brown and lacks extended plumes in the tail. Her slim neck and long wedge-shaped tail, however, distinguish her from the many similarly plumaged female ducks. Both sexes are generally silent, although the hen sometimes utters a muffled *quack,* and the drake employs a variety of mellow whistles.

Pintails migrate and winter throughout Texas. They frequent grainfields as well as marshes and ponds and are even seen in large flocks on the open saltwater bays. A few linger through the summer, and breeding has been recorded in scattered locations, particularly in the northern portions of the state. For the most part, however, pintails are migratory "snowbirds" in Texas.

Circumpolar in their range, northern pintails occur in Europe and Asia as well as across most of North America. They migrate as far south as Africa, India and South America. In the United States, they are more common in the western states than in the East.

Its long, pointed tail characterizes the male northern pintail.

BLUE-WINGED TEAL
Anas discors

These tiny ducks are among the earliest fall migrants to reach Texas, with some of them arriving in late August from their breeding grounds in Canada and the northern states. When the first cold snap touches the reed-lined potholes of the prairie provinces and the upper Great Plains, the blue-winged teal head southward. Most will cross our borders and continue as far as Central and South America. But some will remain in Texas through the winter, particularly along the coast and inland to the Edwards Plateau. Reluctant to return again until the waters have warmed, they may linger here into late April or early May. A few have even remained to breed within our state, particularly in the northern half.

With such a short nesting season, the young must mature quickly. The whitish or buffy eggs hatch in about 24 days, and the precocial, downy young follow their mother to the water. Within six weeks they will be flying. The female incubates the eggs and cares for her ducklings alone, for the male deserts her during the incubation period. If her brood is threatened, she frequently feigns injury to lure the predator away, while the young seek shelter in the reeds.

Male blue-wings retain their eclipse plumage longer than most other ducks. Consequently, the two sexes look much alike when they arrive here in the fall. They can be separated by their vocalizations, for the female converses with soft quacking sounds, while the male has a repertoire of peeping and twittering calls.

In flight, both show a broad, powder-blue patch on the upper side of the wing ahead of a metallic green speculum. Those blue patches are readily visible and mark the blue-winged and cinnamon teal and the northern shoveler. As the male blue-wing molts his body feathers again to breeding plumage, he gets a blue-gray head with a broad white crescent before the eye. In that plumage he is unmistakable.

GREEN-WINGED TEAL *Anas crecca*

The smallest of all our dabbling ducks, the green-winged teal breeds from Alaska and northern Canada through the western and northeastern states. It winters southward to Central America and the West Indies. Flocks of the tiny teal fly with marvelous precision, leaping into flight from the surface of ponds and marshes and twisting and turning in perfect unison. "Like feathered minnows," writes ornithologist S. Dillon Ripley.

The male green-wing sports a dark green ear patch on his chestnut head. This can be difficult to see in poor light, however, and the most useful field marks at a distance are the white vertical bar in front of the wing and the golden patch on each side of the tail. The female is the usual drab and mottled brown, best recognized by her small size and by her associates. Both sexes in flight flash iridescent green specula bordered with buff on the leading edge and white on the trailing edge.

Green-winged teal spend the winter throughout Texas, and a few summer occasionally in the West. They frequent marshes, lakes, ponds and bays, where they tip tail-up to feed on aquatic vegetation and invertebrates. Grain, grasses and other green shoots are also included in the diet.

Young green-wings are the fastest growing of all North American ducks. The eggs hatch in 21 to 23 days, and the immatures can fly within five or six weeks. The male usually deserts the nest when incubation begins, leaving his mate to raise the brood alone. While such behavior may at first seem irresponsible in human terms, it is the habit of many ducks. There is no place for their flashy, resplendent plumage around a carefully hidden nest. The drakes withdraw to molt into eclipse plumage and spend a period of a few weeks of flightlessness in solitude.

Male green-winged teal in breeding plumage.

CINNAMON TEAL
Anas cyanoptera

The male cinnamon teal in breeding plumage poses no problem in identification. His head, neck and underparts are a bright cinnamon-red. The wing pattern is virtually identical to that of the blue-winged teal, with a broad powder-blue patch on the leading edge and a green speculum.

The female and the eclipse-plumaged male, however, resemble the female blue-wing and are very difficult to distinguish. Roger Tory Peterson, in his 1960 *Field Guide to the Birds of Texas*, took a cautious approach: the female cinnamon teal, he wrote, "cannot be separated from female Blue-wing except by her associates." The most recent field guides, however, take up the problem, noting that the female cinnamon is a richer brown than the blue-wing, the eye line is less distinct, and the bill is larger and more spatulate. Those are fine points that are difficult for a novice to invoke in the field, especially without a direct comparison.

The cinnamon teal ranges from southern Canada to South America. It breeds in most of the states west of the Great Plains and migrates throughout Texas, although it is rare in the eastern parts. It winters in South Texas and sparingly along the lower coast, as well as locally inland to El Paso. Breeding records exist for western Texas, but they are rare.

Nests of the cinnamon teal are frequently parasitized by other ducks. The redhead is the most notorious of the brood parasites among waterfowl, but mallards and ruddy ducks may also lay an egg in teal nests, occasionally removing an egg of the host as well. The biological benefits of the trait are not entirely clear and require additional study. Some birds recognize the presence of alien eggs; others apparently do not.

Blue-winged teal pair (top).
Male cinnamon teal (right)
in breeding plumage.

NORTHERN SHOVELER *Anas clypeata*

Its oversize, spatulate bill is the chief claim to fame of the northern shoveler. Only slightly larger than a teal, this common little duck sports a bill that would do justice to a much bigger bird. Hunters across the country call it the "spoonbill," but birders reserve that name for the roseate spoonbill, the pink, long-legged wader of the Texas Gulf Coast. The shoveler's beak is not as bizarre as that of the spoonbill, but it is certainly a distinctive enough appendage.

The shoveler sits low in the water, with its bill angled downward as if too heavy to hold up. It only rarely feeds by tipping up, but instead garners small plants and animals from the surface by straining water and debris through the comblike edges of its bill. It also feeds along the edges of mud flats in a similar manner. The low opinion some hunters have of the shoveler as table fare may be due to the taste of morsels gleaned from the muck and mire.

Northern shovelers are widespread across North America, Europe and Asia and migrate into South America and Africa. They breed on this continent in Alaska, Canada and the western states and are apparently increasing in the East as well. They migrate throughout Texas and spend the winters here in all but the coldest regions of the Panhandle. Some remain through the summer in scattered locations and have nested on occasion.

The colorful male shoveler has a dark head glossed with green, a white breast and rusty-brown sides. Blue forewing patches are visible in flight, much like those of the blue-winged and cinnamon teal. The female is the typical mottled brown of most other female ducks, but her outsized bill makes identification relatively easy.

Northern shovelers
in flight.

GADWALL   *Anas strepera*

The gadwall sports none of the gaudy colors that ornament most of our other wild ducks, yet it has a subtle beauty all its own. The drake is attired primarily in gray, with a white belly, black tail coverts, and pale brownish patches on the wings. Up close, it looks as if it has been painstakingly drawn in pen-and-ink, with delicate tracings and flecks in shades of gray. No flash, no glitter. Just a finely detailed bird in its own special niche.

The black rump of the male gadwall contrasts sharply with the gray plumage and provides the best field mark on swimming birds. The female wears the typical mottled-brown hen plumage, much like that of the female mallard. Both sexes have white inner secondaries that sometimes show as small patches while sitting and that provide diagnostic white specula on the trailing edges of the wings in flight.

The drake makes the most of his subtle coloring during courtship displays. He raises his black posterior and waves his white-splashed wings, all the while bobbing his head up and down. Such displays characterize the courtship of many waterfowl and provide fascinating areas for field observation and analysis. The male carries on with a vocal repertoire of whistling calls, while the female quacks loudly, *kaaak-kaaak-kak-kak-kak*. The gadwall's scientific name, in fact, comes from the Latin *streperus,* or "noisy," as in "obstreperous." The word gadwall is of obscure origin, but was used as early as 1676.

Like many other ducks, gadwalls are circumpolar, breeding in northern Europe and Asia as well as in North America. They winter southward into Africa, India and Mexico. The Canadian prairie provinces and the potholes of the Great Plains are the strongholds of the gadwalls on this continent. They also appear to be expanding their range eastward. Historically, they have had a fairly high rate of nesting success, although the nests are sometimes parasitized by other gadwalls and by scaup.

Gadwalls migrate and winter throughout Texas, on almost any marsh, pond, lake or bay. A few remain through the summer, and nesting has been recorded near Amarillo and Dallas. It is likely that many such attempts of uncommon birds go unrecorded, and a massive statewide effort to prepare an atlas of Texas breeding birds is presently under way. Such a county-by-county survey will reveal a great deal about bird populations within the state.

Gadwalls dive more for their food than most other dabbling ducks. Consequently, they often feed farther from shore, submerging in search of water plants and aquatic insects and other invertebrates. On the other hand, they also walk well on land, and they frequently wander through open woodlands and fields in search of nuts, acorns and grain.

Female gadwalls feed on algae.

AMERICAN WIGEON   *Anas americana*

Out on the open water a mixed flock of redheads and canvasbacks dive repeatedly for food, bringing up aquatic plants from the bottom in their spatulate bills. Other ducks among them do not dive, but rather ride high on the waves, picking at scattered debris floating on the surface. The white crowns of the males mark them as American wigeons. As a canvasback dives, however, a wigeon seems to anticipate where it will emerge and swims over to be ready. When the canvasback pops to the surface, strings of greenery hanging from its bill, the smaller wigeon darts in and grabs a strand. He turns quickly and darts away, nibbling at his stolen prize. The diving ducks seem strangely unperturbed by this piracy, perhaps accepting it as small compensation for an early warning system. Wigeons are more wary and restless than many other ducks and can be counted on to sound the alarm if danger threatens.

Male American wigeon in breeding plumage.

CANVASBACK
Aythya valisineria

One of our largest ducks, the canvasback looks as if it is wearing a white saddle blanket, its black chest and rump in stark contrast to the white back and sides. The head and neck are a bright chestnut hue. The female and eclipse male are less strikingly marked than the male in breeding plumage, with pale brown heads and grayish brown bodies. Both sexes can be easily distinguished from other diving ducks with similar patterns, however, by their unmistakable profiles. The forehead of a canvasback slopes directly into the curve of the long, dark bill; it is not rounded as in other species. That characteristic is visible at a great distance and in failing light where color patterns are not discernible.

Canvasbacks are exclusively North American birds. They breed in Alaska, western Canada, and the northwestern states and migrate to wintering grounds along the coasts and in the southern states and Mexico. The prairies of Canada harbor the majority of nesting birds, which seek marshy ponds surrounded by emergent reeds. The nests are half-floating rafts of vegetation or platforms secured above the water. Muskrat houses are often used, but canvasbacks seldom nest on dry ground. As typical of diving ducks, their legs are set too far back for easy walking.

Females exhibit a high degree of "philopatric" instinct, meaning they often return to the areas in which they were reared. The males do not share these instincts, but instead follow the females of their choice. The pair bond is not a lifetime one, and mates do not pair again in subsequent years. The male deserts his mate shortly after the clutch is complete. The female then incubates and rears her brood alone, often losing 70 percent of her body-fat reserves while remaining on her nest.

When canvasbacks leave the breeding grounds in autumn, they fan out along several pathways. Some go

The American wigeon is often called "baldpate," for the male's gleaming white forehead and crown that make him instantly recognizable in a mixed flock of ducks. He has green patches on the sides of his gray head as well, and his breast and sides are a rich pinkish brown. In flight, he flashes large white patches on the upper wings. The female is mottled brown, but her contrasting gray head and neck usually serve to distinguish her from female gadwalls and pintails. Her wing-patches are more dingy gray but still recognizable.

Unlike many of the local ducks, which range around the Northern Hemisphere, the American wigeon is largely limited to North America, as its scientific name would indicate. Its counterpart is the Eurasian wigeon (*Anas penelope*), distinguished by a rich red-brown head and buffy cap. The latter occurs only as a very rare straggler to our coast. It is always searched for, but never expected.

Our wigeon species breeds in Alaska, Canada and the northwestern states. It seems to be expanding its range toward the East Coast and migrates as far as northern South America. It spends the winter throughout Texas and is common on most marshes, ponds and shallow bays. In addition to feeding on the surface and shadowing other flocks of ducks, it grazes in grasslands and cut-over grainfields.

The etymology of the word wigeon is complex, according to Edward Gruson in his *Words for Birds*. The name apparently developed from the Latin *vipionem* as used by Pliny to mean "small crane." It then became *vigeon* and *gingeon* in French to refer to a "whistling duck." From there, it became *widgeon* and *wigeon* in English. The male wigeon is, indeed, a whistling duck in the vocal, if not the taxonomic, sense. Its calls are a series of musical, whistled notes, *whee-whee-whee*. The female is the noisier of the sexes, uttering a loud *qua-ack* when alarmed.

east to winter on the Atlantic Coast. Others wing southward in long lines and ragged V-formations to spread across the southern states and the Gulf Coast. Canvasbacks migrate throughout Texas. They are most abundant along the coast in winter but may be found locally inland.

Large flocks assemble on the coastal bays, floating in close-packed rafts and diving actively to feed. Hunters rank them among the tastiest of ducks—if they have been eating properly. Flocks on the East Coast dine heavily on eelgrass (Vallisneria), and the canvasback has even taken its scientific name from that favored food, although Alexander Wilson misspelled it when he described the bird in 1814. A water plant often called "wild celery," eelgrass is plentiful on Chesapeake Bay, and the ducks of that region are famous for their flavor. Some authors, however, report that canvasbacks of the Pacific Northwest that select a diet of shellfish and rotting salmon are far less palatable.

Numbers of canvasbacks still seek winter shelter along the Texas coast, but the declining population has been a subject of serious concern. The species was placed on the Audubon Society's Blue List in the 1970s and 1980s as warranting special attention. Draining and cultivation of the prairie potholes and marshes has severely reduced the suitable breeding habitat, and that trend will be difficult to counteract.

Male canvasbacks court passing females.

REDHEAD *Aythya americana*

Redheads are the most notorious of the brood parasites among waterfowl. They lay eggs in other birds' nests and let the involuntary foster parents raise their young. Canvasbacks are their favorite targets, but others fall victim, too. In one study in Utah's Bear River marshes, biologists found that redheads had laid eggs in 70 percent of the mallard nests and 79 percent of the cinnamon teal nests.

Such parasitism is not the redhead's only reproductive strategy. Some females rely entirely on other birds, but some build nests amidst the marsh vegetation and incubate their own clutches of about a dozen eggs. Still others combine the techniques, raising only part of the brood themselves. One researcher watched 13 different females deposit eggs in a single nest, and one such "dump nest" contained 83 eggs, far more than any bird could incubate.

Redheads breed in the marshes and prairie potholes of western Canada and the northwestern states and spend the winter in the southern states, Mexico and the West Indies. In Texas, redheads migrate throughout the state and winter primarily on the coastal bays. In fact, half of the world's population spends the winter months on the lower Texas coast, from Rockport and Corpus Christi southward to Laguna Atascosa Refuge. As is the case with many other diving ducks, they prefer the open water of the bays, lakes and large reservoirs.

The male redhead in breeding plumage has a rusty-red head and neck, black chest and rump, and pale smoky-gray back and sides. It is not unlike the larger male canvasback, but it is not as starkly white. The best aid to separating the two at a distance is the profile. The canvasback's fore-

head slopes directly into the long dark bill, without a distinct break, while the redhead has a rounded head and smaller, bluish bill. Females and eclipse-plumage males are brown.

Redhead populations have declined so severely in recent decades that hunting had to be curtailed in many crucial areas. Drought and development have decreased the available prairie-pothole habitat and nesting sites. As the wetlands dry up, the birds suffer from a number of effects ranging from increased accessibility of nests and young to predators to epidemic diseases caused by overcrowding on the wintering grounds.

Redheads rise in flight from a Padre Island marsh where much of the world's population spends the winter.

RING-NECKED DUCK   *Aythya collaris*

If birders were to name this handsome little duck, it would be called the "ring-billed duck." The collar for which it was originally named is a cinnamon band, barely visible against the black head, neck and chest. The most striking field marks are a broad white ring around the bill, another thin white line at its base, and a white crescent at the waterline that separates the black breast and pale gray sides. The female is brown with a white eye-ring and whitish mottling on the face. Both sexes have rather triangular, peaked heads. In flight they flash broad gray wing stripes, the only black-backed ducks with such markings.

Ring-necked ducks breed across Canada and the northern states and winter through the southern U.S. into Central America. They migrate throughout much of Texas. Wintering populations are largest along the coast but range locally inland except in the Panhandle.

Unlike many of the other diving ducks of their genus, which form large rafts on open bay waters, ring-necks seem to prefer more secluded niches on freshwater ponds and in the coastal marshes. They are most likely to be seen on woodland ponds and small lakes. Here they dive and probe for the seeds and roots of aquatic plants and for insects and snails.

Their feeding preferences place ring-necked ducks at extraordinary risk from lead poisoning. Shot fired decades ago is still proving fatal, even after lead is no longer in use. An estimated 6,000 tons of lead was fired each year over our wetlands before its gradual phasing-out in favor of nontoxic steel shot. The annual death toll by lead poisoning has been placed at up to three million birds. Even a flock of endangered trumpeter swans recently reintroduced to the wild in Minnesota was decimated by the toxic metal when droughts decreased water depths and made the old pellets more accessible.

The male ring-necked duck (right) has a prominent white ring around its bill. Pair of lesser scaup (below).

LESSER SCAUP
Aythya affinis

Roger Tory Peterson aptly describes the scaup in his field guide as "black at both ends and white in the middle." The back is faintly lined with darker feather edgings, but it appears white at a distance. The black head reflects an iridescent purple gloss, and the bill is pale blue, giving rise to the colloquial name "bluebill." The female is somber brown, with a pale area on the face around the bill.

The lesser scaup is one of the most abundant ducks along the Texas coast, winging its way from its breeding grounds in the Northwest to winter here from mid-October into April and early May. It is also fairly common inland across the state. Although scaups mass in large rafts on the open waters of bays and larger lakes, they might be found on almost any pond or puddle. There they dive for a mixed diet of aquatic plants, seeds, mollusks and crustaceans.

The lesser scaup is the common scaup of Texas. The greater scaup (*Aythya marila*) occurs here only rarely, for it winters primarily on the Atlantic and Pacific coasts. The latter bird has a green-glossed head, and detailed field guides call attention to minor differences in the bill. How-

ever, these distinctions require an experienced eye.

The greater scaup also flashes white wing-stripes in flight that reach well out onto the primaries. The wing-stripes of the lesser scaup are shorter and cover only the secondaries. It is a definitive difference, but one that is difficult to assess as the birds flush in a whir of wings. The greater scaup is another of those Texas birds that should always be looked for, never expected, and reported only with great caution.

COMMON GOLDENEYE
Bucephala clangula

The scientific name of the lovely common goldeneye results from an interesting blend of classical languages. *Bucephala* is from the Greek *boukephalos,* meaning "ox-headed." And *clangula* is the diminutive of the Latin *clangor,* or "noise." Thus the goldeneye is officially a noisy little ox-headed duck. The distinctive whirring of the wings in flight has also resulted in the popular hunters' name of "whistler," and "goldeneye" is equally appropriate.

The large, puffy head of the male goldeneye shines glossy green. A round white spot ornaments the face between the bill and the bright yellow eye. The breast is immaculately white; the black upperparts are patterned with white by the scapular feathers at the bases of the wings. White wing-patches also serve as a distinctive field mark in flight. All in all, the common goldeneye presents a clean, neatly drawn image as it bobs on the water or runs on the surface to take off across the waves.

Females and eclipse males also have a big-headed look, but their heads are brown and separated from the gray-brown body plumage by white collars. Their eyes, too, are shining golden orbs, and they flash white patches in their wings in flight.

Common goldeneyes nest in wooded, waterfront habitats across Canada and the northern edge of the United States. The eggs are laid in tree cavities, and females readily adopt nest boxes when they are made available. When nest sites are scarce, goldeneyes parasitize each other, laying eggs in another female's ready nest. Studies show that if this is done early enough in the laying cycle, the host may reduce her own clutch to accommodate the foreign eggs.

Goldeneyes are hardy birds. They migrate only to find open water, and winter across most of the U.S. and far northward along the coasts. In Texas, they are most common along the upper and middle coast but also occur

SURF SCOTER   *Melanitta perspicillata*

None of the three scoter species is a common bird in Texas. Breeding in Alaska and Canada, they migrate southward along the Pacific and Atlantic coasts. Oberholser, in *The Bird Life of Texas,* calls the surf scoter "rare and irregular" during the winter months. In recent years, however, birders have discovered that it is more frequent along the coast than was once believed. From vantage points on jetties and piers, it is sometimes possible to see long lines of the dark-bodied sea ducks flying low over the water. Others float just beyond the breaking waves, diving repeatedly for the shellfish that make up the bulk of their winter diet. *A Birder's Checklist of the Upper Texas Coast,* published by the Ornithology Group of the Houston Outdoor Nature Club, now lists the surf scoter as "uncommon" from December through early April, a term defined as "To be expected, but not always present in proper season and habitat."

The male surf scoter is a bizarre-looking bird. Largely black, it has orange legs and a sloping forehead that blends directly into a large, harlequin-patterned bill. White patches ornament the forehead and nape, giving rise to the undignified sobriquet "skunkhead coot." The female is cloaked in drab brown plumage, with two light patches on each side of the head.

Two other scoters of the same genus, the black scoter (*Melanitta nigra*) and the white-winged scoter *(M. fusca),* sometimes share the off-shore waves with the surf scoter. They, too, are dark, chunky seabirds with unusual bills. The latter has white patches in the wings. Scoters can best be seen by spending long hours scanning the open Gulf waters with a spotting scope, but they sometimes turn up on inland lakes and reservoirs across the state.

Male surf scoter.

on inland rivers and lakes in the northern portions of the state. On the saltwater bays, they feed primarily on crustaceans and mollusks. Aquatic insects, crayfish and small fish make up their diet in freshwater environments.

A cold, wintry day might find a small flock of common goldeneyes swimming buoyantly on an open Texas bay. They dive and splash, chasing back and forth, seemingly oblivious to the driving wind and biting spray. Their crisp black-and-white plumage brightens the otherwise gray day and lifts the spirits of all who chance to see them.

BUFFLEHEAD
Bucephala albeola

These charming, active little birds are the smallest of all our diving ducks. Riding the waves, they dive repeatedly in search of the aquatic invertebrates on which they feed. They pop to the surface and rest for a moment, then disappear again, only to pop up somewhere else. It can be a frustrating experience for the novice birder trying to get that first good look at a bufflehead.

When they are in a flock, however, there is usually one sentry that stays alert as the others dive. He may appear to doze, with his head tucked beneath a wing, but a closer look will show an eye peering out now and then. Biologists have studied these periods of "quiet sleep" and found that ducks peek once every few seconds. The smaller the flock, the more often each member must peek. Males keep a closer watch than females, especially during courtship season. They must be alert not only for predators but to what the other males are doing.

Buffleheads form long-term pair bonds and often return to the same breeding sites in Alaska and western Canada each year. The nest is usually in a natural tree cavity or old woodpecker hole near a small lake or pond, which the male defends as his territory. The female then incubates her eggs and raises her young alone, while the drake goes off to molt his breeding plumage with other males. His consort will later join them with her growing brood.

Buffleheads do not fear icy temperatures as long as they find open water. They spend the winter throughout the southern states and far up the Mississippi Valley and the coasts. Migrants range across Texas. They winter mainly along the coast but may also appear on inland lakes and streams. Although buffleheads prefer quiet ponds in summer, they are equally at ease on the larger bays in winter.

The male is black above and white below, with a large white patch over the top of his head behind the eyes. It is this large, round, puffy head from which the bufflehead gets its name. It is short for "buffalo-head." The female is a duller black and dingy gray, with a smaller, elongated white ear patch. Where one goes, the other usually follows, and they make an engaging couple on Texas' winter wetlands and waterways.

Common goldeneyes (top) in eclipse plumage. Male bufflehead (above) in breeding plumage.

Common mergansers in eclipse plumage.

COMMON MERGANSER *Mergus merganser*

Mergansers are large ducks with long necks and long, thin, serrated bills. They use these bills to catch and hold small fish, giving rise to names like "fish ducks" and "sawbills." The word merganser combines the Latin *merger,* "to dive," with *anser,* or "goose." Hence, a "diving-goose."

The common merganser is the most widespread of the group. It nests across Canada and the northern U.S., ranging southward in the Rocky Mountains. It also occurs in Europe and northern Asia, where it is called "goosander." A hardy bird, it moves southward only to seek open water and winters across most of the United States and north along the coasts. It can be common in winter in the Texas Panhandle and Trans-Pecos, but is irregular and local through the remainder of the state. Only scattered records exist for the upper Texas coast, where the red-breasted merganser is much more abundant. The common merganser prefers freshwater lakes and rivers to the saline bays and surf.

In breeding plumage, the male common merganser sports an iridescent green head, black back, and white sides and breast. The thin bill and the feet are red. Females, eclipse males and immatures are gray with rusty-red, crested heads. This is the plumage most often seen in Texas. They can be distinguished from the red-breasted merganser by the contrasting white chin and the sharp line separating the red head and neck from the white breast. White wing-patches are evident in flight.

The hooded merganser (*Lophodytes cucullatus*) also occurs irregularly in winter, primarily in the northern parts of the state. A lovely duck with a large crest, it inhabits wooded ponds and river bottoms, much in the manner of the wood duck.

RED-BREASTED MERGANSER
Mergus serrator

This "sawbill" or "saltwater sheldrake" is a common winter resident along the Texas coast and occurs irregularly across the remainder of the state. Through most of the season, all wear the female plumage common to eclipse males and immatures as well. They are large, gray ducks with thin, hooked bills and reddish, shaggy-crested heads. They resemble the female common merganser except for the absence of a sharp line of demarcation between the reddish head and neck and the white breast. The pale neck and breast of the red-breasted merganser are smudged with rust to the water line.

Once the male attains his breeding plumage, he is beautifully adorned in black and white, with reddish streaks on the breast and a white collar setting off the crested, glossy green head. His slender, serrated bill is red. The nuptial molt usually begins before the birds depart in the spring, so Texans, too, can see them at their best.

Red-breasted mergansers breed across the upper reaches of the continent, from Alaska to Nova Scotia, and southward to the Great Lakes. They also inhabit northern Europe and Asia. They seek woodlands beside lakes and rivers or sheltered coastlines and build their nests under bushes and piles of timber. Unlike most ducks, which defend larger territories, the highly gregarious mergansers often nest close together. Broods of young are frequently combined under the watchful eyes of one or more females while the others go off to feed. Later, they assemble in large flocks along the coasts to feed near the mouths of rivers and in the surf on small fish, crustaceans and aquatic insects. They then disperse southward along the U.S. coastlines.

On the Texas beaches and in the bays, the small flocks of mergansers might at first be mistaken for cormorants or loons. A closer look, however, reveals the shaggy, crested heads and thin bills. The birds fish actively underwater, leaping forward in graceful dives that would do justice to any Olympian. Red-breasted mergansers have been known to feed cooperatively, driving schools of fish into shallow water where they grasp the prey with their flashing beaks. It is a water ballet worth watching on a winter day along the shore.

Ruddy Duck
Oxyura jamaicensis

The chubby little ruddy duck belongs to a group generally known as the "stifftails." They have long, spiky tails that are often cocked upward above the water. They also have short, thick necks and large heads with very broad bills. Most inhabit swampy, overgrown ponds and marshes in the tropical and temperate regions of the world.

The male ruddy duck is immediately recognizable from his chunky profile and the white cheek patches below a dark cap. In breeding plumage, he is a rich, ruddy chestnut color with a pale blue bill; the winter plumage is a drabber brown. The female shows a single dark line across the cheek below a darker cap.

Ruddy ducks occur across western Canada and the U.S. and southward into tropical America. They migrate and spend the winter throughout Texas, although they are most abundant and predictable along the coast. Some have even remained to nest in South and Central Texas.

The breeding biology of the ruddy duck is unusual in several respects. The male is the only duck with an inflatable air sac in his neck, which he pumps up during his courtship displays. He then circles the female, cocking and fanning his tail over his head, pumping his bill up and down, and wildly splashing water with his flailing feet. He utters a number of chuckling calls, *chuck-chuck-uck-ur-r* or *ip-ip-ip-u-chuck*.

The female lays her six to ten whitish eggs in a woven basket in the reeds above the water—or in some other convenient nest nearby. The ruddy duck is a notorious brood parasite, depositing eggs not only in nests of her own species but in those of other ducks, grebes and even rails. Dump nests with scores of eggs from several females have also been found. The eggs are absurdly large for the size of the bird, even larger than those of a mallard or canvasback, both of which weigh twice as much as the tiny ruddy duck. A one-pound female may lay a clutch of eggs weighing three pounds.

The male deserts his mate early in the incubation process. Some reports indicate that he often remains to aid in the raising of the young, one of the few ducks to do so. However, recent marking studies have shown that such drakes are rarely the fathers of those broods. They have apparently arrived more recently on the scene and taken a liking to the hens.

Male red-breasted merganser (top) in breeding plumage. Male ruddy duck (above) in breeding plumage.

GULL-LIKE WATER BIRDS

To most casual visitors to the coast, "sea gulls" are the prototypical ocean birds. Actually, most gulls do not prefer the open sea. The vast majority remain along the shore, frequenting the beaches and tidal flats and feeding in the shallow water. Some even range far inland to forage and nest in freshwater wetlands. Nor do the flocks along the Texas coast necessarily contain a single species. Several different gulls and terns mingle at the water's edge. They vary in size and plumage and have different personalities and habits. The typical "sea gull" flock is far more diverse and interesting than one might first imagine.

There are some other families that are truly ocean birds. The shearwaters and petrels seldom come to land except to nest. Birders pursue these pelagic species on fishing boats and special birding trips offshore, all in the hopes of adding a new one to their lists. Most of the seabirds are beyond the scope of this book, for they rarely come within sight of the Texas shore. Only a few, the gannets and boobies and the frigatebird, regularly approach our coast and are treated here.

The pelicans are better known, of course. At close range, they are obviously not "gull-like" in their appearance, but they might easily be overlooked in the milling throngs of coastal birds.

Laughing gulls and Sandwich terns on a Texas beach.

GANNETS AND BOOBIES (Family Sulidae)

Immature masked booby.

The Sulidae are not regular residents of Texas. The large, goose-size birds are encountered primarily offshore but can sometimes be seen from the shoreline. Storms occasionally drive them onto the beaches or into the bays, where they loom over the gulls and terns assembled there. They have spindle-shaped bodies, tapered tails and massive, pointed bills. One author describes them as "shaped like fat cigars." Their long, narrow wings and powerful wingbeats carry them effortlessly across the sea, and they feed by diving headlong after fish, sometimes from as much as 100 feet above the waves. Layers of air sacs beneath the skin cushion them from the impact of the dive.

The northern gannet breeds in the cold waters of the North Atlantic and ranges off the Texas coast in winter. Checklists normally refer to it as "uncommon," but it is sometimes seen in fairly large numbers from the beach or jetties. Two other gannet species occupy similar niches on the coasts of South Africa and Australia. Formerly included in the genus *Sula* with the boobies, gannets are now classified in the genus *Morus.*

The six booby species inhabit islands in tropical seas. Some are blown to our beaches in hurricanes; others approach the coast in their normal wanderings across the Gulf. The masked booby (*Sula dactylatra),* formerly called the blue-faced booby, is the most likely to be sighted on our coast. The blue-footed, red-footed and brown boobies are all regarded as "accidental" on the Texas checklist. None is to be expected at any time, but a sulid on the beach is hard to miss. Other than on offshore trips, birders search for them by scanning the horizon above the waves with binoculars and spotting scopes for hours on end.

The name gannet is related to "gander" and comes from various German and Old English words for "sea fowl" and "gooselike sea gull." Booby means "stupid fellow," from the Portuguese and Spanish *bobo.* Early sailors probably bestowed the name because of the ease with which they were able to capture the giant birds.

NORTHERN GANNET   *Morus bassanus*

Far out over the Gulf waters a trio of large birds flies strongly and arrow-straight into the chill winter wind. The birds are barely visible from the beach against the leaden sky and disappear at times in the thick, driving spray. They appear all white, except for black wing-tips, but details are impossible to see. One of the birds wheels and folds its wings, diving headlong into the churning waves. It emerges quickly and rejoins its companions at the focus of a swirling flock of gulls, which are much smaller. The size of the three birds, their long profiles, massive bills, and narrow wings mark them as northern gannets.

Gannets were formerly regarded as very rare visitors to the Texas coast, but birders have found them regularly in recent years, flying just offshore during the winter months. This probably results from an increased awareness by the birders rather than from any changes in the status or habits of the birds.

After breeding in huge, closely packed colonies on the rocky cliffs and islands of eastern Canada, gannets take to the sea. They roost on the water and may not return to land again until the next mating season. They are most likely to appear near shore during the cold, wet, windy days that are fit for neither man nor beast. The chill winds hold no threat for these birds that ornithologist and seabird expert Robert Cushman Murphy called "the kings of the North Atlantic." They are well equipped for a pelagic life with their waterproof, insulating plumage and webbed feet. A special reinforced skull and air sacs beneath the skin cushion the impact as they dive from high in the air in pursuit of the schooling fish on which they live.

Because of their tameness and concentration in large nesting colonies, gannets suffered a serious decline before adequate protection laws were passed. Fishermen on Canada's shores clubbed them to death and used their meat for cod bait. Gannets numbered 150,000 in a historic colony on the Gulf of St. Lawrence "bird rocks" in 1860. By 1904, only 3,000 remained. Decrees by the Canadian government finally ended the slaughter, and populations rose again. It is unlikely, however, that they will ever reach their former levels. Many are still drowned in commercial fishnets while diving for fish to feed their young.

Fully three feet long, and with a six-foot wingspan, the northern gannet is nearly twice the size of the herring gull, the largest gull found commonly along the Texas coast. The body of the adult, including the tapered tail, is white, with a buffy yellow wash on the head. The white wings are tipped with black. The smaller masked booby has a black tail, and the black of the wings extends along the entire trailing edge. These are the adult plumages, however. Gannets acquire their clean white feathers in their third year; younger birds are mottled gray. Boobies go through similar phases, and all too often the distance and conditions make positive identification almost impossible. Even the most expert birders go home occasionally with checklists marked simply "Sulidae species."

Northern gannets in a Canadian nesting colony.

PELICANS (Family Pelecanidae)

Brown pelican.

One can scarcely meet a pelican face to face without recalling Dixon Merritt's 1910 classic, "A wonderful bird is the pelican, / His bill will hold more than his belican." Merritt did not resort to poetic license, for the amazing gular sac, or pouch, of the white pelican holds three gallons, more than twice the capacity of the stomach. The smaller pouch of the brown pelican holds up to a gallon. To regard the pelican only as a comic character, however, does it a grave disservice. It is marvelously adapted for the special ecological niche it occupies.

The bill of a pelican is several times as long as the head, and ends in a clawlike hook. On the underside are long extensions of the lower jawbones. Although fused together in most ordinary birds, these bones, called rami, join only at the tip and can be spread widely. Between them hangs the pouch, which can contract when not in use or expand to serve as a dip-net in catching fish. After scooping up its catch the pelican closes and raises its bill, contracts the pouch to force out the water, and swallows the fish.

It was once believed that pelicans carried home live fish in their pouches to feed their young. In fact, the chicks are fed a half-digested soup that the adults regurgitate and drip into the babies' mouths. Older chicks pursue this mixture by poking their heads into the throats of the adults in what Terence Shortt described as "like a wrestling match, and the writhing and contorting are both alarming and revolting."

There are seven or eight pelican species in the world, depending on which authority you choose to follow. The Peruvian pelican is sometimes regarded as a valid species and sometimes combined with the brown pelican of North America. Two species, the American white pelican and the brown pelican, occur in the United States and in Texas. Early settlers who sailed to Galveston frequently mentioned the thousands of birds that inhabited Pelican Island in Galveston Bay. William Gray, who visited the area in 1836, noted that the pelicans "at a distance resembled companies of soldiers, white and gray; the two colors flock together."

Although pelicans look ludicrous on land, waddling about and hopping awkwardly to take off, they are wonderfully graceful in flight. Heads pulled back to rest on their shoulders, they alternately flap and sail, with some of the slowest wingbeats of any bird. They travel in orderly V-formations and lines, flapping and sailing in rhythm, each picking up the beat from the bird ahead.

The pelican is widely represented in folklore, literature and art. During medieval times it became a symbol for Christ because of the erroneous belief that it picked at its breast until it bled in order to feed the blood to its nestlings. The Spanish name for the pelican, *alcatraz,* has also become a familiar part of our lexicon. The rocky island in San Francisco Bay was named for the brown pelicans that inhabited it. Presumably the birds were more free to come and go than some of the subsequent inhabitants of the rock.

AMERICAN WHITE PELICAN   *Pelecanus erythrorhynchos*

The white pelican is enormous, with a weight of 15 or 20 pounds and a nine-foot wingspan. It looks like a battleship among yachts as it floats high on the water, looming over the cormorants and gulls with which it shares the Texas coastal bays. In spite of its bulk, it is amazingly graceful in the air. The long, black-edged wings enable pelicans to soar to great heights on the thermals, and it is not unusual to see them wheeling in lazy circles up into the clouds until they vanish, seemingly enjoying their release from earth-bound concerns. Harry Oberholser writes of this aerial ballet, "A large flock of White Pelicans circling on a thermal in blue sky is a natural spectacle that is unexcelled in America."

Unlike its brown cousin, the white pelican does not dive for its food. Instead, it floats quietly along, paddling with its webbed feet and scooping up fish with its enormous beak. Flying low over the water, it may also splash down feet-first and scoop quickly at fleeing schools. Cooperative fishing is

---

American white pelicans.

also fairly common. The flock forms a line or semicircle and drives the fish toward shore with much splashing of their flailing wings and feet. Surrounding the confused and helpless prey, they then reap the harvest of their combined efforts. A white pelican consumes about three pounds of fish a day, most of it nongame rough fish.

During the breeding season adults grow a strange fibrous plate or "horn" on their beaks. This drops off after egg-laying is complete but appears to play a function in courtship and perhaps serves as a harmless target during territorial battles.

White pelicans breed in the western half of North America, ranging as far north as the lakes of central Canada and Minnesota and southward to California, Nevada and Colorado. There have also been sporadic breeding records along the Texas coast, but in recent years the state has had only a single colony on an island in the Laguna Madre in Kleberg County. Amazingly, this adjunct population is 1,400 miles from its nearest neighbors in Utah. Other pelicans seen during the summer in Texas appear to be nonbreeding birds that do not bother to migrate northward.

Nests are built on the ground, usually on islands free from mammalian predators. Level areas free of vegetation are required for takeoffs and landings. The breeding behavior is closely synchronized within a given colony, and most pairs begin mating within a few days of each other. Two white eggs form the normal clutch, but seldom is more than one chick raised successfully. The older, more aggressive sibling gets most of the food while the younger starves. Both male and female incubate the eggs and feed the young, and they may fly as much as 150 miles from the colony in search of food. At fledging, the chick is 20 percent larger than its parents, with a stored fat reserve that will see it through meager days of learning to fish for itself.

In the fall the huge birds drift southward, primarily to the coastal regions of California and the Gulf of Mexico. Some continue into Mexico and as far as Guatemala. They may be seen in migrating flocks throughout Texas, flying in long lines or precise V-formations, but they stay to winter mainly along the coast.

Several breeding colonies have been lost due to habitat destruction, and white pelicans were watched with great concern during the 1970s and early 1980s. However, the population was not decimated as was that of the brown pelican. Because most white pelicans move to fresh water during the breeding season and feed in varied locations, they have not suffered as severely from the DDT-caused eggshell thinning that has threatened many large fish-eating birds.

BROWN PELICAN   *Pelecanus occidentalis*

The sky turns pink with the glow of sunset and the water darkens to purple, its mirrored surface broken only by the wake of a passing shrimp boat. Behind the boat flies a cloud of wheeling, screaming gulls, following it between the jetties and up the channel. Low over the water, a line of much larger birds flies slowly by in precise formation, huge dark birds whose wings beat no more than once a second. Heads pulled back on their shoulders and long bills resting on their breasts, they alternate between ponderous, flapping flight and short, arrow-straight glides. As they skim the water, it seems impossible that they can remain airborne with so little effort. Their massive size and majestic manner set pelicans apart from all other birdlife in the bay. Their distinctive profiles make them immediately recognizable, even in silhouette against the darkening sky. These giants are brown pelicans, birds which nearly disappeared from the Texas coast. Now they are returning to these shores in increasing numbers, much to the delight of all who enjoy the outdoor scene.

An estimated 5,000 brown pelicans nested on the Texas coast around 1920. In the 1950s, however, observers noted a disastrous decline. Fewer and fewer adults were seen, and nesting was severely curtailed. The downward spiral continued until no young fledged between 1964 and 1966. An extensive survey in 1969 counted only 116 brown pelicans along the entire Texas coast, with none at all on the upper portion, where they had once been common. In 1969, too, came word of trouble in the pelican colonies of California. Broken eggs littered the ground, their shells too thin to withstand the weight of incubating birds.

It was a disaster presaged by Rachel Carson's 1962 classic, *Silent Spring*. Scientists determined that the decline was due primarily to the buildup of DDT and other chlorinated-hydrocarbon pesticides in the environment and in the birds' food chains. Sprayed on the land in massive amounts, the chemicals and their toxic breakdown products washed into the streams and down to the seas, where they were absorbed by marine micro-organisms. These were eaten by fish, and the fish, in turn, by the pelicans. Each successive step further concentrated the pesticides in the organs and fatty tissues of the hosts.

The concentration was rarely enough to kill the birds outright, but it was sufficient to upset the body chemistry and produce infertile or thin-shelled eggs. Brown pelicans were not the only victims. Bald eagles, ospreys and peregrine falcons all suffered from pesticide poisoning. All declined significantly and were listed as endangered species.

DDT was banned for most uses in the United States in 1972, and bird populations began to recover quickly. Although brown pelicans have returned to the Texas coast in significant numbers, the threat is by no means over, for chlorinated hydrocarbons are still in use in other countries. They also enter the environment as by-products and intermediates in the manufacture of other chemicals. But at least for now, brown pelicans again fly majestically along the surf and over our coastal bays.

The adult brown pelican has a gray-brown body and blackish belly. The head and neck are white, often with a yellow wash. The back of the neck turns a deep chestnut in breeding plumage, and the bill and facial skin flush with hormonal colors. Immatures are entirely brown, with lighter bellies, and do not acquire adult plumage until their third year.

Unlike their larger white cousins, brown pelicans feed by diving, sometimes from heights of 50 or 60 feet. Folding their wings, they plummet headfirst, rotating in the dive so that they may slant into the water almost belly-up. They net the fish in their expanded pouches and surface again to drain the water. Swallowing their catch, they laboriously struggle to take off again. Pelicans can also be seen perching stolidly on boats, piers and pilings, sometimes even begging handouts from neighboring fishermen.

With gulls and terns, brown pelicans plunge headlong into the surf for fish.

FRIGATEBIRDS (Family Fregatidae)

Male magnificent frigatebird.

Five species of frigatebirds inhabit the tropical oceans of the world, but only one, the magnificent frigatebird, reaches the shores of North America. All are masterful fliers, with the longest wings, in proportion to their weight, of any birds. Their seven-foot wing-spreads support three-pound bodies in aerodynamic perfection. Their slender skeletons weigh less than their feathers.

For all their prowess in the air, frigatebirds present a strange anomaly. Although they spend most of their lives at sea, they do not swim, for their feathers are poorly waterproofed. If they were to spend any time on the sur-face, they would quickly become water-logged. Nor can they take off readily from the flat surface of the sea, since they require a deep stroke of their long wings. Thus, they spend most of their lives on the wing. They feed by sweeping low to snatch up prey with long, hook-tipped beaks or by ha-rassing boobies, gulls, terns and other seabirds until they drop or disgorge their fish. The frigates then wheel and catch the booty in midair.

Early sailors apparently named the frigatebirds for the swift sailing ships of their day. Their simi-larity to fleet warships and their piratic habits also gave rise to an alternate name, "man-o'-war birds."

MAGNIFICENT FRIGATEBIRD *Fregata magnificens*

Soaring over the sunlit waters of the Gulf, this dark seabird appears every bit as majestic as its name. It sails ef-fortlessly on the thermals, its long wings bent sharply at the wrists. The long tail is sometimes folded into a single point, sometimes scissored open in a dramatic swallowlike fork. No bird is more graceful on the wing, nor is there a bird with greater need for that aerial ability, for the frigatebird cannot land on the water.

It perches occasionally on pilings and platforms but spends much of its life in the air, presumably even dozing as it flies.

The magnificent frigatebird breeds along the Mexican coast and on is-lands in the Caribbean, wandering northward after the early breeding season. There is at least one record of a nest found in our state, but that is highly unusual. The birds occur from April through October along the Texas coast, with most sightings dur-ing the hot summer months.

The male frigatebird is entirely glossy black, with a small throat pouch that inflates to an enormous red balloon during courtship displays. Although most classic portraits show this red gular sac, it is normally not inflated during the frigatebird's post-breeding wanderings. The female is a duller brownish black with contrast-ing white breast, and immature birds display varying amounts of white on the head and underparts. Juveniles re-quire from four to six years to attain adult plumage.

Magnificent frigatebirds nest in large, closely packed colonies, usually on islands or coastlines with stunted, flat-topped trees and shrubs. The absurdly small, crude stick nests are built atop the trees, where the birds can obtain an elevated takeoff point without entangling their long wings. Both sexes incubate the single white egg, which does not hatch for at least 50 days. Both also care for the chick over some five to six months before it can fly. The nest is never left unguarded. Neighboring frigates quickly move in to steal material from an unattended nest, and they will also eat abandoned eggs and young.

Once nesting chores are over and the young have fledged, the colony takes to the sea. Frigatebirds soar continuously, sweeping down to pick fish, squid and crabs from the surface with their long hook-tipped beaks or chasing other seabirds to steal their catch. They are strong, agile aerial pirates, sailing tropical seas on the wings of the wind.

Juvenile (top) and male magnificent frigatebirds sail on motionless wings.

GULLS, TERNS AND SKIMMERS (Family Laridae)

Laridae comprises a large and cosmopolitan family of about 90 species. Most are known simply as "sea gulls" by nonbirders, but there is wide variation among family members in size, form and function. Although they are usually thought of as coastal birds, many gulls and terns range far inland, breeding on freshwater lakes and marshes. The young are semiprecocial. At hatching they are covered with down and their eyes are open, but they remain in or near the nest for the first two or three weeks to be brooded and fed by the adults.

Many, particularly the terns, breed in large, tightly packed colonies. Several reasons have been proposed for such colonial behavior. One explanation is that the colonies serve as "information centers" where knowledge can be shared. Less effective foragers follow the more adept to productive feeding grounds. Sometimes, too, the juvenile birds assemble in creches, to be watched by a few adults while the others search for food.

Anyone who has ventured into a tern colony amidst swirling wings and sharp, flashing beaks can also affirm that the community provides a measure of protection against predators. Banding studies indicate that the older, more experienced birds occupy the center of the colony where they are most secure. Predators need only reach the perimeter to find sufficient food, and the inner core is protected by the "swamping effect" of the multitudes. This assures the productivity of at least a portion of the colony at the expense of some individuals. Tennyson made such an observation about nature—"So careful of the type she seems, / So careless of the single life."—several years before Charles Darwin used the same idea as a cornerstone of his theories.

The gulls are the best known of the family Laridae. About 40 species occur around the world, many in the North Temperate and Arctic zones. They are robust birds with slightly hooked bills and rounded or squared tails. Gulls are basically scavengers and contribute greatly to beach sanitation. They do not dive headlong into the water as do the terns, but rather scoop food items from the surface in flight or splash down to swim and pick at almost anything that floats.

Several species of gulls and terns line the beach.

Besides the gulls treated in this section, several others live in northern North America and may wander occasionally to Texas. The Thayer's gull is much like the herring gull and can be separated only by careful and detailed observation. The glaucous and Iceland gulls are largely white; the lesser and great black-backed gulls are darker across the back and wings. Intermediates also occur, and the relationships among the various forms remain unclear. The checklists will probably see further revisions in the future.

Another problem in gull identification is that immatures are similarly mottled in shades of brown and gray and require two, three or four years to attain adulthood. Until that time, they look nothing like their parents and can be separated only by size and minor differences in plumage.

Detailed treatment of gull plumages is beyond the scope of this book. Field guides devote many pages to the problem, and other books deal with gulls alone. Learning each and every one takes experience, and even the experts disagree from time to time. It is one of the most difficult of birding's problems; however, that is half the fun. There is always the chance of spotting some rare and unusual gull that wandered far out of its normal range.

With their slender wings and sharp-pointed beaks, terns are generally more streamlined and can maneuver better than the bulkier gulls. Most have forked tails. Terns normally hover while feeding and then plunge headfirst into the water to grasp prey. Although they tend to be smaller than gulls, they range in size from the tiny nine-inch least tern to the huge 21-inch Caspian tern. The lat-

Ring-billed gull.

ter, with a wingspan of more than four feet, is considerably larger than Texas' common laughing gull. Many terns are pearly gray above and white below, with black caps in the breeding season.

The skimmers are sometimes placed in a separate family, Rynchopidae, but are included here as a subfamily of the Laridae. The black skimmer is the local species; there are also African and Indian skimmers. They are unique among the world's birds in having the lower mandible longer than the upper.

Jaegers and skuas, too, rate their own family, Stercorariidae, in some taxonomies. They look much like gulls but are more hawklike in behavior. They fly rapidly after gulls and other birds and steal their catch.

Sandwich and royal terns occupy a common, densely packed colony.

Three jaegers—the pomarine, parasitic and long-tailed—breed on the North American tundra and wander in winter as far south as the Texas coast. All have elongated central tail feathers as adults, but individual variation and complex immature plumages make them extremely difficult to identify. They can best be seen from offshore boats and sometimes from jetties and fishing piers as they course over the waves or harass flocks of gulls and terns. Individual species are not treated here.

LAUGHING GULL *Larus atricilla*

The laughing gull takes its name from its call, which Roger Tory Peterson calls a "strident, hysterical *ha-ha-ha-ha-ha-haah-haah-haah*." "Or are they calling 'half, half, half,' as if demanding tribute from the pelicans diving below?" Austin Rand suggests. Abbreviated versions of the laughing cry are given in flight.

Visitors to the Texas coast can scarcely miss the laughing gull. It is a common year-round resident, the only gull that nests regularly on our shores. Although it has occasionally wandered inland to San Antonio, Austin and Dallas, it is normally confined to the beaches and bays along the Gulf.

In breeding plumage, the laughing gull sports a black hood with a contrasting white eye-ring and red bill and legs. The underparts are immaculately white; the mantle (the upper back and wings) is dark slate-gray, blending into black wing-tips without intervening white bars. In winter, the black head becomes largely white, with only a grayish wash across the nape and on the face. The birds, however, do not always agree upon the season, and a variety of plumages is often apparent.

The laughing gull is termed a "three-year gull," because juveniles do not attain full adult plumage until their third year. They are at first a dingy grayish brown, shedding the mottled plumage and dark tail-band through a series of molts. They are smaller than the young ring-billed and herring gulls that share the beach in winter, and they have dark bills and legs.

Laughing gulls breed all along the Atlantic and Gulf coasts, from Nova Scotia to Yucatán. They migrate from the northeastern portions of their range, where they are called "summer gulls," and reach down into South America.

Nests vary from bulky platforms of grass and debris among the marsh grasses to simple scrapes on beaches and shell banks, the latter rimmed with a few plant stalks and feathers. They are usually in loose colonies, sometimes with the nests of terns and wading birds. Both parents incubate the three olive-brown eggs spotted and flecked with shades of brown. The eggs hatch in about 20 days, and the downy chicks fledge five weeks later.

Laughing gulls consume fish, shrimp, snails, insects and what might in polite terms be called "garbage." As with most other gulls, they also prey at times on the eggs and tiny chicks of other birds. Fully protected by state and federal laws, they play an important part in our coastal ecology as well as providing a lively treat to all who walk along our Texas beaches.

*Two laughing gulls sit
on their nests.*

FRANKLIN'S GULL
Larus pipixcan

Franklin's gull is an inland bird, breeding on the marshes and ponds of Canada's prairie provinces and the northern plains of the United States. Nesting in large colonies, the gulls follow farm machinery through the fields, catching insects chased up in their paths and earthworms exposed by the plow. Worms, in fact, make up a substantial portion of the diet for the downy chicks.

In the fall, the flocks head southward to spend the winter in Central and South America. During both spring and fall migrations, Franklin's gulls occur commonly across the eastern two-thirds of Texas. They are much less abundant in the Trans-Pecos. Only a few remain in winter along the coast, where they are difficult to distinguish from the resident laughing gulls.

In breeding plumage, Franklin's gull has a black hood and dark slate-gray mantle, much like that of the laughing gull. However, a white bar separates the gray of the wing from the black wing-tip. There may also be a pale rosy blush to the white breast. In fall and winter, the same wing pattern is diagnostic, and there is a larger dark patch across the head than in the laughing gull's nonbreeding plumage. Franklin's gull is slightly smaller, but that is almost impossible to judge without a direct comparison. Flocks of small gulls seen well inland from the coast in April and May or from late September into November may very well be Franklin's.

The gull's common name derives from that of Englishman Sir John Franklin, a 19th-century Arctic explorer. His attempt in 1818 to reach the North Pole failed when his ship nearly foundered in the ice. The next year, and again in 1845, he tried to find the Northwest Passage. The last attempt ended in the disappearance of Franklin and his crew, and for a decade scores of expeditions tried to learn their fate.

Franklin's gull shows white bars near the wing-tips.

BONAPARTE'S GULL   *Larus philadelphia*

This smallest of the North American gulls spends the winter in Texas, particularly along the coast. Somewhat ternlike in its flight, it hovers above the crashing surf or bobs buoyantly on the waves, picking up small fish and crustaceans from the surface. It occurs less frequently on inland lakes and ponds across the state, especially in migration.

Adults have black heads in the breeding season, but that plumage is rarely seen in Texas. These hardy little gulls leave early in the spring to return to their nesting grounds in Alaska and western Canada, arriving before the snow is gone. They build their nests of twigs, grasses, mosses and lichens in the tops of conifer trees, an unusual custom for members of this ground-nesting family. After raising their three chicks on the abundant insect life of the region, they migrate southward again in fall, wintering along the U.S. coasts and into the West Indies and Mexico.

Bonaparte's gull in winter plumage.

In its winter plumage, Bonaparte's gull has a white head with a conspicuous round black spot behind the eye. The adult flashes a white wedge on the leading edge of the wing; the immature has a brownish bar on the wing and a black band at the tip of the tail. The small size and slender black bill aid in identification.

Bonaparte's gull was named for Charles Lucien Bonaparte, a nephew of the Emperor Napoleon. Born in Paris in 1803, he was educated in science in Italy and came to the United States at the age of 19. Here he began a set of supplemental volumes to Alexander Wilson's *American Ornithology*. These and subsequent works on comparative zoology published after he returned to Europe earned him the title of "father of systematic ornithology."

RING-BILLED GULL *Larus delawarensis*

So abundant was the ring-billed gull in Audubon's time that he called it simply "the common American gull." It appears to have relinquished a portion of its breeding range in the East since then, but it remains a common and widespread species. Nesting in colonies across Canada and the northern states, the ring-bill winters along the coasts, around the Great Lakes, and through the southern states into Mexico. It migrates and winters throughout most of Texas from September through May. As might be expected, however, it is particularly abundant along the coast and rare in the arid regions of the Trans-Pecos.

At 18 inches in length, and with a four-foot wingspan, the ring-bill is considerably larger than the resident laughing gull. The breeding adult has a pale gray mantle and black wing-tips marked with white spots. The head and underparts are white, the legs yellow or yellow-green. A black ring around the yellow bill near the tip gives the species its name. Winter plumage is much the same, but with brownish streaking on the head and nape.

Immature ring-bills acquire a different plumage in the fall for each of their first three years. Juveniles are heavily mottled with brown and have a black-tipped tail and bill. The legs are flesh-colored or pinkish gray. With each molt, they slowly lose that drab feathering to gain adulthood.

Among Texas' most common gulls, only the herring gull is larger than the ring-bill. The plumages are much the same, but the adult herring gull has pinkish legs and lacks the ring around its massive beak. As is the case with some other groups of birds as well, the color of the bill and legs may be major keys to gull recognition.

Ring-billed gulls undoubtedly owe part of their success to their ability to eat almost anything. Over inland fields, they follow the plow to pick up earthworms and insects, their excited *kre, kree, kree* cries ringing across the plains. On the coast, they eat fish, crustaceans and mollusks floating on the waves or washed up on beaches along their route. They catch small rodents and pirate the untended eggs of other birds. And in the face of advancing urban development, they absolutely delight in scavenging at garbage dumps and fast-food parking lots.

Ring-billed gull.

Herring gulls.

HERRING GULL *Larus argentatus*

The herring gull looms over all the other gulls and terns with which it regularly shares Texas' winter beaches and lakeshores. It is more than two feet in length and has a five-foot wingspread. The pale gray wings of the adult are tipped with black; the head and underparts are white. In addition to being much larger than the similarly plumaged ring-billed gull, it has pale pink instead of yellow legs and lacks the black ring around the bill. A red spot on that heavy, hooked bill serves as a "target" when the adult is feeding young. As the chick pecks at the spot, the parent regurgitates the meal it has carried back.

Immatures do not attain adult plumage until their fourth year. In the process, they go through a series of molts during which they slowly lose their mottled brown plumage and dark tail. They can usually be identified by size alone, especially in Texas where other large gulls are very rare.

The herring gull occurs around the globe in the Northern Hemisphere. In North America it breeds from Alaska to Nova Scotia and southward through the Great Lakes and the northeastern states. It winters through much of the U.S. and into Central America and the West Indies. Common along the Gulf Coast, the herring gull is an irregular visitor to inland lakes east of the Pecos River and much rarer farther west. Immature birds outnumber adults because they tend to wander farther from their established home ranges.

Herring gulls are omnivorous feeders, consuming everything from dead fish to berries. Eggs and young of other gulls and terns are frequent targets in the crowded nesting colonies. Scavenging at garbage dumps supplements their natural diet and undoubtedly accounts in part for an increase in both numbers and range.

Immature black-legged kittiwake.

GULL-BILLED TERN
Sterna nilotica

The white tern hovers on beating wings over the marsh, its stout, almost gull-like bill pointed straight down. It then drops quickly into the long grass and rises again with a grasshopper in its bill. Gulping it down, the bird courses off in search of more insects, which make up the bulk of its varied diet. Its unusual menu includes spiders, frogs, crabs and crayfish, an occasional egg or young bird, and even a mouse or two. It dives for fish much less frequently than other terns.

The gull-billed tern is stockier and paler than most of its relatives, with a shorter and more shallowly forked tail. In breeding plumage, it has a neat black cap; in winter, only some fine dark streaks shade the otherwise white crown. Its call is a sharp *kaywack* or a throaty *za-za-za*. The overall pale plumage and sturdy black bill distinguish it from other medium-sized terns on the Texas coast.

The etymology of the gull-bill's scientific name reveals its worldwide distribution. *Sterna* has its origins in a variety of Norse, Swedish and Danish words for "sea swallow," one of the colloquial names frequently used in this country as well. These names entered the English as "tern" and "stern," and Turner then Latinized them to *sterna* in 1544. In applying his first binomial system to birds, Linnaeus used Turner's name as that of the genus for the terns. *Nilotica,* the gull-billed tern, is from the Latin *niloticus,* "of the Nile," because the type specimen was collected in that region.

The gull-billed tern nests along the U.S. coast from the mid-Atlantic states to the Gulf and on both coasts of Mexico. It formerly ranged to the northeastern states, but plume hunters and egg collectors decimated the population at the turn of the century, when women's hats were adorned with tern wings and the eggs were a favored spring delicacy. The species has never recovered from that onslaught, and the gull-bill is one of the least common of the terns.

BLACK-LEGGED KITTIWAKE *Rissa tridactyla*

"New Englanders say winter begins when the black-legged kittiwake arrives in mid-October, announcing itself with a shrill *kit-ti-wake,*" writes ornithologist Austin Rand. Only winter storms drive the kittiwake to Texas, where it remains one of the prizes awaiting hardy birders. It is listed as "rare" on the checklist for the upper Texas coast, a term described as "Not to be expected more than once or twice per season." Nevertheless, it is sometimes spotted at such vantage points as the Galveston or Freeport jetties or the Texas City Dike, and it might even be encountered on inland lakes and reservoirs.

The kittiwake nests in large colonies on the steep seaside cliffs of Alaska and northern Canada. After the breeding season, it heads far offshore to spend the winter on the waves. One of the few gulls that truly deserves to be called "sea gull," it follows ships and flocks around the fishing boats. It braves howling gales and flies effortlessly over the towering wave crests, dipping into the troughs to search for food. It is the only gull that dives underwater to catch fish.

The adult in winter has a white head with a gray smudge across the back, dark eyes, and an unmarked yellow bill. The gray wings are tipped with black. Most kittiwakes seen in Texas, however, are young birds, which tend to wander farther from their customary routes. The immature has a dark half-collar around the back of the neck and a round black spot behind the eye. The black bill is usually pale at the base. A black band tips the slightly forked tail, and the wings have dark bands forming a "W" across the back of the bird in flight. About the size of a laughing gull, it can be distinguished from the immature Bonaparte's gull by its larger size and dark collar.

The black-legged kittiwake is representative of several rare gulls that show up periodically in Texas. They usually appear after strong winter storms, which drive them southward and inland to our sheltered Gulf shores. It is after such storms that ardent birders prowl the coast, field guides in hand, examining all the flocks in search of something out of place.

Gull-bills breed locally along the Texas coast but are only rarely seen inland. In winter, when the northern populations migrate as far as South America, there are fewer here as well. Nests are shallow scrapes on the beaches of coastal islands, usually lined and rimmed with scattered grasses, sedges and shells. The two or three buffy eggs are spotted with camouflage brown and hatch in 22 or 23 days. Both parents incubate and care for the semiprecocial downy chicks, sheltering them from the hot Texas sun and feeding them for at least two or three months.

CASPIAN TERN
Sterna caspia

A visitor to the Texas Gulf Coast at any season of the year will likely encounter Caspian terns. They stand huddled on the beaches and flats with other gulls and terns or fly overhead with powerful wingbeats, crying *kowk* or *ka-aar* in loud, harsh tones.

The largest tern in the world, the Caspian is nearly two feet long and has a wingspan of more than four feet. A bulky, stocky bird, it dwarfs the smaller terns with which it associates along the beach and is bigger even than the laughing and ring-billed gulls. Among the common Texas Laridae, only the herring gull exceeds it in size.

Its feeding habits are half tern, half gull. It hovers and dives ternlike after fish but also swims like a gull and picks up food from the surface. Gull-like, too, are its habits of stealing the catch from other birds and robbing nests of eggs and chicks.

The Caspian tern has a heavy, bright red or red-orange bill and a black cap in breeding plumage. Winter adults and immatures have foreheads heavily streaked with black. They do not get the white forehead of the nonbreeding royal tern, the only species with which they might be confused. The royal is also a smaller, sleeker bird with a more slender or-

Gull-billed terns (top). A juvenile Caspian tern begs for food from an adult (above).

ange bill and a longer, more deeply forked tail.

While Caspian terns are year-round residents of the Texas coast, they occasionally wander inland, though rarely more than about 100 miles from the Gulf. The least social of the terns, they breed alone or in small colonies on island beaches and shell banks around the coastal bays. The nest is a simple, shallow scrape sparsely lined with grasses and often well concealed among the shells and beach debris. Both parents incubate the two or three pinkish eggs speckled and splotched with shades of brown.

The downy young hatch in three weeks and quickly learn to recognize the calls of their parents as they return with meals of small fish. Adults are strict disciplinarians, punishing their young with sharp pecks and blows of the wings for wandering too

far. It is a lesson well learned, for straying into the territory of a neighboring gull or tern could mean being severely injured or even killed and eaten. Even after the juveniles can fly, they are fed for six months or more by the adults, the longest period of parental care of any of the terns.

Caspian terns nest along the coasts of North America and on inland lakes, rivers and marshes across Canada and the northern states, retreating in winter to the southern coasts and as far as South America. They also range widely through other regions of the world. The name, in fact, comes from the type specimen collected on the Caspian Sea. The large range is typical of many of the water birds such as the gulls, terns, ducks and shorebirds. Powerful fliers accustomed to migrating great distances over water, they easily colonize distant lands.

ROYAL TERN
Sterna maxima

The royal tern is a large, elegant bird with a bright orange bill and shaggy black crest. Smaller and sleeker than the bulky Caspian tern, the royal has a longer, more deeply forked tail and a more slender bill. Although the royal tern has a typical black cap in breeding plumage, that is retained for only a short time. Even when the birds are sitting on their nests, most are already molting. Thus, for most of the year, the royal tern has a white forehead with a black crest across only the back of the head. The Caspian always has dark streaks down the forehead, even in winter.

Royal terns breed along the southern Atlantic and Gulf coasts, through Mexico and the West Indies, and in western Africa. In winter they migrate as far as South America. They are almost exclusively coastal, rather than ranging inland as do Caspian terns. Their shrill *keer* and *kaak* calls are higher pitched than the Caspian's harsh jeers.

Royal terns are resident throughout the year along the Texas coast. They nest in large, closely packed colonies, frequently with Sandwich terns. The nests are simple depressions in the sand or shell, usually on an island or isolated sandbar. Unlike most other tern species, royals normally lay but a single egg, although some clutches contain two. They vary in color from white to buff and are speckled and spotted with reddish brown.

Young royal terns join a large creche within a few days of hatching. While a few adults remain to watch the chicks and herd them protectively back and forth, the others are free to go off fishing. Adults and young recognize each other's voices, and the chicks fight their way to the edge of the milling throng to be fed only by their own returning parents.

Royal terns in their nesting colony.

SANDWICH TERN
Sterna sandvicensis

The Sandwich tern was first described from a specimen taken near Sandwich, England, and owes its name to that location rather than to any particularly tasty aspects of its anatomy. It is best recognized by its long, slender black bill with a contrasting yellow tip. Slightly larger than the Forster's tern that is so abundant on the Texas coast, it looks more like a miniature royal tern, with its trim lines and short black crest.

Royal and Sandwich terns (top) share nesting space on a coastal island. Sandwich tern (right) at nest.

Indeed, Sandwich terns usually associate with the larger royals, both on the breeding grounds and across their winter range. A mixed colony of the two species might contain as many as 10,000 birds, all sitting on their eggs within a few inches of each other. Each nest is just a small depression in the sand, for terns seldom waste much time on fancy architecture. The one or two eggs range in color from white or pale pink to olive-buff, marked with spots and splotches of brown and black. The variation may help each bird locate its own nest, for at any disturbance the entire flock rises into the air in a blizzard of wings. They swoop low at an intruder, their shrill cries almost deafening. Just as quickly they settle back, each unerringly on its own eggs.

Mated birds form long-term pair bonds and share in the incubation chores. The eggs hatch in about 24 or 25 days, and individual downy chicks also display a good deal of color variation. Some are white; others are buff or yellowish, each lightly flecked with darker spots. This, too, may help in recognition, and within four or five days the parents and chicks recognize each other's voices.

The young of both Sandwich and royal terns assemble in a common creche, sometimes containing thousands of birds. The flock roams through the colony, protected by a few adults, while the others fly out to fish. On returning, the parents find their own and call them over to be fed. This continues until fledging at about five weeks of age, when the juveniles begin to learn how to dive for their own meals.

The Sandwich tern breeds along the lower Atlantic Coast and around the Gulf of Mexico. As indicated by the type location, it also inhabits Europe and western Asia. The American population was known as Cabot's tern in older publications. Sandwich terns are fairly common along the Texas coast in summer, but most North American birds head south for the winter, ranging down into South America. Only a few remain along the Gulf at that season, and they can be difficult to find.

Forster's tern on its nest.

FORSTER'S TERN
Sterna forsteri

This is the familiar small white tern of the Texas coast. Whereas many of the other terns have worldwide ranges, Forster's is strictly North American. It breeds in scattered colonies from western Canada to the Gulf Coast and winters along the southern coasts to Guatemala and the West Indies.

Snow-white below and pale silvery gray above, the breeding adult sports a jaunty black cap and bright orange bill tipped with black. In winter plumage, attained by mid-August, it loses the cap and has only an elongated black patch around the dark eye. The bill then becomes dark.

Forster's tern is part of a complex that also includes the Arctic, roseate and common terns. All are of similar size and plumage. The common tern (*Sterna hirundo*) can be found along the Texas coast in winter, but it is much less abundant than the resident Forster's. The common tern in winter plumage has a dark patch extending around the back of the head, and its wings are darker. Forster's has lighter, more silvery wings and black only on the sides of the head. The distinctions are not always easy to see. So similar are the two, in fact, that Forster's tern was not recognized as a separate species until the mid–19th century. The other two North American species, the Arctic (*S. paradisaea*) and roseate (*S. dougallii*) terns, are presently considered "hypothetical" in Texas, since no conclusive documentation of their occurrence exists. Only the bravest birders have the temerity to report seeing them.

Forster's terns nest most frequently among the grasses of the coastal salt marsh. Although colonial, they do not choose sites as closely packed as those of royal and Sandwich terns. The nests are substantial, well-built platforms of grasses and sedges holding the three or four buff-colored eggs mottled with brown. Some birds choose to nest directly on the sand or shell banks, and their nests are more sparsely lined with grasses and beach debris. Both sexes incubate, and the semiprecocial, downy brown chicks hatch in 23 or 24 days. They are fed on small fish, aquatic invertebrates or insects, depending on the location and resources of the colony.

Forster's tern was named for the German-born naturalist Johann Reinhold Forster. After first studying for the ministry, he developed a strong interest in science and was teaching natural history in England when he was selected in 1772 to accompany Captain Cook on his second voyage around the world. Forster also published the first book that attempted to cover American fauna. Published in 1771, *A Catalogue of the Animals of North America* listed 302 species of birds.

LEAST TERN
Sterna antillarum

At nine inches in length, and with a 20-inch wingspan, the least tern ranks as the smallest of all American terns. Until recently, it was considered a race of the worldwide little tern (*Sterna albifrons*), and it is so listed in the older field guides. Not all taxonomists agree with the separation, but the American Ornithologists' Union has accorded the least tern full species status in its *Check-list of North American Birds.*

In breeding plumage, the tiny birds are the typical silvery gray above and white below. The black cap, however, is interrupted by a white patch on the forehead, and the bill and legs are bright yellow. The breeding range extends along the East and Gulf coasts, along the southern California coast, and through the midsection of the country. Many of the colonies are declining dramatically, and the interior subspecies of the least tern is listed as endangered.

Plume hunters nearly exterminated the species before legal protection was obtained in 1913. The feathers, and even whole birds, were popular on women's hats, and 100,000 were shot each year. After recovering from that onslaught, the least tern now suffers from a serious loss of habitat.

Colonies occupy sandy beaches, where the females lay their two speckled eggs in small scrapes directly on the sand or shells. With continued residential and beach development, dogs and cats have become major predators. Fishermen and beachgoers, too, disturb the colonies and keep the birds from their nests while eggs and young perish in the blazing sun. Automobiles and foot traffic take their toll of eggs that are too perfectly camouflaged against the sand.

A few communities have helped offset the nationwide losses by protecting their beachfront colonies with snow fences to provide shade and protect nests from traffic and prowling predators. Similar projects should be implemented in Texas, and the public must be educated to the value of local birdlife. An important step was made in that direction in the spring of 1992, when the Houston Audubon Society signed a long-term lease to manage Bolivar Flats, a vital shorebird and seabird area on the Bolivar Peninsula near Galveston.

The least tern nests in Texas along the coast and at a very few locations on the Red River system on the northern border. The inland sites are threatened by the construction of dams and fluctuating water levels as well as by animal predation and human disturbance. All of the populations winter far southward in Central and South America.

The lovely little least tern needs our concerted efforts for its preservation. Anyone who watches a courting male bring a gift minnow to his chosen mate, or sees it hover on beating wings and then plunge headlong into the surf, cannot but marvel at its grace and beauty. To allow such scenes to vanish from Texas' summer beaches would gravely diminish them.

The least tern is the smallest of all American terns. Its yellow bill and white forehead distinguish it in breeding plumage.

BLACK TERN *Chlidonias niger*

They hover over the marsh on beating wings like large black butterflies on a warm May afternoon. One swoops abruptly into the long grass and emerges with a dragonfly in its slender black bill. Another splashes lightly into a small pond to capture a minnow. Settling onto a line of fence posts beside the marsh, they gulp down their catches and begin to preen their long, slender wings and forked tails. Trim and sleek, these birds are easy to identify, for the black tern is our only dark-bodied tern.

About ten inches long, with a two-foot wingspan, the black tern is scarcely larger than the least tern. Head and body are black; back, wings and forked tail are dark gray. The paler gray wing linings and white undertail coverts contrast sharply with the otherwise dark plumage.

These black terns will not stay for long, for they are migrants through Texas on their return from the wintering grounds in tropical America. They will continue northward to nest in the marshes and ponds of Canada and the upper and middle states. They will return before too long, however, for their breeding season is relatively short. Most pairs raise only a single brood, and the incubation and fledging periods may be as short as three weeks each.

The spring and fall migrations nearly overlap. North-bound birds pass through Texas from April into mid-June, while the return flow occurs from late July until October. The autumn birds look very different after molting from their breeding plumage. In mid-molt, they are dappled black and white. Molt accomplished, they are dark gray above and white below, with a dark cap extending down into an ear-patch behind the eye. Their small size and darker backs distinguish them from the Forster's and other terns with which they might assemble. Migratory black terns are fairly common along the Texas coast and on marshes, lakes and wet fields inland.

The black tern first made the National Audubon Society's Blue List in 1978, a dubious honor denoting special concern for declining populations in certain regions of the country. Reduced hatching success can probably be traced to widespread use of agricultural chemicals, and the loss of wetlands across the continent is having its obvious consequences.

A black tern rests beside a Texas marsh on its way northward to its breeding grounds.

BLACK SKIMMER *Rynchops niger*

It is one of the premier spectacles of nature, a flock of unique birds doing what they alone can do. The black skimmers fly just above the quiet waters of the bay, lower mandibles cutting the surface with their razor edges. Periodically a bird dips its head, beak snapping shut on a fish or shrimp. It gulps its catch and rejoins the throng, tracing an arrow-straight path across the bay. Reaching the opposite bank, the flock wheels on long, narrow wings and sweeps low again. The skimmers retrace their routes, intent on more minnows attracted to the wakes. Swirling up again, appetites satisfied, they alight on a sandbar. There they huddle close together, standing on absurdly short legs, bills pointing into the breeze. They seem suddenly awkward and ill at ease, but they remain ever dignified in their formal dress.

The world's three skimmer species are the only birds whose lower mandibles are longer than the upper. Of these, only *Rynchops niger* occurs in the Americas. The black skimmer ranges along the Atlantic and Gulf coasts from Massachusetts to Texas and through Central and South America. It is a year-round resident in Texas but is less common in the winter. Skim-

mers occasionally wander inland, especially on the winds of summer storms, but most remain along the coastal beaches and bays.

The skimmer is black above and white below. The huge black-tipped red beak is laterally compressed to cut the water like a knife. Juveniles are mottled brown above instead of black, but their profiles remain unmistakable.

The black skimmer breeds in colonies on beaches and islands, often with terns and gulls. The nest is a simple scrape in the sand or shellbank; the three to five white or buffy eggs are heavily spotted with brown and gray. Perfectly camouflaged, they blend with the sand, seashells and beach debris and can be very difficult to see. They hatch in about three weeks.

The semiprecocial, downy young are brooded and fed by both parents on regurgitated fish and crustaceans dropped on the ground. Eventually they accept whole fish, but the lower mandible does not begin to elongate until they are nearly full size. In defense of their nests, the parents stand their ground or swoop low at an intruder, uttering sharp, barking cries: *kak, kak, kak*. As the chicks begin to wander from the nest, they hide by scratching hollows in the sand and stretching out flat in them, kicking up sand to partially cover themselves. This may also help to keep them cool in the broiling sun.

Development and increased beach traffic pose a major threat to many of the black skimmer's traditional nesting grounds. Even a slight disturbance in the colony reduces the rate of nesting success. Oil and chemical spills kill both adults and young, and summer storms flood many nests. Occasionally, however, an industrial plant or community helps the species by setting aside and protecting parking lots or other open areas that skimmers have begun to colonize.

Black skimmers guard their egg and chick.

SHOREBIRDS

To the beginning birder, the shorebirds can seem an enormously confusing group. The numerous species fall into four major family groups—the plovers, oystercatchers, stilts and avocets, and sandpipers—mostly small- to medium-sized birds that can look remarkably alike. Although a few are strikingly marked and immediately recognizable, most wear subtle shades of brown and gray. This is especially true in the

A large mixed flock of shorebirds huddles on the beach.

winter plumage they adopt during much of their stay in Texas. Indeed, even the most experienced birders find shorebirds challenging, often recording them simply as "sandpiper species" in their field notes.

Identifications frequently hinge on such factors as the length and color of the bill and legs, or on wing and tail markings visible only when the bird is in flight. Occasionally, the best distinction between two species is the difference in their voices. Plumage variations due to sex, age and season add to the confusion. Several books are devoted solely to the finer points of shorebird classification, and the serious bird student will want to acquire them. Shorebirds comprise, in fact, a fascinating group with remarkable achievements and unique adaptations to a specialized way of life. They constantly test one's powers of observation, but that is part of the joy of the sport. There is always something new to be learned.

A few of the shorebird species remain in Texas throughout the year, but most are winter residents or pass through only in migration. Many nest on the Arctic tundra and stage spectacular long-distance migrations to Central and South America, only to return again to the Arctic in the spring. They may cover more than 15,000 miles a year, flying at speeds approaching 50 miles an hour. Banding studies have tracked birds flying nonstop for 2,000 miles in less than two days.

An estimated 20 million shorebirds migrate across the U.S. to the high Arctic every year. Along the way, they assemble in huge numbers at well-known staging areas to rest and feed. Virtually all of the western sandpipers and dunlins, for example, stop in Alaska's Copper River Delta. Nearly 1.5 million other shorebirds reach Delaware Bay in the spring. Their migration is synchronized with the breeding cycle of the horseshoe crabs that abound in the bay. For three or four weeks in the spring the birds gorge themselves on crab eggs before continuing their journey northward.

Texas' Bolivar Flats, across the ship channel from Galveston, has become a world-renowned shorebird area. More than a score of species and thousands of individuals can be seen, particularly during the spring and fall migrations. Many remain through the winter as well, feeding on the prolific marine life. Combined with herons and egrets, pelicans, cormorants, gulls and terns, they provide an awesome spectacle at virtually any time of year.

Other great shorebird areas dot the Texas coastline. Beaches, mud flats and salt marshes all attract specific avian clienteles. Inland flocks use flooded rice fields and wet pastures, freshwater marshes and lakeshores. Even city sewage-treatment ponds draw shorebirds, gulls and waterfowl. In every location, too, one might chance upon a rare and unexpected visitor, for shorebirds, with their long migration routes, are notorious wanderers.

These feathered hordes apportion the food resources according to their individual characteristics, and direct competition occurs less frequently than one might expect. Oystercatchers use their strong beaks to pry open clams and mussels, while turnstones flip over rocks and shells to grab the invertebrates hiding beneath. Avocets swing their scythelike bills back and forth in the water and snatch up morsels from the bottom, and curlews probe with long, decurved beaks for worms and shellfish buried deep within the sand or mud. Tiny sandpipers scamper about to pick at food lying on the surface; larger ones wade farther out and probe more deeply with longer bills. Each has its own niche based on a specialized anatomy and instinctive behavior.

Except for a few species, most shorebirds nest on the ground, relying on camouflage colors and patterns to hide their eggs. The eggs are large for the size of the bird, and the well-developed, precocial hatchlings wear a coat of down. Their eyes are open, and they can scamper about shortly after emerging. Birds that nest in secure locations among the trees or in cavities lay smaller eggs that hatch into naked, blind young. These helpless, altricial babies remain in the nest and develop after hatching. The precocial babies of ground-nesting birds remain longer and develop more fully inside their larger eggs. Shorebirds generally lay four rather pointed eggs that fit together in the nest like quarters of a pie, enabling the incubating bird to cover them with its body.

Shorebirds were once hunted for their plumage, and tens of thousands were shot for food as well. Curlews and plovers graced tables from New York to Galveston, along with more traditional game birds like quail, ducks and grouse. Fortunately, the market-hunting days are gone, but other threats continue to multiply. The birds require not only nesting habitat but feeding and staging areas along their traditional migration routes. If wetlands and estuaries disappear, the plovers and sandpipers will not be far behind.

Sanderlings (opposite) doze under a midday sun. A feeding willet (right) flashes its bright wing pattern.

PLOVERS (Family Charadriidae)

These members of the large shorebird complex are chunky, compact birds with short, thick necks and large eyes. Their movements identify them as readily as their appearance. Plovers run quickly across the ground, stopping to pick at tasty morsels with their short, pigeonlike bills. Then they dart off again—stop and start, stop and start.

The smaller ringed plovers are usually found near water, although the most familiar, the killdeer, occurs in a wide variety of habitats across the continent. The brown backs of these species blend with the sand in an excellent example of protective coloration. North American species lack a hind toe and have at least a small amount of webbing between the other three.

Larger family members include the black-bellied plover and lesser golden-plover, both of which are seasonally common in Texas. They have mottled backs and black underparts in breeding plumage. The mountain plover (*Charadrius montanus*), a bird of the western plains, is less common but occurs in the western and southern portions of the state in migration and during the winter months. A few mountain plovers have also remained within the state to breed.

The Charadriidae includes the lapwings, but none occurs regularly in North America. Older references placed the turnstones here as well; they are now listed with the sandpipers.

Their camouflage patterns hide these killdeer eggs and hatchling (top). This black-bellied plover (left) is just beginning its spring molt.

BLACK-BELLIED PLOVER *Pluvialis squatarola*

This largest of the North American plovers is also one of the most cosmopolitan of about 65 species found throughout the world. In the New World, the black-belly breeds on the Arctic tundra of Alaska and Canada and winters along the U.S. coasts and southward through Central and South America and the West Indies. It also nests in the northern regions of Eurasia, where it is called the "grey plover," and migrates to Africa, southern Asia and Australia.

Resembling a gorgeously detailed drawing in pen and ink, the well-named black-bellied plover is unmistakable in breeding plumage. Its back and wings are spangled black and white; the breast and face are solid black. A broad white stripe runs from the forehead and crown down the neck and along the sides of the breast. That plumage, however, is seen in Texas only in late spring as the birds head northward and in late summer as they return. For most of the year, they dress in more somber shades of gray.

The winter plumage is mottled darker gray above and dingy, pale gray below. The stocky build and pigeonlike bill provide the best clues to its identity. In flight the black-belly shows bold white wing-stripes, a white rump, and a white tail barred with gray. Diagnostic, too, are what ornithologists call "black axillaries." Birders often use the less elegant term "dirty armpits."

Black-bellied plovers migrate through Texas from March through May and from August into November. They might be seen across the state on lakeshores, marshes and wet fields, but they are most abundant on the beaches and mud flats along the coast. Some of the coastal birds remain throughout the winter.

On their breeding grounds, these large plovers fiercely defend the territories around their nests. The four large camouflaged eggs hatch in 26 or 27 days, and the downy chicks are fed primarily on insects. The female leaves her brood after about 12 days, but the male remains until the young can fend for themselves. They fledge at about five or six weeks of age and soon head southward for the winter.

In inland fields, they consume insects, worms and berries. Along the coast, they feed primarily on small clams and snails, marine worms and other invertebrates. There, too, they establish territories and defend them against other feeding birds. Black-bellied plovers are usually seen alone or in small groups. They dash quickly across the beaches and mud flats or stand hunch-shouldered on the sand, huddled against the wind and spray.

LESSER GOLDEN-PLOVER *Pluvialis dominica*

The lesser golden-plover makes one of the most astonishing migrations of any of our North American birds. Nesting on the Arctic tundra of northern Alaska and Canada, it winters on the plains of central South America. Some, in fact, may fly nonstop from James Bay, Canada, to the Argentine pampas, reaching speeds of 70 miles per hour. The bulk of the population apparently flies a Great Circle oceanic route, moving across Canada to the East Coast and then striking out in a wide swing southward across the Atlantic. A smaller number, including more of the immatures, migrate later along a broader inland front, working southward through the prairies. In the spring, however, most golden-plovers head back along the inland route, working up through Texas and across the Great Plains. The total round-trip journey may be as much as 20,000 miles.

For this reason, the lesser golden-plover is an abundant spring migrant through Texas but occurs only rarely

*Lesser golden-plover
in winter plumage.*

in the fall. It is seen most commonly near the coast and with diminishing frequency westward across the state. Open fields are the favored habitats, but flocks are also encountered on mud flats and along the shores, darting back and forth after the insects and other invertebrates that fuel their prodigious flights.

Slightly smaller than the foot-long black-bellied plover, the golden-plover in breeding plumage is black below and spangled with gold above. A white stripe reaches from the forehead over the eyes and down the sides of the breast. Immature and nonbreeding birds are mottled golden brown, darker above than below. In these plumages, the golden-plover is browner than the grayish black-belly and lacks the white rump and tail and the dark "armpits" apparent when in flight. Spring migrants sport an array of intermediate plumages as they traverse Texas.

The lesser golden-plover (hyphenated) was formerly called the American golden plover (unhyphenated). The hyphen, the bane of editors who have to deal with such things, is used in the official nomenclature of the American Ornithologists' Union to indicate that this is one species in a complex of golden-plovers. Another, the greater golden-plover, is a Eurasian resident. And, in fact, there may be a third. Some taxonomists lobby for a division of our present North American species into two. The race *dominica* breeds from Alaska eastward into Canada. Another, *fulva,* breeds from Alaska across into Siberia and winters in Hawaii and the South Pacific. Where the two ranges overlap on Alaska's Bering Coast, the races do not appear to interbreed, one test for the separation into full species. This is of great interest to the scientific community and to birders with wide-ranging lists. However, it does not affect the Texas checklist, since only *dominica* occurs within our borders. Books which presently give *Pluvialis fulva* species status call it the Pacific golden-plover.

Once present in enormous flocks that "darkened the sky," the lesser golden-plover was decimated by the early market hunters. One report cites the shooting of 48,000 on a single day in 1861 near New Orleans. Another notes that plovers were killed by boys in the Midwest and sold on the streets of Chicago for 50 cents per hundred. Fortunately, those days are over, and the golden-plover is coming back. The 11-inch, 6-ounce birds are far more attractive in a Texas field in breeding plumage than naked on a dinner plate, however tasty they might be.

WILSON'S PLOVER *Charadrius wilsonia*

Wilson's plover, at about eight inches in length, is the largest of our small "ringed" plovers. It has also been called the "thick-billed plover," and its relatively long, heavy black bill separates it from the other three species found in Texas. The neck band—black on the males, brown on females and immatures—is also much broader than on the others. The legs are grayish pink. Wilson's is a darker brown than the pale, sandy-colored snowy and piping plovers. The brown semipalmated plover *(Charadrius semipalmatus)* has a short, stubby little bill and yellow or orange legs.

Named for early ornithologist Alexander Wilson, Wilson's plover breeds from the mid-Atlantic states southward along the coasts to South America. It nests all along the Texas Gulf Coast and also inhabits the Pacific side of the continents from California south. U.S. birds migrate in the fall, but some remain in Florida and Texas throughout the winter. A resident of open beaches and tidal flats, it rarely wanders inland. It can be fairly common in our state throughout the year, but like the other small plovers, it seems to be declining.

The female lays her eggs in a simple scrape in the sand or shells or even on a gravel roadway. Sometimes she hides them among beach plants or driftwood, but often they are out in

Male Wilson's plover.

the open, relying on the natural camouflage of the three cream or pale buff eggs marked with brown and black. The female incubates most of the day; the male, at night. The downy, precocial chicks hatch after 23 or 24 days and soon scamper around with their parents, feeding both day and night on crabs, worms and insects. Should her eggs or young be threatened, the female stages a convincing distraction display punctuated by sharp whistled calls of *wheet* or *quip*, lying on her side or dragging a wing as she leads the intruder away.

PIPING PLOVER

Charadrius melodus

In January 1991, a team of biologists and volunteer birders launched an unprecedented ten-day census of the piping plovers along the Texas Coast. By airboat and all-terrain vehicles and on foot, the crew combed the beaches and sandy flats to identify and count the tiny seven-inch birds. The final tally was 1,904 piping plovers, half of the remaining world total and virtually the entire breeding population of the Great Plains.

"The survey once again emphasizes the importance of the Texas Coast to so many coastal avian species," notes Houstonian Ted Eubanks, coordinator of the census and a member of the federal recovery team for the piping plover, in the newsletter of the Texas Ornithological Society. "The reddish egret, whooping crane, piping plover and the eastern subspecies of the snowy plover are examples of coastal species whose very existence in the United States may depend upon Texas coastal marshes, beaches and tidal flats."

The piping plover breeds in disjunct ranges on the Great Plains of the U.S. and southern Canada and on the upper Atlantic Coast. Another group in the Great Lakes region is nearly gone. In winter, the plovers move southward to the lower Atlantic

and Gulf states. Because the breeding season is very short, piping plovers begin arriving on the wintering grounds in late July and remain until April. Thus Texas is home to half of all these severely endangered birds for nine months of the year.

First depleted by hunters in the late 1800s, the plovers now suffer from conversion of their inland breeding areas to agriculture and from development and increasing recreational uses of the beaches. The biggest threats on the Texas coast, according to Eubanks, are probably the ever-present hazard of oil spills and the four-wheel-drive vehicles that tear up the food-bearing substrate of its preferred beaches and sand flats.

Pale, sandy tan on the back and head, and countershaded white below, the piping plover matches the color of the dry beach sand that it inhabits. Darting along, start and stop, dashing after an insect or little crab and then freezing motionless against a dune, it seems perfectly camouflaged. In breeding plumage, a narrow dark

band crosses the breast, although it is sometimes incomplete, especially on the females. The breast band is lacking in winter plumage. Orange-yellow legs distinguish the piping plover from the slightly smaller snowy plover (*Charadrius alexandrinus*), which always has dark legs.

The latter, too, was counted in the 1991 piping plover census. The final count of snowy plovers barely exceeded 1,400 individuals, "a paltry sum if one considers that the coast of Texas (and the northern Gulf Coast of Mexico) is the center of the eastern snowy plover's wintering range," says Eubanks. "Circumstantial evidence indicates that the snowy plover may be in greater danger of extinction in the United States than the piping plover."

Half the world's piping plovers spend the winter on Texas beaches.

KILLDEER   *Charadrius vociferus*

The frantic birds circle low overhead, uttering loud, piercing calls of *kill-dee, kill-dee* and *dee-dee-dee*. One of the pair lands suddenly and flops to the ground, obviously with a serious injury. Raising one wing, it beats the other in the dirt, flashing white wing-stripes and a bright orange rump. It continues to scramble pitifully for several yards and then, miraculously, takes flight again. The broken wing has been an act. Somewhere behind the startled and confused intruder is a nest with four buffy eggs spotted and mottled with dark brown, wonderfully camouflaged and almost invisible on the graveled ground. The killdeer is not the only bird to employ a distraction display in defense of its nest, but it deserves the award for acting ability.

The killdeer is undoubtedly one of the best known of North American and Texas birds. It ranges across Canada and the U.S., from Atlantic to Pacific, and through Mexico and the West Indies. In winter, it withdraws from the northern portions of that range and ventures as far as South America. The killdeer occurs across the entire state of Texas throughout the year and breeds from sea level at the Gulf to an elevation of 6,000 feet in the West.

Farm fields, pastures, mud flats, airports, lawns and even urban parking lots provide space for nesting killdeers. The eggs are laid in a shallow scrape in the ground, sometimes lined with a few blades of grass, pebbles, shells or pieces of cow chip. Both parents incubate, cooling the eggs in hot weather by "belly-soaking" and dripping water from their moistened underparts. The eggs are very large for the size of the bird, as is the case with most shorebirds, and hatch in 24 to 28 days into well-developed, precocial chicks. After drying out, the fluffy puffballs stand on toothpick legs and absurdly large feet and scamper after their parents. They quickly learn to pick at the insects that make up the bulk of a killdeer's diet. Unfortunately, people often pick up killdeer babies, assuming them to be abandoned. They should be left strictly alone, for the parents are usually waiting nearby.

About 11 inches long, the killdeer differs from the smaller ringed plovers in the same genus by having two black breast bands instead of one. The downy chicks, however, have but one in juvenile plumage. Brown above and white below, adults are easily recognized by the double breast-band, harlequin face pattern and orange rump. The loud call, too, is unmistakable, giving the bird its common name as well as the scientific one, *vociferus*.

The killdeer sports two black breast bands; the smaller plovers have but one.

OYSTERCATCHERS (Family Haematopodidae)

Once seen, the large, flashy oystercatchers are not easily forgotten. They have bright red, laterally flattened bills used for prying open the shells of oysters, clams and mussels and for probing in the sand for crabs and marine worms. Some authors list six species throughout the world; others name as many as 10 or 11. They disagree on whether some of those should be accorded full species status or are merely geographical races of a more wide-ranging species. All are black and white or entirely slate black, with red bills and red eye-rings. Two, the black-and-white American oystercatcher and the all-dark black oystercatcher, occur in the United States. The former ranges along the Atlantic and Gulf coasts; the latter inhabits the Pacific Coast.

The unique bill of the oystercatchers is long, knifelike and chisel-tipped. It has been described as "nature's original oyster knife." Careful observations of the Eurasian oystercatcher (*Haematopus ostralegus*), a bird much like our own species, revealed that it depends on one of two learned feeding techniques. It is either a stabber or a hammerer.

Stabbers approach open mollusks and plunge their bills between the two halves of the shell before they can close. They snip the strong adductor muscles and then pick out and eat the meat. Hammerers, however, pull loose the mollusk and shatter one valve with a series of powerful blows. The bill is then inserted through the broken shell to cut the adductors and pry the two halves apart. Young oystercatchers apparently learn one of the two techniques by watching their parents, who assist them as they learn to feed.

AMERICAN OYSTERCATCHER *Haematopus palliatus*

This is one of the most striking of all our shorebirds and, at 18 to 20 inches in length, one of our largest. It paces the beaches and exposed shell reefs alone or in small groups, prying open mollusks with its flattened bill or picking out crabs and marine worms. The adult has a black head and neck, a dark brown back, and white underparts. The bill is bright red-orange; the legs, pink. Immatures have dark-tipped bills for the first year of their lives. In flight, the oystercatcher flashes large white patches in the wings and tail. It can be a noisy bird, uttering loud *pic, pic, pic* alarm notes and piercing cries of *wheep-wheep-wheep.*

The American oystercatcher ranges along the entire Texas shoreline and virtually never strays inland from tidal waters. It is most common on the central coast. A scrape on a sandy beach or shell bank serves as a nest, and the olive-buff eggs marked with brown are laid directly on the ground. The normal clutch consists of three eggs; however, if something happens to them and the pair renests, as many birds do, the female normally lays only two more. The parents share the incubation chores and the care and feeding of the young. Juveniles take a long time in learning to pry open the bivalves that make up a substantial portion of their diet. The extended period of intensive parental care may be one reason for the small clutch, since shorebirds typically lay four eggs.

American oystercatchers appear to be expanding their range northward along the Atlantic Coast. They occur from New Jersey all the way down the eastern coasts of the Americas to Argentina, as well as from Baja California south to Chile on the Pacific side. On the U.S. Pacific Coast, they are replaced by black oystercatchers

(*Haematopus bachmani*). Where the two overlap on the Baja peninsula, hybrids are sometimes found. Biologists disagree on whether the two are valid species, merely subspecies, or members of what they call a "superspecies." The last term implies two species of common descent but with different geographical ranges. It is not clear whether they have evolved enough to present a barrier to interbreeding.

American oystercatchers use their colorful, laterally flattened bills to pry open shellfish.

STILTS AND AVOCETS (Family Recurvirostridae)

If it is possible to appear both graceful and awkward at the same time, the stilts and avocets accomplish just such a feat. They are slim, elegant birds with long, slender bills. Their legs seem absurdly long, but they manage to use them with amazing aplomb.

The nearly cosmopolitan family contains seven or eight species: four avocets and three or four stilts, depending on the authority followed. Two, the black-necked stilt and the American avocet, occur in North America and in Texas.

The scientific family name comes from the Latin *recurvus*, meaning "bent back," and *rostrum*, or "bill." It describes the long, upswept bill of the avocets and provides the name of that genus as well.

Black-necked stilt.

BLACK-NECKED STILT *Himantopus mexicanus*

The coastal marsh swelters under the early-summer sun, and the silence is broken only by the persistent hum of mosquitoes. Then, at some slight disturbance, a half-dozen lanky black-and-white birds rise into the air and circle low over the grass, trailing their pinkish red legs behind them. Their loud *kek, kek, kek* calls become sharper and more frenzied, *kip, kip, kip, kip,* until they suddenly cease their display and drop back to the ground. The intruder, real or imagined, is gone. The marsh again settles into torpor.

One of the elegant birds strides on its absurd stiltlike legs to a hummock of grass and stares down at the four large buffy eggs heavily spotted with brown and black. She bends to turn them gently with her needle bill and then sits over them to incubate. Her improbable legs seem to fold forever as she settles down on the nest and gazes alertly all around.

Within a few minutes, her mate joins her. The change-over requires careful planning and dexterity. Two pairs of such legs can become almost inextricably tangled. The plumage of the two birds is much the same, except for a more brownish hue to the female's back and wings. The male now settles in to incubate, the female feeding casually nearby. When she returns, her underparts are dripping wet, and her next stint will serve to cool the eggs. This "belly-soaking" may be repeated a hundred times a day as the adults protect their clutch and themselves from the Texas heat.

When the precocial babies hatch, they will follow their parents through the marsh for a month before they can fly. They will hide from danger as the adults stage their aerial distraction displays, and occasionally the young will swim to safety by using their downy wings like oars.

The black-necked stilt is unmistakable. No other bird is so cleanly black above and white below, with a long, slender black bill and amazing pink or red legs. It breeds along the Texas coast and inland locally in the southern and western portions of the state. Wintering birds are relatively common in the Rio Grande Valley but are less frequently seen along the central and upper coast. Migrants range across the Panhandle as well. Grassy marshes, mud flats, rice fields, and shallow lakes and ponds all provide appropriate habitat.

Stilts nest across the western states and along the lower Atlantic and Gulf coasts, then southward as far as South America. Most of the U.S. population migrates toward the tropics in the fall. Southern South America and Hawaii are home to two other stilts which the AOU checklist considers subspecies of the black-necked stilt. Other taxonomists go so far as to include the American form with the Old World black-winged and pied stilts. In the extreme, all of the world's stilts could be considered members of a single "superspecies." Except for the scientific names, these taxonomic differences have no effect on the Texas list. Only a single form occurs within our borders.

AMERICAN AVOCET *Recurvirostra americana*

One of the most beautiful and fascinating sights in the avian world is a flock of feeding avocets. Hundreds, even thousands, gather en masse on Texas' Bolivar Flats in the wintertime, foraging for small crustaceans, worms and other aquatic invertebrates. Their wings are striped black and white and, as spring approaches, their heads and necks take on a rusty wash. Long blue-gray legs enable them to feed in deeper water than most other shorebirds, tapping a resource all their own. As if in a chorus line, they stride together through the water, heads down, swinging their upturned bills from side to side. The scythelike motion stirs up the muddy bottom, and their sensitive bills grasp the tasty morsels thus exposed.

Avocets nest mainly across southwestern Canada and the western states. They are rare east of the Mississippi. In winter they retreat to our southern coasts and Mexico. Migrants can be seen from March through May and from July into October throughout most of Texas, and flocks remain to winter in the marshes and on the flats and beaches along the Gulf. Avocets breed in the Texas Panhandle and high plains and, to a much lesser extent, along the lower coast.

The nest is a shallow depression on a dry mud flat or along the bank of a playa lake or prairie pond. The four olive-buff eggs are spotted with brown and hatch in 22 to 29 days. Newly hatched chicks follow their parents shortly after emerging.

Although the American avocet loses the rusty wash on its head after the breeding season, it is still easily recognized. No other large, lanky shorebird has a similar black-and-white pattern, stiltlike legs, and thin, upswept bill. The bill of the female is curved more than that of the male, the only difference in their outward appearance.

American avocets.

SANDPIPERS (Family Scolopacidae)

They rise from the sandy beach in a swirling cloud and wheel as one across the waves. They fly with incredible precision, close together and seemingly responding to each other's every move. The compact flock contains a variety of species, for some flash white wing-stripes, and several types of tail patterns can be seen. Then they drop back to the sand and begin to forage up and down the beach. They are of different sizes, but most are garbed in gray or brown. Individual identifications are not always an easy matter.

The sandpipers comprise a large and complex family, ranging from the six-inch least sandpiper to the two-foot long-billed curlew. Some of them are distinctively marked, but many fit the generic family mold. The smaller ones are collectively called "peeps," a useful term when all else fails.

A gregarious lot, most sandpipers associate in large groups in migration and on the marshes and seashores of the wintering ground, taking advantage of rich feeding areas and apportioning the provisions according to their physical characteristics and individual feeding habits. They frequently nest far inland, however, many of them on the high Arctic tundra. The young are on their own within a month and may not leave the nesting grounds until after the adults are gone. They migrate instinctively, without leadership, winging their way southward for thousands of miles to a predestined location where the others wait.

Most sandpipers have at least three distinct plumages. Breeding and nonbreeding adults can differ greatly, and juveniles frequently resemble neither. Slimmer than the chunky plovers, with longer necks and legs and longer, more slender bills, sandpipers also have more sensitive bills than plovers. The soft skin allows tactile feeding as the birds probe deep into the sand or mud.

Dowitchers (above) probe the bottom for tasty morsels. A greater yellowlegs (right) captures a minnow.

GREATER YELLOWLEGS   *Tringa melanoleuca*
LESSER YELLOWLEGS   *Tringa flavipes*

Both yellowlegs species nest in Alaska and Canada and spend the winter as far away as southern South America. They can be seen throughout Texas during migration and commonly remain through the winter in the marshes and on the mud flats along the coast. They also winter locally on lakeshores and ponds across the southern half of the state.

The scientific names collectively define both of these lanky, long-legged sandpipers. The genus name *Tringa* comes from the Greek *tryngas,* as used by Aristotle for a "waterbird with a white rump," according to Edward Gruson's *Words for Birds. Melanoleuca* is from the Greek *melanos,* for "black," and *leukos,* "white," denoting the checkered appearance of the upperparts, particularly in breeding plumage. The lesser yellowlegs' *flavipes* derives from the Latin: *flavus,* "yellow," and

pes, or "foot." Both species are streaked on the breast and sides in breeding plumage but appear more uniformly gray in winter.

The long, bright yellow legs serve to distinguish them from most other shorebirds, as do the uniformly dark wings in flight and the whitish rump and tail. As might be expected, the greater yellowlegs, at 14 inches long, is larger than the 10- or 11-inch lesser. That comparison can easily be made if the two are standing side by side, but it is much more difficult on a single bird. Vocalizations sometimes provide a key, for the greater gives a loud series of three or more notes, *tew-tew-tew,* as compared with the lesser's slightly higher-pitched single *tew.*

The easiest distinction, however, is in the relative lengths of the bills. The greater yellowlegs' bill is longer than the head and sometimes curves

slightly upward. That of the lesser yellowlegs is shorter and straight. To judge, imagine folding back the bill at its base so that it projects backward through the eye. If the tip would just reach the back of the head, the bird is a lesser; if the bill would project well beyond, it is a greater.

WILLET
Catoptrophorus semipalmatus

"The Willet has the distinction of being the only species among Texas' twenty-four regular sandpipers which breeds enthusiastically within the Lone Star State," writes Harry Oberholser in his monumental two-volume *The Bird Life of Texas*. When other shorebirds head north in spring, the large, noisy willet settles down to raise its brood in the salt marshes or among the dune grasses behind the beach. Its loud *pill-will-willet, pill-will-willet* and rapid *kip-kip-kip* alarm calls can be heard all along the Gulf Coast.

Finding a nest, however, is quite another story. The parents steal from the site if danger threatens and fly low around the intruder, venting their anger loudly. Only when the threat is over and all is quiet do they return, landing well away from the nest and walking cautiously to it through the grass. The four large olive-colored eggs are camouflaged with brown markings, and the streaked and barred gray-brown adults easily conceal themselves amidst the vegetation while they incubate. Willets show a strong fidelity to their mates and to their nesting sites and feeding territories from year to year.

The willet migrates through most sections of Texas from March to May and July to November. Substantial numbers winter along the coast, and many stay to "breed enthusiastically," as Oberholser states. The entire breeding range extends from Canada to the southern Atlantic and Gulf states, with the greatest numbers in the western U.S. and along the Gulf Coast. Northern populations winter southward as far as South America.

In winter plumage, the plump 15-inch willet is uniformly gray above and whitish below, with blue-gray legs and a heavy gray bill. Although common and widespread, it is inconspicuous until it flies; then it flashes a bright wing pattern of black and white. The genus name stems from the Greek *katoptrophorus,* or "mirror-bearing," referring to the startling white patches on the blackish wings. *Semipalmatus* refers to the willet's "half-webbed" feet.

SPOTTED SANDPIPER

Actitis macularia

The spotted sandpiper usually forgoes the sociability of shorebird flocks to forage alone on the beaches, riverbanks and lakeshores within its range. In breeding plumage, its white breast bears large, round brown spots, the maculations from which it gets its scientific name. The spots disappear in winter plumage, but a vertical white bar in front of the wing is a good field mark. Even more diagnostic are the bird's actions. The spotted sandpiper flies with shallow strokes, its wings stiff and bowed, flicking rapidly in contrast to the deeper wingbeats of other shorebirds. On landing, it teeters up and down, as if trying not to overbalance, and it continues this characteristic teetering as it walks slowly along the bank.

The most widespread of all the North American sandpipers, the spotted breeds across much of the continent, from Alaska and northern Canada through the central states. In the winter, this seven-inch bird ranges down into South America. It migrates through most of Texas and stays to winter in the southern half and along the coast. There are even a few scattered breeding records, particularly in the Panhandle. Because it lives near water from sea level to the alpine

The greater yellowlegs (top, opposite) has a proportionately longer bill than the lesser yellowlegs. Willet (above) in winter plumage. Spotted sandpiper (left) in breeding plumage.

zones, its diet is of necessity highly varied. It is adept at catching flying insects, but it also picks tidbits from the surface and probes the mud. Worms, small fish, crustaceans, mollusks and even carrion go to fuel its flickering wings.

Although the spotted sandpiper is a familiar bird across the continent, it was not until the 1970s that ornithologists discovered just how unusual its breeding habits really are. The polyandrous females arrive first on the breeding grounds and court the males as they appear. Once a female has mated and laid her full clutch of four eggs, she leaves to court again. The male incubates the eggs and raises the downy chicks virtually alone. Mating with another newly arrived male, the female repeats the process. She may lay as many as five clutches during a single season, each tended by one of her mates. This unusual avian lifestyle is apparently a way to maximize the reproductive potential of each female, for she would not have time to raise that many consecutive broods herself. The average is about eight eggs for each female in a summer, but as might be expected, the older, more experienced females are most successful in courting and winning several mates.

Upland sandpiper.

UPLAND SANDPIPER
Bartramia longicauda

The upland sandpiper must have a severe identity crisis. For many years it was called the upland plover, and it appears under that name in older field guides. It is also a shorebird that seldom goes near the water, preferring open upland prairies and fields where it feeds on insects, grain and weed seeds. It undoubtedly performs a valuable agricultural pest-control service as it consumes quantities of grasshoppers, armyworms, cutworms and weevils.

The plumage is buffy brown, mottled and streaked in camouflage pattern. The upland sandpiper lacks distinctive plumage field marks, but its unique shape renders it unmistakable. The absurdly small head sits atop a long neck, giving rise to the nickname "pinhead" among many birders. The very large, prominent eyes, relatively long tail, long wings, and yellow legs complete the strangely shaped "shorebird," which is most often seen walking across the fields or perched atop a roadside fence post or pole. It flies "on the tips of its wings," with shallow, quivering wingbeats similar to those of a spotted sandpiper, and it often holds its wings raised after landing on a post.

Upland sandpipers nest from Alaska and western Canada through the northern states, but the bastion of their breeding range is the Great Plains. Populations are declining in the East, and the Audubon Society has included the species on its Blue List as warranting special concern. Upland sandpipers migrate throughout most of Texas on their prodigious journeys to and from the pampas of South America, but rarely stray west of the Pecos River. Birds are seen occasionally in summer in the Panhandle and North Texas, but the degree to which they nest within our borders is not clear. The breeding-bird atlas of Texas, now in preparation, should help clear up such uncertainties.

When the once-abundant supply of passenger pigeons gave out, market hunters of the 1880s turned to the upland sandpiper as a source of revenue. It, too, was on the verge of extinction until saved by modern migratory-bird laws. The loss of old fields to development in the East, however, has proved an even more difficult threat to counteract.

The upland sandpiper has also been known as the Bartramian, or Bartram's, sandpiper. It was named for William Bartram, born in Philadelphia in 1739. The son of John Bartram, one of the first great botanists to work in America, he tried a number of business endeavors without success. Eventually, he traveled in the southeastern states to study and draw the birds and plants, at last finding his true calling. The genus *Bartramia,* of which the upland sandpiper is the lone member, still bears his name. The species name, *longicauda,* refers to the tail, which is unusually long for a sandpiper.

Long-billed curlew.

LONG-BILLED CURLEW

Numenius americanus

Our largest shorebird, the long-billed curlew seems equally at home along the beaches and bay fronts or on the open prairies. Its amazing down-curved bill can measure more than eight inches long, with those of the females averaging longer than the males. Juveniles, of course, have shorter bills. With these prodigious tweezers, the curlews deftly catch insects or probe for worms, burrowing crustaceans and mollusks well beyond the depth of other sandpipers.

Rich cinnamon-brown above and buffy below, the "sickle-bill" has distinctive cinnamon wing linings easily seen in flight. The call is a loud, ascending *cur-lee, cur-lee,* while the even more melodious "song" is a drawn-out *curleeeeuuu.*

Long-billed curlews breed in southwestern Canada and the western states and winter from the southern U.S. to Guatemala. They migrate virtually throughout Texas, where many remain through the winter. A small population breeds in the northwestern Panhandle, and scattered nesting records exist for the lower Texas coast.

The nest is hidden in the grass and holds four eggs ranging in color from olive-green to buffy white marked with brown. Both parents incubate and care for the downy, precocial chicks that hatch in about four weeks. It is another five weeks or more before they fly, though few chicks survive that long. Hawks, ravens, badgers, coyotes, weasels and snakes all relish curlew eggs or young. In one study on the rangeland of Idaho, an average of only one fledgling survived from every two nests.

The long-billed curlew once migrated in large flocks through the Atlantic states, where market hunters shot them over decoys in enormous numbers. The two-foot, one-and-one-half-pound birds made tasty fare for the tables of eastern restaurants. The eastern population never recovered. More serious, however, may be the continued loss of breeding habitat across the American West.

The whimbrel *(Numenius phaeopus),* once called the Hudsonian curlew, also migrates through Texas in the spring and, less commonly, in the fall. It is most often seen along the coast. Smaller and with a shorter bill than the long-billed curlew, it has dark brown stripes on the head.

Birders still search for the little Eskimo curlew *(N. borealis)* as well, primarily on the coastal prairies near Galveston and Houston. Nesting on the Arctic tundra, it winters in South America. The species is almost extinct, but most sightings in this century were along the Texas coast in spring. At this writing, recent searches have proved futile.

Marbled godwit.

MARBLED GODWIT *Limosa fedoa*

Only slightly smaller than the long-billed curlew, the marbled godwit shares the curlew's tawny brown plumage mottled and barred with black. The curlew's bill bends sharply down, however, while the godwit's bill curves gently upward. Both prowl the coastal beaches and tidal flats, probing the shallow waters for the marine worms, crustaceans and mollusks that make up a major portion of their winter diets.

Marbled godwits breed on the northern Great Plains and in Canada's prairie provinces, making their nests in grassy meadows near lakes and ponds. They leave those frozen regions in the fall and spend the winter along the U.S. coasts and southward as far as South America. Most common on the Pacific and Gulf coasts, they have never recovered from market hunting and are rare along the eastern seaboard. Marbled godwits migrate and winter along the Texas coast, appearing only rarely farther inland.

The source of the name godwit is not clear. According to Gruson and to Choate, the word may owe its origins to the Old English phrase *god wiht,* or "good creature," referring to the bird's popularity on the menus of the 15th and 16th centuries. Elliot Coues doubted this interpretation, however, and Olin Sewall Pettingill wrote, "Listen! This bird tells you who he is. *God-wit! god-wit!* he calls, accenting the last syllable."

The Hudsonian godwit (*Limosa haemastica*) also migrates northward along the Texas coast in spring. Slightly smaller than the marbled godwit but with the same upturned bill, it is distinguished by its black tail and white rump. It has a chestnut breast in breeding plumage but is a drab gray in winter. The Hudsonian godwit flies a circular migration route much like that of the lesser golden-plover. Leaving its Arctic breeding grounds in autumn, it migrates off the Atlantic Coast to South America. Returning in late spring through the midsection of the country, it appears in Texas in late April and early May.

RUDDY TURNSTONE
Arenaria interpres

The ruddy turnstone ranks among the most beautiful of birds in its harlequin breeding plumage. The white head bears a bold black pattern, and the white underparts are broken by a wide black bib. The back is rich, ruddy chestnut, again patterned with black; the short legs, a shocking, brilliant orange. In flight, the turnstone flashes a complex wing and tail pattern of all those colors, leading to such old regional names as "calico back" and "checkered snipe." Immatures and nonbreeding birds are duller gray-brown, but they retain the orange leg color and enough of the black bib and flight pattern to be easily recognizable.

Ruddy turnstones are common migrants along the Texas coast, and many remain through the winter. They appear inland much less frequently. They breed in the Arctic regions around the world and spend the winter on almost every ice-free coastline. North American birds nest on the tundra of northern Alaska and Canada and migrate along both the Atlantic and Pacific coasts as far south as Tierra del Fuego. The other turnstone species, the black turnstone (*Arenaria melanocephala*), nests in Alaska and spends the winter on the Pacific Coast.

The chunky little turnstones were formerly placed in the family of the plovers, but recent books include them with the sandpipers. With their uniquely chisel-shaped and slightly upturned beaks, they flip over pebbles and shells to search for food underneath. So common and striking is the habit that the turnstone's name in many different languages translates exactly the same, "turn stone."

Flipping stones is not their only feeding method, however. There is not much that ruddy turnstones will not eat. They catch insects and probe for worms. On their northern breeding grounds, they climb into the stunted shrubs to eat the berries; along the East Coast, they dig in the sand for the eggs of horseshoe crabs. The sharp beaks work equally well for hammering open limpets and barnacles on the rocks or for breaking apart a tough sea urchin. On our present-day beaches they seem to favor sandwich remnants, French fries and chicken bones.

While they may not be the bird world's most sophisticated gourmets, ruddy turnstones certainly rank among the most charming of our Texas shorebirds. They are well worth watching as they scamper along our beaches and tidal flats or prowl the stone jetties and fishing piers, particularly in the spring as they molt to breeding plumage.

Ruddy turnstone (right). Juvenile red knot (below).

RED KNOT

Calidris canutus

This chunky, rather short-legged sandpiper is unmistakable in breeding plumage. Chestnut and black feathers checker its back; its face and breast gleam rusty red, giving rise to the old hunter's name of "robin snipe." Most of the birds seen along the Texas beaches, however, do not wear that colorful plumage. Juveniles and winter birds appear pale gray above and white below, and must be identified almost by default. Larger and stockier than the little "peeps," red knots are smaller than the dowitchers and have shorter bills. In flight, they flash whitish rumps finely barred with gray.

North American populations of this worldwide shorebird breed in the northern Canadian Arctic. The first authentic nest with eggs, in fact, was found on northern Ellesmere Island in June 1909 by Robert E. Peary as he returned from the initial journey to the North Pole. Those same birds, a few weeks later, might well have begun a 19,000-mile round-trip migration to spend the winter in the relatively hospitable climate of Tierra del Fuego at the southernmost tip of South America.

The hardy little red knot, formerly

called simply the "knot," was once the most abundant shorebird in all of North America. Enormous numbers migrated along the Atlantic Coast, and the plump little birds were slaughtered by gunners around the turn of the century. The population has never recovered, but tens of thousands of "beach robins" still return northward along the eastern seaboard in the spring, timing their arrival on Delaware Bay to feed on the freshly laid eggs of horseshoe crabs. During that time, 80 percent of North America's red knots assemble for the feast.

Much less common along the Texas coast, knots can nevertheless be seen in spring and fall. Some remain through the winter as well, striding along the sandy beaches and tidal flats or standing huddled against the wind and spray, somewhat dumpy and nondescript in their pale gray garb.

SANDERLING *Calidris alba*

It is a common scene on almost any sandy Texas beach. Small gray shorebirds scamper along behind a retreating wave, picking quickly at tiny marine worms, crustaceans and mollusks exposed in its wash. Then, as another wave comes rushing in, they dash back up the beach ahead of it, as if afraid of wetting their feet. Back and forth, back and forth, like tiny wind-up toys, seeming never to tire of the chase. Appetites sated, they cluster together in a closely packed flock, some on one leg with heads tucked beneath their wings.

These eight-inch shorebirds with black bills and legs are sanderlings; light gray above and white below, they are the palest of all our winter sandpipers. If flushed from the beach, they wheel as one, flashing prominent white stripes along their wings.

Sanderlings breed on Arctic islands and barren coasts around the Northern Hemisphere and migrate far to the south. There is scarcely a beach in the world unvisited by the plump, active little birds. Their sharp *kip* or *quit* calls are as widely heard as the sounds of the surf.

Sanderlings migrate throughout most of Texas but occur only rarely in the Panhandle and the far western counties. They are particularly abundant on the coast and remain there through the winter. *A Birder's Checklist of the Upper Texas Coast* describes them as "abundant" from mid-August into May, and they are listed as "common" even through the summer. Most of those that linger are probably nonbreeding birds, although the ones that depart latest in the spring nearly meet the first ones to return.

They begin to take on breeding plumage before they head north, their heads, backs and breasts turning a lovely rusty gold. Arriving on the tundra of northern Canada, they lay their eggs in nests hidden among the grasses and moss. Recent studies show that sanderlings employ a number of reproductive strategies, depending on the situation and the abundance of potential mates. Food supply and available nest sites may also play a role. Most mated pairs are monogamous, but a few females practice polyandry, mating with more than one male and laying separate clutches of eggs for each. Both male and female may also incubate separate clutches and care for the resulting young. The breeding season is only eight or ten weeks long, but that is quite enough. The downy chicks grow rapidly and are capable of flight in only 17 days.

As the early autumn winds begin to rake the tundra, the sanderlings and their broods head south again, intent on specific wintering grounds to which they show strong fidelity from year to year. There they set up feeding territories and defend them against intruders. Many return to patrol Texas beaches, delighting us all with their endless, charming antics.

A sanderling feeds on a ripening fish.

WESTERN SANDPIPER
Calidris mauri

The appropriately named western sandpiper breeds in the tundra on the northwestern coast of Alaska. After the short nesting season, during which it makes maximum use of the long days and bountiful food supply, it heads southeastward to the southern U.S. coasts, sometimes continuing as far as South America. It migrates across most of Texas and remains through the winter along the Gulf, where it is abundant from late July or early August until the following May. Patrolling the beaches, mud flats and marshy ponds, it replaces its summer insect diet with small marine invertebrates. A few nonbreeding birds even remain throughout the summer months rather than making the long return flight to the Arctic.

At six and one-half inches in length, the western sandpiper is slightly larger than the very similar

semipalmated and least sandpipers. The least, however, has yellowish legs, while the legs of the western and semipalmated are black. The latter two are almost identical in winter plumage. Both pass through Texas in migration, and the older field guides use the bill length as the distinctive feature for identification. That of the western is somewhat longer and droops slightly at the tip. Looking back through Christmas Bird Count records for the Texas coast from a few years ago, one finds that large numbers of both western and semipalmated sandpipers were reported.

More recent studies have shown that the bill sizes overlap, with females of both species having longer bills than males. A re-examination of winter semipalmated specimens from the U.S. showed they had been misidentified. Most Christmas counts now report only western sandpipers rather than both species. It takes a confident birder indeed to claim a semipalmated sandpiper (*Calidris pusilla*) in Texas in midwinter.

In breeding plumage, the western is washed with rusty red on the back and head and is easily distinguished. During the peak migration times—from late July into September and in April and May—when both are abundant along the Texas coast, the longer, slightly drooping bill of the western sandpiper serves as the best characteristic for juveniles and nonbreeding birds. Remember, however, that it is not infallible. "Peep" is a handy term to use, not only for the western, semipalmated and least, but for several other small sandpipers that all look very much alike.

The western sandpiper (*C. mauri*) takes its name from Italian botanist Ernesto Mauri, according to Edward Gruson in *Words for Birds*. Director of the Botanical Gardens in Rome, Mauri was a close friend of Charles Lucien Bonaparte (Bonaparte's gull) and collaborated with him on publications about Italian fauna. Upon Mauri's death, Bonaparte named both a fish and a sandpiper after him. The latter was first described in a publication with the improbable title *Comparative List of Birds of Rome and Philadelphia*.

Western sandpipers have black legs and longer bills than most small sandpipers.

The yellowish legs of the least sandpiper (top) are often camouflaged with mud. The dunlin's bill (above) is long and drooping.

DUNLIN
Calidris alpina

Dunlins fly unusually short migration routes compared with other Arctic-nesting sandpipers. Many species that nest in far northern Canada and Alaska spend the winter in South America, but dunlins remain along the U.S. and upper Mexican coasts. They are circumpolar in their distribution, with other populations in Europe and Asia. Dunlins arrive on the Texas coast in October, much later than most other shorebirds, and leave again in early May. They are seen occasionally inland during migration but are much more abundant in marshes and tidal flats along the Gulf.

Larger than the western sandpiper and other common "peeps," the dunlin is a chunky, short-necked sandpiper that often assumes a "hunch-backed" posture as it feeds. The sturdy bill is longer than those of its smaller relatives and droops downward at the tip. It is much shorter, however, than the bills of the larger dowitchers, with which dunlins sometimes associate.

Dunlin was originally "dunling," meaning a little dun-colored bird, which describes perfectly the winter plumage most often seen along our shores. Dull gray-brown above and white below, it has a grayish wash across the breast. As it takes on breeding plumage in the spring, the dunlin acquires a distinctive black belly-patch and a reddish back, the reason it was sometimes called the "red-backed sandpiper."

LEAST SANDPIPER
Calidris minutilla

Minutilla, Latin for "very small," describes the least sandpiper perfectly. At six inches in length, it is the smallest of the several sandpiper species collectively called "peeps." The size difference between the least and the western and semipalmated sandpipers, however, is difficult to judge. A better distinction is in the color of the legs. Least sandpipers have yellowish or yellow-green legs; western and semipalmated have black. The least also has a short, thin bill that droops very slightly at the tip, a darker brown back than the others, and a band of brownish streaks across the white breast in winter plumage.

After breeding in Alaska and northern Canada, the least sandpiper spends the winter from the southern states to South America. It migrates throughout Texas in both spring and fall. Winter residents are most abundant along the coast, but they also occur inland across the state. Although the shorebirds often mix in enormous flocks, the least sandpiper is more likely to be seen on bayside mud flats, marshes and muddy ponds than on surfside beaches. It has been called the "mud peep," while the larger semipalmated sandpiper (*Calidris pusilla*) is the "sand peep."

Flushing in compact flocks from tidal flats or freshwater ponds, least sandpipers fly with rapid wingbeats, zigzagging erratically but in perfect control. Their alarm cries, *kree-eet, kree, kree,* are sharp and shrill. Just as quickly, they alight again and dash off together along the bank, probing incessantly with their slender bills.

SHORT-BILLED DOWITCHER *Limnodromus griseus*
LONG-BILLED DOWITCHER *Limnodromus scolopaceus*

The foot-long, chunky shorebirds move through the shallow water in a compact group, their long bills stabbing repeatedly downward into the mud. Like toy sewing machines, they stitch their way across the flats. The birds are obviously dowitchers, because no other members of the tribe have such enormously long bills for their size. Alas, further identification is not quite so simple, for the question is, "How long is long?"

The AOU checklist first split the short-billed and long-billed dowitchers into two separate species in 1957. Actually, the bill lengths overlap, and such measurements are of questionable value except in the extremes. Ornithologists have written treatises on the finer points of dowitcher identification, but a number of subspecies and plumages make those treatments even more complex. They are too lengthy and detailed to quote here. A few simple tips, however, might help in many cases.

Short-billed dowitchers breed across Canada and southern Alaska and migrate as far as South America. They funnel down along the Texas coast, and many remain here through the winter, preferring to feed in the saltwater marshes and tidal flats rather than in fresh water.

Long-billed dowitchers breed in far northwestern Canada and Alaska and in Siberia. They winter southward only as far as Mexico and Guatemala. Long-bills migrate across most of Texas but winter mainly in the coastal regions. In spite of this proximity to saltwater environments, they prefer freshwater ponds, marshes and flooded rice fields to saline bays and beaches and occur more frequently inland from the Gulf shores.

Birders normally identify dowitchers by their diagnostic calls. The call of the short-billed is a mellow, repeated *tu-tu-tu*, while the long-billed utters a sharp, high-pitched *keek*, either as a single note or a rapid series. Texas birders usually list them as

Long, straight bills distinguish the dowitchers from other sandpipers, but the two dowitcher species are best separated by voice.

"dowitcher species" if they do not hear them.

In winter, both species appear dark brownish gray above and whitish below, with a gray wash across the breast. In breeding plumage, they become a checkered rusty brown above and reddish below. Experienced birders recognize dowitchers at any time of year, and in any plumage, by their relatively large size and their very long, straight bills. In flight, both dowitcher species display white tails and rumps, with the white pattern extending far up the back in a long, tapering wedge. That combination resembles the flight pattern of no other sandpiper.

ber until April. They prefer grassy marshes and wet meadows and are often shy and secretive. Flushing close under foot, with harsh cries of *scape* or *scipe*, they dart away in rapid, zigzag flight. They have extremely long, straight bills and probe deeply in the mud for the earthworms, insects, crustaceans and mollusks that make up the bulk of their diet. The pliable, sensitive bill allows snipe to feed by touch, opening the flexible tip and grasping their prey to pull it from the ground. Small pellets of the indigestible parts are regurgitated later.

By mid-April the common snipe leaves Texas for its breeding grounds farther north. There the male stages his spectacular courtship display, circling high in the air and then diving toward the ground, his tail feathers widely spread. The wind through those feathers produces strange pulsating tones, *who-who, who-who,* the famous mating "song" of the snipe.

The name snipe has its complex origin in the old Germanic languages, according to Gruson. It is similar to "snip" and "snap" and probably refers to the long beak. *Gallinago,* used twice as the scientific name, is a form of the Latin *gallina,* or "hen."

The common snipe has a boldly striped back and head, streaked breast, and white belly. The rusty orange tail shows in flight. The only other shorebirds of similar size with such long, straight bills are the dowitchers and the woodcock. Dowitchers lack the striped plumage and inhabit open ponds and mud flats rather than heavy grass. They also flash a long, triangular white patch on the lower back in flight.

The American woodcock (*Scolopax minor*) is a "shorebird" only in its familial relationships. It inhabits wet woodlands and thickets rather than open marshes and fields. It winters in eastern Texas and as far west as Fort Worth, Austin and Corpus Christi. A small number remain to breed in the woodlands of East Texas.

COMMON SNIPE *Gallinago gallinago*

Yes, Virginia, there is a snipe, in spite of what many young boys and girls may think after enduring their first midnight snipe hunt at summer camp. Formerly called Wilson's snipe, the common snipe remains a popular game bird through many sections of the country. It breeds in Canada and the northern and western U.S., as well as in Europe and Asia, and winters in this hemisphere from the southern states to South America.

Snipe spend the winter across most of Texas, remaining from Octo-

The flexible tip of the common snipe's bill aids in pulling worms from the muddy soil.

WILSON'S PHALAROPE

Phalaropus tricolor

Phalaropes employ a remarkable reversal of the normal avian sex roles. It is the female of each species that is the more brightly colored, and she flaunts her nuptial plumage in extravagant aerial displays and water ballets, fluffing her feathers and singing a strange "chugging" song. Seemingly unimpressed, the male refuses to submit, until she chases him down and captures him. After mating, the male makes several nest scrapes on the ground, and the female chooses one in which to lay her clutch of four spotted eggs. The nest is lined with grasses after the first egg is laid. Her duty done, the female wanders off, leaving her mate to incubate and rear the brood alone. She may occasionally mate again with another male, or she may join a group of other females who are also free from family chores.

Wilson's phalarope is a slim, elegant bird with a long, thin black bill and legs and a long neck. In the breeding plumage, a bold black stripe runs through the eye and down the side of the neck, blending to rich chestnut-brown on the back and sides of the breast. In winter, both sexes appear dark gray above and white below, with a thin dark line through the eye.

Wilson's phalarope breeds on the prairie ponds and marshes of western Canada and the U.S. and spends the winter in South America. It can be relatively common throughout Texas in spring and fall migrations. Phalaropes have partially lobed toes and are equally at home wading or swimming. They often spin around and around

Wilson's phalarope is a slender, elegant shorebird.

like tops while swimming, stirring up insect larvae and other aquatic invertebrates, which they then pick from the surface with their slender bills.

The name, pronounced *FAL-uh-rope,* comes from the Greek meaning "coot-footed." The Greek *phalaris* signifies "white" or "shining" and was the name applied to the coot, apparently because of its white bill and forehead shield. *Pous* means "foot." This became *phalaropus* in the Latin and then passed into English from a French adaptation. Although the AOU checklist classifies the phalaropes as a subfamily of the sandpipers, some other authors accord them full

family status as the Phalaropodidae because of their unique breeding biology.

The two other phalarope species breed in the Arctic and are mainly oceanic in their migrations. Both the red-necked (formerly northern) phalarope (*Phalaropus lobatus*) and the red phalarope (*P. fulicaria*) are seen occasionally in Texas, the former more often than the latter. Slightly smaller than Wilson's phalarope, they have shorter bills and display a larger black patch behind the eye in winter plumage. Both show white wing-stripes in flight, while the Wilson's wings are entirely dark.

BIRDS OF PREY

Birds of prey rank among the most magnificent of all the world's creatures. Few seem more perfectly suited to the ecological niche they fill than these feathered hunters of the skies. Long celebrated in song and story, they have come to symbolize strength, wisdom and freedom of spirit. People of many cultures around the world have considered them sacred and worshiped them as deities through the centuries. Yet in spite of all their magnificence and the useful roles they play in our environment, hawks and owls face continued persecution and remain in need of stepped-up conservation efforts and widespread understanding.

Our birds of prey, often called raptors, are killed by farmers and ranchers who consider them predators of domestic animals. "Hunters" looking for large and easy targets shoot them when they become bored with legal game. Many are taken for illegal taxidermy, and others bring high prices in the extensive and lucrative black-market trade in falconry, particularly from foreign countries where hunting-birds are highly prized.

Raptors feed high on the food chains and accumulate the toxic pesticides and pollutants we spew out. Some die outright from poisoning, while many more fail to reproduce. Such was the havoc that DDT and other chlorinated hydrocarbons wrought on the bald eagle, the osprey and the peregrine. The large hunters, too, require larger territories in which to nest and raise their young, and they suffer the most from habitat destruction. Modern laws protect all these birds of prey, but only education can assure their preservation. As long as eagles, hawks and owls fly free, hope remains for the environment we all must share.

This grouping as "Birds of Prey" follows function rather than strict taxonomic form, for the families of the hawks and owls are not closely related. The nocturnal owls have certain adaptations not shared by the diurnal raptors, yet each group has evolved the flashing talons and sharp beaks necessary to hunt successfully.

_____

The osprey is a majestic master of the air.

HAWKS AND EAGLES (Family Accipitridae)

Young Harris' hawks feed voraciously on rodents.

The Accipitridae comprises a worldwide family of more than 200 species of diurnal raptors, or birds of prey. They range in size from huge eagles to tiny accipiters and kites and can sometimes be difficult to identify in the field. Females average larger than the males of the same species, and immature plumages differ from those of the adults. A wide range of individual variation further complicates the birder's problems. Nevertheless, the family contains some of the most spectacular and beautiful birds in the world. True masters of the air, they fly swiftly on powerful wings and soar lazily aloft on the wings of the wind.

Hawks and eagles have developed special adaptations to make possible their lives as hunters, whatever the size and nature of their prey. Strong, sharp talons grasp that prey, and hooked beaks tear away bits of flesh. Raptors' eyes are immense for the size of their heads. Mounted well forward on the face, they give hawks the binocular vision and depth perception necessary to swoop to a point in space. The eyes are also packed with a higher density of receptors than those of other animals, resulting in the keen vision responsible for such stock terms as "eagle eye" and "eyes like a hawk." Bony ridges above the eyes give them a hooded appearance and make the raptor's piercing gaze seem even more steely and fierce.

Size and shape distinguish members of the various subfamilies and genera within the Accipitridae. Some have long, pointed wings for swift flight in open country. Others have shorter, broader wings for greater maneuverability. The key to raptor identification lies in first noting that shape and putting the bird in its proper group. Then such factors as wing-pattern and the color and pattern of the tail become important.

OSPREY: Many authors place the osprey in its own family, the Pandionidae. The AOU checklist, however, still regards it as the lone member of a subfamily with the hawks and eagles. The wide-ranging, cosmopolitan species is large and eaglelike and plunges into the water feet-first for fish.

EAGLES: North America's two largest birds of prey, the bald and golden eagles, have wingspans of up to seven and one-half feet. Their massive size and broad wings held flat while soaring make them unmistakable, even at a distance.

KITES: Graceful birds with long, pointed wings, kites resemble falcons in their general shape. The snail kite is limited to Florida and tropical America, but the American swallow-tailed kite, the black-shouldered kite and the Mississippi kite all occur in Texas. A fifth species, the hook-billed kite, provides one of the rare birding prizes in the lower Rio Grande Valley. It has broader wings than the others and looks more like a buteo.

HARRIERS: The northern harrier, formerly called the marsh hawk, is the only U.S. representative of its genus. It has long wings and a long tail and soars low over the prairies and marshes. A large white patch on the rump of both the pale gray male and the brown female and immatures provides the most distinctive field mark.

ACCIPITERS: *Accipiter* is the Latin word for "bird of prey." These aggressive, forest-dwelling raptors have short, rounded wings and long tails. Highly maneuverable, they dart swiftly through the thickets in pursuit of smaller birds.

BUTEOS: These large broad-winged, broad-tailed hawks soar high in the sky or perch on poles and in treetops, watching for careless prey. Authorities place most of them in the genus *Buteo,* but the term also refers more loosely to other closely related hawks. Because these majestic hawks are called "buzzards" in Europe, North American birders do not use that term for the vultures, in spite of its common usage in Texas and elsewhere in the United States. Several buteo species have both light and dark phases as well as intermediate plumages. Immatures vary as well. *Hawks,* a book by William Clark and Brian Wheeler, provides useful information and keys for identification of the diurnal raptors.

White head and tail distinguish the adult bald eagle (opposite). Crows give chase to a red-tailed hawk (right).

Osprey with fish.

OSPREY *Pandion haliaetus*

The large raptor flies slowly along the shore of South Texas' Laguna Madre, its long wings arched and bent back sharply at the wrists, much like those of the gulls. It is dark brown above and white below, with a white head and short, shaggy crest. A broad, dark line runs through the eye and down the neck. With its six-foot wingspan, the bird appears almost big enough to be an eagle, but its contrasting pattern and characteristic wing shape mark it clearly as an osprey. It is probably on its way from its nesting territory farther north to spend the winter in tropical America.

Its keen eyes scan the water below. Shrill, whistled cries, *kyew kyew kyew,* warn off the gulls that circle near. The osprey hovers on beating wings and then drops feet-first to the surface with a splash. Wings flailing, it rises and gives a sudden shudder to shake the water from its plumage. The long talons of one foot securely grasp a foot-long mullet. Carefully the osprey rotates the fish to grip it with its head pointing forward and then flies ponderously to a small grassy island. Settling on the muddy bank, the bird tears pieces from the fish with its sharp hooked bill and wolfs them down.

From the 1950s to the 1970s, such scenes became increasingly rare across the continent as the osprey population plunged. Decimated by DDT, which rendered it and several other fish-eating birds incapable of reproducing, the osprey was listed as endangered. After federal bans on chlorinated-hydrocarbon pesticides, and with other conservation measures, it has now returned in good numbers.

The osprey ranges throughout the Northern Hemisphere. In North America, it breeds across Canada and the northern and western states and in Florida. A few scattered nesting records exist for Texas, but its present breeding status needs further study. Ospreys migrate throughout the state, and a few remain through the winter, particularly along the coast.

Nests are bulky structures of sticks and debris placed in trees or on towers and poles near freshwater lakes and rivers or along the coasts. Added to and reused year after year, they become very large. Artificial nesting platforms in the eastern states have helped restore the vanishing birds. The two to four large eggs are white or pinkish and spotted with olive-brown. Although the female plays the major role in incubation and in brooding her young chicks, the male takes his turn. He also brings food to the nest. Incubation requires from 32 to 43 days; fledging of the young takes up to two months more.

Some authorities place the osprey in its own family, separated from the eagles and hawks by several anatomical differences. Sharp spicules cover the lower surfaces of its toes, and it can reverse the outer toes at will to point them backward. Both adaptations aid in catching and grasping slippery fish, the major item on the osprey's menu.

The name osprey came from the Latin *ossifraga,* meaning "bone-breaker," which was first applied to a quite different species, the massive lammergeier *(Gypaetus barbatus)* of the Eurasian mountains. That bird is far more deserving of the name than the osprey, which consumes primarily fish. *Pandion* refers to the mythical King of Athens whose daughters were transformed into birds, and *haliaetus* is from the Greek for "sea eagle."

BALD EAGLE *Haliaeetus leucocephalus*

It was on June 20, 1782, that the U.S. Congress approved the "American eagle" as our national emblem. The designer of the seal originally proposed using the image of the golden eagle, but Congress noted that the latter cosmopolitan bird had served for centuries on the seals and flags of several European states. Instead, it chose the strictly North American bald eagle.

The selection was not without opposition. Benjamin Franklin, for one, insisted the eagle did not deserve its reputation as a powerful and noble bird of prey. He denounced it as a coward, bully and thief, feeding on carrion or stealing fish from the smaller osprey. The wild turkey, Franklin insisted, would be a far better choice for the honor. But Congress overruled him, and the eagle was approved.

Despite its honored and symbolic status, the eagle has been severely persecuted, along with other large birds of prey. Not until 1940 did it gain full protection under federal laws. Habitat loss also contributed to the population decline, as did toxic pesticides and heavy-metal residues. In 1982, the breeding population of bald eagles outside Alaska was estimated at fewer than 1,500 pairs. Major conservation efforts in the last decade have begun to reverse the downward slide.

Its white head and tail and its massive yellow bill make the adult bald eagle immediately recognizable. Immatures, however, are mostly dark, with irregular white patches in the wings and at the base of the tail. They do not gain adult plumage until their fourth year and, until then, can easily be confused with immature golden eagles, which also show white in the underwings and tail. The common name comes from the Old English *balde,* meaning "white," and the scientific name reflects the same striking feature: *Haliaeetus* is Greek for "sea eagle," while *leucocephalus* means "white head."

Its white head and massive yellow bill make the adult bald eagle unmistakable.

Flying on broad, flat wings spanning nearly eight feet, bald eagles range along the coasts and inland near lakes and rivers. They feed primarily on fish but also take small mammals and water birds as well as carrion. The eagle's cry is a shrill *kweek-kik-ik-ik-ik*. A pair establishes long-term bonds and performs spectacular aerial courtship displays, locking talons and somersaulting toward the ground.

The mated pair returns to the same site year after year, adding new material to the stick nest, called an aerie, until it reaches incredible proportions. One such nest proved to be nearly ten feet across and twenty feet deep. Another weighed more than two tons and contained branches six feet long and several inches in diameter. Perched high in the tops of trees, these enormous structures sometimes plummet to earth as the trees snap under the weight.

The female lays from one to three large bluish white eggs. The normal clutch is two, but because the chicks hatch at different times, the first to hatch has the advantage, and the second often dies. Incubation requires from 34 to 36 days, with both parents taking part, and the young are about three months old before they leave the security of the nest.

Texas hosts a small resident population of bald eagles that nests along the coastal plain between Corpus Christi and Houston and on some of the larger wooded lakes and reservoirs in the eastern portion of the state. In 1991, there were 29 nesting pairs under close observation by Texas Parks and Wildlife biologists.

Winter brings down a larger number from the North. Some move onto the lakes in eastern and central Texas, where they feed primarily on fish. Others hunt on the prairies west of Houston, surviving on wounded ducks and geese left by human hunters. A January 1991 survey by 200 volunteers counted 327 bald eagles at 15 survey sites, but some estimates indicate there might be twice that many within the state.

GOLDEN EAGLE *Aquila chrysaetos*

A long time ago when the world was new, says a legend of the Brule Sioux, the water monster caused a great flood that killed all the people. Only a beautiful girl survived, for an eagle swept down and lifted her from the hilltop where everyone had taken refuge. The eagle flew to a high stone pinnacle, the only spot that was not inundated, and he and the girl were spared. Later they married, and the eagle's wife bore him twins, a boy and a girl. The eagle, Wanblee Galeshka, helped them down from the pinnacle and put them on earth, telling them to "become a great nation." They, in turn, married and had children, and a new nation was born.

There are many such legends among Native Americans, for the golden eagle was considered a powerful god. Other peoples of the world, too, have honored the bird in song and story, and it has adorned the banners of several nations. Found in the mountainous terrain around the Northern Hemisphere, the golden eagle is a fitting symbol of the rugged wilderness. Few have captured its spirit better than Tennyson: "He watches from his mountain walls, / And like a thunderbolt he falls."

Indeed, the thunderbolt dive of the eagle is remarkably swift and powerful. Hunting over open country, it swoops to capture jackrabbits, ground squirrels, prairie dogs and other small mammals. Birds, snakes and carrion also add to the diet. The eagle does, on occasion, take larger animals including lambs, a trait that has won it no favors from the nation's sheep ranchers. Texas naturalist Roy Bedichek wrote of a pilot in the Davis Mountains who reported shooting 1,875 golden eagles in two years from his small plane. Other reports claim that more than 20,000 eagles were killed in ten years throughout the West. Although protected by federal laws since 1962, golden eagles remain unpopular in many sectors. Careful observations indicate, however, that they are unfairly blamed for many assaults on domestic stock that actually died from other causes.

The golden eagle soars on long, flat wings spanning seven feet or more. The adult is entirely dark brown, with a golden wash on the head and neck. The immature shows well-defined white patches in the wings and at the base of the tail. It does not attain adult plumage until its fourth year and is easily mistaken for the immature bald eagle.

Nesting across Alaska and Canada and in the western U.S., the golden eagle may wander more widely in the fall. Nesting records exist for the Texas Panhandle, Trans-Pecos and Edwards Plateau, and in the fall and winter golden eagles occasionally stray eastward to the Gulf. The bald eagle is more common in the eastern half of the state; the golden, in the west.

Golden eagles form long-term pair bonds and build their bulky nests on rocky cliffs, adding to them and reusing them from season to season. Two eggs form the normal clutch, and the female does most of the incubating, while the male hunts and feeds her on the nest. The chicks fledge in 66 to 75 days, but because they do not hatch at the same time, the larger sibling gets most of the food if provisions are scarce. It may even kill the smaller one as it grows weaker. While such a reproductive strategy may seem cruel by human standards, it assures at least one healthy fledgling when times are particularly hard.

The adult golden eagle (opposite, top) sports tawny feathers on its head and neck. An immature golden eagle in flight (opposite) shows white patches in its wings and tail.

AMERICAN SWALLOW-TAILED KITE

Elanoides forficatus

In a 1991 poll, *American Birds* magazine asked ten well-known artists to name the ten most beautiful birds in the world. Out of approximately 9,000 birds, the swallow-tailed kite finished in a first-place tie with the resplendent quetzal of Central America. Bird illustrator Dale Zimmerman called this handsome raptor "the epitome of grace and ethereal beauty." Doug Pratt cited the bird's grace as "a wonderful acrobat. Wherever you see it, it's a joy."

Certainly no one can forget his first view of the swallow-tailed kite gliding across the sky on four-foot wings, primaries feeling gently for the breeze, long forked tail tilting from side to side. Its aerial grace is unequaled, its clean black-and-white pattern supremely elegant. The kite is a deep, glossy black above and white below, with a white head. The forked tail and the trailing edges of the wings are black as well. Usually silent, it occasionally whistles a shrill *kee-klee-klee.*

The swallow-tailed kite breeds along the southern Atlantic Coast from South Carolina to Florida and westward along the Gulf of Mexico. It once ranged across most of the eastern U.S., as far north as Minnesota, but declined rapidly in the path of lumbering and land clearing, drainage programs, wanton shooting and other intrusions on its habitat. It then sought refuge in the southern swamps and river bottoms, where it nests in the tops of tall trees.

Kites build their nest of twigs broken off with the feet in flight and line it with Spanish moss and other soft materials. The two to four white eggs are marked with brown. Incubation by both parents requires four weeks, and the young kites fledge five or six weeks after hatching. Surprisingly gregarious for birds of prey, swallow-tailed kites often breed in loose colonies of several pairs and share common feeding grounds. They catch large insects in the air and swoop to snatch up snakes, lizards and frogs. Observers report kites will even grab a bird's nest from a tree to eat the young within. Most of their food is eaten on the wing, and they drink and bathe by swooping down to dip in flight.

Most of the U.S. population is concentrated in southern Florida, while other subspecies occur through Central and South America. The northern kites, too, winter in South America, and they pass through Texas occasionally in migration. Until the early 20th century, they nested on the Texas coastal plain and along wooded river drainages to the central portion of the state. The last substantiated breeding record, however, was in Harris County in 1914.

Then, in 1989, several kites were seen north of Hamshire in Jefferson County. Birders flocked to the site and watched them carrying nesting material in their talons as they sailed above the heavily wooded tracts along Taylor's Bayou. Residents of the area had been seeing them for several years, and there is every indication that they were nesting. Texas Parks and Wildlife Department biologists have been monitoring the birds, hoping to prevent disturbance in the nesting area. Road sightings have increased, particularly in April and early May. Apparently the elegant American swallow-tailed kite has once again returned to Texas as a breeding resident, however tenuous its hold.

Few birds are as graceful and elegant as the swallow-tailed kite.

BLACK-SHOULDERED KITE *Elanus caeruleus*

At first glance, the dapper black-and-white bird might be mistaken for a gull flying buoyantly over the South Texas coastal prairie. Suddenly it wheels around and hovers in one place, facing into the brisk wind, wings beating rapidly. The morning sun behind it filters through the white tail feathers and glints off the long, pointed, falcon-shaped wings. The bird drops feet-first into the grass and rises again with a cotton rat grasped in its sharp talons. Flying to the edge of the field, it lands on a fence post with its still-struggling prey.

This small raptor is about 16 inches long; its wings span three and one-half feet. Pale gray above and white below, it has a white head with a small black patch around the eye. Black epaulettes adorn the shoulders. The small size, dainty features and distinctive black-and-white pattern mark it as a black-shouldered kite.

One of the prettiest of our birds of prey, it was formerly named the white-tailed kite *(Elanus leucurus)*. The AOU, however, now considers it part of a single worldwide complex with the black-winged kite of Africa and Eurasia and the black-shouldered kite of the Australian region. All are collectively designated the black-shouldered kite.

Perhaps the only raptor to benefit from agricultural expansion, it seems to adapt readily to habitat disruption and thrives on the abundance of rodents around farms and ranches. Mice and small rats, along with grasshoppers and other insects, make up the bulk of the kite's diet. Populations are subject to wide fluctuations, but the black-shouldered kite has expanded its range dramatically in recent years. In the U.S., it has traditionally been found along the lower Texas coast and in southern California. Now it has spread eastward around the Gulf of Mexico and northward and eastward from California. Although still most common in South Texas, from the Rio Grande to about the Corpus Christi area, it also

occurs frequently along the middle and upper coasts and inland on the prairies. It prefers overgrown grasslands with scattered trees and shrubs on which to perch.

The breeding pair builds a platform of dead twigs and grasses on the top of a dense tree or in a tall yucca, and the female lays four or five white eggs marked with brown. Only the female incubates, while the male does all the hunting for his mate and their brood. The eggs hatch in 30 to 32 days, and the young fledge four or five weeks later. Juveniles have a rusty wash on the head and underparts but are easily recognizable. They gain adult plumage within a few months.

According to Dawn Conway Carrie, who studied black-shouldered kites at Laguna Atascosa National Wildlife Refuge for her master's thesis at Texas A&M, a pair may have more than one brood a season. The nest success rate is low, however, due in part to predation by great-tailed grackles and snakes. Carrie also observed as many as a hundred kites roosting communally at night.

A black-shouldered kite tends its young.

An adult Mississippi kite (left) eats a cicada picked from a tree limb. Immature Mississippi kites (below) are boldly streaked.

MISSISSIPPI KITE *Ictinia mississippiensis*

Few sights in nature are more thrilling than hawks on the wing, and among the most graceful of all these birds of prey is the Mississippi kite. Sailing effortlessly on the thermals, it glides and wheels into the wind, sometimes swooping to catch an insect in midair or to snatch a noisy cicada from a treetop.

The long, pointed wings of this streamlined, falcon-shaped hawk span slightly less than three feet. Dark gray above and paler gray below, it has a long black tail and a pale gray or whitish head. From below, the bird in flight appears entirely dark except for the lighter head. Immature birds are heavily streaked and spotted, with pale bands across the tail. Their shape, however, and their association with other kites make identification easier.

Mississippi kites nest across the southeastern United States, ranging along the Atlantic Coast to North Carolina, up the Mississippi Valley to southern Illinois, and through the Great Plains as far north as central Kansas. In Texas, they breed locally in the Panhandle and northern counties, usually forming loose colonies where they congregate at communal perches and favorite foraging areas.

Nest sites include large trees in open rangeland and along wooded creeks. The bulky, flat nests are built of twigs and lined with leaves to hold the two or three whitish eggs. The young hatch in 31 or 32 days and require another five weeks of care before they fly.

In late summer and early fall, these graceful raptors begin their southward migration, staging an aerial circus for all to see. Scores of kites swirl overhead on motionless wings, tilting their tails rudderlike to drift with the wind. They move across Texas from the Panhandle to the Rio Grande, sometimes purposefully, sometimes in their characteristic lazy glide, headed for their winter range in South America. Along the way they consume the grasshoppers, cicadas and other insects that make up the major portion of their diet, along with occasional mice, lizards, small snakes and frogs.

I will never forget my first view of Mississippi kites one morning many years ago. It was Labor Day weekend, and we were relaxing in the quiet little town of George West when we looked up to see a swirling flock of about 400 kites hanging like a giant mobile directly overhead. They were catching large moths that had been attracted to the streetlights through the night and were consuming them in the air, talons to beak, while gliding smoothly along.

At a time when many other species are declining, Mississippi kites appear to be increasing in both numbers and range, probably because they do not demand large tracts of forested land and because their insect prey remains plentiful in settled areas. Tree planting for windbreaks and erosion control on the open plains has also provided additional nest sites that enable them to spread westward.

The northern harrier hunts by sailing on uplifted wings.

NORTHERN HARRIER *Circus cyaneus*

Formerly called the marsh hawk, the harrier was renamed to coincide with European usage: the Eurasian race of this species is called the hen harrier. The name comes from the Old English *hergian,* meaning to harass or harry by constant attacks. The genus *Circus* stems from the Greek *kirkos,* or "circle," for the habit of flying in low circles while hunting. *Cyaneus* refers to the pale blue-gray back of the male harrier.

The adult male is a beautiful raptor, pale gray above and white below, with long, slender wings tipped in black. It has a long tail and a large white patch on the rump. Females are brown above and heavily streaked below; immatures resemble females, but with cinnamon breasts. All, however, have slender bodies, long wings and tails, and the white rumps easily visible in flight. As with many hawks, the female is larger than the male, with a wingspread of up to four feet.

A characteristic ruff around the face gives the harrier an owllike facial disk. Such disks serve as sound reflectors, and recent studies have shown that harriers rely heavily on sound while hunting. Thus, they cruise low over the marshes and fields, gliding buoyantly on long wings tilted upward in a dihedral similar to that of soaring turkey vultures. They rock gently in the breeze, taking advantage of every air current, quartering back and forth over their feeding territories. Spotting a rat or mouse, the harrier drops feet-first to the ground to grasp its hapless prey. Frogs, small snakes, insects and occasional birds are also taken when available.

Harriers range from Canada to the midsection of the United States, migrating to the southern states and as far as South America for the winter. They occur virtually throughout Texas from September into May, with the males arriving later than the females in the fall and leaving earlier in the spring. They nest locally in the northern half of the state but are much more abundant through the winter.

The northern harrier is the only North American raptor that regularly practices polygyny. In one lengthy study, a substantial number of the males mated with two or three females. The four to nine (usually five) bluish white eggs are laid in a crude nest platform of reeds and grasses on the ground in a marsh or shrubby field. The eggs hatch in about 32 days, and the young fledge five weeks later. The female incubates her eggs and broods her downy white chicks alone, while the male hunts and brings her food. Returning from a successful hunt, the male is met by his mate. He drops his catch, and she rolls on her back to catch it deftly in the air.

Northern harriers declined during the 1970s and 1980s, probably because of habitat loss and the heavy use of pesticides. Their place atop the food chain with other birds of prey puts them at risk from the toxins that accumulate in the tissues of smaller animals. Nevertheless, the harrier remains a common sight across Texas through a major portion of the year. Gliding on uplifted wings over the marshes and fields, it flashes the white rump patch that makes it so easily recognizable.

SHARP-SHINNED HAWK *Accipiter striatus*
COOPER'S HAWK *Accipiter cooperii*

The sharp-shinned and Cooper's hawks look much alike and differ mainly in size. The tiny sharp-shinned is 10 to 14 inches long and has a wingspan of 20 to 28 inches. Cooper's hawk ranges from 14 to 20 inches in length, with a proportionately longer wingspan of up to three feet. As with many hawks, however, females are larger than males, and a female sharpie may be nearly as large as a male Cooper's. The former also has a shorter, square-tipped tail, while the tip of the Cooper's long tail appears rounded. That is perhaps the most reliable field mark.

Adults of both species are blue-gray above with rusty barring across the white under-

The keen eyes of a sharp-shinned hawk aid greatly in its hunt for prey.

parts. Cooper's hawk, unlike the sharp-shinned, has a dark crown that contrasts with the bluish back. Immatures of both species are brown above with brown streaks on the lighter breast and belly. The distinctions are not easy ones to make in the field, and even the experts are confused at times by the similarity of these two accipiters. A third species, the northern goshawk *(Accipiter gentilis)*, is even larger than the Cooper's hawk and occurs as a rare winter visitor to the Panhandle and northern Texas.

The accipiters are bird hunters. They inhabit wooded areas, where their short, rounded wings and long tails give them great maneuverability among the trees. They perch quietly on branches or cruise low over the woods, hoping to surprise an unwary songbird and win the ensuing chase. They supplement their diet with small mammals.

The sharp-shinned hawk breeds throughout the northern and western portions of North America and moves southward in the fall. It occurs across most of Texas during the winter season but is uncommon in places without woodlands or brush. Nesting records exist for the northern half of the state, but most sharp-shins leave Texas in the spring.

Cooper's hawk, named for a 19th-century New York zoologist, ranges even more widely than the sharpie. It nests from southern Canada to northern Mexico and withdraws only from the northern edge of its territory. It migrates throughout Texas and winters everywhere except the northern Panhandle. Breeding records exist for most parts of the state, but the Cooper's hawk occurs less frequently in summer than in the fall and winter.

Both accipiters build their nests of sticks and line them with strips of bark, grasses and leaves. The four or five whitish eggs are usually spotted with brown. Females do most of the incubating and feeding of the chicks, while their mates hunt and return to the nest with food. Both species declined dramatically in the 1970s and early 1980s, but reversed the trend when the use of DDT was curtailed.

Harris' Hawk

Parabuteo unicinctus

Harris' hawks are amazingly social birds, a rare trait among the raptors. They sometimes practice what has been termed "simultaneous polyandry," with two males mating with the same female and remaining together through the nesting season. The nest is a platform of sticks in a yucca or low tree, usually lined with green leaves or bark. The three to five white eggs may be either unmarked or spotted with brown and lavender. In the case of a polyandrous trio, all three birds share in the incubation and help to brood and feed the young, which remain with the adults for at least three to six months after fledging. These family groups often hunt cooperatively, working together to flush rabbits from their hiding places and swooping quickly to catch them in rapier talons. They also eat other small mammals, snakes, birds and even large insects.

The female is larger than the male, but the plumages are alike: dark chocolate brown both above and below, with bright chestnut wing linings, thighs and shoulder patches. The shoulder color accounts for an older name, bay-winged hawk. In addition, Harris' hawk displays a broad white band at the base of the tail and a narrower white terminal band. Immature birds are streaked with brown beneath, but the rusty shoulders usually prove diagnostic. Leaner bodied than the large *Buteo* hawks with which it might be confused, Harris' hawk has long yellow legs and appears lankier and less compact when perched. Its long wings span nearly four feet.

Harris' hawk ranges from the arid southwestern states to Chile and Argentina. In this country, it occurs primarily in southern Texas and Arizona. It inhabits the brushlands and mesquite thickets from the lower Rio Grande Valley to the central coast, ranging less commonly to the Edwards Plateau and the Trans-Pecos. Wanderers occur throughout the state on rare occasions. Those en-

countered in other parts of the country, far from their normal range, may be escapees from captivity, for Harris' hawks are popular with falconers.

This large and distinctive raptor was named for Edward Harris, a New Jersey gentleman farmer and natural-

ist. A patron and friend of Audubon, Harris accompanied him on some of his collecting expeditions.

A mockingbird harasses Harris' hawks at their nest.

half of Texas, from the Red River to the Rio Grande.

A medium-sized buteo, smaller than the red-tailed hawk but larger than the broad-winged, it measures 18 to 20 inches long with a wingspan of about three and one-half feet. Adults are brown above with reddish barring across the light breast. Rufous shoulders give it its name, although they are not always visible when the hawk is perched. In flight, the red-shouldered hawk displays rufous wing-linings and pale crescent-shaped patches at the base of the primaries. The dark tail crossed by narrow white bands is also diagnostic. The broad-winged hawk has similar red barring on the breast, but its white tail bands appear nearly as wide as the dark bands.

Red-shouldered hawks nest in tall woodland trees and show considerable loyalty to each other and to the nesting site. Pairs may reuse their stick nest from year to year, adding to it and lining it with grasses, moss and green leaves. The two to four white eggs are marked with brown and hatch in 28 days. Both parents incubate and care for the downy white chicks, feeding them on snakes, frogs, crayfish, small mammals and birds. Such food items as frogs and crayfish are unusual fare for large raptors and reflect their wet bottomland habitat. The young hawks clamber about in the treetop as they develop and fledge at about six weeks of age. In their immature plumage, their breasts are streaked with brown.

Red-shouldered hawks are frequently noisy, giving a loud, clear series of calls, *kee-yar kee-yar kee-yar,* or *kah kah kah.* Blue jays in eastern Texas and brown jays in the Rio Grande Valley mimic them effectively, until the birder is not sure whether he is pursuing a hawk or jay. The hawk population has decreased in recent decades, probably from a combination of toxic pesticides and loss of timbered habitats.

Rusty epaulettes and barring on the breast mark the adult red-shouldered hawk.

RED-SHOULDERED HAWK *Buteo lineatus*

This is the hawk most likely to be encountered in the forests of East Texas. Unlike many of the large buteos that prefer open country, the red-shouldered hawk inhabits moist woodlands, swamps and river bottoms. It ranges across the eastern half of the continent, from southeastern Canada into Mexico, moving southward for the winter from only the northern edge of its territory. It is a year-round resident in the eastern

Broad-winged Hawk

Buteo platypterus

High overhead they swirl in lazy circles, silhouettes against the blue autumn sky. Hundreds of birds drift slowly southward, wings set and tails flared to ride the thermals.

This is the fall migration of the broad-winged hawks. They come from across the eastern half of the continent, from southern Canada to the Gulf States, funneling through Texas and down the Central American land bridge to South America. There they will spend the winter before retracing their aerial pathway in the spring.

The broad-winged hawk is the smallest of our common buteo hawks. Crow-sized, it measures 16 to 18 inches long and has a 34-inch wingspread. Plain brown above, it sports rusty barring on the breast and a tail with wide black-and-white bands. The broad-wing is smaller than the similar red-shouldered hawk, and its white tail bands are wider. Immature birds are streaked beneath, with indistinct tail bars.

Broad-winged hawks breed in wooded areas, frequently near water. They build their nests of twigs high in the trees and line them with strips of bark, lichens or green leaves to cradle the two or three white eggs splotched with brown and purple. Incubation requires 28 to 30 days, and the young remain in the nest for five or six weeks after hatching.

A rather tame bird, the broad-wing perches low in the trees near a stream or pond to wait for prey. It specializes in frogs and toads but also takes small rodents, snakes, crayfish, insects and an occasional small bird. The reliance on cold-blooded prey forces it to abandon northern forests early in the fall, and the birds begin their southward drift toward tropical America. Flocks build into the hundreds, even thousands, as the migration progresses.

Although broad-winged hawks nest in Texas only in the woodlands along the Louisiana border, the main migration route takes them through the eastern half of the state. In September and October they ride the winds, stopping at night in trees along creek beds and river bottoms, taking wing again in midmorning when the land warms and the thermals begin to rise. The huge flocks roll and boil in the sky, giving rise to the descriptive term "kettle" for a swirling group of hawks. Their flight seems leisurely and effortless, yet they must cover thousands of miles in the weeks ahead.

Even as I write this passage early in October, there is a report on the Texas Rare Bird Alert, the recorded telephone message describing unusual sightings, of an immense flight of 20,000 broad-wings over the levee at Santa Ana National Wildlife Refuge in the Rio Grande Valley. Volunteers man "hawkwatch" stations at Smith Point in Galveston Bay and at Hazel Bazemore County Park near Corpus Christi, where 10,000 hawks a day can be expected from mid-September into October.

Hawk-census data indicate the health of bird populations and the overall state of the environment. From a purely aesthetic point of view, however, the migration of the broad-winged hawks through Texas is a spectacle of grace and beauty, an aerial circus without equal.

Broad-winged hawks.

SWAINSON'S HAWK   *Buteo swainsoni*

A gnarled cottonwood tree stands alone on the open prairie, its branches and trunk bearing the scars of summer drought and harsh winter storms. The tree contains a large, rather untidy platform of sticks and weedy stalks lined with strips of bark, feathers and a few green leaves. Atop the nest sits a large hawk, brown above and whitish below, but with a sharply marked brown bib across the chest. It is a Swainson's hawk, a bird of the western plains, incubating her three white eggs speckled with brown while her mate hunts nearby.

Swainson's hawk breeds on the open grasslands across the western half of North America and winters mainly on the pampas of South America. Its annual round-trip migration of up to 17,000 miles makes it one of the truly long-distance avian commuters. It ranges throughout Texas during those spring and fall migration flights, but it is most common in the western half of the state. There, large flocks of migrating Swainson's hawks replace the kettles of broad-winged hawks that funnel through the eastern counties. Swainson's hawk remains to nest, too, in the western half of Texas.

The plumage is extremely variable, and a number of color forms occur. The light phase predominates, with the striking dark bib contrasting with white or pale buff underparts. However, there is a less common dark phase that is entirely chocolate brown, and a wide range of intermediate plumages between the two extremes also exist. To further complicate the picture, immatures are heavily streaked below. We often see that plumage because it takes two years for the young hawks to reach adulthood. Such variation is not uncommon in the buteos, and careful attention must be paid to the shape and color patterns of the underwings and tails of hawks in flight. Field guides and specialized books on hawks detail these finer points of identification.

Swainson's hawks fly magnificently, soaring on long wings that are narrower and more pointed than those of the red-tailed hawk and some of the other large buteos. They raise their wings above the horizontal while soaring, forming a dihedral much like that of a turkey vulture or harrier, and the bird rocks from side to side to utilize air currents. In the light-phase plumage the pale, unmarked winglinings contrast with darker, barred flight feathers.

Swainson's hawks often hunt on the wing but also perch on posts and rocks to watch for prey. Spotting movement, they pounce quickly from their perches, taking a wide variety of rodents, rabbits, snakes, lizards, fledgling birds and even large insects. The insects, in fact, may make up a substantial part of the diet, and it is not uncommon to see a migrating flock of Swainson's hawks drop into a field to

Immature Swainson's hawk.

feed on grasshoppers or crickets. They even follow plows or mowers to pick up morsels thus exposed.

In spite of their apparent tameness at such times, the adults are extremely wary and defensive around their nests. Even a slight disturbance may cause abandonment before the eggs have hatched.

Swainson's hawk was named for William Swainson, a widely published English naturalist and artist born in 1789. He scored what might be considered an ornithological hat trick; a hawk, a warbler and a thrush now bear his name.

WHITE-TAILED HAWK

Buteo albicaudatus

Birders come from across the country to see the specialty species of Texas, birds found nowhere else in the United States. One of those prizes is the beautiful white-tailed hawk, a tropical species that ranges northward from South America and crosses our borders in the lower Rio Grande Valley, extending its territory sparingly to the Houston area. The grasslands of the lower coast and the semi-arid brush country of southern Texas offer the best chances for spotting this large and uniquely marked raptor.

The head and upperparts of the white-tailed hawk are dark gray, the underparts white. The shoulders bear epaulettes of a rich chestnut color, and the immaculate white tail displays a single black band near the tip. In flight, the clear white underparts and wing-linings and the black-tipped white tail prove diagnostic. Immatures, however, are dark brown above and heavily streaked and mottled with blackish brown on the breast and belly. The light tail is faintly barred and lacks the black tip. This and the transition plumages can be confusing, as is the case with many of the immature hawks.

At nearly two feet in length, and with a wingspan exceeding four feet,

the white-tail equals the more common red-tailed hawk in size, but its wings appear more pointed and the tail is proportionately shorter. It hunts from a perch or on the wing, either by gliding slowly over the fields or by hovering in one place on beating wings, dropping feet-first into the grass after its prey. Small mammals, especially rabbits and woodrats, make up the bulk of its diet in South Texas, although it also utilizes snakes, lizards, frogs, birds and large insects. The white-tail is attracted to prairie fires, where it hunts the edges for fleeing animals.

The white-tailed hawk suffered a marked decline in Texas from the 1930s into the 1960s, due primarily to habitat loss over the inland portions of its range. Eggshell thinning was also detected and may have contributed to lack of nesting success. A few records exist from the far corners of the state, but the nonmigratory whitetail is rare outside extreme South Texas and the coastal plain.

A bulky platform of sticks in the top of a low tree or yucca serves as a nest, and the same pair often refurbishes and reuses it from year to year.

A white-tailed hawk lands at its nest.

The building of a new nest reportedly occupies up to five weeks of intermittent work. About two-thirds of the white or bluish white eggs are marked with brown, while the other one-third is unmarked. A clutch ranges in size from one to four eggs, with two or three being most common. The breeding biology has not been studied as thoroughly as that of many birds, and the incubation and fledging periods are not well known.

Although severely restricted in its range and numbers, the white-tailed hawk can usually be found on a trip across the King Ranch into South Texas or at such refuges as Laguna Atascosa on the lower coast. Perched on a roadside post or hovering over the prairie, it is a real prize for the observant birder or anyone else who appreciates beauty on the wing. Its series of cries, *kil-la kil-la,* is surprisingly high-pitched and musical for so large and powerful a bird of prey.

Red-tailed Hawk

Buteo jamaicensis

The red-tailed hawk is the most widespread and abundant of all our large buteo hawks. It ranges across the continent, from Alaska and Canada southward to Panama, and withdraws only from the northernmost portions of that range in winter. The scientific name refers to the first specimen, which was collected in Jamaica.

Texas birders often say that any large hawk should be considered a red-tail until proven otherwise, especially in the open country that it prefers. The major problem, however, is that the red-tail is also highly variable, and plumages range from extremely pale to almost black. A number of named races occur across the country, and the picture is further complicated by individual variations within a given range.

The typical adult red-tailed hawk appears white underneath, with a series of short brown streaks forming a "belly-band" that shows up easily

against the pale plumage. The upperparts are brown, often with pale mottling on the scapulars that forms a light V across the back of the perching bird. The rusty red top of the tail flashes in the sunlight as a soaring bird banks and rolls; however, the underside is paler, with only hints of red showing through. At least one of those three features—the belly-band, the pale V on the back, or the red tail—can usually be seen from any angle, making a tentative identification possible. In flight overhead, a dark bar on the leading edge of the wing is also visible, contrasting with the pale wing linings. Immature red-tails display heavier brown streaking on the underparts and have gray-brown tails with several blackish bands.

The pale race found in the Big Bend region and in South Texas was named *fuertesi* for Louis Agassiz Fuertes, the famous American bird artist. Less heavily marked below, it may lack the belly-band entirely. The reddish race *calurus* inhabits western Texas, and an extremely light race called "Krider's hawk" *(kriderii)* moves into Texas in the winter from its nesting grounds on the Great Plains. The latter has a whitish tail with only a pale reddish wash near the tip. Melanistic, almost black, birds are also known; however, they usually exhibit a deep red shading on the tail.

One form of the red-tail was considered a separate species until recently. "Harlan's hawk" (formerly *Buteo harlani*) breeds in Alaska and northwestern Canada and occasionally wanders into eastern and central Texas in the winter. It is largely black, with a whitish or mottled gray tail blending into a broad, dark band at the tip. Biologists now regard it, too, as a race of the widespread red-tail.

Ill-advised bounties severely reduced populations in the eastern United States, and persecution and habitat loss contribute to a continued decline. Red-tailed hawks have often taken the blame as "chicken hawks" when, in fact, the culprits more likely were Cooper's hawks or other smaller raptors. Red-tails feed primarily on rodents, a trait that actually makes them valuable to farmers. With their bulky two-foot bodies and wide wings spanning more than four feet, they are not agile enough to be a serious threat to many birds.

Red-tailed hawks build large stick nests in tall trees on the edge of open woodlands, in isolated trees on the plains, or on rocky cliff faces, wherever they have a commanding view of their domains. The two or three whitish eggs, often spotted with brown, are incubated mainly by the female, with the protective male helping at times. Both parents feed the downy white chicks that hatch in about 30 days, and the young fledge 45 days later.

The red-tailed hawk nests widely across Texas, but it is rare or absent in the lower Rio Grande delta and on portions of the coast during the summer. For example, the checklist for the Houston area lists it as "rare" from May through August. At other times of year, however, the red-tail is abundant across the state. It perches on telephone poles and fence posts along every roadway and hunts over open woodlands, cultivated fields, pastures and desert scrub. High in the air, it soars on broad, flat wings, flashing its rusty tail and calling in its harsh voice, *keee-yrr, keee-yrr, keee-yrr.*

Red-tailed hawk (above and opposite).

CARACARAS AND FALCONS (Family Falconidae)

Crested caracara.

The family Falconidae contains two widely disparate groups of birds, the true falcons and the caracaras. Taxonomists combine them in a common family based on certain shared skeletal characteristics that are not found in other birds of prey. However, the appearance and habits of the two differ markedly.

The falcons are the most streamlined of the hawks, with long, narrow, pointed wings and long tails. Along with the swifts, they are considered the fastest of all birds, reaching speeds of more than 100 miles per hour in a dive, or "stoop." Their common name and the genus name *Falco* stem from the Latin *falx,* or "sickle." Some authors relate it to the wing shape, while others believe the name refers to the sharp, curved talons. Either would be appropriate.

The falcons constitute a world-wide group of more than 50 species and have long been admired for their speed, fierce beauty, and hunting ability. Ancient Egyptians deified a falcon as the god Horus, and the peoples of central Asia trained falcons to hunt for sport and food as early as 2000 B.C. The sport of falconry remains popular in many countries today, but illegal trade in birds of prey poses a threat to several rare and endangered species.

The caracaras, on the other hand, are limited to the warmer regions of the Americas. Only one species, the crested caracara, ranges northward to the United States. In appearance and habits, the caracaras are distinctly vulturelike, and convergent evolution has given them similarly naked faces and weak feet and claws more suitable for feeding on carrion than for catching living prey. The long-legged birds have large heads and wide, rounded wings. The name comes from a native word in South America and presumably imitates the harsh, cackling call.

Male American kestrel.

CRESTED CARACARA   *Polyborus plancus*

The crested caracara is the national bird of Mexico, and most Texans know it as the "Mexican eagle." It is, however, structurally related to the falcons, while being distinctly vulturine in many of its habits. Older books refer to it as Audubon's caracara and apply an outdated scientific name,

Caracara cheriway. The newer name, *Polyborus plancus,* comes from the Greek *poly,* or "many," and *boros,* or "gluttonous," indicating a voracious appetite. The Latin *plancus* means "flat-footed." The caracara may, indeed, be a flat-footed glutton, but it is a very striking one.

Two feet long, and with a wing-span of more than four feet, the crested caracara matches the common red-tailed hawk in size. It has long legs and a long neck. The large head has a black crest and bare red or orange facial skin around the massive, hooked beak. In flight the caracara shows white at all four corners of a blackish cross: on the head and neck, on the black-banded tail, and near the tips of the broad, rounded wings.

Immatures are browner and heavily streaked, but the combination of other field marks makes them unmistakable.

This largely tropical species ranges northward from South America to southern Texas and Arizona and to central Florida. It is a year-round resident from the Rio Grande delta northward along the coast and inland sparingly to Austin, Waco and Dallas. Stragglers have been reported in many other sections of the state; however, the prairies and rangelands of the lower coastal plain remain its major stronghold.

The caracara feeds primarily on carrion with the vultures and frequently harasses them until they disgorge their food. It also spends a good deal of time foraging on the ground, where with its long legs and flat claws, it can run fast enough to catch insects, lizards, snakes and small mammals. It flies with slow, methodical wingbeats and soars like an eagle with wings held flat.

The nest is a bulky bowl of sticks and vines in the top of a tree or yucca, and the two or three white eggs marked with brown hatch in about 28 days. Both parents share in the incubation and in the feeding of the young, but a great deal remains to be learned about the breeding biology of this bizarre but handsome bird of prey.

A crested caracara watches for prey.

PEREGRINE FALCON *Falco peregrinus*

The sleek, slate-gray bird stands on the shell-covered Texas beach, looking vaguely out of place amidst the passing gulls and terns. A small flock of shorebirds wheels over the breakers along the shore, and the keen-eyed raptor launches in pursuit. It climbs quickly above the frantic flock on long, slender, swept-back wings and then folds into a lightning dive. Like a guided missile locked on target, it plunges into the flock in a burst of feathers. The flock flies on, but the handsome peregrine falcon lands atop a sand dune with a plump black-bellied plover in its talons. There it proceeds to pluck its prize, sending soft feathers adrift on the sea breeze across the sand.

The peregrine falcon subsists mainly on a diet of birds, which it captures on the wing. Once called the "duck hawk," it is one of the fastest of all birds. Estimates of its speed in a dive range upward to 150 or 200 miles per hour. In flat, powered flight it maintains speeds of 60 mph and covers enormous distances, the reason for the name *peregrinus*, Latin for "wandering." The peregrine's worldwide range is more extensive than that of any other bird. It inhabits all of the continents except Antarctica and reaches many of the oceanic island groups.

In North America, the tundra subspecies of the peregrine breeds in Arctic Alaska and Canada, and other subspecies nest on the rocky cliffs of the Pacific Coast and through the mountains of the West. A few birds breed in the rugged Chisos and Guadalupe mountains of Trans-Pecos Texas and in the canyons along the Rio Grande, but most seen in Texas are migrants across the state. Some

An immature peregrine falcon prepares to eat a fresh duck dinner.

remain through the winter, particularly along the coast, although the majority continue southward as far as Argentina.

The peregrine falcon is an endangered species that suffered greatly from pesticide accumulations in its system, causing eggshell thinning and reproductive failure. By the mid-1960s, the eastern population was extirpated; no peregrines were breeding east of the Mississippi. The ban on DDT has contributed to a slow recovery, as have captive breeding and reintroduction programs. Peregrines now occur sparingly through the East, and some are even breeding in large cities, where they prey on flocks of feral pigeons and utilize bridge spans and tall buildings instead of their customary rocky ledges.

The adult peregrine falcon is a slaty bluish-gray above, while its pale underparts are heavily barred with gray. Most distinctive is a black cap that extends in broad wedges, often called "mustaches," below the eyes. The effect is not unlike an aviator's helmet, appropriate attire for this master of the skies. Males and females look alike, but as with other falcons, females are considerably larger than their mates. They range from 16 to 20 inches long and have wingspans of 40 to 46 inches. Immature peregrines are dark brown above and heavily streaked with brown below. The helmet, however, remains diagnostic in any plumage.

The prairie falcon (*Falco mexicanus*) also occurs in Texas, where it prefers grasslands at higher elevations. A species of western North America, it breeds sparingly in the Trans-Pecos and Panhandle and occasionally wanders eastward across the state. Much like the peregrine in size, shape and actions, it is a paler sandy-brown color with thin "mustache" marks below a pale crown. Blackish patches in the "armpits" distinguish it from other falcons in flight.

AMERICAN KESTREL

Falco sparverius

This smallest of the North American hawks was formerly called the sparrow hawk. The name has been changed to bring it into line with the nomenclature used in Europe, where the sparrow hawk is an accipiter related to our sharp-shinned hawk, and the tiny falcons are called kestrels.

A jay-sized raptor, the American kestrel has a wingspan of less than two feet. The male is smaller than his mate. Both have russet backs and tails, the only species of small hawk so colored. The female is barred with black above; the male has a black-tipped, unbarred tail and lighter barring on the back. His blue-gray wing coverts contrast sharply with the otherwise rusty plumage. Both sexes have two vertical stripes on each side of the white face, a double "mustache" where other falcons have but one.

Kestrels range throughout the Americas, from the Arctic treeline to Tierra del Fuego at the tip of South America. They breed in the northern and western portions of our state but are strangely absent along the coast and in South Texas. During migration and in the winter, however, kestrels are common almost everywhere in Texas. They prefer open prairies, farmlands and desert scrub but even move into busy cities. There they perch on fences and telephone lines and on the tops of trees with an unobstructed view. They also feed by hovering in place on beating wings before plunging after their prey. Insects constitute the bulk of the summer diet, with small snakes and lizards for variety. Small mammals and birds serve as winter prey in colder regions where insects are not readily available.

Kestrels nest in cavities, utilizing old woodpecker holes and niches in buildings to hold their four or five white eggs marked with brown. The female does most of the incubation, but both sexes attend the young. Competition with other hole-nesting

The female American kestrel lacks the blue-gray wing coverts of her mate.

birds, such as the introduced starling, has probably contributed to a slow decline of the kestrel in some regions of the country. It readily accepts nesting boxes, which are proving successful in restoring this tiny and lovely falcon to its former range.

The merlin *(Falco columbarius)*, formerly called the pigeon hawk, is only slightly larger than the kestrel, but its plumage is more like that of the peregrine. Males are blue-gray above with broad black bands across the gray tail. Females and immatures are brown. Both sexes have heavy streaking on the underparts and lack the strong facial markings of both kestrels and peregrines. The narrow, often obscure "mustache" mark extends downward from the eye.

AMERICAN VULTURES (Family Cathartidae)

Turkey vulture.

The American vultures are simply "buzzards" to most Texans, but that is an unfortunate misnomer. It's not that there is anything wrong with the term, but it was first applied to a common buteo hawk in Europe. Our red-tailed hawk would be a "red-tailed buzzard" over there. Noting some similarities, early settlers to this country called the newly discovered vultures "buzzards," and the name has persisted to the present day. However, New World vultures rate a family of their own, distinct from the hawks and from the Old World vultures of Europe, Asia and Africa. The latter group is actually more closely related to the hawks and eagles of the family Accipitridae than to our American vultures.

Three vulture species occupy North America. The largest, with a wingspread of up to ten feet, is the California condor *(Gymnogyps californianus).* When it reached near extinction in the wild, the remainder of the condor population was trapped for captive breeding. The ultimate aim is the reintroduction of captive-raised birds in enough suitable habitat to guarantee their future. The other two species, the turkey vulture and the black vulture, occur commonly in Texas.

American vultures have small, unfeathered heads and hooked beaks, both of which are useful adaptations for feeding on the carrion that makes up the major portion of their diets. Their talons are weak and poorly suited for grasping the living prey taken by most hawks and their close relatives. Vultures are gregarious birds, feeding together and assembling in large flocks to roost at night. During the nesting season, however, they become solitary. They do not build nest structures, but instead lay their eggs in sheltered nooks on rocky ledges, in hollow logs or trees, or even in deserted buildings.

TURKEY VULTURE *Cathartes aura*

A flock of huge dark birds sits huddled in a gnarled tree overlooking the Texas prairie. A light fog has soaked the grasses, and spider webs glisten in the cool, clear dawn. The turkey vultures slowly rouse themselves, but they remain quietly on their perches. They have maintained a lower body temperature through the night and are not yet ready to leave the roost. As the rising sun warms the air and chases the fog, they raise their long wings and hold them extended to dry. The added surface area also aids in thermoregulation, absorbing solar heat and warming bodies chilled by the long autumn night. Only when the sun is well up in the sky do the vultures launch themselves into flight.

With slow, deliberate beats of their six-foot wings, they seek a thermal to carry them aloft. Then, high above the ground, they sweep in wide circles within the bounds of the rising column of warm ascending air. The vultures sail with long, narrow wings tilted upward in a shallow V, rocking back and forth as they drift with the breeze. They spread their primary feathers like fingers, lowering wing-tip turbulence to permit slower flight without stalling. With scarcely a wingbeat they drift across the sky, watching with keen eyes for a morning meal far below.

The turkey vulture is a near-perfect sailplane with extremely low wing loading, the ratio of body weight to wing area. Able to soar effectively on weak thermals, it extends its summer range all the way into the cooler climate of southern Canada. The shorter-winged black vulture is less efficient in flight and is restricted to the warm South, where higher temperatures result in stronger thermals.

The turkey vulture has a naked red head and a long tail. Its slender wings appear two-toned from below, the steel-gray flight feathers contrasting with black wing linings. In contrast, the shorter, broader wings of the black vulture have white patches near the tips.

The turkey vulture breeds throughout Texas and withdraws from the colder Panhandle and Trans-Pecos regions in the winter. It lays its two white eggs, sometimes spotted and splotched with brown, in a sheltered niche, where both parents share the incubation chores. Hatching in 38 to 41 days, the downy white chicks have bare black faces. They are fed by regurgitation and mature slowly, not leaving the nest area until they are about 11 weeks old. Immature birds have blackish heads and lack the facial wrinkles of the adults.

Ornithologists have long wondered whether vultures locate their decaying food by sight or smell. Birds are particularly attuned to sight and sound. They do retain the necessary olfactory apparatus in their nasal passages, but most display little sense of smell. The turkey vulture seems to be an exception. It has a particularly well-developed olfactory lobe in its brain, and experiments indicate a keen sense of smell. Even so, it seems unlikely that odor can play a major role in detecting carrion from the altitude at which the vulture often forages. In that case, it seems more likely that one vulture spots a carcass and others within sight are guided by its actions.

Whatever the detection method, turkey vultures are important factors in nature's sanitation scheme. The genus name *Cathartes* is from the Greek *kathartes,* "a purifier." Gregarious birds except when nesting, vultures assemble peacefully for dinner, a few grunts and hisses sufficing for table talk. At the end of the day, when the earth cools and there are no thermals left to ride, they gather at communal roosts to sit stoically through the night.

Turkey vultures congregate at their evening roost. Some sit preening, while others spread their wings to the last warming rays of the setting sun.

BLACK VULTURE *Coragyps atratus*

To most Texans they are simply "buzzards," but the black and turkey vultures differ greatly in both their physical attributes and their habits. Both range widely across the state; however, the black vulture is an infrequent visitor to the Panhandle and the northern Trans-Pecos. Largely nonmigratory, it occupies much the same territory year-round, while the turkey vulture ranges farther north during the summer months and retreats southward for the winter.

The wings of the black vulture span less than five feet and have white patches near their tips. Its shorter wings and short tail make the black vulture less efficient in soaring, and while the turkey vulture sails endlessly on slender, two-toned wings, the black customarily alternates rapid flapping flight with short glides. These features—the short, white tipped wings; the very short, wide tail; and the characteristic flight—all serve to identify the black vulture well before its black head color can be seen.

The black vulture is essentially a bird of the South, ranging from the mid-Atlantic coast to Texas and down through the tropics to Chile and Argentina. More gregarious and aggressive than the turkey vulture, it frequently establishes itself near human settlements, where it feeds on garbage and refuse. It also descends en masse on carrion spotted by rival turkey vultures and keeps them away until it eats its fill. No carcass is too old. "The riper, the better," as one author put it. Unlike its red-headed relative, however, the black vulture is also known to capture small mammals, reptiles and young birds.

The nesting habits resemble those of the turkey vulture, but the eggs are light grayish green liberally marked with brown. Buff-colored down covers the hatchling chicks.

The black vulture is even more colonial, particularly on its winter roost, which may also serve as an information center. Well-fed birds, having found a good foraging area, are more likely to be followed as they leave the next day. When the day ends, however, the vultures come streaming in from all directions to take their places in the funereal assemblage. That, in fact, is what the name *atratus* means in Latin, "clothed in black, as if for mourning."

Black vultures lack the red head of the turkey vulture and have shorter, broader wings and tail.

According to Iroquois legend, Raweno, the Everything-Maker, was hard at work creating Rabbit while Owl, still unformed, watched from a nearby tree. Owl demanded a long neck like Swan's, bright red feathers like Cardinal's, a long beak like Egret's and plumes like Heron's. "Be quiet and turn around," warned Raweno, for no one was allowed to watch him work. When Owl persisted, Raweno grabbed him angrily. He pushed his head down onto his body, shook him until his eyes grew huge with fright, and pulled his ears until they stuck up straight. Since Raweno worked by day, he sentenced Owl to be awake only at night, and he rubbed mud across his body to make him a dingy gray. Once released, Owl flew off moaning, "Whoo, whoo, whoo."

Owls abound in the folklore of the world. An owl was one of the symbols in Egyptian hieroglyphics, and owls played a prominent part in ancient Mayan art and ritual. The Romans considered the owl an evil omen, a messenger of death and a companion of witches. Pima Indians believed that at death the human spirit passed into the body of an owl, and they gave owl feathers to a dying person to help him on his way.

Truth is almost stranger than the fiction, for owls are remarkable birds, uniquely adapted to their particular niche in nature. Their large, immobile eyes are set facing forward in their large heads, giving them the binocular vision necessary to judge distance and to pounce on their prey. To look around, however, they must swivel their heads, an amazing feat to watch. This forward-facing look, a caricature of the human face, accounts in part for the wide appeal of owls.

Young great horned owls try to intimidate an intruder.

In many species, the large external ear openings are asymmetrical. Not only do they have different shapes, but they are mounted at different heights on the sides of the head. This allows an owl to judge accurately the direction and distance of a sound, a valuable asset for nocturnal foraging. The upright feather tufts commonly called "ears" or "horns" do not play a part in the hearing process in any way, but their early characterization as "devil's horns" may have contributed to the owl's role in evil superstitions.

Soft feathers allow owls to fly silently, and the leading edge of the forward primary is serrated to disrupt the flow of air and further eliminate wing-tip noise. Thus owls arrive unannounced and swoop down on their unsuspecting prey with long, sharp talons. They gulp down smaller food items whole and tear larger ones into pieces with their strong, hooked beaks. Undigestible portions like fur and bones are later regurgitated as oval pellets, the biologists' key to tabulating a menu of their prey.

Approximately 130 species of owls occur throughout the world. The Texas checklist includes 15 in this family, although some of these are rare or accidental wanderers. The barn owl is in a separate family, the Tytonidae.

EASTERN SCREECH-OWL *Otus asio*
WESTERN SCREECH-OWL *Otus kennicottii*

Both gray (above) and red (right) phases of the eastern screech-owl occur in Texas, sometimes even in the same brood.

These common little owls were formerly considered a single species known simply as the screech owl (*Otus asio*), but they are now separated into two distinct species. Their ranges overlap in Texas near the Pecos River. The eastern screech-owl inhabits woodlands, parks and suburban yards throughout much of the state, although it is rare in the lower Panhandle. The western screech-owl replaces it in similar habitats in the Trans-Pecos. The two are most easily separated by their calls.

The eastern screech-owl, which ranges across the entire eastern half of the United States, has two different vocalizations. The first is a series of quavering whistles descending in pitch; the second is a long, single trill. The western screech-owl, found west of the Great Plains, utters a series of short whistles that accelerates in tempo, and its trill song consists of a short trill followed immediately by a longer one.

The screech-owls stand about eight inches tall. Blending with tree branches and foliage, they erect their feathered "ear" tufts and close their eyes to narrow slits. When threatened, they snap their bills to produce a loud popping sound. The bill of the eastern screech-owl is usually a pale greenish yellow; that of the western species is black.

Both red and gray phases of the eastern screech-owl occur. The color is not related to sex or age, and both phases may be present in the same brood. The rusty red form predominates in the southern states, while the gray one is more common in the North and, for some unknown reason, in southern Texas. The western screech-owl occurs only in the gray phase, although some birds of the

Pacific Northwest have browner plumage.

Screech-owls nest in tree cavities and old woodpecker holes and accept nest boxes readily. The four or five eggs are white and almost round, as is typical for most owl species. Cavity nesters have no need for camouflage colors, nor can rounded eggs roll from the nest. The male feeds the incubating female, and both feed and tend the downy white chicks that fledge four weeks after hatching.

The most nocturnal of the owls, screech-owls do most of their hunting in the first few hours after dark. They are opportunistic feeders, and their diets depend on their specific environments. Large insects and small mammals occupy a prominent place on a menu that also includes reptiles, amphibians, spiders, scorpions, earthworms, snails and an occasional bird. Frequent bathers, these little owls also plunge into shallow water after small fish and crayfish.

As with other owl species, screech-owls are often "mobbed" on their daytime roosts by jays and flocks of small songbirds. Birders, in fact, imitate their calls to lure other species within view.

GREAT HORNED OWL

Bubo virginianus

No bird is more impressive in a face-to-face encounter than the great horned owl. The massive owl is as big as our largest hawks, and its enormous yellow eyes glow like embers from beneath hooded brows. Long "ear" tufts are raised alertly, and the powerful feathered feet grip the perch with rapier talons. Approached too closely, it bobs and weaves, snapping its beak in a protest that must be heeded. Encountered on its daytime roost, it will fly away with slow, measured wingbeats, but it is fiercely protective around its nest and will attack if pressed. One need never wonder

why the great horned owl has been called "the tiger of the woods."

It ranges from the Arctic treeline in Alaska and Canada to the Strait of Magellan at the southern tip of South America. A year-round resident throughout Texas, it inhabits forests, prairies, deserts and even suburban parks and yards. As with other owls, the great horned does not build a nest, but lays its eggs in hollow trees or logs, on ledges, in shallow caves, or directly on the ground. It also utilizes old stick nests of crows, ravens and hawks. The nesting season begins very early, and Texas owls may already be incubating in late December or early January. Farther north, it is not unusual to see a great horned owl sitting covered with drifting snow. The slow development of the young makes an early start necessary.

Both parents share in the nest chores, although the female incubates more than her mate. The two or three rounded white eggs hatch asynchronously, as do those of other owls. Because incubation starts before the clutch is complete, the chicks emerge at different times, providing a set of stair-step siblings. When food is plentiful, they all survive. But when prey is difficult to find, the largest siblings take it all. While that may seem a harsh reproductive strategy, it assures that at least one young bird will grow up strong and healthy. That is enough to perpetuate the line, for great horned owls have been known to live for more than 28 years.

The nearby hoots of a great horned owl rank with the coyote chorus among the most thrilling songs of the Texas night. The characteristic call is a series of three to eight loud, deep hoots, the second and third combined as a short, quick phrase: *hoo hoohoo hoo hoo.*

Although chiefly nocturnal, these owls may also hunt during the day when opportunity permits. Rabbits and rodents are favored prey, but great horned owls take a variety of animals including snakes, lizards, large insects, birds and even fish. They are the principal predators of screech-owls, and they frequently

take skunks, a trait that is not difficult to ascertain, even among some old museum specimens. Not even porcupines are immune to surprise attacks, but the owl does not always win such encounters.

When prey is plentiful, great horned owls stock their nests with food or cache some in other locations, "incubating" a frozen cache in winter to thaw it before consumption. Nineteenth-century ornithologist Charles Bendire reported one nest that contained "a mouse, a young muskrat, two eels, four bullheads, a woodcock, four ruffed grouse, one rabbit, and eleven rats." The provisions totaled 18 pounds.

Young great horned owls (above) peer down at the world from near their nest cavity in an old willow tree. A West Texas great horned owl (following page) roosts through the day in a shady mesquite thicket.

BURROWING OWL

Speotyto cunicularia

One of the strangest and most beguiling members of the owl family is the burrowing owl. It lives in a hole in the ground, often on a treeless prairie or desert, and is most frequently seen standing beside its burrow or perched on a nearby fence post. Its long legs distinguish it from all other small owls.

Standing nine to ten inches tall, the burrowing owl is about the size of the common screech-owl, but its round head lacks the feathered "ear" tufts. Its face is framed with white and set off by a dark collar. White spots ornament the brown upperparts; the light underparts are spotted and barred in brown.

Burrowing owls occur over an amazingly wide range, from the prairie provinces of Canada southward through the western United States and the drier regions of Central and South America to Tierra del Fuego. Isolated populations also inhabit Florida and the West Indies. Those found in the northern states migrate southward for the winter.

These charming little owls breed locally in the Panhandle and West Texas, frequently associated with prairie dog villages, where they utilize the ready-made burrows and tunnel systems. Others adapt abandoned homes of ground squirrels and pocket gophers, enlarging them by kicking dirt out backwards with their feet.

They often form small colonies, probably because of available space among colonial rodents rather than through any social inclinations. Grasses, roots and pieces of dried cow dung line the burrow and cushion the five to nine white eggs. Both parents care for the young, capturing insects, mice, lizards and other tasty morsels with their sharp raptorial talons.

Burrowing owls winter throughout Texas but are most frequent in the western portions of the state. However, I have encountered them in a plowed field near Brownsville and in a concrete culvert draining a country road near Rockport. They have even

been found among the rocks of Galveston jetties and the Texas City Dike. One particular owl proved partial to a drain tile in the middle of Houston, while another spent several winter seasons in a trash heap on the Bolivar Peninsula, perching on a discarded bed spring to survey its coastal domain.

Pacific Coast and the isolated Florida populations are declining, probably due in part to poisoning and nest-site loss from efforts to control prairie dogs and ground squirrels. The species has been on the National Audubon Society's Blue List as rating special concern because of that decline.

I vividly recall a summer day when I spent the late afternoon hours sprawled in the grass of a prairie-dog town, watching a pair of burrowing owls with their young. At my cautious approach, one adult flew off a short distance and landed on a post. The other stood on the pile of dirt beside its home, bowing and bobbing in agitation, sometimes crouching low and uttering a series of chuckling sounds and a rapid chatter much like a rattlesnake's rattle. Soon, however, they quieted down and returned to stand at the mouth of the burrow.

Within minutes, two young owls marched out. Although nearly grown, and with the long-legged stride of their parents, they had the unmarked breasts and buffy wing-patches of juvenile plumage. There they all stood, sharing with me the fading day, until I crept slowly away.

I was reminded of a short passage written many years ago by ornithologist Alexander Wetmore: "Like an elderly couple enjoying the sunset on the porch, a pair of long-legged, stub-tailed owls stand on a mound of earth and peer into the twilight. Their heads swivel nearly full circle as they scan the plains."

A burrowing owl stands beside its hole in a fallow field.

Normally a denizen of woodlands and swamps, this barred owl chose to roost in the rafters of an old shed.

BARRED OWL
Strix varia

Almost everyone who has ventured out into the East Texas countryside at night has heard the deep, resonant call of the "eight-hooter": *Hoohoo-hoohoo, hoohoo-hoohooaw.* The song is usually interpreted as, "Who cooks for you? Who cooks for you-all?", the last *hoo-aw* drawn out in appropriate southern fashion. At other times the barred owl gives vent to an eerie assortment of squawks, barks and screeches that results in the name "crazy owl" in some regions.

This large, chunky owl is more frequently heard than seen. It remains well hidden on its daytime roost but is sometimes flushed from the woodlands, river bottoms, wooded swamps and parklands that it prefers. About 21 inches long, it has a large round head without the feather-tuft "horns" of the great horned owl, and its huge, limpid eyes are dark brown. The upper breast is barred crosswise with brown; the lower breast and belly are streaked lengthwise.

The barred owl ranges across Canada and throughout the eastern U.S., occurring southward to Honduras. It inhabits the northern and eastern parts of Texas, as far west as the Panhandle and the Edwards Plateau and south to Corpus Christi. A similar species, a southern race of the spotted owl (*Strix occidentalis*) made famous in the Pacific Northwest logging controversy, occurs as a very rare resident of the high Guadalupe Mountains.

Barred owls nest in tree cavities or appropriate old nests of hawks, crows and squirrels. The female incubates the two or three white eggs, while her mate brings her food. The chicks hatch in about four weeks and fledge six weeks later. They eat small mammals such as mice, squirrels, rabbits and shrews as well as reptiles, amphibians, large insects, crayfish and occasional fish. Regurgitated pellets of fur and bones around the nest and below feeding perches enable biologists to assess the food habits easily.

SHORT-EARED OWL

Asio flammeus

A red sun is sinking toward the western horizon, and the light on the coastal marsh begins to fade. It is time for the changing of the guard. The northern harrier that has been coursing back and forth above the reeds retires to its nighttime roost, and another large raptor takes its place. Nearly the size of a crow, it is pale buffy brown, and it flies with erratic, fluttering wingbeats, like a giant moth in the gathering dusk. The short-eared owl is on the hunt.

Less nocturnal than many other owls, it hunts primarily at dawn and dusk, roosting on the ground or on low perches during the day. It prefers open country instead of woodland habitats and is most frequently seen over the marshes, weedy fields and coastal dunes. The small "ear" tufts for which it was named are seldom noticed, but the dark facial disk makes its blazing yellow eyes particularly prominent. The long wings in flight show buffy patches on the upper side and black carpal patches at the wrists below.

The short-eared owl is nearly cosmopolitan, colonizing several continents and oceanic island groups. In North America, it breeds from coast to coast, from the high Arctic regions of Alaska and Canada to the central United States. It moves southward in the winter and ranges across most of the U.S. into Mexico. The short-eared owl migrates throughout Texas and remains in scattered locations through the winter. Most common along the coast, it begins arriving in early October and leaves again in April. Normally silent except in the breeding territory, it has an un-owllike call consisting of raspy, sneezy barks.

The short-eared owl feeds primarily on rodents but takes occasional birds and insects. It sets up winter feeding territories if prey is plentiful enough and may engage in communal hunting. Because it is declining over much of its range, it has been in-

The golden eyes of a short-eared owl blaze from within the dark facial disk.

cluded on the Audubon Society's Blue List of species that warrant special concern.

The long-eared owl (*Asio otus*) breeds occasionally in northern and western Texas and is a rare wanderer in winter across the state. Its long "ear" tufts are set close together, and

it looks somewhat like a small, crow-sized great horned owl. Its breast, however, is streaked lengthwise rather than being barred crosswise. Unlike the short-eared owl, it prefers to roost in trees in dense woodlands and thickets and hunts at night over nearby clearings and fields.

Barn Owls (Family Tytonidae)

Distinctive heart-shaped faces give the members of the Tytonidae the widespread name of "monkey-faced owls." The facial disks are more complete than those of the family Strigidae and serve as parabolic reflectors, funneling sounds to ear openings hidden beneath the soft feathers. So acute is their hearing that barn owls can detect and capture prey by sound alone. Long legs with bristly feathers on the toes and comb-edged middle claws are also family characteristics.

The single U.S. species, the barn owl, ranges widely around the world. Others encountered abroad are also recognizable by their facial similarities.

A barn owl found roosting on the ground bobs and weaves and snaps its beak at all intruders.

Barn Owl

Tyto alba

The barn owl is far more tolerant of people than most other owls. It nests and roosts in farm buildings, garage lofts, church steeples, and even in industrial plants and factories within the boundaries of our largest cities. This is the bird that Tennyson described: "Alone and warming his five wits, / The white owl in the belfry sits."

Its human neighbors often remain unaware of the owl's presence, however, because of its silent, nocturnal habits. It does not often call unless confronted near its nest, and then its cry of rage and warning is a raspy, hissing screech. This is the bird that should have been named the "screech owl," although "barn owl" is also appropriate. One reference notes that it probably serves as the source of many popular haunted-house stories.

This pale, long-legged owl has a distinctive heart-shaped face and dark eyes. The upperparts are rusty brown or golden buff, finely marked with tiny white spots and darker tracings. At close range, the intricately patterned feathers are some of the most beautiful in all the avian world. The underparts vary from white to pale cinnamon, and males tend to be paler than the females. In automobile headlights or in urban floodlights at night, the barn owl appears ghostly white, and such sightings lead to erroneous reports of snowy owls (*Nyctea scandiaca*). The latter, a wanderer from the Arctic, has been seen in Texas only on very rare occasions.

The barn owl occurs throughout the world. It breeds across most of the United States and withdraws only from the northern edge of its range in winter. It is a year-round resident in virtually all of Texas, except for the higher mountains, and nests in hollow trees and cliff niches in areas devoid of human habitation.

The white, elliptical eggs often rest on a cushion of regurgitated fur pellets and number from three to eleven. From five to seven is the average clutch; however, clutch size reflects

The heart-shaped facial disk distinguishes the barn owl from other owls.

the availability of prey. When food is scarce, particularly after severe winters, the owls seem able to reduce accordingly the number of eggs they lay.

The female incubates for about 32 days, with her mate attending and feeding her. Because incubation starts when the first egg is laid, the downy white chicks hatch at intervals and may differ in age by as much as two weeks. If food is plentiful most will survive, but during hard times the smaller babies fail to get their share. It will be nearly eight weeks before they leave the nest, and they face many threats in the weeks ahead. One study found that 60 percent of all barn owl young died within their first year.

Barn owls are considered the most beneficial of all North American owls in terms of our own human interests. Their diet consists largely of rodents, and they consume enormous quantities of rats and mice. Rollin Baker of Eagle Lake published a study in the September 1991 issue of *The Southwestern Naturalist* in which he determined the feeding habits of barn owls in six counties along the length of the Texas coast. By analyzing the contents of owl pellets collected at various roosts, he identified 20 different species of small mammals that had been consumed. These included shrews, young rabbits and opossums, pocket gophers, pocket mice, and a number of other native rats and mice. Skulls from house mice and Norway and roof rats were also prominent at roosts near residential areas and landfills. Baker found that the hispid cotton rat is the barn owl's chief source of food along the Texas coastal plain.

With their facial disks acting as parabolic reflectors to focus sounds on their sensitive ears, barn owls have amazingly acute hearing. Experiments have shown, in fact, that they are able to capture mice in total darkness, unaided by their sight. Their sensitive eyes and ears, combined with silent flight and raking talons, make them superb nocturnal hunters. The barn owl is nature's design for building a better mousetrap.

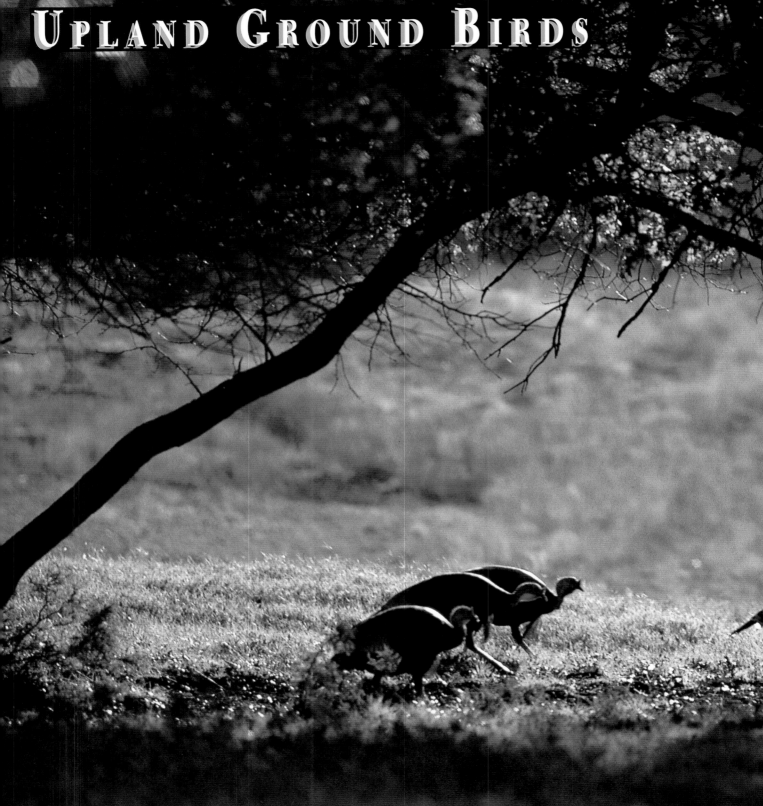

UPLAND GROUND BIRDS

irds of several different families are included in this section, and they have no close taxonomic relationships. They share common habits and habitats, however, and might prove confusing to the beginning birder. All are primarily ground-dwelling birds, occupying the drier upland prairies and woodlands or the arid desert regions. Most are patterned in shades of brown. They vary from game birds like the turkey and quail to the nighthawk and its relatives. The familiar roadrunner is also included here because of its appearance and habits, although its familial relationships are with the cuckoos and anis.

Wild turkeys.

PHEASANTS, GROUSE, TURKEYS AND QUAIL (Family Phasianidae)

The family Phasianidae includes a number of popular game birds and domestic fowl used as food around the world. They are chickenlike, ground-dwelling birds that fly strongly when pursued but seldom travel far. All possess short, strong bills and feed primarily on insects, seeds, berries and buds. Many have evolved elaborate courtship rituals, such as the intricate dances of the grouse and the posturing and strutting of the turkeys. Some taxonomists divide the group into several families; however, the AOU checklist presently lumps them into a single large, worldwide family. It includes the pheas-

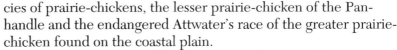

ants, grouse, turkeys and quail, as well as the wild precursors of such domestic birds as guineafowl, peafowl and chickens.

None of the Old World pheasants and partridges of the subfamily Phasianinae is native to America, but several have been introduced as game birds. The ring-necked pheasant has naturalized in the Panhandle, while efforts to establish the chukar (*Alectoris chukar*) in West Texas have been less successful.

The grouse, subfamily Tetraoninae, are restricted to the Northern Hemisphere, and several species occur across the northern states and Canada, including the three Arctic ptarmigans that molt to a snow-white winter plumage. Texas grouse are limited to the two species of prairie-chickens, the lesser prairie-chicken of the Panhandle and the endangered Attwater's race of the greater prairie-chicken found on the coastal plain.

Subfamily Meleagridinae contains only two turkey species. One, the wild turkey, is fairly common in many sections of Texas. The other, the ocellated turkey (*Agriocharis ocellata*), is restricted to the Yucatán Peninsula and adjacent regions.

Several species of quail (Odontophorinae) inhabit the United States. Two, the northern bobwhite and the scaled quail, range widely in Texas, while two others, the Montezuma quail and Gambel's quail, can be found in the western Trans-Pecos.

A ring-necked pheasant hen (above) alertly watches from the edge of the corn. From its perch on a rock, a scaled quail (left) greets the sunrise.

RING-NECKED PHEASANT

Phasianus colchicus

The ring-necked pheasant has traveled a long and tortuous route from its Asian homeland to the prairies and farmlands of the United States. Today it is a popular game bird in many of the northern and western states and even serves as the state bird of South Dakota. It has become a naturalized resident of the Texas Panhandle, but the population has been declining in recent years.

The large, gaudy rooster is unmistakable in its glossy bronze plumage marked with black, brown and green. The iridescent green head has fleshy red wattles around the eyes and feathered "ear" tufts, and there is usually a white ring around the neck. The long, pointed tail feathers give it an overall length of nearly three feet. Smaller and duller, the hen is buffy brown, with a shorter tail than her mate. The hen could be confused with the prairie-chicken, but the latter has an even shorter, square-tipped tail.

Pheasants feed in grainfields and weedy pastures and seek cover along overgrown fencerows and among the weeds and grasses of sloughs and creek beds. Roosters defend their territories and attempt to claim harems of several hens, each of which incubates her eggs and raises her chicks alone. The 6 to 15 olive-colored eggs are laid in a grass-lined nest, usually well hidden in the long grass, and hatch in 23 to 25 days. The downy chicks follow their mother soon after hatching and are independent at about ten weeks of age.

Pheasants often assemble in small flocks during the fall and winter months before separating again for the nesting season. Flushed from cover, they rise in a roar of wings with hoarse, cackling alarm calls.

The ring-necked pheasant was introduced into Europe from Asia by the ancient Greeks and Romans and may have reached Britain by the 11th century. It soon became a universal

The dark plumage of a male ring-necked pheasant suggests a mixture of genetic strains.

game bird throughout the European continent. Unsuccessful attempts to introduce it to America began as early as the 1730s, when the Governor of New York released a half dozen pairs from England. Benjamin Franklin's son-in-law, Richard Bache, also attempted to establish pheasants on his land in New Jersey in 1790. Similarly unsuccessful introductions took place in California in the 1870s.

But in 1882, Judge Owen Denny, Consul General in Shanghai, sent several dozen birds from China for release in Oregon's Willamette Valley. Another shipment followed in 1884. These pheasants multiplied in spectacular fashion, and when a hunting season was declared a decade later, an astounding 50,000 birds were shot on opening day. Hunters took as many as half a million during the 75-day season.

Since that initial success, state game agencies across the country have introduced pheasants for hunting purposes. Texas is no exception and, as Harry Oberholser notes in *The Bird Life of Texas*, they were "released relentlessly in many localities." A population survived for many years along the upper Texas coast, but pheasants are seldom seen there now.

By 1940, however, they were naturalized in the northern Panhandle.

A survey by the Texas Parks and Wildlife Department in October 1990 revealed that the Panhandle pheasant population has dwindled in recent years. Biologists believe the major cause to be the replacement of irrigated crops like corn and milo by dryland wheat and other grains. In addition, recent dry weather has resulted in egg failure and low nesting success as well as crop failures and reduced food resources.

According to some studies, much of Texas is too hot and dry to allow pheasant eggs to hatch properly. In 1969-70, state biologists released an Iranian pheasant strain tolerant of such conditions, and some of that genetic material may remain in the present population.

Not all ornithologists support the introduction of exotic birds to compete with native species, no matter what the recreational demands. Oberholser wrote of the various pheasant projects, "All sincere friends of native Texas birds hope that this naturalization experiment will fail completely." His sentiment, of course, is not shared by hunters across the continent.

GREATER PRAIRIE-CHICKEN   *Tympanuchus cupido*

Attwater's prairie-chicken (*Tympa-nuchus cupido attwateri*) is the most critically endangered bird in Texas. In spite of determined conservation efforts, the population continues to decline at a perilous rate. At the present rate, this Texan will become extinct within the decade.

Biologists regard Attwater's prairie-chicken as a subspecies or race of the greater prairie-chicken, a wide-ranging species found on remnant tall-grass prairies across the Midwest and Great Plains. The latter, too, is now uncommon, local, and seriously declining. Another race, the heath hen, vanished from the East Coast in 1932.

An estimated one million Attwater's prairie-chickens once occupied seven million acres of prairie along the Texas and Louisiana coasts. They were hunted heavily for food and sport until they received protection under modern game laws. But native tall-grass prairies, this bird's essential habitat, have all but vanished, posing the greatest threat to this remarkable species. Their numbers began to drop in the early 1900s, and by 1937 only 8,700 birds were found on 45,000 acres. Since then, continued urbanization, ranching and agriculture have chipped away at the coastal prairie.

Attwater's prairie-chicken was offi-cially declared endangered on March 11, 1967, and five years later the 8,000-acre Attwater's Prairie-Chicken National Wildlife Refuge was established near Eagle Lake. At that time, a census found 1,772 birds on the Texas coast. By 1988, that number dropped to 926; and in 1991, to 480. All that remained were in four major populations in only seven counties.

The question is not "What happened to the prairie-chicken?" notes a recent status report from the federal refuge. It is "What happened to the prairie?" At present, only two tracts of federal land—the Eagle Lake site and a portion of the Aransas National Wildlife Refuge—have been set aside

---

A male Attwater's prairie-chicken dances at dawn.

for prairie-chicken management. Together they provide a paltry 15,000 acres—one-fifth of one percent of the original seven-million-acre range.

But government biologists fear the bird cannot be saved on public lands alone. Sixty-five percent of the remaining population exists on private ranches in Goliad and Refugio counties. Thus any effective recovery plan must include incentives for proper management of those lands as well as an urgent public education program.

The prairie-chicken's springtime courtship display ranks as one of nature's greatest spectacles. The males patrol their sections of the lek, puffing out their orange neck pouches and dancing in competition for the females. Their feet beat so rapidly they are just a blur; the "booming" from the air sacs carries for half a mile.

The mated females steal away to lay their spotted eggs in shallow depressions among the tall, concealing prairie grasses. The clutch varies from 7 to 17 eggs, and the female incubates for 23 to 26 days. The downy, precocial chicks remain with their mother for several weeks, feeding on insects, seeds, berries and tender leaves. Predators, fire ants, parasites and disease all take a heavy toll on both the eggs and chicks.

A new program begun in the spring of 1992 may offer one last chance to save Attwater's prairie-chicken. Forty-nine eggs gathered from nesting areas in Colorado and Galveston counties, and incubated at Fossil Rim Wildlife Center near Glen Rose, produced 35 healthy chicks. They will form part of a captive-breeding program aimed at eventually returning prairie-chickens to the wild in other locations along the Texas coast.

The lesser prairie-chicken (*T. pallidicinctus*) resembles its slightly larger relative, but is paler and less heavily barred on the breast and belly. The male displays neck sacs of a darker reddish orange hue than those of Attwater's prairie-chicken. Found locally on the sandhills and short-grass prairie of the Panhandle, the lesser prairie-chicken, too, is slowly declining in its range and numbers.

WILD TURKEY *Meleagris gallopavo*

The largest game bird in North America is slightly smaller and more slender than the domesticated turkey derived from it. The dark-plumaged, iridescent tom is up to four feet long, with white barring on its flight feathers and a blackish "beard" protruding from its breast. Fleshy red wattles adorn the bare blue-and-pink head. The smaller, duller hen often lacks the breast tuft of the male.

Residents of open woodlands, turkeys forage on the ground for nuts, acorns, seeds and insects. They usually run rather than fly from danger, moving rapidly on long, powerful legs. However, they often fly up to roost in trees at night.

A displaying male erects his fan-shaped tail and struts about, chest thrown out, wings drooping and rattling violently. The warty growths and wattles on the head become swollen and intensely colored. Thus do the toms compete for hens to join their harems, and the courtship goes on day after day.

Once mated, the female steals off to make her nest in a shallow depression on the ground, laying an egg a day until she reaches a clutch of 8 to 15. During that time, she may return to the courtship arena each day at dawn, covering her eggs to hide them while she is gone. She incubates them for about four weeks, and the precocial chicks scamper after her soon after hatching. Although they grow rapidly and can make short flights within two weeks, they roost beneath their mother's wings, protected from chilling rains that could prove fatal. The brood remains together through the winter, often joining other hens and their chicks in a larger flock.

The wild turkey was introduced to Europe from its native America about 1530, when the conquistadores brought some back to Spain. Within a decade, the "turkie-fowle" graced British royal tables. According to Edward Gruson, "turkey" was a vague term used to describe foreign imports that were strange and exotic, especially those from Tartary and Asia Minor. The American turkey was apparently confused with the African guineafowl, which had come to Europe via the Turkish Empire, and both were called "turkey." Early English dictionaries, as well as those in other European languages, often mixed the words for turkey, guineafowl and peafowl. Thus this strictly North American bird, which failed to become our national bird by only one vote in a congressional ballot, still bears an alien name.

Turkeys reputedly were part of the first Thanksgiving dinner, and they were hunted relentlessly for food throughout the East. Overshooting and the clearing of woodland habitats took their inevitable toll, but more recent reintroductions have established

Wild turkeys (above and following page) are the largest of Texas' native upland birds.

wild turkeys again in most eastern states and throughout much of the West.

The eastern race of the turkey was extirpated in East Texas by 1930, and another, called Merriam's turkey, vanished from the Guadalupe Mountains. Only the Rio Grande race of the wild turkey remained as a viable population in Texas, particularly on the Edwards Plateau and on the large ranches of the southern coastal plain.

Since the early 1940s, thousands of Rio Grande turkeys have been trapped and transplanted to various portions of Texas, establishing the giant bird over a much wider range. That race will not reproduce in the wetter climate of East Texas, however, so that region is being restocked with eastern birds.

The Texas Parks and Wildlife De-partment began its eastern turkey restoration program in 1987. With the assistance of timber companies, sportsmen's groups and conservation organizations, more than 2,000 wild-trapped turkeys had been obtained from other states and released in 26 East Texas counties by the fall of 1991. The efforts continue, and the wild turkey can once again be spotted across a wide range of Texas habitats.

NORTHERN BOBWHITE
Colinus virginianus

Its clear, whistled call is a familiar sound in the farmlands, thickets and open woodlands of the eastern and central states. *Bob-white, bob-white, poor-bob-white,* the charming little quail calls its name. To most people it is simply "bobwhite" or "quail," for no other quail species is native to the East. The full name, northern bobwhite, is applied by ornithologists because related bobwhite species occur in tropical America. One race of the northern bobwhite, called the masked bobwhite, is severely endangered and is being reintroduced into southern Arizona from Mexico.

The chunky, short-tailed northern bobwhite is a rich reddish brown, mottled and flecked with black, buff and white. The male has a white throat and facial stripe; those of the female are buff-colored. The species ranges across most of Texas but rarely occurs west of the Pecos River. Nonmigratory, it remains throughout the year and breeds from early March into October.

This ten-inch eastern quail is a popular game bird. In 1981, 2.9 million bobwhites were taken by 267,000 Texas hunters. Because it breeds prolifically, however, the population can withstand heavy hunting pressure. Habitat loss, the scarcity of food, and nest failure from drought or flooding present far more serious threats than controlled hunting.

A grass-lined hollow in long grass or brush serves as a nest for the northern bobwhite, which often conceals it by weaving an arch of grasses. The clutch consists of 10 to 20 white or pale buffy eggs that hatch in 23 or 24 days. Both parents share in the incubation, and both care for the precocial, downy chicks. Although the young take their first short flights in only a few days, they remain together, often forming larger coveys with one or more other families when the chicks reach about three weeks of age.

The male northern bobwhite has a white face pattern; the female, buffy yellow.

Bobwhites feed and roost in coveys except during the nesting season. Freezing motionless at the first sign of danger, the covey explodes into the air with a loud whirring of wings when threatened. The birds roost in a compact circle, heads all pointing outward, sharing their warmth and maintaining a clear flight path for each should they need to escape.

SCALED QUAIL *Callipepla squamata*

The scaled quail replaces the northern bobwhite in arid regions of Texas, although the two species overlap widely in their ranges. Also called "blue quail" and "cotton-top," the scaled quail prefers the desert scrub and dry, brushy grasslands, where it feeds on weed seeds, green leaves and shoots, berries and insects. Long-legged and slightly larger than the bobwhite, it runs rapidly and resorts to flight only when pressed.

The name comes from the dark edging on the blue-gray feathers of the breast and upper back, which gives the bird a scaly appearance. The head bears a conspicuous crest tipped with white.

Except during the breeding season, scaled quail form large coveys, often with 30 or more birds. They communicate with loud location calls, variously written as *chip-chur* and *kuck-yur,* and low whistles usually syllabized as *pay-cos.* Scaled quail reside year-round in the Panhandle and Trans-Pecos Texas, ranging eastward onto the Edwards Plateau and south through the brush country to the lower Rio Grande.

The nest is a grass-lined hollow hidden beneath a bush. The 9 to 16 white eggs sometimes have brown spots, and they hatch in about three weeks. Although the female incubates more than her mate, both parents care for the precocial chicks. Juvenile birds resemble the adults but have more dark mottling and less conspicuous scaling.

Two other quail occur sparingly in far West Texas. Gambel's quail (*Callipepla gambelii*) inhabits the desert from El Paso southward along the Rio Grande to Big Bend. Although rare within our state, it becomes more common westward in the Sonoran Desert. The grayish male has a black face and rusty crown, while a long plume curves forward above the forehead of both sexes.

The Montezuma quail (*Cyrtonyx montezumae)* inhabits open woodlands and grassy slopes in the West Texas mountains. A rare and secretive bird, it is most frequently seen in the Davis Mountains. Plump and short-tailed, it has a crest at the back of the head. The male has a clownish black-and-white face pattern and spotted sides; the female appears browner and less distinctively marked. The species has also been called Mearns' quail and harlequin quail.

Scaled quail are also called "blue quail" or "cotton-tops."

CHACHALACAS AND GUANS (Family Cracidae)

These large birds of the tropical forests have long tails and short, rounded wings. Their strong legs carry them quickly through the underbrush, and they can be difficult to see, even though they are sometimes highly vocal. Although they resemble somewhat the Phasianidae in their large size and chickenlike habits, they are also at home in the trees, where they stride easily along the branches. Only the plain chachalaca occurs north of Mexico.

PLAIN CHACHALACA

Ortalis vetula

No one sleeps late in Bentsen–Rio Grande State Park when the chachalacas are around. The dawn chorus of tropical birds usually awakens campers, but that of these "Mexican pheasants" is almost deafening. From the treetops the cacophony begins—*cha-cha-lac, cha-cha-lac*—harsh, ringing tones audible throughout the campground. Famed ornithologist Dr. Arthur Allen once described their sounds as raucous cries of "keep-it-up, keep-it-up," followed by a lower "cut-it-out, cut-it-out."

Descending to the ground, the males strut among the flock as it parades through the campsites and picnic areas in search of breakfast snacks. The two-foot-long chachalacas are equally at home on the ground or in the trees, where they feed on fruits, buds, leaves and insects. Despite their size and raucous manner, they can be disconcertingly secretive and difficult to find at times, especially during the breeding season.

The nest is a crude mass of sticks, grasses, leaves and other debris installed in a tree or tangle of vines. Chachalacas often appropriate and add to an old nest of another bird. The female incubates her two or three unmarked white eggs, but both parents care for the young. The chicks hatch in about 25 days and leave the nest within two hours; in three weeks, they can fly.

One of several chachalaca species

A plain chachalaca fans its tail in a courtship pose.

found in tropical America, the plain chachalaca is dark gray-brown above and a richer buffy brown below. The long, rounded tail is tipped with white, and a slight crest may be raised at times.

The plain chachalaca is the sole U.S. representative of a family that includes the guans and curassows. Because of their large size and palatability, and because of major habitat losses, many of these cracids are vanishing from the forests of Central and South America. Texas chachalacas range along the Rio Grande from Falcon Dam to Brownsville and northward to Raymondville.

Along with many other tropical birds of similar distribution, they are sought by birders from around the world who come to such birding hot spots as Bentsen–Rio Grande State Park, Santa Ana and Laguna Atascosa National Wildlife Refuges, and the Sabal Palm Grove Sanctuary near Brownsville.

CUCKOOS (Family Cuculidae)

The cuckoo family comprises a large, widespread group of strangely disparate birds that includes the cuckoos, the anis and the roadrunners. The greater roadrunner is included here because of its similarities in appearance and habitat to some of the gallinaceous, chickenlike ground birds, although it differs anatomically. The other cuckoos are discussed in the section on the perching birds.

GREATER ROADRUNNER   *Geococcyx californianus*

Most Texans need no introduction to the roadrunner. It occurs throughout the Southwest, from Kansas to California, and southward to central Mexico. It resides year-round in most sections of Texas, but less commonly in the eastern portions of the state. This slender, long-legged ground cuckoo can be seen dashing across the desert or plains and may even be encountered in the East Texas Piney Woods. Capable of sprinting up to 15 miles an hour, it flies only under duress. When alarmed or curious, it slowly raises its shaggy crest and long, white-edged tail, uttering a strangely dovelike series of *coo*'s, or clattering its beak.

The roadrunner eats almost anything that moves—insects, spiders, scorpions, lizards, rodents and small birds. It is also famous as a snake killer. Legend has the roadrunner building a fence of cactus pieces around a snake so that it cannot escape, and while that technique is fictional, the bird's quick agility lets it capture even highly venomous prey. Darting in to stab a snake's head, it then grabs the squirming reptile in its powerful beak and thrashes it on the ground. About 90 percent of its food is animal matter, while fruit and seeds make up the other 10 percent.

Roadrunners remain paired and territorial throughout the year and may form lifelong bonds. They hide their stick nest in a cactus, shrubby bush or low tree and line it with grasses and leaves. The three to six white eggs hatch into homely, altricial chicks in 20 days. They grow rapidly and make their first flights at about 18 days of age. Soon after that, they begin catching their own food.

The greater roadrunner is so named to distinguish it from a similar species, the lesser roadrunner (*Geococcyx velox*), that occurs in portions of Mexico and Central America. Other regional names include "paisano" and "chaparral cock." Roy Bedichek, in *Adventures with a Texas Naturalist*, writes that he prefers the name "paisano" because it is euphonious and because this large bird will travel with you for miles across the lonely desert, where company is scarce, staying only a few yards ahead. "Paisano," Bedichek notes, suggests congenial companionship, a fellow traveler.

Few birds have more "personality" than the greater roadrunner (above left and opposite).

NIGHTJARS (Family Caprimulgidae)

Common nighthawk.

Few bird families are as poorly known and as misunderstood as the Caprimulgidae. Most people across the continent have seen the common nighthawk in action, but they give little thought to its familial relationships or its unique habits. With its tiny bill and small, weak feet, it bears no resemblance to the hawks—fierce raptors with hooked beaks and flashing talons. Conversely, another nightjar, the whip-poor-will, is well known from song and story, but few have encountered the live bird in the wild. Most birds of this family remain mysterious voices of the night, and that is a shame, for their special adaptations and subtle, understated beauty make them a fascinating group.

It is difficult even to select a name for this interesting worldwide family of nearly 70 species, for none in common usage is self-explanatory. "Nightjar" is the European name and comes from the nocturnal "churring" songs of several species, which are said to be "jarring the night."

Another common name, "goatsucker," dates back to ancient times when these birds were thought to suck at the udders of goats. Aristotle, in fact, wrote that "flying to the udders of she-goats, it sucked them and so gets its name. They say that the udder withers when it has sucked at it and that the goat goes blind." Even the scientific name, Caprimulgidae, means "milker of goats" in Latin. The myth probably began when people saw birds swooping among grazing goats, catching flies attracted to them. The birds would then be blamed if any nanny turned up dry.

Terence Shortt, in his *Wild Birds of the Americas,* comments on the validity of the legend: "Since a nightjar stomach might hold a teaspoonful, it would require a queue of about eighty 'goatsuckers' drinking in rapid succession to drain a good milch nanny (never mind that their mouths possess no sucking lips)."

Actually, their mouths are edged with long, stiff bristles that serve as efficient flytraps. Although the nightjars have tiny beaks, their gapes are very wide. With their enormous mouths and the rictal bristles, they scoop flying insects from the air as handily as a Golden-Glove first baseman nabs an errant throw. They also have the large eyes expected of nocturnal hunters.

By day, nightjars roost on the ground or sit lengthwise along low tree branches, where their beautifully marked, cryptic dead-leaf patterns provide near-perfect camouflage. They are most easily located and identified by their distinctive calls. The common North American nightjars, except for the nighthawks, are all named for their nocturnal vocalizations: whip-poor-will, chuck-will's-widow, poorwill and pauraque. They repeat their names over and over again. Early naturalist John Burroughs reported hearing one whip-poor-will call 1,088 times, pause for a moment, and then add 390 more.

Shortt comments that many campers have been delighted to learn they pitched camp within the territory of a whip-poor-will; however, the feeling is often short-lived. "An hour or so later, as the whip-poor-will begins its sixth or seventh series of no-pause, hundred-plus reiterations of its name, the enchantment palls and ears are covered in an attempt to escape . . . ." The chuck-will's-widow of East Texas, the common poorwill of the West, and the pauraque of the lower Rio Grande Valley all have similar persistent, onomatopoeic songs.

COMMON NIGHTHAWK   *Chordeiles minor*

The common nighthawk occurs throughout Texas, from sea level to an elevation of more than 8,000 feet. Many Texans know it as the "bullbat." Most frequently seen over open grasslands and fields, it also inhabits cities and towns, where it wheels across the sky on long, pointed wings, swooping and whirling erratically to catch insects in midair. A familiar summer resident across North America, from Canada into Mexico, it departs to spend the winter in South America.

Nighthawks are gray-brown above, mottled with a cryptic black pattern. The white underparts are barred with dusky gray. The male has a white throat and a white bar near the tip of the shallowly notched tail; the female's throat is buff-colored. Both sexes display a distinctive white bar on both upper and lower wing surfaces that serves as the best field mark in flight.

Nighthawks lack the long rictal bristles of other nightjars and are more active during daylight hours. Although they prefer to forage at dusk, they might be seen even at midday, especially when storm clouds build and rain

threatens. The aerial circus takes place, too, around the lights of parking lots and sports stadiums, where nighthawks pursue insects attracted to the light.

By day, the common nighthawk roosts on the ground and on posts, or perches lengthwise on tree limbs and wires. Flat roofs of city buildings provide habitats for nesting as well as roosting, for the two speckled eggs are simply laid on the bare ground. The eggs hatch in about 19 days, and the downy young make their first flights three weeks after hatching.

Unlike the other nightjars, which call their names repeatedly through the night, the common nighthawk utters a simple nasal *peent* in flight. That is often accompanied by a hollow booming sound caused by the wings. Throughout the nesting season, the male stages a courtship dis-

play in which he dives toward the ground and then pulls up quickly. The rush of air makes the primary feathers vibrate and creates the sound.

Although the common nighthawk ranges across most of the country, it has been slowly declining in many places. Concern for its future has prompted its recent inclusion on the Audubon Society Blue List.

The lesser nighthawk *(Chordeiles acutipennis)* resembles the common nighthawk, but it is slightly smaller and paler, and the white bar across the wing is closer to the tip. A bird of the arid southwestern deserts and scrublands, it tends to fly lower and with a more fluttering wingbeat. It also lacks the characteristic *peent* call of the common nighthawk and utters a low *chuck chuck* or a soft whinnying sound somewhat like the trilling song of a toad. Sometimes called the "trilling nighthawk" or the "Texas nighthawk," it is a summer resident of the western and southern portions of the state.

A common nighthawk dozes through a sunny day on a roadside fence post.

CHUCK-WILL'S-WIDOW   *Caprimulgus carolinensis*

The chuck-will's-widow is more often heard than seen in the woodlands, river bottoms and cedar-covered hills of eastern and central Texas. If spotted in the beam of a flashlight, its enormous eyes glow with an eerie luminescence. It is a beautiful and intriguing denizen of the night woods.

The foot-long chuck-will's-widow is the largest of our nightjars. A southern cousin of the whip-poor-will, it ranges from Kansas and New Jersey southward to the Gulf States. Many people confuse the two species, and both are collectively called "whip-poor-will" by nonbirders in many areas. Birders often refer to them by the shorter and more familiar "chuck" and "whip."

The chuck is larger and more reddish brown than the whip, and its throat, above a white necklace, is buff-colored rather than black. Both have long tails and rounded wings and

fly with a characteristic mothlike flutter, flushing from the forest floor or from low branches to fly a short distance before dropping to the ground again. Their cryptic, mottled plumage provides perfect camouflage among fallen leaves. Males have white on the outer tail feathers, and that white is more extensive on the whip-poor-will. Females' outer tail feathers are tipped with buff.

The loud song of the chuck is a distinctly four-syllabled, whistled *chuck-will's-wi-dow,* with the accent on the second and third syllables. The initial *chuck* is lower in pitch and often inaudible at a distance. Although not as persistent as the whip-poor-will in its nocturnal vocalizations, the chuck-will's-widow can often be heard calling its name again and again in the woodlands of eastern Texas.

A migrant through the eastern half of the state, it remains through the

summer to nest in northeastern and central Texas and sparingly southward. The full extent of its breeding range will be better defined on completion of the forthcoming atlas of Texas breeding birds. The chuck-will's-widow winters in Central and South America and the West Indies.

The huge mouth of the chuck-will's-widow opens to a gaping cavern more than two inches across and is surrounded by long, stiff rictal bristles that help funnel in food. Its diet consists primarily of insects captured in flight, but the chuck occasionally catches small birds and swallows them whole.

The two buff, pink or whitish eggs are blotched with camouflage brown or gray and are laid directly on the leaf-covered ground. The female incubates them alone and receives little or no help from her mate in raising her two young. The downy chicks hatch in about 20 days and are capable of sustained flight in about 17 days more. At first they remain near the nest location, but they move about as they grow, "hopping like toads," as one author describes them.

The whip-poor-will (*Caprimulgus vociferus*) ranges northward to the Canadian border and is less abundant through the Gulf States. It migrates through eastern Texas and remains to breed sparingly along the northern edge of the state. A disjunct population also nests in the Guadalupe and Chisos mountains of West Texas.

The pauraque (*Nyctidromus albicollis*) of the lower Rio Grande Valley resembles the chuck-will's-widow in form and habits but has broad white bars across the wings, like those of the nighthawks. It ranges northward sparingly to the Corpus Christi area and can sometimes be spotted along the roadsides at dawn and dusk. The loop roads at Bentsen–Rio Grande State Park remain a favorite place to see this South Texas specialty, whose nocturnal song is a low *pur* note followed by a higher *wheeer.*

Camouflage plumage of a chuck-will's-widow conceals it among fallen leaves.

COMMON POORWILL   *Phalaenoptilus nuttallii*

The classical Greeks believed that swallows burrowed into the mud at the bottom of ponds and lakes to hibernate through the winter. How else, they reasoned, could the seasonal disappearance of such species be explained? Much later, of course, scientists discovered and tracked avian migration routes, and the mystery was solved. Birds simply flew to more hospitable climes. They certainly did not hibernate.

Then, on December 29, 1946, biologist Edmund Jaeger and two of his students made a startling discovery. In a hollow in a canyon wall in the Chuckawalla Mountains of southern California, they found a poorwill. "When we had observed the bird quietly for more than ten minutes without noticing any motion, I reached forward and touched the bird without evoking any response," wrote Jaeger in the January-February 1948 issue of *The Condor*. "I even stroked the back feathers without noticing the slightest movement. Was our bird dead, sick or just deep in winter sleep? We left the place for awhile, then about two hours later returned. The Poor-will was still in its same position. I now reached forward and picked it up, freely turning it about in my hands. It seemed to be of unusually light weight and the feet and eye-lids when touched felt cold. We made no further attempt to be quiet; we even shouted to see if we could arouse our avian 'sleeper.' I finally returned it to its place in the crypt; but while I was doing this I noticed that it lazily opened and shut an eye, the only sign I had that it was a living bird."

Ten days later Jaeger returned to find the poorwill still in its niche, but when picked up it "opened an eye and began to make a variety of queer high-pitched whining or squeaky mouse-like sounds. After some moments it opened its mouth widely as if yawning and then resumed its quiet." That afternoon, when picked up again for photographs, it "whipped open its wings and flew out of hand in per-

fectly normal flight . . . ." The following year Jaeger found what was presumably the same bird in the same little hollow, again lethargic with the cold.

Jaeger's discovery shocked ornithologists, for the poorwill is the only bird known to hibernate for long periods of time. While most migrate from their summer range, some apparently survive by dropping their body temperature and lapsing into a state of torpor to conserve energy.

The seven- to eight-inch common poorwill is the smallest of our nightjars. Brownish gray in color, it has a white band across the throat and white tips on the outer tail feathers. The tail and wings are short and rounded, and the flight is fluttering and mothlike. Roosting on the ground, the poorwill flutters up to snatch flying insects from the air and

returns to its station, where it blends perfectly with its surroundings.

The poorwill breeds in the West, from British Columbia to Mexico, and winters mainly south of the U.S. In Texas, it ranges across the western half of the state and locally eastward to Austin, San Antonio and Beeville. A few remain through the winter in the southern counties. Inhabiting dry hillsides, canyons and deserts, it lays its two eggs directly on the ground or atop a flat rock, where both parents share the incubation and chick-rearing chores.

Although the common poorwill frequents roadsides and is sometimes spotted in the headlights of approaching cars, it is more often heard than seen. At a distance the song is a characteristic loud, repeated *poor-will,* but at close range a softer third note is audible, *poor-will-ip.*

Only the sharpest eyes would spot this common poorwill on the ground.

PIGEONS AND DOVES

The pigeons and doves, together with a few Old World relatives not found in North America, form a scientific order of their own, the Columbiformes. They are not closely related to any other group of birds. Because of their status as a separate order, and because most people recognize the generic "dove" by its form and habits, this group is treated separately. There is no clear-cut distinction between pigeons and doves, and the names are often used interchangeably. The wild ancestor of the ubiquitous domestic pigeon is known to ornithologists and birders as the rock dove. For the most part, however, "pigeon" is used for the larger species; "dove," for the smaller. All have plump, muscular bodies and small, rounded heads that bob back and forth as they walk. Strong, fast fliers, the larger species are popular as game birds.

One native American species, the passenger pigeon (*Ectopistes migratorius*), was apparently the most abundant bird in the world during the early days of our country's history. Ornithologist Alexander Wilson estimated that one flight contained two billion birds, while John James Audubon watched a single flock pass overhead for three days and estimated that at times as many as 300 million pigeons flew past in an hour.

Texas shared in this avian bounty. According to Robin Doughty's *Wildlife and Man in Texas*, a professional hunter named Captain Flack likewise reported a flock flying over Washington County for three consecutive days in 1853. Another hunter brought down 87 birds with one blast from his shotgun. Charles Terrell wrote that during his boyhood in Wise County in 1870 enormous numbers of pigeons congregated to roost in the evening, and large trees toppled under their weight.

Shaped much like the smaller mourning dove, the passenger pigeon measured about 16 inches long and weighed about nine ounces. Beautifully colored, with a slaty blue back and deep rosy pink breast, it was slim and elegant. The long, slender, graduated tail was edged with white.

Passenger pigeons provided a valuable food resource for early American settlers, and no one could imagine the eventual extinction of the species. It came with amazing rapidity. As the railroads stretched across the Midwest, millions of pigeons were shipped to markets on the Atlantic Coast. A single Michigan market hunter shipped three million birds in 1878; 11 years later, the species was extirpated in that state. When a flock numbering 250,000 pigeons was discovered in the Great Lakes Region, a mob of hunters arrived, alerted by telegraph. Fewer than 10,000 birds survived.

By 1900, the passenger pigeon was gone from Texas and the nation. Some references list records for that year; others assert the last verified sighting of a wild bird was in 1899. The last individual, a female named Martha, died at the Cincinnati Zoo in 1914, and what was once this planet's most numerous bird was extinct.

It seems unlikely that hunting pressure alone could have exterminated every bird, but the full details of the event remain a mystery. Passenger pigeons normally laid a single egg and had a very low reproductive rate. There were apparently survival advantages to assembling in such enormous flocks for breeding and foraging. Once those flocks were decimated and the surviving birds broken up into smaller groups, the passenger pigeons could not maintain a reproductive rate sufficient to sustain themselves.

Two common ground-doves join a larger mourning dove for a drink.

PIGEONS AND DOVES (Family Columbidae)

Nearly 300 species of the family Columbidae populate the world. A dozen occupy the Texas checklist, although a few of those species occur only as rare wanderers from other regions. The rock dove, or domestic pigeon, was introduced to the U.S. from the Old World and now lives virtually throughout the state while the ringed turtle-dove (*Streptopelia risoria*) has escaped captivity to colonize several Texas cities. The latter has creamy tan or whitish plumage with a narrow black band across the back of the neck. Two of the larger doves, the mourning dove and the white-winged dove, are abundant enough to support widespread hunting.

These chunky, fast-flying birds feed primarily on grain, weed seeds and berries. Rather than feeding their young on insects as do most other seed-eating birds, they feed them "pigeon's milk," a nourishing liquid produced from the lining of the crop. The milk contains more protein and fat than cow or human milk and is fed exclusively to the young hatchlings by both parents. The production of crop milk is an unusual trait shared by two other widely disparate types of birds, the flamingos and the penguins.

Doves exhibit an unusual method of drinking as well. While most birds dip their bills and then tip their heads back to let the water run down their throats, doves immerse their bills and suck up the water without raising their heads.

The low, rather melancholy calls of the various doves and pigeons contain a variety of cooing notes, the tempo and sequence unique to each species. Long considered symbols of peace, family members are in reality anything but peaceable. Terence Shortt, in *Wild Birds of the Americas*, writes of the "dove of peace": "Few birds are less qualified: they are aggressively amorous and, while tender and devoted to their young, their love is marked by irritability and pugnacity."

Young Inca doves (above) in a patio hanging basket. White-winged doves (right) line a backyard fence.

ROCK DOVE
Columba livia

With a thunder of wings, the local pigeon flock descends on our backyard bird feeder. More than a dozen birds crowd onto the raised platform only 18 inches square, some standing on the backs of others, all squabbling for the choicest seeds. Startled by some movement or sound, they fly up to perch in a row on the power line, a few swelling their necks and bowing to the others in a frenzy of courtship passion. Then they are off again, winging en masse across the neighborhood.

There probably are no more universally recognized birds in the world than the common domestic pigeons. They inhabit virtually every city, wandering along the sidewalks and descending on building roofs and backyard patios. I have waded through throngs of them in the parks of New York City and walked with them along the streets of Ushuaia, Tierra del Fuego, the southernmost town in the world.

This portly urban bird descended from the wild rock dove of Eurasia and northern Africa. Once found from the British Isles through the Mediterranean region, it inhabited sea cliffs and rocky slopes. Truly wild rock doves still exist in that region, but their lineage is blurred by the myriad domestic forms now found among the millions of feral birds of the brick-lined city canyons.

In its original form, the rock dove is gray, with the head and neck darker than the back. There are black bars on the wings, a broad black band at the tip of the tail, and a white patch on the rump. Many of the feral birds retain that general pattern, but a host of multicolored forms have developed through centuries of domestication and selective breeding. Neighborhood flocks contain nearly black birds, brown ones and brindled grays and tans. Many have an iridescent green or purple sheen on the neck.

Pigeons have been domesticated

Feral pigeons display a variety of plumages.

for thousands of years. Since the days of Solomon they have been bred and trained for their homing ability. They helped Caesar conquer Gaul and served the Saracens against the Crusaders. According to one account, the Sultan of Baghdad set up a pigeon post in 1150 to link his empire.

Parisians, under siege by the Prussian army in 1870, sent out crated pigeons by balloon, the birds returning with vital information. Thousands of combat pigeons flew over the trenches during World War I, and the most famous, Cher Ami, won the Croix de Guerre for carrying a message that saved the American "Lost Battalion." Although badly wounded, it flew 25 miles across enemy lines. Carrier pigeons were vital messengers even with the technology of World War II.

Hobbyists now train homing pigeons as racers; others, as fancy show breeds. Well-trained homing pigeons, air-expressed 1,500 miles, have returned to their lofts three days after release.

Domestic pigeons first reached North America in 1606, when Lescarbot brought them to Nova Scotia.

They were probably introduced to the United States as early as 1621. Now they are everywhere, building their crude nests of twigs, straw and even nails on window ledges, under bridges and in old barns, laying two white eggs as often as five times a year in warmer climates.

The pride of pigeon fanciers, they may also be the bane of city officials as they foul buildings, statues and water supplies. Whether a delight or a curse, however, we must give the offspring of the rock dove credit for being amazingly adaptable.

BAND-TAILED PIGEON
Columba fasciata

The large, handsome band-tailed pigeon has a purplish sheen on the head and breast and a broad, pale gray band on the rounded tail. Juvenile birds lack the narrow white collar on the nape of the neck displayed by adults. Gregarious birds, band-tails often assemble in large flocks and might be mistaken for feral rock doves. However, they are slightly larger and lack the black band on the tip of the tail and the white rump patch of the latter. Its wilder habitat and its tendency to land in trees also aid in identification.

A native western species, the band-tailed pigeon occupies the coniferous forests of the Northwest and the oak woodlands of the more arid Southwest, ranging from British Columbia to Central America. It is also becoming increasingly common in parks and suburban areas. In Texas, it inhabits the Guadalupe, Davis and Chisos mountains of the Trans-Pecos and descends to lower elevations in the winter to wander more widely through the western portions of the state. Its call is a low, repeated, owllike *whoo-whoo* or *whoo-oo-whoo*.

A crude stick platform on a horizontal branch or in the fork of a tree serves as a nest and usually contains a single white egg. Both parents incubate the egg and care for the helpless, altricial chick, feeding it on pigeon's milk from their crops for about three weeks. Mature birds consume great quantities of acorns, berries and seeds.

Another large species, the dark gray red-billed pigeon *(Columba flavirostris),* occurs as a very rare spring and summer resident of the lower Rio Grande Valley. It sings a drawn-out song with a long *coooo* followed by three repeated *up-cup-a-coo's.* A largely migratory species, it is one of the true birding prizes of the remnant woodlands of deep South Texas.

Band-tailed pigeon.

WHITE-WINGED DOVE
Zenaida asiatica

Accounts of early settlers in Texas state that from about 1870 to 1920 there were several million white-winged doves in the lower Rio Grande Valley. However, wholesale clearing of the land destroyed most of the scrub woodlands used for nesting and, according to Oberholser, hordes of hunters had contests to see who could kill the most. By 1930, the population had begun to decline.

With conversion of the native brushlands to farming, the doves moved to mature citrus groves and by 1950, 80 percent of the white-wings were nesting in orange and grapefruit trees. Increasing crop diversity, periodic freezes that killed old groves, and saturation spraying with pesticides and herbicides subsequently took a heavy toll. Although the dove population will never again reach its former numbers, the white-wing remains a popular game bird in South Texas, and tracts of land are being purchased to serve as refuges for doves and other declining species.

The white-winged dove is a summer resident north to Uvalde, San Antonio and Beeville and ranges along the Rio Grande to El Paso and westward through the desert Southwest. It occasionally wanders onto the Edwards Plateau and along the upper coast; a small colony has become established in Galveston. Most spend the winter far southward in Central America.

The heavy-bodied white-wing can be distinguished from the mourning dove by the large white wing-patches and by its shorter, rounded tail with broad white corners. The wing-patches, however, show only as narrow white lines on the folded wings of perching birds. There are several variations of the loud, low-pitched cooing calls. One of the most frequent is usually interpreted as *Who-cooks-for-you?*

White-winged doves nest singly or in colonies, building their crude stick nests in mesquite, citrus or other leafy

A white-winged dove perches on a spiny ocotillo stalk.

trees. Farther west, they colonize the saguaro-paloverde desert scrub, and they move freely into towns. Both parents incubate the two white to pale buff eggs that hatch in two weeks, and both feed the hatchlings on pigeon's milk. Within four days the chicks also consume seeds, and they leave the nest at about two weeks of age. Grain and other seeds and the fruits of cacti then make up the major portion of the white-wing's diet.

MOURNING DOVE

Zenaida macroura

The mourning dove is the most abundant and widespread dove in Texas and across the continent. Harry Oberholser notes in *The Bird Life of Texas* (1974) that it is the only native Texas bird that has been documented as occurring in every one of the state's 254 counties; only the imported house sparrow is equally ubiquitous. The most widely hunted of all game birds across the country, millions of mourning doves are shot each year. They manage to maintain their population because they adapt to virtually every habitat and nest at least twice a year. Texas birds breed virtually year-round, with a peak season from March through September.

The mourning dove ranges from Canada to Panama and continues to expand northward, although the northern population is at least partially migratory. It inhabits farmyards, cultivated fields, prairies, open woodlands, deserts and suburban parks and yards. The crude twig nest is placed in a tree, shrub or cactus, but mourning doves may also nest directly on the ground in treeless areas. Built by the female as the male brings materials, the nest is so flimsy that the two white eggs can often be seen through it from below. Both adults incubate, the male during the day and the female at night, and the eggs hatch in about 13 or 14 days. Fed first on pigeon's milk and then on seeds, the fledglings leave the nest in about two weeks.

The trim-bodied mourning dove has a small, round head and slender neck. The long, pointed tail is edged with white. Although the overall plumage is a soft brown, there are black spots on the upper wings of the adults. A pinkish tint on the breast, a subtle wash of shimmering, iridescent colors on the neck, and blue rings around the eyes make it a surprisingly lovely bird when seen up close. Its familiar low, mellow call, *ooah-coo-coo-coo,* is mournful yet pleasing and brings forth images of warm country evenings and the smell of new-mown hay.

The genus of the mourning and white-winged doves, *Zenaida,* was named for Princess Zenaide Charlotte Julie Bonaparte, according to Gruson. The daughter of Joseph Bonaparte, the King of Spain from 1808 to 1813, Zenaide married her cousin, Charles Lucien Bonaparte, in 1822. The latter was one of Europe's greatest early ornithologists and worked in America for eight years. The other portion of the mourning dove's scientific name, *macroura,* is from the Greek for "long-tailed."

Mourning dove (opposite).
Inca dove (below).

INCA DOVE

Columbina inca

At a time of declining wildlife populations and threatened or endangered species, a few birds are expanding their ranges against the trend. One of these is the dainty, delightful Inca dove. It has moved gradually northward from Mexico and Texas' Rio Grande Valley with settlement and agricultural expansion. A friendly bird, it frequents suburban yards and even nests in patio flower boxes. It prefers to eat on the ground or on platform-type bird feeders and consumes a wide variety of seeds.

The Inca dove measures only eight

inches long and weighs less than two ounces. The gray body feathers have dark edges and impart a conspicuous scaly appearance that readily distinguishes the Inca from the larger mourning dove. Chestnut wing-patches show in flight, while the comparatively long, squared tail has white edges when spread. The even smaller ground-dove also flashes rusty wings but has a short, dark tail.

Inca doves inhabit the semi-arid southwestern states and range through Mexico and Central America to Costa Rica. In Texas, they have moved northward to Austin and the Houston-Galveston area and along the Rio Grande to El Paso. In the early 1960s, a small colony was centered around Kempner Park in Galveston, but the birds were difficult to find elsewhere on the upper coast. Now the Inca dove is a common resident of that region, and wanderers have been spotted as far north as Kansas and Arkansas.

Like most of the others in its family, the Inca dove builds a flimsy twig platform for its two white eggs, and both parents incubate them and care for the newly hatched chicks. Adults are aggressive during courtship and battle furiously among themselves; however, in cold weather they often huddle together in a feathered pyramid to keep warm, some birds perching on the backs of others until the pile is three or four layers deep.

Males puff out their chests and strut regally before the females of their choice, bowing and cooing with tails fanned. The song is a distinctive, double *ooh-coo* call that Roger Tory Peterson claimed sufferers of Texas' summer heat might interpret as, "no hope." It is a mellow, pleasing song, however, that is becoming increasingly common in the state.

COMMON GROUND-DOVE
Columbina passerina

The chunky little ground-dove, at six inches, is the smallest of all our native doves. Scarcely larger than a sparrow, it has scaly feathering on the head and breast. In flight it flashes bright chestnut primaries and wing linings and a short, blackish tail. The latter distinguishes it from the slightly larger, longer-tailed Inca dove. The soft, two-syllable call has been described in various field guides as a repeated, ascending *coo-oo, woo-oo* or *wah-up,* illustrating the difficulty of translating avian songs to human words.

The common ground-dove inhabits southern Texas from the Rio Grande to the central coast, Austin and the Big Bend region, and wanders less commonly to the Houston-Galveston area, particularly in winter. A few records exist for extreme northern Texas and the Panhandle. Its range extends across the southern edge of the United States from Florida to California and southward to Costa Rica and South America.

In the southeastern U.S., the ground-dove prefers farmlands and orchards, but the Inca dove occupies that niche in Texas. The ground-dove, instead, seems more at home in the brushy rangeland, open woodlands and desert scrub. It is largely terrestrial, as the name implies,

Its short, dark tail and tiny size identify the common ground-dove.

and forages for seeds and berries, often in small groups. It seems a tame, friendly little bird as it walks along, head nodding with each stride, but an old Creole superstition threatens misfortune to anyone who cages a ground-dove. In modern times, of course, the superstition is backed by laws that prohibit keeping any of our native wild birds.

Common ground-doves make only a half-hearted attempt at nest-building, constructing a flimsy platform of a few twigs and weed stalks in a tangle of vines, a cactus or a low tree. Some lay their two white eggs directly on the ground with even less preparation. Both sexes share the incubation chores, and the eggs hatch in only 12 to 14 days. Presumably fed on "milk" from their parents' crops, the young grow rapidly and are ready to leave the nest in about 11 days. The adults soon nest again, raising two or more broods each year.

The ruddy ground-dove (*Columbina talpacoti*) is a similar, Latin American species that has been reported a few times in the Rio Grande Valley and in the Big Bend region. It lacks the scaly, dark-edged feathering of the common ground-dove, and the male has rusty upperparts. A number of other related ground-doves range through Central and South America.

WHITE-TIPPED DOVE

Leptotila verreauxi

The white-tipped dove inhabits the dense thorn-scrub woodlands and river thickets of the lower Rio Grande Valley and ranges as far southward as Argentina. It is the only U.S. representative of the genus *Leptotila*, which contains several very similar tropical species. Birders come to Texas from across the continent to search for it at Santa Ana and Laguna Atascosa National Wildlife Refuges, the Sabal Palm Grove Sanctuary near Brownsville, and Bentsen–Rio Grande State Park, for it can be found nowhere else in the country.

A large, plump dove about the size of a white-winged dove, it has a dark gray-brown back and pale underparts. It lacks the white wing-patches of the white-wing and the long, pointed tail of the mourning dove. Instead, its tail is rounded and has white corners when fanned in flight. The white-tipped dove was known until recently as the white-fronted dove, for the white forehead just above the bill.

This shy, secretive bird feeds on the ground, seldom venturing far from the protective undergrowth. The best sign of its presence is its ghostly call, *oo-wooooo,* like the sound produced by blowing across the top of a bottle.

The female lays her two creamy-buff eggs in the flimsy nest typical of the dove family, but not all of the breeding biology has been studied. Presumably it is much like that of the other doves.

The white-tipped dove is a Texas resident only in the Rio Grande Valley.

HUMMINGBIRDS

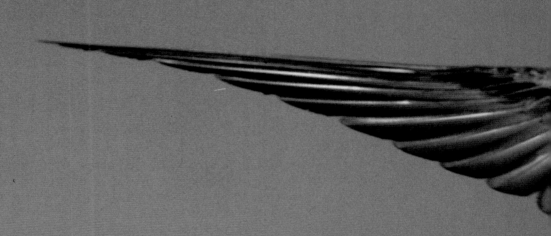

These smallest of all birds rank among the most popular with birders and nonbirders alike, yet they are often poorly understood. Hummingbirds range throughout the Americas, from Alaska to Tierra del Fuego and across the Caribbean, but they do not occur in the Old World. Thus they were looked on with amazement by early explorers and settlers to this land.

In his book *Hummingbirds,* Andrew Cleave cites William Wood's 1634 description of the ruby-throated hummingbird: ". . . one of the wonders of the Countrey, being no bigger than a Hornet, yet hath all the demensions of a Bird, as bill, and wings, with quills, spider-like legges, small clawes; for color she is as glorious as the Raine-bow; as she flies, she makes a little humming noise like a Humble-bee; wherefore she is called the Humbird."

More recently, Roy Bedichek commented in *Adventures with a Texas Naturalist* that hardly a year passed that he did not hear accounts of hummingbirds hitchhiking on migration, concealed in the feathers of larger birds. One woman wrote to say that she saw them

Blue-throated hummingbird.

doing it regularly in the spring and fall, while a man was enraged that anyone should doubt the phenomenon. He claimed to have shot a great horned owl and 14 tiny hummingbirds tumbled out from beneath its wings. The story simply would not die, Bedichek noted. "It is too pleasing a fancy, too human."

As fanciful as such stories are, the facts are equally amazing. "The wonder, indeed, is not that hummingbirds sometimes drop exhausted, but that they stay aloft," writes Donald Culross Peattie in *A Cup of Sky*. "Their feats are possible because they have proportionately immense wing muscles, and are—for their size—the biggest-hearted little birds in the world."

Their small size does not necessarily mean that hummingbirds are delicate. Some are capable of long migration flights, and others live at elevations of up to 15,000 feet in the South American Andes, where nightly temperatures fall below freezing and the air is thin. The hummingbird's heart is indeed the largest in the world in proportion to body size, and it beats about 500 times a minute while resting and up to 1,200 times a minute (20 beats a second) in full flight. So rapid is the hummingbird metabolism that Esther and Robert Tyrrell note in their book *Hummingbirds: Their Life and Behavior*, "If man had as high a weight-specific metabolic rate as a hummingbird, his daily intake of food would have to be approximately twice his body weight. Also, his temperature would be over 750 degrees F and he would use up 155,000 calories per day." At night, however, hummingbirds sometimes descend into a state of torpor whereby their body temperatures drop and metabolic rates slow to a fraction of the waking rate, thereby conserving energy.

With wings beating nearly 80 times a second, these mites of the bird world are masters of controlled flight. They can hover in one place, fly backward, and even fly upside-down. They react quickly, but their apparent speed is something of an optical illusion. Hummingbirds probably average no more than 25 or 30 miles per hour in level flight.

Hummingbirds live on the edge, constantly searching for food to fuel that incredible metabolism. They perch to rest and preen but soon zoom off again, visiting flower after flower to sip at nectar reservoirs. In return, they carry pollen from one flower to another, although they are relatively inefficient from the plant's point of view. The interactions shape the behavior and natural selection of both bird and plant.

Flower nectar consists primarily of a solution of sugar in water, with a few trace minerals and amino acids as well. Most of the bird's energy comes from this nectar, while small insects and spiders supply necessary protein. In his research on hummingbirds in Texas' Big Bend National Park, Peter Scott found they devoted 90 percent of their feeding time to obtaining nectar, and the remaining 10 percent to hawking insects. Scott measured the nectar content of individual flowers and calculated that a hummingbird requires nectar from about 2,000 flowers a day to balance its energy budget. And that is optimistic, since many plants are visited by other birds or insects first. A more realistic total is probably 5,000 flower visits each and every day.

In turn, the plants must balance their rewards of nectar for the pollination service with their other needs. Much of their energies and resources must go to growth and seed production once that pollination is accomplished. "The sugar reward is barely profitable for hummingbirds," says Scott. "It's in the plants' best interests to keep hummingbirds lean and hungry and moving around." It is a delicate balance that has evolved for the benefit of both, and it is just one of many fascinating interactions in the natural world.

HUMMINGBIRDS (Family Trochilidae)

More than 320 species of these feathered gems inhabit the New World, where they have long been favorites of Native Americans. Hummingbird feathers adorned the regal robes of Montezuma, and several tribes honored deities in hummingbird form. Most numerous and varied in the equatorial tropics, hummingbirds decrease both northward and southward into the temperate zones. One, the rufous hummingbird, breeds as far north as the Alaskan coast, while another, the green-backed firecrown, reaches the tip of South America. They range in size from the two-and-one-half-inch bee hummingbird of Cuba, the smallest bird in the world, to the eight-and-one-half-inch giant hummingbird of the Andes.

Their names mirror the gemlike splendor of their glistening plumage: emerald, sapphire, ruby, topaz. One could expect nothing but breathtaking beauty from a tropical bird named the amethyst-throated sunangel or from a golden-bellied starfrontlet. The glittering, iridescent colors, however, are structural in nature. Unlike the pigmented red color of a cardinal, they are produced by the reflection of light from tiny platelets in the feathers. The thickness of the platelets, the amount of air contained in tiny bubbles within them, and the angle of the light determine the colors seen. It is much the same as the iridescent rainbow produced by a drop of oil in water. Specialized feathers on the crown and on the throat (the gorget) of hummingbirds are frequently the most colorful, but they are also very flat and have the most critical angle of iridescence. With the sun behind the viewer, the gorget sparkles at its best; but in oblique or dim light, it may appear entirely black.

Female black-chinned hummingbird on nest.

Sexual dimorphism is common among hummingbirds. While males have distinctively colored gorgets, females are typically green above and whitish below, lacking the bright feathering of their consorts. Some of the North American species look very much alike in female and immature plumages. These two factors—color dependence on the angle of the light, and the similarity of many females and immatures—make hummingbird identification difficult. No one will succeed in identifying every individual.

A typical North American hummingbird can scarcely be mistaken for any other kind of bird, but confusion with sphinx moths happens frequently. Some of the latter, also called "hawk moths" or "hummingbird moths," are large and long-winged, and they hover to sip nectar from flowers. Although moths are generally nocturnal, many also feed during the day, especially at dawn and dusk. More than one photograph of such an insect has been submitted to bird-record committees for verification of a rare hummingbird sighting.

Hummingbird nests are generally tiny cups of soft plant fibers and spider webs lined with cottony down. Lichens may ornament the exterior, creating additional camouflage to make them appear nothing more than small knots on tree limbs. Two white eggs make up the typical clutch, and although they are the smallest of all bird eggs, they are really quite large in comparison to body size. Many females lay clutches weighing as much as 20 percent of their own weight.

Eighteen hummingbird species occupy the state checklist of the Texas Ornithological Society, and more will undoubtedly be added with time. Eight of those species, however, are listed as either "accidental" or "hypothetical," unsubstantiated by photographs or specimens. Some, like the ruby-throated hummingbird and the black-chinned hummingbird, range widely in the state, while others are strictly local in their distributions. The Lucifer hummingbird, for example, is limited in Texas to the Chisos Mountains of Big Bend National Park. A few of the more widely distributed and distinctive species are treated here, but others might be encountered on rare occasions. Most U.S. hummingbirds wander into the Trans-Pecos region, and many have also turned up on the central coast near Rockport.

RUBY-THROATED HUMMINGBIRD *Archilochus colubris*

The familiar ruby-throated hummingbird migrates through the eastern two-thirds of Texas from September to December and March to May, ranging as far west as the Pecos River and the Panhandle. It remains to breed in summer east of the Edwards Plateau, from the Red River to the central coast. This is the common hummingbird of eastern Texas, and a few remain through the winter; however, visitors to winter hummingbird feeders in that section of the state are just as frequently wandering species from the West. The only hummingbird nesting east of the Mississippi, the ruby-throat ranges from southern Canada to the Gulf States and spends the winter in Mexico and Central America.

Male ruby-throated hummingbird.

The adult male ruby-throat is aptly named for its brilliant red gorget. Metallic green above and whitish below, it has a black, shallowly forked tail. The female lacks the ruby gorget and has a rounded tail with white-tipped corners. Both females and immatures resemble similarly plumaged black-chinned hummingbirds, and it is extremely difficult to separate the two species except by range. The ruby-throat is much more numerous in eastern Texas; the black-chin, in the West.

Ruby-throated hummingbirds make an astonishing migration for birds so small. Feeding heartily in the fall to add up to 50 percent to their body weight, birds in the eastern states then launch into nonstop flight across the Gulf of Mexico. Those that nest in Texas or that funnel down along our coast, however, may continue inland into Mexico instead of flying across the corner of the Gulf. Authorities still argue about the relative prominence of these circum-Gulf and trans-Gulf migration routes.

As with most hummingbird species, males migrate before females and immatures on both legs of their round-trip journey. Arriving in the North before flowers, small insects, and spiders are abundant enough to fuel their incredible metabolisms, they sometimes subsist on tree sap gleaned from the drillings of sapsuckers and other woodpeckers. Declining over many portions of its range, the lovely ruby-throat has been included on the Audubon Society's Blue List of birds that need careful attention.

Male black-chinned hummingbird.

BLACK-CHINNED HUMMINGBIRD *Archilochus alexandri*

Only in the best of light can one see the beautiful purple band below the black-chinned hummingbird's dark chin and throat. Glistening green above and whitish below, with its black and purple gorget, the adult male black-chin is the western counterpart of the closely related eastern ruby-throat. Indeed, the females and immatures can be separated by experts only after careful study. It is important, too, to remember that the ruby-throat's gorget may also appear black except in direct sunlight from behind the observer.

The black-chinned hummingbird breeds across the semi-arid portions of the West, from British Columbia to Mexico, and winters well south in Mexico. A few also wander eastward at that time, where they are often mistaken for lingering ruby-throats.

In Texas, the black-chin nests across the western and central counties, as far east as Dallas, Austin and San Antonio. Migrants then range to the central coast and through the Rio Grande delta.

One of the most vocal of all hummingbirds, the black-chin has a high-pitched song that sounds much like a person whistling through his teeth, and its angry chase note is an excited, repeated chip. After an aerial courtship in which the male performs a series of looping dives and figure 8s before his chosen mate, the female builds a tiny walnut-sized nest of plant down and spider webs on a horizontal branch. While the ruby-throat adorns the exterior of her nest with lichens, the black-chin uses occasional small leaves or flowers or disdains such artifice entirely. She incubates her two pea-sized white eggs with no help from the male.

Hatching in about 16 days, the tiny altricial, helpless babies grow quickly on a diet of nectar, insects and spiders regurgitated by the mother. It is amazing and frightening to see her perch on the side of the nest and plunge her needle beak deep into the gullets of the begging chicks, but they seem no worse for their sword-swallowing routines.

Unlike most other birds, baby hummingbirds do not develop a downy plumage. Born naked and with tiny bills, they have only a few strands of down and rely entirely on their mother for body warmth. In a few days they develop pinfeathers, and their bills begin to lengthen, while the nest stretches and bulges to accommodate them. Within two weeks they are exercising their wings and practicing the moves that will help them develop into such wondrous flying machines.

the male has a rose-red gorget. The wing-tips of the male also produce a unique, trilling "whistle" that heralds its approach and aids in identification.

Its rusty plumage clearly marks the male rufous hummingbird, here visiting a backyard feeder.

BLUE-THROATED HUMMINGBIRD
Lampornis clemenciae

The five-inch blue-throated hummingbird seems huge in comparison to the common three-and-three-fourths-inch *Archilochus* and *Selasphorus* species. The large size, uniformly gray underparts and broad white eye-stripe are characteristic, as is the big tail with broad white outer tips. The male sports a beautiful bright blue throat.

A Mexican species found along the southern U.S. border, it breeds in the higher canyons of Big Bend's Chisos Mountains, where hikers search for it around Boot Spring. The male's call, a high-pitched, squeaky *seep*, aids in locating it. Less frequent in the Davis Mountains than in the Chisos, the blue-throat occasionally wanders across the state and has even been sighted along the coast.

The genus name *Lampornis* is Greek for "torch bird" and alludes to the brilliance of hummingbird plumage. R.P. Lesson, a French naturalist and doctor, named the species *clemenciae* for his wife, who was a talented nature artist.

The magnificent hummingbird (*Eugenes fulgens*), formerly called Rivoli's hummingbird, is another very large, dark hummer that is seen less frequently than the blue-throat in the mountains of West Texas. The male has a purple crown and an iridescent green throat. The female is duller, lacks the purple crown, and has small light tips on the outer tail feathers.

RUFOUS HUMMINGBIRD   *Selasphorus rufus*

The rufous hummingbird ranges farther north than any other member of the family Trochilidae, breeding in the Pacific Northwest and through western Canada to the coast of Alaska. There it inhabits the forest edges and feeds in the flower-filled mountain meadows, before departing in midsummer on its leisurely migration through the western U.S. to Mexico.

Fairly common fall migrants through West Texas and the Panhandle, rufous hummingbirds occasionally range all the way to the Texas coast. Finding nectar-rich flowers and hospitable feeders, they might even forgo the remainder of their journey southward and remain throughout the winter.

The adult male has a distinctive reddish brown back, tail and flanks and a flaming orange-red gorget. Iridescent green feathers adorn the crown and spangle the back of some individuals. Females resemble those of other common hummingbird species, green above and whitish below, but their tail feathers are rust-colored at the base and there is a rufous wash on the flanks.

The similar Allen's hummingbird (*Selasphorus sasin*) of the Pacific Coast is an accidental wanderer to Texas. The adult male has a greener back and crown, but females and immatures are virtually inseparable from rufous hummingbirds.

Broad-tailed hummingbirds (*S. platycercus*) breed throughout the mountains of the West, including the Guadalupe, Davis and Chisos mountains of Trans-Pecos Texas. Both sexes are metallic green above, and

Another Mexican species breeding in Big Bend Park is the Lucifer hummingbird (*Calothorax lucifer*). A small (three-and-one-half-inch) bird, it is the only North American species with a downcurved bill. The male has a flaring purple gorget; the female, a buffy breast and a pale streak behind the eye. Lucifer hummingbirds inhabit the dry foothills and canyon mouths around the Chisos Mountains and have been recorded from March into November.

BUFF-BELLIED HUMMINGBIRD

Amazilia yucatanensis

The relatively large, four-and-one-fourth-inch buff-bellied hummingbird represents a tropical genus that reaches its northern limits along our southern border. A Mexican species encountered nowhere else in the U.S., it can usually be found in the parks and remnant woodlands of the lower Rio Grande Valley, particularly around Brownsville and at the nearby Sabal Palm Grove Sanctuary. Occasional wanderers range up the Gulf Coast into Louisiana in the fall and winter months.

The sexes have similar plumages and are bronzy green above with a chestnut tail and buffy belly. The throat and upper breast are bright, metallic green. The black-tipped red or coral-pink bill and shrill, squeaky call notes are also diagnostic.

The nest is constructed of plant fibers and down, bound with spider silk and covered with lichens or shreds of bark. Perched on the limb of a tree or shrub, it cradles the typical clutch of two white eggs. The breeding biology of the buff-bellied hummingbird has not been studied fully, but the female presumably incubates her eggs and broods and feeds her young alone.

Blue-throated hummingbird (above left). Buff-bellied hummingbird feeding young (above).

he woodpeckers compose the most abundant and widespread family of climbing birds. However, there are a few other species that also cling to tree trunks and branches to work their way slowly along in search of their next meal. Chief among these are the nuthatches and the brown creeper. These three families share no close taxonomic ties, but they have each evolved methods of foraging that set them apart from most other birds.

Acorn woodpeckers study new park regulations.

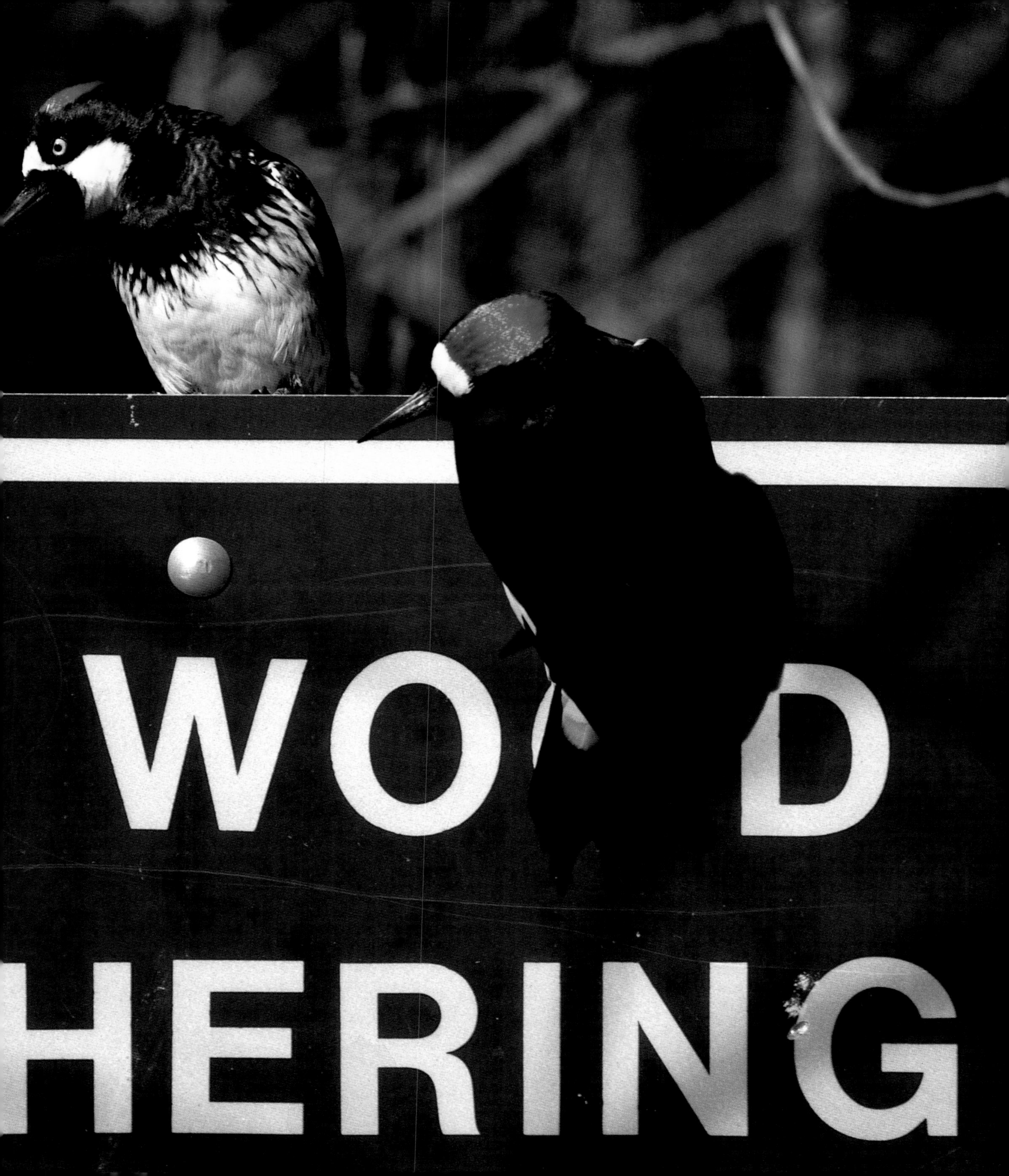
WO D
HERING

WOODPECKERS (Family Picidae)

A male red-bellied woodpecker shows his barbed tongue.

Few birds are more uniquely adapted for the ecological niche they fill than these "jackhammers of the forest." Their strong chisel bills enable them to dig for boring insects in the trunks of trees and to hew out nest holes in solid wood. Those holes provide homes not only for their original occupants but for a host of other birds ranging in size from chickadees to wood ducks and for other wildlife as well.

The bones of a woodpecker's skull are thick and heavily ossified to withstand the vigorous pounding, and the tongue is like that of no other bird. Hyoid bones at the base of the tongue are not anchored to the bottom of the skull. Instead they wrap around and over the cranium and anchor near the base of the bill. Elastic muscles encase the long, flexible rods of bone, and the woodpecker can thrust out its tongue several inches past the tip of its beak. Backward-pointing barbs allow most woodpeckers to spear insects in their burrows and pull them free. Others have modified tongues for specialized feeding habits. The long tongue of the flicker has fewer barbs and is coated with a sticky secretion for licking up ants, while that of the sapsucker is bristled like a brush for lapping up sap oozing from holes drilled through the bark of living trees.

Woodpeckers have short legs and strong claws for clinging to tree trunks, while unusually stiff tail feathers serve as props when climbing. Instead of having the normal arrangement of three toes pointing forward and one backward, they have a reversible toe that is usually directed backward. That X-shaped toe arrangement facilitates vertical climbing. A few species have only three toes and usually arrange them in an open Y position.

Woodpeckers typically make nest cavities in trees and poles or in large cacti and old agave bloomstalks in arid regions where trees are scarce. The eggs are glossy white and rounder than those of most other birds, for there is no need for camouflage colors or for a pointed shape that prevents rolling from the nest. The clutch of four to seven eggs is usually laid on the unlined floor of the cavity, and both parents incubate and feed the young.

More than 200 woodpeckers and their relatives range throughout the wooded regions of the world. Fourteen occur in Texas, while another former resident, the ivory-billed woodpecker, is now presumed to be extinct in the United States.

Most people recognize the generic woodpecker from its characteristic appearance and tree-climbing habits. Woodpeckers also fly with a peculiar undulating, roller-coaster flight. Most males have some red color on the head, and each has its own vocal calls that are as distinctive as its plumage. The staccato drumming, too, serves as a territorial challenge, and various cadences have coded significance in courtship. It takes the place of song in woodpecker communication.

RED-HEADED WOODPECKER   *Melanerpes erythrocephalus*

Most woodpeckers display some red on the head and are collectively called "red-headed woodpeckers" by many casual observers. The true red-head, however, has the entire head, neck and throat a vivid scarlet, set off by a black back and immaculately white underparts. In flight it flashes large white patches in the wings and on the rump. The two sexes have similar plumages, but the immatures are dusky brown. So different do they appear that early naturalists thought them to be a separate species. They acquire the red head during a gradual winter molt. The call is a loud *queark* or *queer,* somewhat harsher than that of the red-bellied woodpecker.

The red-headed woodpecker is an eastern species, ranging from Canada to the Gulf States and from the Great Plains to the Atlantic Coast. A year-round resident in Texas, it inhabits the eastern and central portions of the state, occurring westward to the Panhandle, Fort Worth, Waco and Austin and south to the upper coast.

Red-heads prefer open deciduous woodlands, farmlands, parks and even wooded suburban yards. The construction of East Texas reservoirs provided added habitat in the dead trees left standing as the waters rose. The birds forage on tree trunks but also descend to the ground to gather insects, berries and acorns. The latter are harvested in the fall and stored for winter in tree cavities and crevices. Red-headed woodpeckers also flycatch from treetops and poles. While frequenting roadsides to feed on grasshoppers and other insects killed by cars, they all too often fall victim themselves to onrushing traffic.

Unlike some species that excavate nest holes in living trees, red-headed woodpeckers prefer dead trees or barkless stubs. They also utilize utility poles and fence posts in agricultural areas and on the open plains. The nesting pair requires a week or two to hew out a suitable cavity, and the clutch of four or five white eggs is laid on a bed of wood chips. Both parents incubate the eggs, and the helpless,

altricial babies hatch in 12 or 13 days. They remain in the security of the nest for about four weeks before taking flight, growing slowly on a diet of insects, spiders, worms and berries.

The red-headed woodpecker appears to be declining in the Northeast due to loss of habitat and competition with the introduced starling. The aggressive starling not only challenges several other species of birds for old nest holes but evicts woodpeckers from those recently constructed.

A red-headed woodpecker brings food to its young.

ACORN WOODPECKER
Melanerpes formicivorus

The bird world abounds with beautiful and interesting characters, but one of the real charmers is the acorn woodpecker with its circus-clown face and unusual habits.

The black-and-white face pattern is unique among woodpeckers, with white eyes gleaming from within the black mask. The crown is flaming red, more extensive on the male than on the female. In flight, white rump and wing-patches flash brightly against the contrasting black plumage.

The acorn woodpecker is a resident of the Pacific Coast, from Oregon to Baja California, and of the Southwest down through Central America. In Texas, it is fairly common in the Trans-Pecos, ranging eastward occasionally to the Edwards Plateau. Anyone visiting the western mountains of our state will probably encounter this colorful, noisy character.

It is most easily located by its raucous, raspy call, variously described as *Ja-cob Ja-cob* or *whack-up whack-up*. Because the birds are sociable and live in small colonies, the resulting racket can be considerable.

Members of the colony work together in excavating nest holes and feeding young. There is some indication that they may even share incubation chores. Typical colonies probably consist of at least one older breeding pair, young from previous nestings, and subsequent members of the extended family.

Certain trees within the perimeter of the territory serve as "granary" trees and are used year after year. In them, the birds store enormous numbers of acorns. They drill small holes into the tree and hammer in the acorns, pointed end first, until the surface is studded with nuts. One famous tree in California was found to be inlaid with more than 50,000 acorns. The stores seem to be primarily emergency rations for winter, since the woodpeckers are usually observed feeding on insects during mild weather.

On an October afternoon in the Chisos Basin of Big Bend National Park, I sat on a hillside and watched four acorn woodpeckers pounding acorns into the top of a power pole. They foraged through the Chisos red oaks in a small ravine, then flew with the acorns to the pole and worked them into existing crevices and into holes they chiseled in the treated wood. The troop would work furiously for a while in the warm sun, then rest quietly on shaded branches before continuing to stock the pantry.

A few days later, near my campsite in Davis Mountains State Park, a band of six birds was working on its winter stores. Four of the woodpeckers used the dead stub of an oak tree, but two repeatedly returned with their acorns to a nearby maintenance building, where they hammered them into cracks between the wooden door or window frames and the plaster wall. One young male then found a convenient slot beneath the eaves and proceeded to stuff acorn after acorn into it. His enthusiastic efforts were doomed to failure, however, for I could hear the acorns dropping far down inside the wall.

Acorn woodpeckers (opposite) store provisions in "granary" trees. A golden-fronted woodpecker (below) visits its nest in a roof support above a picnic table.

GOLDEN-FRONTED WOODPECKER *Melanerpes aurifrons*

The large, zebra-backed woodpecker works diligently away at a nest hole in the trunk of a dead mesquite, chopping vigorously with his sturdy bill and flinging chips in all directions. His mate takes over when he stops to rest and feed in a nearby thicket. Working together, the pair will take a week or more to excavate their nest, and they will then share in the incubation of their four to seven eggs and the raising of their young. Starting with an opening about two inches across, they dig straight back and then down, perhaps for a foot or more, finally enlarging the cavity at the bottom and leaving a few wood chips as the only pallet for their pending brood.

The golden-fronted woodpecker ranges from extreme southwestern Oklahoma to Nicaragua; thus most of the U.S. population resides in Texas. It is a year-round resident from the eastern Panhandle to the Rio Grande delta, occurring westward to Big Spring and the Big Bend area and eastward to Austin and the central coast. The golden-fronted woodpecker is the southwestern counterpart of the more eastern red-bellied woodpecker, and the two species sometimes hybridize where their ranges overlap.

Ten inches long, and with a black-and-white barred back, the golden-fronted woodpecker has light underparts, a white rump and an all-black tail. A large golden orange patch ornaments the nape, and there is a smaller yellow patch above the bill, the "golden front." In addition, the male sports a small, round red cap that is lacking on the female.

Golden-fronted woodpeckers are the common larger woodpeckers of dry woodlands, mesquite brushlands and pecan groves throughout the midsection of Texas. Their calls, a rolling *churr-churr* and a raucous, cackling *kek-kek-kek* are familiar sounds from the ranches of the Panhandle and the rolling plains to the Tamaulipan thorn-scrub forest of the lower Rio Grande.

RED-BELLIED WOODPECKER

Melanerpes carolinus

Residents of East Texas mistakenly call this common ten-inch bird the "red-headed woodpecker" or "ladder-backed woodpecker," and while those names do seem more appropriate than the proper one, they are reserved for two other very different species. The "red belly" is at most a rosy blush on the lower abdomen and is seldom noticed in the field. Others simply call the bird "pecker-wood," for it is the most abundant woodpecker in the northeastern portion of the state.

The red-belly has a zebra-barred black-and-white back and pale buff underparts. A scarlet cap extends from the forehead to the nape of the neck on the male, while the female is red only on the nape. The call is a distinctive, repeated *chuck chuck* or *chiv chiv* and at times a rattled *churrr*, hardly a musical song but diagnostic of the species. In its undulating flight, it flashes a white rump patch.

The red-bellied woodpecker ranges throughout the eastern half of the United States, from Minnesota and Connecticut southward to Florida and the Gulf Coast. In recent years it has extended its range northward into New York and New England, probably because of the increasing use of bird feeders.

Found in open or swampy woodlands, farm groves, parks and wooded city neighborhoods, the red-belly is a common visitor to backyard feeders. There it accepts seeds, bread, fruit, suet and even sugarwater intended for hummingbirds. Its natural foods include vast numbers of wood-boring beetles and their larvae, grasshoppers, ants, wild fruits, and acorns, which it habitually stores in cracks and crevices for future use. It also pecks into ripening oranges in the citrus groves of Florida, where it is considered a pest.

In Texas the red-bellied woodpecker occurs throughout the eastern woodlands, west to the Panhandle and the Austin area and south to the central coast, where it is replaced by the closely related golden-fronted woodpecker. The latter has a golden-orange nape rather than red and a black tail. The central tail feathers of the red-belly are barred black and white.

A red-bellied woodpecker (opposite) brings home an insect. Yellow-bellied sapsuckers (above right) drill holes in trees to lick the sap.

YELLOW-BELLIED SAPSUCKER   *Sphyrapicus varius*

Like its other woodpecker relatives, the sapsucker clambers up and down the trunks of trees and hammers away with its chisel bill; however, it has a very different purpose in its carpentry. Instead of digging in pursuit of insects concealed within the wood, it methodically drills neat rows of holes through the bark and into the cambium layer of the tree. It then eats portions of this tender layer and laps up the sweet sap that flows. To this end, it has a brushlike, bristle-tipped tongue rather than the barbed spear of others in the family.

The yellow-bellied sapsucker is a winter resident in most of Texas. Breeding across Canada and through the northeastern states, it migrates much farther than most woodpeckers to winter from the southern U.S. to Central America and the West Indies.

The adult yellow-bellied sapsucker can be recognized by its red forehead, a black-and-white face pattern, and the large white wing-patch seen as a longitudinal stripe down the wing when the bird perches upright on a tree trunk. The male displays a red throat; the female, a white one. Both have a black bib across the upper breast and a pale yellow wash on the belly. Juveniles are brownish until their first spring molt, but the white wing-patches remain diagnostic.

Sapsuckers frequent deciduous woodlands and parks as well as tree-lined neighborhoods, collecting syrup from a wide variety of trees and shrubs. Biologists, in fact, have cataloged some 250 species bearing the checkerboard scars that are the trademark of foraging sapsuckers. Returning repeatedly to collect the tree sap that has accumulated, the birds also consume ants, beetles and other insects attracted to the sweets. Small mammals, hummingbirds and butterflies also show up to dine at this energy-rich food source.

Two other forms once considered subspecies of the yellow-bellied sapsucker have recently been assigned full species status of their own. One, the red-breasted sapsucker (*Sphyrapicus ruber*), is confined to the Pacific Coast and does not occur in Texas. However the other, now called the red-naped sapsucker (*S. nuchalis*), is a Rocky Mountain species that also breeds at higher elevations in the Trans-Pecos and wanders through West Texas during the winter. It is distinguished from the yellow-bellied sapsucker by a variable red patch on the back of the head and by the white chin and red throat of the female. The two species are diffi-

cult to separate in the field, and the range of overlap is not fully known.

Yet another species, Williamson's sapsucker (*S. thyroideus*), occurs as a rare migrant and winter visitor to western Texas. The distinctive male is largely black, with a white rump and wing-patches, yellow belly and bright red throat. The female has a brown head, and her back, wings and flanks are barred dark brown and white.

The genus name of these aberrant woodpeckers is a hybrid of Greek and Latin. It combines the Greek *sphyra,* "hammer," with the Latin *picus,* for "woodpecker," according to Gruson. The yellow-bellied sapsucker's *varius* refers to the highly variable plumage within the species. Some of those variations, however, have now been separated as new species, and the name is less appropriate.

LADDER-BACKED WOODPECKER
Picoides scalaris

The seven-inch ladder-back is the common small woodpecker of the Desert Southwest, sharing much of its range in Texas with the larger golden-fronted woodpecker. It is a year-round resident of arid brushlands, mesquite woodlands and deserts from California to Texas and south through lowland Mexico. In Texas, it ranges through the western two-thirds of the state, from the Panhandle to the Rio Grande Valley and eastward to Dallas, Waco and the central coast.

The black-and-white-barred back and black-striped face distinguish the ladder-backed woodpecker from others in similar habitats. The male has a red crown; the female's crown is black. Foraging through the trees and shrubs for the insects that make up the major portion of their diet, they communicate with sharp, crisp *pik* calls and a descending whinny much like those of the slightly smaller downy woodpecker. The latter species shares a small portion of the ladder-back's range in central Texas but can be easily distinguished by its white, unbarred back.

Male and female ladder-backed woodpeckers share in the incubation of their four or five white eggs, and both feed the altricial young that hatch in only 13 days. They customarily excavate their nest in the dead or decaying limb of a small tree but also use fence posts, large cacti, or the stalks of large yuccas and agaves where trees are not available.

The pair divides its foraging activities in remarkable fashion. The female tends to search higher in the trees and gleans insects from the bark and leaves. The male, on the other hand, probes and pecks beneath the

A red crown distinguishes the male ladder-backed woodpecker from his mate.

bark of the trunk and lower limbs. Although the ladder-backed woodpecker consumes the fruits of cacti and other plants and even descends to the ground in search of insects, it specializes in extracting the larvae of beetles from small trees. How it finds this hidden food reserve remains the subject of much debate among biologists. Some contend the bird listens for movement beneath the bark, while others suspect it locates burrows by tapping on the wood and detecting the resonance below.

The little downy woodpecker is a backyard favorite across much of the continent.

DOWNY WOODPECKER *Picoides pubescens*

This smallest of all our woodpeckers also ranks as one of the favorites, for it is a familiar visitor to backyard feeders throughout most of the country. A rather tame bird, it inhabits suburban yards and parks as well as larger forested tracts. The downy woodpecker ranges across North America, from Alaska and Canada to the southern states, avoiding only the arid regions of the Desert Southwest. It resides year-round in eastern and northern Texas, occurring westward to the Panhandle and Austin and south to Victoria and the central coast. It is one of the few Texas birds that does not also range into Mexico.

The seven-inch downy woodpecker has a distinctive white back, white-spotted wings, and black facial stripes. The male also displays a small red patch on the back of the head. The hairy woodpecker is similarly marked and shares much of the downy's range, but it is larger and has a proportionately longer, heavier bill.

Vocalizations of the downy woodpecker include a soft *pick* call and a rapid, descending whinny. However, as with other woodpeckers, a great

deal of the communication is done by drumming. It is used to establish claims to a territory and in courtship, when the pair often drums in duet. The drum rhythm of each woodpecker species is distinctive, and that of the downy is an unbroken, rapid roll lasting about two seconds. Mated pairs also use a slower tapping signal to stay in contact with each other as they roam through the treetops.

The sexes forage separately, with males preferring the smaller upper branches of the tree. This division presumably allows a pair to work more efficiently and keeps a bird from searching for food in locations already covered by its mate. Insects make up 75 to 85 percent of the downy woodpecker's diet; the remainder includes fruit, seeds, and sap garnered from the drillings of sapsuckers.

downy, but its larger size and more massive bill are diagnostic. The outer tail feathers of the hairy are entirely white, while those of the downy usually have dark bars or spots. That difference should be used to confirm the identification, for relative size can be difficult to determine in the field. The male hairy woodpecker, like the male downy, has a small red patch on the back of the head. The two species are the only Texas woodpeckers with white backs.

The hairy woodpecker ranges from the tree line of Alaska and Canada through the U.S. into Mexico. Essentially nonmigratory, it resides year-round in the northeastern third of Texas, occurring west to Fort Worth and Waco and south sparingly to Houston. A southwestern race also occurs in the Guadalupe Mountains.

Less likely to turn up in urban settings than the tamer little downy woodpecker, it inhabits both open woodlands and denser forests across the country. Its loud, sharp *peek* calls and its drumming usually reveal its presence before it is seen.

HAIRY WOODPECKER *Picoides villosus*

Courtship and pair-bonding for the hairy woodpecker begin in midwinter, well before the nesting season. The male drums sharply on his favorite trees, proclaiming his territory and inviting females to visit him. An interested female answers, and the two commence a long-distance conversation of duet drumming that may last for weeks. Finally entering the male's territory, the female performs her stylized aerial courtship flights, quivering her wings and fluttering like a butterfly to attract her suitor. She makes her rounds and taps at potential nest sites, indicating her willingness to mate. The male apparently makes the final site selection, and they then begin to excavate a cavity, a

project that may require two or three weeks of intermittent work.

Once the female has laid her three to six white eggs on a bed of wood chips, both sexes share the incubation chores. The male sits through the night; his mate, for most of the day. She feeds nearby at dawn and dusk, seldom straying far from the nest. The naked, helpless babies hatch in 11 to 15 days, and are brooded and fed by both parents. The two distribute the territory between them, the male ranging farther afield and returning less frequently with larger prey. The female remains within hearing of her young and makes more frequent trips to the nest. Studies have shown that 75 to 95 percent of the hairy woodpecker's diet consists of insects, with acorns, nuts and berries added in the winter.

The nine- to ten-inch hairy woodpecker is patterned like the smaller seven-inch

The hairy woodpecker has a longer, more massive bill than does the smaller downy woodpecker.

RED-COCKADED WOODPECKER

Picoides borealis

First named to the endangered species list in 1970, the red-cockaded woodpecker of the southeastern U.S. continues to decline dramatically. It owes its precarious status to its highly specialized nesting habits. This small woodpecker inhabits mature, open pine forests and excavates its nest cavities primarily in living pines infected with red-heart disease, a fungus that attacks older trees. Modern forest management techniques, however, call for cutting the mature stands and also exclude natural fires that remove undergrowth and keep the pines well spaced. As a result, red-cockaded woodpeckers have abandoned nesting colonies throughout a major portion of their range.

These eight-and-one-half-inch woodpeckers live in family groups composed of a mated pair, their off-spring, and occasional unmated male helpers. They remain territorial throughout the year and defend areas of about 100 to 200 acres, reusing their cavity trees year after year. After making the nest holes, the birds then drill small holes around the entrances to increase the flow of sap. The sticky resin coats the trunks, marking the nesting trees distinctively and pre-sumably helping to repel predators.

Prior to 1989, there were an esti-mated 2,000 active woodpecker colo-nies in the southeastern states, most of them in unlogged national forests. South Carolina's Francis Marion Na-tional Forest contained 562 of those colonies when Hurricane Hugo dev-astated the region that year. Hugo leveled 100,000 acres of the forest and destroyed the cavity trees of over half the resident colonies. Only one percent of the colonies survived un-touched.

All national forest units are now reviewing their management policies for the preservation of this rare spe-cies. Experiments are underway in Texas to install artificial nesting cavi-ties in stands of pines and to move captured birds into appropriate new areas of the forests. Clearly, timber cutting must be curtailed near estab-lished colonies, and mature forests must be maintained free from undue activity if the endangered red-cockaded woodpecker is to survive.

This charming, active little bird is a local resident in the East Texas Piney Woods, ranging westward to Tyler and Conroe. It has a black-and-white barred back, a black cap, and a white cheek patch that serves as the most distinctive field mark. Tiny red patches on the head of the male, for which the species was named, are barely visible. Downy and hairy woodpeckers also inhabit the pine for-ests of East Texas, but they can be differentiated by their white backs and black cheeks surrounded by white.

Red-cockaded woodpeckers forage in living pines for the wood-boring beetles and grubs that make up the bulk of their diet. Males feed prima-

An endangered species, the red-cockaded woodpecker nests only in pines in the southeastern states.

rily in the upper portions of the trees; females, along the lower trunk. As they troop through the woods, they can be located by the sounds of their tapping and by their nasal calls, a raspy *sripp* and a high-pitched *tsick,* quite unlike the notes of other wood-peckers in their range.

Black mustaches and a red patch on the nape mark this northern flicker as a male of the yellow-shafted form.

NORTHERN FLICKER *Colaptes auratus*

The northern flicker comprises three distinct forms that until recently were considered different species: the yellow-shafted flicker of the eastern states, the red-shafted flicker of the West, and the gilded flicker of the Desert Southwest. The yellow- and red-shafted forms apparently developed on opposite sides of the Great Plains, separated by treeless prairies that precluded breeding by cavity-nesting species. As settlers planted farm groves and shelterbelts, however, the twain did meet, and numerous hybrids were discovered that combined the characteristics of the

two. With no biological barrier to interbreeding, the yellow-shafted and red-shafted flickers became one in the eyes of the ornithological gods. They included the gilded flicker, too, as simply a form adapted to the tree-like saguaro cactus of the Arizona desert. Because the yellow-shafted flicker had been named first, the new collective species took its scientific name, *auratus,* Latin for "golden."

The flicker is a large, foot-long brown woodpecker with a black-barred back, round black spots on the breast, and a black bib on the chest. A white rump patch is conspicuous in

flight. The three forms differ in the color beneath the wings and tail and in the facial markings. The yellow-shafted and gilded races have yellow linings; the red-shafted, salmon red. Male red-shafted and gilded flickers also have red "mustache" marks at the base of the bill, while the male yellow-shafted has black mustaches and a red crescent on the back of the head. Ever ladylike, females of all forms lack the mustaches of their mates.

The combined forms of the northern flicker range across virtually all of North America, from the tree limit in Alaska and Canada to southern Mexico, migrating in winter from the higher latitudes. Indeed, south-central Texas is virtually the only area in the United States without a regularly breeding flicker population. The yellow-shafted form occurs westward to Dallas, Waco and Austin, while the red-shafted ranges through the Panhandle and the Trans-Pecos. Both wander widely in winter and combine with migrants from the North to blanket virtually the entire state, although each race is by far the more common in its own breeding range.

The flicker inhabits open woodlands, farm groves and suburban areas, and in the delightful words of John Burroughs' *Wake Robin* in 1895, "obtains most of his subsistence from the ground, probing it for ants and crickets. He is not quite satisfied with being a woodpecker. He courts the society of the robin and the finches, abandons the trees for the meadow, and feeds eagerly upon berries and grain. What will be the final upshot of this course of living is a question worthy of Darwin."

The flicker is indeed fond of ants and has a specialized tongue for lapping them up after tearing open the mound with its long dagger bill. The extensible tongue has fewer barbs than that of most other woodpeckers and is covered with sticky secretions. One biologist opened the stomach of a bird he collected to count 5,000 ants inside.

Although the northern flicker feeds extensively on the ground, it nests in a cavity in a tree or post in typical woodpecker fashion. The clutch, however, is larger than most and normally contains from five to eight eggs. In a classic experiment quoted by A.C. Bent in his series of books on the life histories of North American birds, a yellow-shafted flicker was induced to lay 71 eggs in 73 days by removing them as rapidly as they were laid but always leaving one "nest egg."

With its unique plumage, extensive range and raucous voice, the flicker is well known throughout the country. Its calls include a loud *wicker, wick-er, wick-er* and *wick-wick-wick* as well as a shrill *klee-yer*. The late Louisiana ornithologist George Lowery counted 132 local names by which the flicker had "endeared himself to Americans from Florida to Alaska." They included "yarrup," "high-hole," and "golden-winged woodpecker." Alabama made the flicker the state bird, and Lowery noted that "her soldiers marched off to the Civil War with feathers of the 'yellowhammer' stuck in their hats."

PILEATED WOODPECKER *Dryocopus pileatus*

Roy Bedichek, in *Adventures with a Texas Naturalist,* described his encounter with a pair of pileated woodpeckers along the Neches River near Lufkin in 1937. When he first heard their "unearthly clamor," Bedichek asked a native what bird it was. "A *good* God," the fellow replied, with emphasis on the "good." "You see, people ain't usta seein' a woodpecker as big as a crow; so when they do see one, they jes' natchally say, 'Good God'!"

The pileated is indeed the largest and most impressive of our woodpeckers, since the ivory-bill has apparently vanished from U.S. forests. From 17 to 20 inches in length, it has a 30-inch wingspan and flies with powerful beats, flashing a bright red crest and large white patches beneath its black wings. Other vernacular names include "Indian hen," "logcock" and "stump-breaker," the latter two alluding to its prowess with its formidable chisel bill. The call is a loud, resonant *wuck-a-wuck-a-wuck-a* or an irregular *kuk-kuk—kukkuk-kuk.*

The pileated woodpecker ranges across Canada and southward through the eastern states to Florida and the Gulf States. It is less common in the Pacific Northwest and along the West Coast. In Texas, it is a year-round resident through the eastern third of the state, west to Denton, Fort Worth and Bastrop and south to Victoria and Goliad. The name (pronounced *PIE-lee-a-ted*) refers to the crest covering the pileum, or the top of the head.

Once common in eastern North America, the pileated woodpecker declined rapidly in the path of lumbering and the clearing of the land for farming. Some were also shot and offered for sale in eastern markets, although Audubon remarked that they were "tough and extremely unpalatable." Rare by the beginning of the 20th century, the pileated woodpecker staged a gradual resurgence as lumbering practices changed and second growth woodlands reclaimed abandoned farms.

Highly adaptable, the pileated has become more common in parks and small woodlots and even in suburban yards. This is an adaptability the ivory-billed woodpecker lacked. The latter inhabited remote bottomland forests and swamps of the South and vanished as its territory was invaded. Instead of eating a varied diet as does the pileated, it depended primarily on the larvae of boring beetles found in large dead trees. The pileated supplements its insect fare with fruit, nuts, acorns and sap. Carpenter ants gathered from old stumps and logs are a mainstay, especially in winter when the ants are dormant.

Perched on a tree trunk, the pileated woodpecker appears mostly black on the back and wings. A white stripe runs up the side of the neck and across the cheek, and the throat is also white. Both sexes possess a red crest, but the female has a dark forehead and lacks the red mustache mark of the male. In flight, the white area beneath is limited to the leading edge of the wing; above, only the bases of the primaries are white.

In contrast, the even larger ivory-billed woodpecker (*Campephilus principalis*) has a large white border on the rear of the wing that is visible both from above and from below. The white also shows as a large wing-patch on the perching bird. Both sexes have the characteristic white bill, but only the male has a red crest; that of the female is black. The call is a loud, nasal *yank,* like the tooting of a tin horn,

quite unlike the rolling calls of the pileated woodpecker.

Reports of ivory-bills continue to emerge from the river bottoms of East Texas, but most are undoubtedly due to confusion with the pileated. At least one such report appears to involve a partial albino pileated woodpecker with larger than normal white areas in the wings. There have been no unequivocal sightings of the ivory-bill since the 1950s, and most authorities consider it extinct in the U.S., although a few have been found in Cuba.

Meanwhile, the pileated woodpecker continues to adapt and flourish in the face of human encroachment. It leaves its mark in the form of large rectangular or oval holes it chisels in search of grubs and ants, and it excavates its nest holes high on the trunks of large trees. Old cavities are reused by a variety of wildlife including wood ducks, owls and flying squirrels.

Adult pileated woodpeckers form lasting pair bonds and defend their territory throughout the year. Both incubate their three to five eggs, the male taking the night shift, the female sitting more frequently by day. They brood the young for up to ten days after hatching, and it is about four weeks before they are ready to leave the nest.

A remarkable series of photographs recently documented an unusual case of egg transport by the pileated woodpecker. When the nest tree suddenly collapsed, the female retrieved her three eggs within 20 minutes and carried them one by one in her bill to another nest cavity. Returning nearly two hours later, the male searched actively until he located the female, and the pair resumed their normal routine.

A male pileated woodpecker arrives to feed its young high in a towering East Texas oak.

These small, stout tree-climbers have no respect for the laws of gravity. They are the only birds that habitually climb down tree trunks headfirst, relying on their large feet and powerful toes for support. The nuthatch stretches one foot forward under the breast and the other back under the tail, rotating it outward and backward to grip the bark. It then hitches nimbly along, switching feet as it works around the trunk, probing for small insects that make up a major portion of its diet. The nuthatch's short, stubby tail is not used as a prop as are the longer stiff-shafted tails of the woodpeckers and creepers. And, although nuthatches forage in somewhat the same manner as the woodpeckers, they are not closely related. The etymology of the name is not clear, but it presumably comes from "nuthack," an old term applied from watching the European species wedge a nut into a crevice and hack it open with its sharp, stout bill.

There are about 30 species in the world, most of them in the Northern Hemisphere. North America and Texas have four. In addition to the red-breasted and white-breasted nuthatches treated here, Texas hosts the tiny brown-headed and pygmy nuthatches. The former, *Sitta pusilla,* inhabits the pine woodlands of East Texas. The latter, *S . pygmaea,* is an uncommon resident of the Guadalupe Mountains and ranges occasionally through the Trans-Pecos and into the Panhandle. In the winter these little "upside-down birds" often roam with small mixed flocks of chickadees, titmice and kinglets, climbing up and down the tree trunks and hanging from branches, stoking their inner fires with hibernating insects, seeds and berries.

The red-breasted nuthatch never seems to know up from down.

RED-BREASTED NUTHATCH

Sitta canadensis

The red-breasted nuthatch inhabits the coniferous forests of Canada and the northern states and ranges southward in the mountains of both the East and West. It is an irregular winter visitor to Texas from October through April, most frequently in the eastern portions of the state.

This four-and-one-half-inch bird is an example of an "irruptive migrant," varying greatly in its range and numbers each year. If food supplies are plentiful, it remains on its breeding grounds, with no need to migrate at all. However, if the year's cone crop should be sparse, it ranges far afield in search of new resources. Such birds migrate not to keep warm in cold weather but to find food. Feeding primarily on insects through the breeding season, they rely heavily on the seeds of the conifers when insects are no longer available.

The red-breasted nuthatch is blue-gray above and rusty beneath, the females and immatures duller and paler than the males. A black cap and eyestripe, with a white eyebrow separating the two, distinguish the red-breasted from all other nuthatch species. The nasal call notes, *ank* or *enk,* sound like the blowing of a little tin horn. Like others of the family Sittidae, the red-breasted nuthatch visits feeders for sunflower seeds and other offerings, sometimes storing the seeds in trees behind bits of flaking bark. It also joins other species of winter birds that troop through the treetops in mixed feeding flocks.

This little nuthatch excavates its own nest cavity in a rotting branch or stump with its sharp, chisellike bill, and lines it with soft grasses and shreds of bark. Occasionally it uses an abandoned woodpecker hole. It then brings small droplets of pitch and smears them around the entrance with its bill. The purpose of this artistry remains unknown, although it might help to bar ants and other pests. The four to seven brown-spotted eggs hatch in 12 days, and the young leave the nest about three weeks later. The breeding pair may then remain together on their territory through winter if food is adequate.

WHITE-BREASTED NUTHATCH *Sitta carolinensis*

It is a cold, blustery winter day in northeast Texas, and a white-breasted nuthatch descends on a backyard feeder. Unlike the accompanying chickadees, which hurriedly grab a sunflower seed and dart off with it to a nearby branch, the nuthatch makes his selection carefully. He picks up several seeds and drops them again before finding one to his liking. Having chosen one that fits some unknown criteria, the nuthatch flies to the trunk of a tree and wedges his bounty into a crevice in the bark, hammering it in solidly with his upturned, chisel-shaped beak. He returns to claim and store several more seeds and then resumes the hunt for other fare, creeping headfirst down the trunk and flying to another tree to repeat his acrobatic antics.

The white-breasted nuthatch is blue-gray above and white below, with chestnut shading beneath the short, stubby tail. A black cap and nape frame an all-white face. Six inches long, it is the largest of the North American nuthatches and lacks the black eye-line of its red-breasted cousin. Its call consists of a nasal, repeated *yank,* while its song is a series of whistles on a constant pitch, *whi-whi-whi.*

Breeding from southern Canada to southern Mexico, the white-breasted nuthatch is a year-round resident in the eastern third of Texas, ranging westward to Fort Worth and Bryan; however, it does not breed along the upper coast. Other races inhabit the mountains of the Trans-Pecos. Both eastern and western populations frequent woodlands, farm groves and tree-lined yards in search of the insects and spiders that make up the major portion of their warm-weather diets. In winter they turn to seeds, nuts and acorns when other food is scarce.

A natural cavity or old woodpecker hole serves as a nest site, and the pair lines it with a soft bed of bark fibers, hair and feathers. The five to eight eggs spotted with reddish brown hatch in about 12 days, and the young fledge two weeks later. The pair frequently maintains its feeding territory throughout the year, but nuthatches are more prone to wander in the winter. They may then turn up in the Panhandle, on the Edwards Plateau or along the coast, visiting feeders and creeping up and down the tree trunks and branches as if they never heard of gravity.

White-breasted nuthatch.

Only a half-dozen of these small, slender tree-climbers inhabit the cooler portions of the Northern Hemisphere and only one, the brown creeper, occurs in North America. The creepers have moderately long, slightly downcurved bills, which they use to pry insects from the bark. Like woodpeckers, they have stiff tail feathers that serve as props while climbing.

BROWN CREEPER

Certhia americana

The slender, five-inch bird perches on an oak tree in the backyard, scarcely visible until it moves. Brown, streaked plumage provides near perfect camouflage against the bark, and the whitish underparts are hidden in shadow as the bird hugs the trunk. Slowly it spirals upward, poking and probing into the crevices with its slender, curved bill. It stops to eat a caterpillar it has found and rests comfortably for a moment, gripping the bark with sharp claws and propping itself against the tree with stiff, pointed tail feathers, much in the manner of a woodpecker. Its snack finished, it continues in search of more, hitching its way up the trunk with a jerky gait. Reaching the upper branches, it flutters down like a wind-blown leaf to the base of another tree and again begins to climb.

Such is the slow, silent, often unseen search of the lovely little brown creeper. Occasionally it utters a soft *see* call, and in courtship it may sing a high-pitched *see-see-see-titi-see* song. It may also join a winter feeding flock of chickadees, titmice, nuthatches and others as they forage through the woods. But for the most part, it goes quietly about its business, attracting little attention with its secretive, solitary ways.

The brown creeper occurs across the continent, breeding from Alaska to Newfoundland. In the East, it ranges southward to the Appalachians; in the West, through the higher mountains into Central America. It has been found nesting in

Sharp claws and stiff tail feathers aid the brown creeper in its climb.

Texas only in the Guadalupe Mountains. During the winter, however, it moves southward to the Gulf and can be found virtually throughout the state.

Older bird books call it *Certhia familiaris* and consider it the same species as the European tree creeper; however, some recent studies indicate a closer relationship to another Old World species, the short-toed tree creeper *(C. brachydactyla)*. The AOU *Check-list of North American Birds* suggests that, "Until relationships in the entire complex are studied, it seems best to retain all three forms as species."

The brown creeper breeds in co-niferous and swampy forests, where it normally builds a nest behind a peeling slab of bark. Constructed of shredded bark, grasses, feathers and mosses, the cup cradles a half-dozen white eggs sparsely flecked with reddish brown. The male feeds his incubating mate, and her brood hatches in 14 to 17 days. The young quickly learn to creep upward along the trunk, leaving the nest in about two weeks to begin foraging for the insects and their eggs and larvae that make up most of the creeper's diet.

PERCHING BIRDS

To the professional ornithologist, the term "perching bird" refers to members of the scientific order Passeriformes, usually called the passerines. The huge order comprises such diverse families as the flycatchers, jays, thrushes, warblers, blackbirds, finches and sparrows. It is the group we normally think of as our smaller "songbirds."

All of the above plus four additional families are included here because the beginning birder is likely to regard them as "perching birds." They are: the parrots (Psittacidae), the cuckoos (Cuculidae), the kingfishers (Alcedinidae) and the swifts (Apodidae). The swifts actually share their order with the hummingbirds, to which they are anatomically similar, but birders are more likely to mistake swifts for swallows.

The perching birds form a very large and complex group, but most of its members can be readily divided into their different families by physical characteristics and by their habits and habitats. The warblers and vireos, for example, are small birds that look much alike; however, the vireos have heavier bills. Once an unknown bird is assigned to its proper family, the problem of identification becomes much simpler.

A male common yellowthroat looks over the realm he claimed by song.

PARROTS (Family Psittacidae)

As amazing as it may now seem, flocks of wild parrots once swarmed across the eastern and southern portions of the United States. This was the Carolina parakeet *(Conuropsis carolinensis)*, a green bird the size of a mourning dove with an orange and yellow head. In the 19th century, it ranged from Nebraska to New York and southward to Florida and the Gulf States. The AOU checklist notes, "Texas records doubtful," but Oberholser lists far too many occurrences for its former presence to be seriously in doubt. He wrote that until about 1890 it was a fairly common summer resident along the Red River, and he cited "a number seen and 1 taken" near Corpus Christi in 1895.

The Carolina parakeet inhabited bottomland forests and wooded swamps, nesting in tree cavities and feeding on fruits and seeds. However, it also proved partial to citrus, pecans, grapes, corn and other orchard and garden crops. Parakeets swarmed over piles of grain until, in Audubon's words, it looked as if "a brilliantly coloured carpet had been thrown over them." Farmers shot them relent-

Green parakeets nest in a South Texas palm.

lessly, and many more were captured as cage birds. By the early 1900s, the Carolina parakeet was gone from the wild. A few were reported from southern forests into the 1930s, but these were probably similar species that had escaped from captivity. The last known individual expired in the Cincinnati Zoo in 1914. Ironically, the last passenger pigeon died there that same year.

Present-day Texas parrots are limited to escapees from captivity or strays from across the Rio Grande. One of the former, the monk parakeet, has established itself in various locations across the state and seems to be reproducing and maintaining a viable population. Others, like the green parakeet and the red-crowned parrot, occur in significant numbers in the lower Rio Grande Valley, particularly in Brownsville and McAllen. Arguments still rage as to whether these flocks resulted from a natural range extension by wild Mexican birds or from either deliberate or accidental introduction by humans. The truth may be a combination of the two. Although their checklist status as Texas residents remains in doubt, many birders take the time to see these free-flying parrots while seeking other exotic birdlife in deep South Texas.

Countless other parrots and their relatives turn up from time to time across the state. Budgerigars, cockatiels, even cockatoos, wander through the neighborhoods. All are escapees, and most quickly vanish; they have little ornithological significance except as curiosities. Indeed, it is probably in the best interests of our native birds that these exotics do not become established in the wild.

More than 300 species of parrots occur worldwide, most of them in tropical regions. With their striking plumages and unique beaks, they are easily recognized. Many are popular as cage birds. The trade in wild birds, however, threatens species around the world, and such exotic pets should be limited to birds produced in captive-breeding programs.

In addition to their heavy, hooked beaks, parrots have "yoked" toes, with two pointing forward and two turned backward. This provides a viselike grip for climbing and great dexterity in picking up food. The tongue is thick and fleshy and has a horny growth like a human fingernail below. Both tongue and hinged upper mandible are used skillfully to grasp food items in clawlike fashion against the short, thick lower mandible.

The voices of the parrots are notoriously strident and grating, yet these birds have an amazing ability to mimic sounds and articulate human speech. With their ability to clamber through the trees, using both feet and beak, they are sometimes called the monkeys of the bird world.

There are no clear-cut rules of parrot nomenclature. Larger forms with squared tails are usually called "parrots"; smaller ones with proportionately long, slender tails are "parakeets." Local names blur these guidelines. At the extremes of the parrot family are the large, long-tailed macaws and the tiny parrotlets.

Monk parakeets have escaped from captivity to colonize several areas.

MONK PARAKEET *Myiopsitta monachus*

The monk parakeet is also known in the pet trade as the "Quaker parakeet" and the "gray-headed parakeet." A native of southern South America, it has been released at several locations in the United States and has established small populations in Houston, Dallas and elsewhere in Texas. These recent immigrants have nested in several cities in the state, but their current status is difficult to assess. They are most conspicuous because of their exotic appearance, loud shrieks, and large, bulky nests of sticks and green leaves placed in trees or atop utility poles.

The foot-long monk parakeet is green, with a gray face and throat. The gray breast is lightly barred with darker feather edgings, while the belly is yellowish green. In flight this small parrot flashes bright blue primaries and secondaries.

Because it is adapted to the temperate regions of South America, the monk parakeet does not depend on a tropical climate as do many exotic cage birds. Thus there are fewer barriers to its naturalization in the North. It was first reported in the U.S. in 1967, and by 1972 parakeets were found across the continent, from New York to California. During the period from 1968 to 1970, nearly 35,000 monk parakeets were legally imported. Broken crates at Kennedy Airport contributed to the initial spread; other birds escaped or were released from pet shops and homes. Press reports indicated a population of nearly 5,000 free-flying parakeets by 1973.

Because the species has proved a major agricultural pest in Argentina, several states including New York, New Jersey, Virginia and California began a coordinated program of eradication. They "retrieved" fewer birds than expected, but the program was apparently successful. The threat may have been more imagined than real, but there are inevitable problems with introducing exotic wildlife species. Had the parakeet become more abundant, agencies estimate the damage to agricultural crops would have equaled two million dollars in California alone.

The monk parakeet remains most abundant in southern Florida, where it shares the hospitable, subtropical climate with the canary-winged parakeet, budgerigar, rose-ringed parakeet and a host of other liberated pets. A number roam the thickets and suburban neighborhoods of Texas, too, surprising birders unaccustomed to having parrots within view.

GREEN PARAKEET *Aratinga holochlora*

The sun is setting in an orange sky as the parakeets come in to roost. Their shrill, noisy chatter precedes them and alerts the birder to their arrival. They come in groups of three, four, a half dozen, their long-tailed forms outlined against the sky. Screeching loudly, they pile into the treetops, green plumage gleaming in the last rays of the sun. It is a scene straight out of tropical Mexico or Central America, but the cast is Texan; the setting, a tree-lined street in Brownsville.

Authorities disagree on the history of these foot-long, all-green parakeets that normally range through Mexico to Nicaragua. Some ornithologists and birders trace their origins to escaped or liberated cage birds; others insist that they crossed the Rio Grande on their own. The latter course seems possible, for the green parakeet is a year-round resident along the Rio Corona in Tamaulipas, less than 180 miles southwest of the border. With wild habitat disappearing rapidly in Mexico, the birds are perhaps being forced to expand their range.

Whatever their origin, green parakeets have become well established in the lower Rio Grande Valley in recent years. Oberholser lists a carefully observed single bird in Santa Ana National Wildlife Refuge in 1960. Fred Webster recorded ten in Brownsville in 1976, and flocks of up to 100 parakeets are now being seen regularly in McAllen and Brownsville. Pairs have also been observed nesting in those cities, and the population is undoubtedly increasing.

The red-crowned parrot (*Amazona viridigenalis*) staged a similar invasion of southern Texas. A chunky, short-tailed parrot with a bright red crown and red patches on the wings, it was recorded in Brownsville in the mid-1970s. Nesting has been confirmed in Brownsville, Harlingen and McAllen, with the breeding pairs using holes in dead palm trees. Although not as abundant as the green parakeet at the present time, the red-crowned parrot can also be seen regularly in small flocks.

The red-lored parrot (*Amazona autumnalis*) and the yellow-headed parrot (*A. oratrix*) are occasionally spotted in the Valley with the others. These species are less likely to have arrived under their own power and are regarded as escaped cagebirds. They, too, may become established in the future.

The flocks of parrots and parakeets move with the seasons and the conditions within their adopted cities. Area refuges, rare-bird alerts and local birders can usually provide information on their current locations.

Green parakeets (opposite) lend a tropical air to Brownsville neighborhoods.

CUCKOOS (Family Cuculidae)

A young groove-billed ani spreads its growing wings to the warm sun.

No other bird family in North America contains such an odd assortment of species. There are the sleek, streamlined, brown-and-white cuckoos; the black parrot-billed anis; and the ground-dwelling roadrunner, which was included in the section on Upland Ground Birds because of its terrestrial habits. The Cuculidae comprises a large family of more than 120 members that are widely distributed in the Old World, but only a few reside in the United States.

While this may seem at first to be a strangely disparate group, there are many anatomical similarities. All are relatively slender birds with long, floppy tails and large beaks. They also have two toes pointing forward and two back; perching birds typically have three forward, one back. Many are brood parasites, laying their eggs in the nests of other birds; however, that trait is less prominent in New World species.

The common European cuckoo (*Cuculus canorus*) was named in ancient times for its call, and that name has insinuated itself into our lexicon in many ways. We build cuckoo clocks with birds that announce the hour in the cuckoo's repetitive voice, and we use the term cuckoo for someone we perceive to have more than the usual eccentricities. A cuckold is the deceived husband of an unfaithful wife, alluding to the female cuckoo's habit of laying her eggs in other nests. The Greek word for the cuckoo was borrowed for our tailbone, the coccyx, when some early anatomist saw a similarity between the fused, rudimentary human vertebrae and the curved beak of the bird.

YELLOW-BILLED CUCKOO   *Coccyzus americanus*

The yellow-billed cuckoo is a migrant and summer resident throughout Texas and is more common than most people realize. A skulker, it sits motionless in dense thickets, then darts out in fast, direct flight. More often heard than seen, it calls in a series of loud, hollow notes, *kuk-kuk-kuk,* gradually slowing to a more deliberate *kowp-kowp-kowp.* The cuckoo frequently sings when storm clouds are building and has acquired the name "rain crow" across the countryside.

Unlike the European cuckoos, which are brood parasites and lay their eggs in the nests of other birds, North American species do so only rarely. They ordinarily incubate their own eggs and raise their own young. The nest is a crude, frail platform of twigs in a tree or bush and usually contains four pale greenish blue eggs.

Both parents share in the nest chores and feed their chicks on regurgitated insects. Cuckoos consume large quantities of hairy caterpillars that many birds ignore, and they are important controls of such pests as tent caterpillars and the imported gypsy moth.

The yellow-billed cuckoo ranges from southern Canada to Mexico. It appears to be declining throughout much of its U.S. range and has been proposed for endangered status in the West. Twelve inches long, it is brown above and white below and flashes rufous primaries in flight. The yellow lower mandible and large white spots on the underside of the tail are diagnostic.

The similar black-billed cuckoo *(Coccyzus erythropthalmus)* is a less common migrant through the eastern half of Texas. It lacks the rusty primaries of the yellow-billed cuckoo and has smaller white tail-spots and a black bill. A few breeding records of the black-bill exist for the northern edge of the state, but it occurs primarily as a spring migrant in late April and early May. A reclusive, secretive bird, it is always a prize for the alert birder.

A third species, the mangrove cuckoo *(C. minor)*, inhabits southern Florida and the Caribbean. It has buffy underparts and a black mask through the eye. Only a very few records exist for Texas.

Rufous wing-patches and white tail-spots mark the yellow-billed cuckoo.

GROOVE-BILLED ANI

Crotophaga sulcirostris

The groove-billed ani is one of Texas' strangest birds, even by cuckoo standards. An all-black, jay-sized bird with a long tail, the ani (pronounced *AH-nee*) might be mistaken for a grackle by the casual observer. However, its absurd, almost puffinlike beak is flattened and deeply ridged, giving a comical air to what Oberholser called a "lizardlike facial expression." Adding to the comic effect are the ani's loose-jointed actions. It flies weakly with a rapid flapping of its short wings followed by a long glide. On landing, its long tail flies up over its head, almost knocking the ani from its precarious perch. It looks, quite literally, as if it is falling apart.

The groove-billed ani ranges from the Rio Grande Valley southward through the tropics to Peru. Although it normally breeds in the U.S. only in deep South Texas, it wanders up the length of the coast and along the Rio Grande to the Big Bend. There are sporadic records for other portions of the state and, in spite of their awkward flight, anis have turned up as far away as Minnesota. While most species migrate toward warmer climates for the winter, the groove-billed ani tends to disperse northward after the breeding season. It then spends the fall and winter in thickets and tamarisk mottes all along the Texas coastal plain.

Long, floppy tails and strangely shaped beaks give groove-billed anis a comical appearance matched by their ungainly antics.

The name ani comes from the Tupi Indian language of Brazil, while the genus name, *Crotophaga*, means "tick eater." Some references state that anis commonly perch on the backs of cattle to pick off ticks, while other authors assert the behavior is rare. Indeed, habits seem to vary with the region. The insect diet is varied with seeds and fruits, and it is this omnivorous behavior that enables anis to move into colder climates in the winter, when insects are normally scarce.

Groove-billed anis are gregarious and often gather in small flocks. Sitting motionless in thickets, they betray their presence with a repertoire of soft, liquid, gurgling notes and a chorus of two-syllable calls usually described as *tee-ho* or *pee-oh*. When disturbed, they utter harsh alarm cries and flutter off in their frantic flap-and-sail manner.

Even during the breeding season, when most other birds defend individual territories, anis may band together in small groups of two to four pairs. The communal nests are bulky masses of dead twigs lined with green leaves. Females each lay three or four pale bluish eggs and take turns incubating them. Newly hatched babies are blind, naked and helpless, with parchment black skin. As they grow, they scramble about in the foliage, clinging awkwardly to the thorny branches.

The groove-billed ani takes its name from the shallow grooves on the surface of its beak. However, these are visible only at close range and may be lacking entirely on young birds and a few adults. The similar smooth-billed ani *(C. ani)* of southern Florida has an even higher bill, but without the grooves. Because the normal ranges of the two do not overlap, there is little chance for confusion. There are a few unsubstantiated sight records of the smooth-billed for the upper coast, but the only ani to be expected in Texas is the groove-billed.

KINGFISHERS (Family Alcedinidae)

Belted kingfisher.

Kingfishers are typically stocky, short-legged birds with large heads and large, heronlike beaks. Many have ragged crests. The family contains more than 80 species, but only a half dozen occur in the Western Hemisphere. A single kingfisher, the belted, is widely distributed in North America, while the green and ringed kingfishers are tropical birds that reach their northern limits in Texas. Thus the lower Rio Grande Valley remains the only place in the U.S. where birders can expect to encounter all three North American kingfishers at one time.

As the name implies, New World kingfishers feed primarily on fish. Hovering over the water or watching intently from low perches, they plunge headlong to catch their prey. Some Old World species, however, range far from any permanent water and consume mainly insects, lizards, or other animal prey.

The family name, Alcedinidae, stems from classical Greek mythology. Alcyone, daughter of Aeolus, God of the Wind, was so distraught when her husband perished in a shipwreck that she threw herself into the sea. Both were then transformed into kingfishers and roamed the waves together. When they nested on the open sea, the winds remained calm and the weather balmy. Unusually peaceful days at sea are still called "halcyon days," a variant spelling of Alcyone. *Alcyon,* too, serves as the specific name of the belted kingfisher.

BELTED KINGFISHER   *Ceryle alcyon*

The belted kingfisher is the only member of its family in most of North America. It breeds from Alaska and Canada to the southern states, inhabiting saline marshes and bays as well as freshwater streams, ponds and lakes. Because it depends on fishing for the major portion of its diet, it withdraws from the northern, ice-bound regions in winter and moves southward, ranging from the midsec-tion of the country through Central America. In Texas, it nests across the northern and eastern portions of the state, south to Pecos, San Antonio and Corpus Christi. It spreads out across much of the state in winter but occurs infrequently on the arid plains and in western desert regions.

More than a foot long, with a large beak and bushy crest, the belted kingfisher is slate blue above and white below. The name comes from a blue-gray band across the breast of both sexes. The female also has a chestnut band across the belly. Normally solitary except during the breeding season, it perches on branches, posts or wires near the water and plunges headlong after passing fish. Its distinctive call is a loud, raspy rattle, described appropriately by one author as like the clicking of a fisherman's reel.

The belted kingfisher nests in a burrow dug into the bank. Male and female alternate in the digging, tun-

A female belted kingfisher perches on a bayfront fishing pier. The male kingfisher lacks the rusty belly-band.

neling with their beaks and pushing the excavated soil backward with their feet. Burrows average three to six feet long but may reach 15 feet, sloping slightly upward for drainage and ending in a domed chamber where the female lays her five to eight white eggs. Both sexes incubate, and the naked, helpless babies hatch in about 24 days. Brooded by the female, they also cling together in a ball for warmth until their feathers develop. Minnows, with occasional insects, frogs and lizards, make up their diet. Bones are regurgitated as pellets and soon carpet the floor of the den.

Leaving the burrow at about five weeks of age, young kingfishers are taught to fish by their parents. Some authorities report seeing adults drop dead prey into the water for their fledglings, forcing them to dive after it. Once they learn to feed themselves, they are forced out to seek their own territories.

An even larger bird, the ringed kingfisher (*Ceryle torquata*), has invaded the Rio Grande Valley from Mexico. When Roger Tory Peterson wrote *A Field Guide to the Birds of Texas* in 1960, he described it as "Casual in s. Texas (at least 7 records)." The ringed kingfisher was found nesting on the Texas side of the Rio Grande two miles below Falcon Dam in April 1970, and it has become more common ever since. Although still one of the birding prizes of the Valley, it is regularly seen below Falcon Dam and at various locations along the river to Brownsville.

In addition to its 16-inch length and greater bulk, the ringed kingfisher can be distinguished from the belted by its rusty belly. The male is entirely rusty red below; the female has a slate-blue breast separated by a narrow white band from the rust-colored belly and undertail coverts. Its harsh rattling calls are slower and lower in pitch than those of the belted kingfisher, and it utters a loud series of *chack* notes in flight.

GREEN KINGFISHER *Chloroceryle americana*

To anyone familiar with the common belted kingfisher, its eight-inch green relative seems absurdly small. The large head and disproportionately large bill, however, mark it immediately as a kingfisher. Dark green above and white below, it has a short, inconspicuous crest at the back of the head. The male sports a rust-colored breast band; the female, a band of green spots. The call of the green kingfisher is a soft but sharp *tick tick,* much like the striking together of two pebbles. Flushed from its perch, it utters a squeaky *cheep* and flashes white outer tail feathers as it darts away in rapid flight.

The green kingfisher haunts the banks of freshwater streams and resacas, utilizing shallower water than does the larger belted kingfisher. It perches on low, sheltered branches or streamside rocks and dives for its catch in typical kingfisher fashion. It also darts out for insects to vary its piscine diet. The nest burrow in a sandy bank averages two to three feet long and shelters four to six white eggs. Rising water presents an obvious threat to nest success, but recent studies show that imported fire ants destroy more broods than all other enemies combined.

A tropical species, the green kingfisher ranges from Argentina and Uruguay northward to Texas. It is an uncommon resident along the lower Rio Grande, from Brownsville to the Pecos River, and also fishes in the clear streams of the Edwards Plateau. Never easy to find, this charming, colorful little kingfisher is a prize well worth a patient search.

Although very small, the green kingfisher displays the classic family profile.

FLYCATCHERS (Family Tyrannidae)

A western kingbird scans the prairie for insects.

The name "tyrant flycatchers" describes this large family perfectly. Always alert and pugnacious, they rigorously rule their territories, darting out to chase off other birds that venture near. Some are also known as "kingbirds," an equally appropriate name, for they readily attack much larger hawks and crows that unwittingly invade their air space.

More than 360 flycatcher species inhabit the Americas from Alaska to Tierra del Fuego. Most are tropical residents, but about 35 range into Texas. A few of those on the state checklist, however, occur only as rare vagrants. The tyrant flycatchers present some of the most difficult of all identification problems for the birder. With such notable exceptions as the distinctive scissor-tailed flycatcher and the brilliant vermilion flycatcher, they wear drab plumages in shades of brown or gray. Some, in fact, are so similar in appearance that they must be identified primarily by voice. The flycatchers tend to be a noisy, vociferous group, and their calls are not particularly musical.

Family members can be recognized by their general appearance and habits. They tend to perch in an upright posture on exposed tree limbs or wires and fly out to catch passing insects in the air. Their heads are large and often slightly crested, and they have broad, flat bills surrounded by long rictal bristles, or "whiskers," that help to funnel insects into their gaping mouths. Small prey is captured with an audible snap of the mandibles; larger insects are carried back to the perch and beaten on a limb until tender enough to swallow. Most Texas flycatchers migrate southward for the winter to assure a plentiful supply of food.

SCISSOR-TAILED FLYCATCHER *Tyrannus forficatus*

Few birds equal the subtle beauty and graceful elegance of the scissor-tailed flycatcher. Although it is officially the state bird of Oklahoma, people south of the Red River have long called it "the Texas bird of paradise."

Certainly I will never forget my first encounter with a scissor-tail more than 30 years ago. Newly arrived in Texas, I went out on a warm spring afternoon to wander through the countryside. Along a quiet country road in Chambers County I found the bird perched on a fence, and as I stopped to watch, it darted up to catch a fluttering grasshopper in its beak. In flight its long black-and-white tail scissored open and closed, and I thought I had never seen such a splendid bird.

I followed close behind it for half a mile as it moved along the fence, flying out several times across the field and returning to its perch. Its upperparts were pale pearl gray, its whitish underparts flushed with salmon pink. Then, in response to a nearby scissortail, it began what I could only assume was a courtship display. Rising high in the air on fluttering wings to reveal their salmon-colored linings, it stalled at the top of its rise and then performed two complete backward loops and a sweeping dive. Pulling out just above the ground, it flared its streaming tail and settled gracefully back on the wire. I had no way of knowing if the other bird was suitably impressed, but I was instantly in love. My fascination with the scissor-tail has not diminished to this day.

The scissor-tailed flycatcher ranges from southern Nebraska to southern Texas, migrating southward in the fall to Mexico and Central America. During that migration, flocks of up to 50 or more birds assemble across the Texas plains and line the roadside fences with autumn elegance. Returning in the spring, they fan out across most of Texas to nest and raise their young. Scissor-tails prefer ranches and farms, mesquite savannahs, and other semi-open areas, but are rare in the far western corner of the state.

The nest is a grass-lined cup of twigs and weed stems in a tree or bush. The four to six whitish eggs are richly mottled with brown, violet or gray and are incubated by the female. Hatching in about 14 days, the ravenous young consume vast quantities of insects brought to the nest by both attentive parents. They fledge at two weeks of age. Immature scissor-tails have short tails and resemble western kingbirds; however, their underparts are washed with pink rather than yellow.

From April through October, the scissor-tailed flycatcher ornaments the Texas countryside, catching insects on the wing and dropping frequently to the ground in pursuit of grasshoppers, crickets, beetles and other fare. A few berries supplement the diet, but flycatchers are largely insectivores.

The scissor-tail's beauty belies its pugnacious personality. It fiercely defends its territory against intruders and does not hesitate to chase off a passing crow or hawk. Swooping repeatedly amidst a tirade of shrill, bickering notes or harsh *keck* or *kew* calls, it pecks at the less mobile subject of its wrath until the harried target is only too happy to escape.

The lovely scissor-tailed flycatcher has been called "the Texas bird of paradise."

Black above and white below, the eastern kingbird has a white-tipped tail.

Eastern Kingbird   *Tyrannus tyrannus*

Some birds are named for their color patterns or songs; some, for their preferred habitats. The eastern kingbird is named for its despotic personality. *Tyrannus* comes from the Latin term for an absolute ruler, passing into English as "tyrant." Thus this kingbird, *Tyrannus tyrannus,* is the ruler of rulers, lord of lords, and it asserts its regal authority at every opportunity.

Not that it causes any harm to other species, but the eastern kingbird tolerates no invasion of its territory. Sitting alertly upright on an exposed perch, it darts out at any intruder with an excited tirade of shrill cries. *Kit-kit-kitter-kitter* and *dzee-dzee-dzee* approximate some of its more vocal phrases. Size is no deterrent, and this eight- to nine-inch monarch does not hesitate to skirmish with the largest hawk, diving at it from above and even landing on its broad back to deliver a peck or two. Once the interloper flees, the victorious kingbird returns to its perch, surveying its realm for both insect prey and avian trespassers.

The eastern kingbird can be mistaken for no other bird. It is black above and white below, with a white terminal band on the black tail. A small crown of red-orange feathers remains hidden beneath the black cap and is seldom visible in the field, although it is often portrayed in field guides.

A resident of open woodlands, farms and orchards, the eastern kingbird ranges from Canada to the Gulf States. As the name implies, it is most abundant east of the Rocky Mountains and is absent from the Pacific Coast and the Desert Southwest. In Texas, it migrates throughout the state, except for the Trans-Pecos, but it occurs most abundantly along the coast. It also remains to nest in the eastern and northern portions of Texas, west to the Panhandle and Kerrville and south to Houston and the upper coast.

It builds a nest of twigs and weed stems on a limb and lines it well with soft grasses, rootlets and feathers. The three or four white eggs are blotched with brown. The eastern kingbird is a common host for the troublesome brown-headed cowbird, but it often recognizes and ejects the cowbird egg from its nest. Hatching in about two weeks, kingbird babies feed on insects brought by both attentive parents and fledge two weeks after hatching. Insects continue to provide the major portion of their diet, but berries are also added when in season. It is not unusual to see eastern kingbirds flying around a mulberry tree, plucking ripe fruits and swallowing them whole.

Western Kingbird

Tyrannus verticalis

The western kingbird, as the name implies, ranges widely across western North America, from Canada to Mexico and from the Great Plains to the Pacific Coast. An inhabitant of dry, open country, it has expanded its range considerably in the 20th century with the settlement of the land and the creation of added nesting sites. The trees of farm groves and shelterbelts, utility poles, windmills and barns all serve as suitable locations for the saucer-shaped nests of twigs and grasses. This kingbird is at home on the prairies or in the scrubby deserts, but it may also nest on light poles along busy streets. Although it normally winters in Mexico and Central America, stragglers wander widely in the fall and early winter to turn up at scattered locations in the East.

The western kingbird commonly breeds across the western two-thirds of Texas, east to Denton and Austin. However, nesting pairs are occasionally encountered in the Houston area and along the coast as well. It has also become more common in South Texas in recent years. As with the other flycatchers, the kingbird's diet consists of insects and, to a lesser extent, berries and other fruits.

The western kingbird has ashy gray upperparts tinged with olive-green on the back. The throat and breast are pale gray, the belly lemon yellow. A red-orange crown patch is often shown in paintings of the species, but that mark is usually concealed and seldom visible in the field. The black tail has white edges, distinguishing the wide-ranging western kingbird from the similar Cassin's kingbird *(Tyrannus vociferans)* of the Trans-Pecos and Couch's kingbird of far South Texas. Both of the latter species lack the white edgings, and Couch's also has a notched tail. Also distinctive is the call of the western kingbird, a sharp, whistled *whit.*

COUCH'S KINGBIRD

Tyrannus couchii

Couch's kingbird is the common nesting kingbird of the lower Rio Grande Valley, ranging northward to Laredo, Kingsville and, on rare occasions, the upper coast. It was long considered a subspecies of the tropical kingbird *(Tyrannus melancholicus)* and appears under that name in older field guides. However, biologists have determined that both forms merit species status. Couch's kingbird occurs in deep South Texas and southward along the eastern coast of Mexico, while the tropical kingbird ranges into southeastern Arizona from western Mexico.

Although almost identical in appearance, Couch's and tropical kingbirds can be separated by voice, a factor that probably serves to inhibit interbreeding. Texas' Couch's kingbird has a shrill, rolling *breeeer* or *queeer* call and a sharp *kip,* the latter given singly or in a series. The tropical kingbird's normal vocalization is a rapid, twittering *pip-pip-pip-pip.*

Couch's kingbird can be separated from the other yellow-bellied kingbirds in Texas, the western and Cassin's, by its dark brown, rather than black, tail that is slightly notched and lacks white edges. It also has a larger bill and a darker ear-patch on

Ever vigilant for an insect meal, a western kingbird pauses on a fence wire.

Couch's kingbird occurs primarily in deep South Texas.

its gray head. Fairly common in the Rio Grande Valley during the summer, it is rare in winter, when it moves southward into Mexico. Couch's kingbird inhabits groves and thickets, usually near water, and flies out from its treetop perches to capture insects on the wing. Like other tyrant flycatchers, it is territorial and aggressive toward intruders.

GREAT KISKADEE *Pitangus sulphuratus*

This large, colorful flycatcher can be mistaken for no other Texas species. Brown above and bright yellow below, it has reddish brown wings and tail and a boldly striped black-and-white head. A yellow crown-patch is often concealed. The kiskadee's namesake call is a loud, deliberate *kis-ka-dee.* It also utters a loud *whank* and a persistent, raucous chatter that betray its presence in the wet woodlands and thickets of deep South Texas. An abundant tropical species that ranges southward to Argentina, it crosses the U.S. border only in the lower Rio Grande Valley and wanders occasionally as far as the Big Bend region and the central coast.

The great kiskadee was called the kiskadee flycatcher in earlier field guides and has also been known casually as the "derby flycatcher." In the tropics, it has a number of similarly plumaged relatives that vary greatly in size. According to Gruson, the genus name comes from the South American Tupi Indian word for "flycatcher," *pitangua. Sulphuratus* refers to the vivid lemon yellow underparts.

Usually found near water, kiskadees often dive for minnows, frogs and tadpoles in addition to catching insects. They do not dive deep enough to submerge, but their behavior resembles that of the kingfishers, a comparison heightened by the large head and bill. The nest is an untidy globe of grasses, weed stems, mosses and feathers in a thorny tree and is entered through an opening on the side. The four or five white eggs are speckled with brown, but the breeding biology and the incubation and fledging periods require further study.

A noisy, aggressive resident of the lower Valley, this unique flycatcher shares its habitat with many other colorful South Texas specialties including the green jay and the Altamira oriole. It remains in Texas throughout the year and is relatively easy to find in such refuges as Santa Ana and Bentsen–Rio Grande State Park.

ASH-THROATED FLYCATCHER
Myiarchus cinerascens

The ash-throated flycatcher is the West Texas representative of the genus *Myiarchus.* The great crested flycatcher represents the group in East Texas; the brown-crested flycatcher, in South Texas. These three species and several others in tropical America share bushy crests, brownish upperparts and yellowish bellies. They differ slightly in size and color, particularly in the amount of rufous in the tail. Vocalizations are usually distinctive.

About eight inches in length, the ash-throated flycatcher is the smallest of the state's regular *Myiarchus* species. It has a grayish brown head and back, pale gray throat and breast, and pale yellow belly. The tail feathers have reddish inner webs. Calls include a rolling *prrrt* and a burry *ke-wheer.*

Ash-throated flycatchers inhabit the deserts and brushlands of the southwestern U.S., from the Pacific Coast to Texas. In winter they range through Mexico to Costa Rica. The species breeds commonly in western Texas, eastward to Austin, Beeville and Laredo. It nests less frequently in the southern portion of the state and along the lower coast. There it is replaced by the larger brown-crested flycatcher *(M. tyrannulus).* The latter, formerly known as Weid's crested flycatcher, has a distinctly larger bill, brighter yellow underparts, and less rufous in the tail.

The ash-throated flycatcher is a cavity nester, using not only natural openings and old woodpecker holes in

No other North American bird shares the great kiskadee's striking pattern.

trees and posts but niches in buildings, eaves, old pipes, and even empty mailboxes. Ornithologist Olin Sewall Pettingill described one pair in California that "raised a family in the knotted leg of a pair of hanging overalls." A nest of grass, hair, fur and feathers cushions the creamy, brown-streaked eggs, and a snakeskin is sometimes added. The female incubates her four or five eggs alone, but both parents feed the nestlings. Incubation requires about 15 days; the young fledge 14 to 17 days later.

GREAT CRESTED FLYCATCHER

Myiarchus crinitus

From high in the top of a large oak comes a medley of loud, whistled calls, *wheeep wheeep wheep*, followed by a rolling *prrreet*. It is a birdsong that 18th-century naturalist Mark Catesby called an "ungrateful brawling noise." The singer is olive-brown above, with a gray throat and breast and a bright yellow belly. As he moves about in agitation, he raises a short, shaggy crest and flashes cinnamon patches in his wings and tail. He drops to a lower limb and continues his tirade, proclaiming ownership of this patch of East Texas woodland, venting his wrath on any who intrude.

Nearby in a hollow tree, his mate incubates her half dozen white eggs that are streaked and blotched with brown and purple. Below the small entrance hole, a bulky nest of leaves, grass, feathers and bits of rabbit fur fills the cavity. A snakeskin is woven through the untidy mass. The pair has twice repelled starlings that sought to usurp their nesting site, and they will continue to defend it through two weeks of incubation and another two weeks of feeding their young before they fledge.

The snakeskin is a well-known trademark of the great crested flycatcher's nest, and it was once thought to scare away potential predators. In recent times, however, flycatchers are as likely to substitute strips of plastic wrap or bits of aluminum foil. Apparently they merely seek the shiny decoration rather than assuming any protective benefit.

The great crested flycatcher nests from the forests of southern Canada to the Gulf of Mexico and from the farm groves of the Great Plains to the Atlantic Coast. In summer it inhabits the eastern half of Texas, ranging west to the Panhandle and the Edwards Plateau and south at least to Beeville and Rockport. South of that range, it is replaced by the brown-crested flycatcher; to the west, by the ash-throated flycatcher.

Its scientific name mirrors the common name of this large eastern flycatcher. *Myiarchus* is from the Greek *myia* for "fly" and *archon,* "ruler" or "chieftain"; hence, "the ruler of flies." *Crinitus* is from the Latin *crinis,* or "hairy," referring to the shaggy crest. The great crested flycatcher does, indeed, feed primarily on flying insects, but also eats berries, fruits and an occasional small lizard. Long bristles around the wide, flat bill help to funnel insects into the gaping mouth.

The western ash-throated flycatcher (top) is smaller and paler than the eastern great crested flycatcher (above).

A close-up view of a male vermilion flycatcher is one of the special treats awaiting the Texas bird watcher. Its plumage seems lighted by some inner fire.

VERMILION FLYCATCHER
Pyrocephalus rubinus

Only the most phlegmatic person can see a vermilion flycatcher for the first time and not gasp with pleasure and surprise, notes Roy Bedichek in *Adventures with a Texas Naturalist*. Indeed, every time I encounter this gleaming gem it seems a special gift, for there are few that equal its surprising beauty, especially in a family that routinely cloaks its members in somber shades.

The male's dark, sooty brown back, wings and tail contrast sharply with the flaming red of its crown and underparts. *Pyrocephalus* in Greek means "fire-headed," while *rubinus* is Latin for "ruby-red." Most descriptive of all, perhaps, is one of several Spanish names for this six-inch flycatcher, *brasita de fuego,* or "little coal of fire." Certainly a flame must come from deep within, for the plumage glows too brilliantly to be mere pigmented color.

Though much less colorful, the female is charming nonetheless. Her upperparts are grayish brown, with a blackish tail; her white underparts are streaked with dusky gray and flushed with salmon pink on the belly and undertail coverts.

I recall witnessing many years ago the courtship flight of the vermilion flycatcher. Perched on an acacia twig beside a pond, the male took off and climbed in sweeping circles high into the air, singing a soft, tinkling song that some authors describe as a repeated *pit-a-zee pit-a-zee.* At the top of his towering rise, he hung on fluttering wings like a giant butterfly, his erect crown feathers glowing in the sun, his tail cocked upward and spread. Puffing out his vermilion chest, he continued to sing, then suddenly fluttered down to land on a branch beside his chosen mate.

This spectacular flycatcher occurs from the southwestern U.S. through Central and South America to southern Argentina. It nests in western

Texas, ranging eastward through the Edwards Plateau to Austin and San Antonio and southward to the Rio Grande. In winter, it wanders more widely, turning up along the Gulf Coast and occasionally in the Panhandle and the northeastern sections of the state. It prefers streamside woodlands and thickets near small ponds and has expanded its range in Texas with the construction of irrigation ditches and stock tanks. It perches frequently on shrubs and fences near the water and darts out to capture flying insects.

The nest is a saucer of twigs on a forked branch, carefully lined with grasses, plant fibers and feathers. The two to four white eggs are blotched with brown and lilac. The female incubates them alone, while her mate feeds her through the two-week period. Both care for the babies that fledge about two weeks after hatching. Juvenile vermilion flycatchers resemble the adult female but are lightly spotted, rather than streaked, below. The young male begins to get his red plumage during his first winter, molting gradually into a flaming "little coal of fire."

EASTERN PHOEBE

Sayornis phoebe

The eastern phoebe is a familiar sight in open woodlands, streamside thickets and suburban neighborhoods, perching on a branch or wire and wagging its tail up and down, darting out occasionally to catch a flying insect with an audible snap of its black beak. It nests in the northern and central sections of Texas, west to the Panhandle and Kerrville and south to San Antonio. In migration, however, phoebes are common throughout the state, except in the Trans-Pecos region. They also remain through the winter south of the Panhandle and are particularly abundant along the coast.

The eastern phoebe inhabits woodlands, farms and towns from

The somber-plumaged eastern phoebe is nonetheless a friendly, charming little bird.

central Canada to the Gulf States. As its name indicates, it occurs from the Great Plains eastward, being replaced in the West by the Say's phoebe. Because of its insect diet, it migrates in the fall to the southern states and Mexico.

This medium-sized, seven-inch flycatcher is brownish gray above and slightly darker on the head, wings and tail. The whitish underparts are washed with pale olive on the sides and breast. In fall and winter plumage, many birds have a strong yellow wash below, but they should not be confused with the tawny-bellied Say's phoebe of the West. The eastern phoebe lacks the distinct light wing-

bars of the smaller wood-pewees and the eye-ring of the *Empidonax* flycatchers, although young birds may have brownish wing-bars for a short time. The repeated wagging of its tail when perched also helps to identify the phoebe, as does its distinctive, emphatic song, *fee-be fee-be,* with the accent on the first syllable. The call note is a sharp *chip*.

The eastern phoebe figured in the first bird-banding study conducted in North America. It was Audubon himself who tied silver threads, "loose enough so as not to hurt," around the legs of a family of phoebes in Pennsylvania and discovered they returned to the same location year after year.

In fact, eastern phoebes frequently renovate their old nests of mud pellets, moss and grasses and reuse them another year. The nest's structure is particularly sturdy, and construction normally requires more than a week of intermittent work. Phoebes often lay their second clutch of the summer in the same nest, especially if the first brood was raised successfully. Such nest re-use is the exception rather than the rule for birds.

Eastern phoebes originally nested in niches on cliffs and banks but have adapted readily to human habitation. Most now build under bridges and eaves or on the rafters of barns and sheds. Almost everyone with a lakeside home or cabin in the northern and eastern states has hosted a family of phoebes under the eaves at some time. The four or five white eggs are incubated by the female and hatch in about 16 days. Fed on insects by their parents, the always-hungry young fledge in 15 or 16 more days.

SAY'S PHOEBE *Sayornis saya*

Say's phoebe is a year-round resident of Texas west of the Pecos River and nests locally in the Panhandle as well. It wanders widely in winter across the western half of the state, as far as Dallas, Austin, San Antonio, Rockport and the Rio Grande Valley. It even turns up as a rare visitor to Houston and the upper coast. Across the continent, Say's phoebe replaces the eastern phoebe west of the Great Plains. It nests from Alaska and northwestern Canada to Mexico, inhabiting open, arid canyons, desert edges and brushy plains.

Grayish brown above, with a black tail, it has a pale grayish breast and a distinctive rust-colored belly and undertail coverts. Restless and active, Say's phoebe constantly flicks its tail while perching and often hovers to catch the insects that constitute the major portion of its diet. Its call is a thin, plaintive whistle, *pee-ee* or *pee-ur*. Like most flycatchers, it is forced to migrate from colder regions in the fall and retreats to the Desert Southwest and into Mexico.

The phoebe weaves its nest of grasses, mosses and other plant fibers, lining it with plant down, wool and hair. Bridges and building ledges have partially replaced traditional cliffside nesting sites, and abandoned houses and sheds in the West frequently harbor a pair of breeding phoebes. Four or five white eggs make up the normal clutch, although the eggs are occasionally flecked with brown.

Say's phoebe and the genus *Sayornis*—Greek for "Say's bird"— were named for Philadelphia naturalist Thomas Say, nephew of distinguished naturalist William Bartram. Despite poor health, Say made two rigorous treks to the Rocky Mountains with Major Stephen Long in 1819 and 1823 on mapping and collecting expeditions. He returned with the first specimens of the mule deer, kit fox and coyote, as well as eight new species of western birds. Say's contributions to several fields of natural history made him one of the premier scholars of his time.

Say's phoebe has a rusty wash beneath.

BLACK PHOEBE
Sayornis nigricans

This charming phoebe ranges through the Southwest, from California to Texas, and as far south as Argentina. It inhabits Trans-Pecos Texas year-round and occurs sparingly eastward onto the Edwards Plateau. The black phoebe and the vermilion flycatcher are the only two North American flycatchers that are not highly migratory. Both, however, wander more widely in our state in winter, and the black phoebe occasionally turns up in the Panhandle and even in the Rio Grande Valley.

Entirely black except for a sharply contrasting white belly, this smallest (at six and three-fourths inches) and most local of the three phoebe species is the only black-breasted flycatcher in the United States. Like the others of the genus *Sayornis*, it is an active bird, constantly wagging its tail while perched and flying out to snap up insects in the air. It usually nests and hunts near water, preferring open streamside woodlands or thickets and rocky canyons. However, it has adapted to small stock tanks and even backyard ponds. One of the most reliable places in West Texas to find the black phoebe is at Balmorhea State Park, where it frequents the giant spring-fed swimming pool and the network of small ditches that drain it.

The nest is the typical phoebe's bracket of mud, grasses and mosses solidly attached to a bridge, ledge or wall in a sheltered niche and lined with soft hair and feathers. The female incubates her three to six white eggs that are occasionally dotted with reddish brown, and they hatch in 15 to 17 days. Fledging in about two weeks, the young are taught by the male to catch insects on the wing, while the female prepares to nest a second time. Although the black phoebe feeds primarily on insects, it sometimes catches small fish at its favorite waterhole.

The black phoebe favors desert streams and ponds.

EASTERN WOOD-PEWEE   *Contopus virens*
WESTERN WOOD-PEWEE   *Contopus sordidulus*

The eastern and western wood-pewees occupy opposite sides of the continent, their ranges separated by the treeless Great Plains. Almost identical in plumage, they are generally indistinguishable except by voice and range. Some authors have considered combining the two into a single species; however, the American Ornithologists' Union still regards them as distinct, placing them together in what is termed a "superspecies."

A superspecies represents what Ehrlich, Dobkin and Wheye called in *The Birder's Handbook*, "a 'snapshot' of the process of speciation—evolution caught in the act, as it were." Because the pewees are woodland birds,

they are isolated from each other by the open plains. Over a relatively short period of time, they have each developed distinctive songs which now, presumably, would tend to prevent courtship and interbreeding. In the limited areas of range overlap, no hybrids have been found; however, the similarity of the plumages makes such a study difficult.

The wood-pewees are dark olive-gray above and pale gray below, with whiter throats and bellies. Adults display two light wing-bars that distinguish them from the larger eastern phoebe, but they lack the white eye-rings of the still smaller *Empidonax* flycatchers. The wood-pewee's upper

The eastern wood-pewee can be distinguished from its western counterpart by its song.

EMPIDONAX FLYCATCHERS
Empidonax species

The tiny *Empidonax* flycatchers are extremely difficult to identify. All are drab olive-gray birds with prominent wing-bars and light eye-rings. They are frequently washed with yellow on the belly, some more intensely than others. Identification depends more on voice, habitat and behavior than on plumage characteristics; however, a number of papers have recently been published on the finer points of their separation using size, bill shape and color, relative wing and tail lengths, and habitual tail movements.

A number of ornithologists have bemoaned the difficulty of identifying these little birds, Peterson noting that during a "wave" of these birds in spring migration, we must let most of them go as simply "*Empidonax* flycatchers." And Ludlow Griscom wrote, "Collecting has proved that it is impossible to be certain in separating Acadian, Traill's and Least Flycatchers by color characteristics even in spring. In fall, it is out of the question . . . ." The songs of all three are easily recognizable, but they seldom sing during migration.

Progress has been made in field identification since those passages were written, but it is significant to note that two new U.S. flycatchers were also discovered masquerading as other species. Both Traill's and western flycatchers were subsequently split.

Ehrlich, Dobkin and Wheye in *The Birder's Handbook* note that even the empids themselves may depend largely on song to sort out their relationships and avoid hybridizing. They are examples of "sibling species" that are similar in appearance but are nonetheless reproductively isolated.

Texas hosts nine of these confusing five- to six-inch empids that the birder can expect to encounter. Some breed in the western mountains and move through West Texas in their migrations to and from tropical America.

mandible is black; the lower, dull orange, in contrast to the phoebe's all-black bill.

The eastern wood-pewee breeds in east and central Texas, ranging westward to about San Angelo and Kerrville and south to San Antonio and Victoria. It migrates through the eastern two-thirds of the state and winters south of the U.S. border in tropical America. Its clear, plaintive song is a whistled *pee-a-wee,* sometimes alternated with a slurred *pee-yer.* Other call notes include a loud *chip* and a rising, whistled *pweee.*

The western wood-pewee occupies West Texas east to the Edwards Plateau and migrates through the Panhandle and plains and along the Rio Grande. Like its eastern counterpart, it does not occur in the U.S. in winter. Its song has been described as *tsweetee-teet* mixed with *peeer* notes.

Both pewees construct neat nests of grasses and weed stems on horizontal limbs far from the tree trunk. However, the eastern species often camouflages its nest with lichens, while the western seldom does. Females incubate their two to four eggs and are fed by their mates.

Also included in the genus *Contopus,* Greek for "short-footed," is the olive-sided flycatcher (*C. borealis*). A northern species, it breeds sparingly in the high Guadalupe Mountains and also crosses Texas in its spring and fall migrations between Canada and South America. Larger than the wood-pewees, it has a more massive head and bill and a whiter throat. Dark patches on the sides of the chest are separated by a white strip down the center, suggesting, as Peterson notes, "a dark jacket unbuttoned down front." White tufts on the rump behind the folded wings are also diagnostic but not always visible.

A similar set of species inhabits Canada and the northern states and migrates primarily through eastern Texas during April and May and again from August into October. Only two, the Acadian flycatcher of the East and the cordilleran (formerly western) flycatcher of the West, nest regularly in Texas. The willow and gray flycatchers have also been recorded breeding in the western portions of the state. Lingering empids are sometimes seen in winter, but most migrate well south of the Rio Grande.

YELLOW-BELLIED FLY-CATCHER *(E. flaviventris)*: More yellow below than other eastern empids, the yellow-belly migrates through the eastern half of Texas and is most abundant near the coast.

ACADIAN FLYCATCHER *(E. virescens)*: The Acadian is the only empid that nests in the forested parts of eastern and central Texas, ranging locally to the Edwards Plateau and south to Houston. It is common in migration throughout the eastern half of the state.

ALDER FLYCATCHER *(E. alnorum)*: A migrant through Texas, the alder flycatcher is combined with the willow flycatcher as Traill's flycatcher in older publications.

WILLOW FLYCATCHER *(E. traillii)*: The willow flycatcher migrates throughout the state and has been found nesting locally in West Texas and in the canyons of the Panhandle.

LEAST FLYCATCHER *(E. minimus)*: As its name suggests, this is the smallest of the empids. Nesting in Canada and the northern states, it migrates through most of Texas east of the Panhandle and Big Bend.

HAMMOND'S FLYCATCHER *(E. hammondii)*: This little bird breeds in the coniferous forests of the western mountains, from Alaska to New Mexico, and is a migrant mainly in the Trans-Pecos.

DUSKY FLYCATCHER *(E. oberholseri)*: A migrant through West Texas, the dusky flycatcher has been found occasionally in summer in the Guadalupe Mountains.

GRAY FLYCATCHER *(E. wrightii)*: Slightly larger and less olive-colored than the similar dusky flycatcher, the gray flycatcher is a western migrant through the Trans-Pecos. A nest has recently been found in the Davis Mountains.

CORDILLERAN FLY-CATCHER *(E. occidentalis)*: Combined with the Pacific-slope flycatcher in pre-1989 books as the western flycatcher, the cordilleran is the western counterpart of the yellow-bellied flycatcher. Brownish green above and yellowish below, it is the only empid that breeds regularly in the mountain woodlands of Trans-Pecos Texas.

The tiny least flycatcher is only one of several in its genus. Most are extremely difficult to identify as they move through Texas.

LARKS (Family Alaudidae)

The 75 members of the lark family are primarily Old World birds, with two-thirds of them in Africa. Only one, the horned lark, is native to North America. The familiar meadowlarks do not belong to the Alaudidae, but instead are classified with the blackbirds and orioles.

A second species, the Eurasian skylark *(Alauda arvensis),* was established on Canada's Vancouver Island in the early 1900s and has colonized the San Juan Islands of Washington as well. Similar attempts to introduce it in Brooklyn in the 1880s were not successful. The skylark is the legendary songster of prose and poetry.

The larks are small, brownish songbirds with musical voices. Primarily ground dwellers, they walk rather than hop and seldom perch in trees or shrubs. Although they have slender bills, they normally feed on a mixture of seeds and insects.

A horned lark feeds its young in their nest beneath a prickly pear.

HORNED LARK *Eremophila alpestris*

Though scarcely seven inches long, the little horned lark is an amazingly hardy bird. It breeds virtually throughout North America, from the Arctic tundra of Alaska and Canada southward into Mexico, and ranges widely around the Northern Hemisphere. In Britain, where it is frequently seen on windswept winter beaches, it is called the "shore lark." Climbers of Mount Everest have found it in almost every Tibetan village and at camps as high as 16,500 feet. The horned lark is equally at home foraging around a stranded iceberg, in the arid desert, or on a warm South Texas beach. It requires open ground, the barer the better, and seeks out dirt fields and shores in preference to woodlands or even grassy prairies. There it feeds on a variety of seeds, insects, spiders and small snails.

Flocks of larks are seen throughout Texas in the winter, and the species breeds widely across the state. It is a particularly abundant nesting bird in the Panhandle, but it also nests through North Texas, on the coastal prairie from Galveston to Brownsville, and locally in far West Texas.

Brown above and pale below, our only native lark sports a pair of devilish black feather-tuft "horns" and a distinctive face pattern. A broad black stripe beneath the eye and a black bib contrast strongly with a yellow or whitish face and throat. The many subspecies differ in the intensity of the yellow color and the amount of streaking on the brown back, but all are recognized by the strongly patterned face. In flight the horned lark flashes a black tail with white outer feathers.

In true lark fashion, the male horned lark stages a spectacular courtship display. Climbing high into the sky, sometimes to several hundred feet, he flies in wide circles, singing his high-pitched twittering, tinkling song. Once the song has ended, he folds his wings and plummets back to earth. At other times the horned lark whistles clear notes usually described as *tsee-ee* and *tsee-titi*.

The nest is a shallow depression in the ground, lined with grasses and sometimes rimmed with small stones or clods of dirt. The three or four spotted eggs are incubated by the female and hatch in 11 days. Within another 9 to 12 days the young leave the nest, and they soon wander off to join a flock of other juveniles. A week later, the female may be ready to nest again.

The genus name of the horned lark, *Eremophila,* is Greek for "solitude loving," a strange name for a bird that often travels in large flocks. However, it is more solitary and secretive during the nesting season, which may explain the choice. *Alpestris* refers to the mountains, an allusion to the northern and high-altitude breeding habitats.

Feather tufts and a black mask give the horned lark a rakish, devilish air.

SWALLOWS (Family Hirundinidae)

A barn swallow feeds its young while on the wing.

Eight of the world's 75 swallow species course the skies over Texas, their slim, streamlined bodies and long, pointed wings adapted to dazzlingly graceful flight. These aerial acrobats feed on insects caught in midair, their mouths gaping wide behind short little bills. Highly migratory because of their food habits, most spend the winter well south of U.S. borders. They often assemble in large numbers for the flight, lining roadside fences and power lines and filling the air with flickering wings.

Most swallows measure less than six inches in length. The purple martin (at eight inches) and the barn swallow (at almost seven) are the exceptions. The sociable purple martin is the best known of our swallows, but others, too, have adapted to the human presence in their territories. Barn swallows, as their name implies, frequently nest around buildings, while cliff swallow colonies have used bridges and culverts to extend their range across the flat and cliffless plains. Farther north, tree swallows have accepted nest boxes as substitutes for hollow trees. Their amazing aerobatics, cheerful chatter, and insect-eating habits make the swallows among the most popular of all our birds.

PURPLE MARTIN *Progne subis*

Perhaps no bird in North America is more popular than this largest (at eight inches) of our swallows, particularly in the eastern and midwestern states. It is certainly the foremost birdhouse species in the country. Native Americans hung hollow gourds near their lodges to attract nesting purple martins, and workers on colonial plantations continued this practice of the Choctaw and Chickasaw. Delighted by the martins' graceful flight, bubbling song and insect-eating habits, homeowners across the country now erect large multi-unit martin houses. Many cities and towns have followed suit. Author Robert Lemmon once described purple martins as "the tenement gossips of the bird world."

The purple martin spends the winter in South America and is one of the earliest of all spring migrants. The vanguard arrives in Texas in February, but a few scattered birds may even turn up in January. Males appear first and squabble over the choicest nesting sites. When the females arrive they apparently select the combination of suitor and apartment that most pleases them; however, late arrivals sometimes evict earlier tenants and move right in. At times there seems to be a curious procession of martins slipping in and out of various compartments, and polygynous males occasionally set up housekeeping with more than one female.

Martins migrate through most of Texas from February through May and again from July into October, but they are most abundant in the eastern and central counties and uncommon in West Texas. Many remain to breed, except in the western and southernmost portions of the state. Others range across North America as far as Canada; however, they are more scattered and local in the West. Hollow trees and old woodpecker holes provide the traditional nesting sites of purple martins, and although birdhouses have largely replaced such habitats in the East, tree cavities are still utilized in the western portions of the martin's range.

The nest is a rather untidy mass of grass, leaves, twigs and feathers, sometimes with a rim of mud in front to keep the eggs from rolling out. The female incubates alone, normally for 16 days. However, the three to five white eggs are sometimes left uncovered at night and may require a longer incubation time. Young martins leave the nest in four or five weeks.

After the breeding season, purple martins gather nightly in enormous colonial roosts for several weeks before migration. Late-summer premigratory colonies of tens of thousands of martins are sometimes formed even in metropolitan Houston, and a roost of more than 20,000 birds slowed motorists on the U.S. Highway 190 bridge at Lake Livingston in 1990. So thick were the birds entering and leaving the roost at sunset and sunrise that many were killed by traffic. The Texas Parks and Wildlife Department issued a warning to motorists until the martins departed for South America.

Male martins are entirely dark glossy blue-black, while females and juveniles are gray beneath with paler bellies. Many females also have a faint collar around the neck. Their shallowly forked tails and long, pointed wings are evident as they fly in sweeping circles, alternating rapid flapping with short glides, to catch insects on the wing. Martins consume prodigious quantities of insects including flies, wasps, beetles, bugs and dragonflies. They drop occasionally to the ground for ants. Arguments still rage over the number of mosquitoes they consume, and their value as mosquito control agents is probably overrated.

The martin's song is a gurgling assortment of low, guttural notes interspersed with throaty calls usually described as *tchew-wew* and *pew pew*.

The purple martin is the only one of its genus to be expected in the United States; however, there are others in tropical America. One, the gray-breasted martin *(Progne chalybea),* has been reported in Texas and is listed as "accidental" on the state checklist.

A purple martin pair adapts to apartment life.

TREE SWALLOW *Tachycineta bicolor*

One of the most distinctively patterned birds of its family is the tree swallow. Its dark, glossy, greenish blue upperparts contrast with immaculately white underparts, the only eastern swallow so colored. The cleanly delineated pattern results in the specific name *bicolor.*

The violet-green swallow *(Tachycineta thalassina),* a western species, is similarly colored; however, the white of its cheeks extends up over the eyes, and white patches adorn the sides of its dark rump. It breeds in the mountains of West Texas and migrates through the Trans-Pecos, only rarely reaching farther eastward across the state.

The tree swallow, on the other hand, nests across the breadth of the continent, from Alaska to Nova Scotia and southward to the central states. Breeding records for Texas are very rare, but large flocks pour across our borders during fall migration and again on their return northward in the spring.

Some even remain through the winter season, particularly in southern Texas and along the coast. While other swallows feed primarily on flying insects and must leave when temperatures begin to drop, the tree swallow supplements its insect diet with fruits and berries. It may even remain as far north as Long Island on the eastern seaboard at times, surviving on the wax-coated fruit of the bayberry tree.

Tree swallows prefer wooded habitats near water, especially where dead trees provide suitable nest holes. They are cavity nesters, competing with house wrens, bluebirds, house sparrows and starlings for old woodpecker holes, tree stubs and birdhouses. The nest is made of dried grasses and lined with soft feathers that curl around the four to six white eggs. Such unmarked eggs are typical of hole-nesting birds, where there is no need for camouflage color or pattern. Incubation, by the female alone, requires about 16 days; the young fledge three weeks later.

Shortly after the juveniles can fly, tree swallows begin assembling in enormous flocks. Thousands of birds congregate along lakeshores, rivers and marshes, hawking insects over the water and alighting on the beaches to glean insects and other invertebrates from the sand. The swirling hordes glide in circles on delta-shaped wings, flapping quickly to gain altitude with each sweeping revolution. From dawn till dusk they patrol the air, their cheerful, chittering calls providing pleasant music for late summer days. At night they mass at communal roosts.

Then, as a chill comes to the northern latitudes, they are gone, winging their way southward. Most will eventually reach Central America, but a few will remain along our borders through the winter. They move across Texas where insects are still plentiful, over fields, pastures, and mosquito-filled marshes and along the shore. The glossy adults bring with them their drab, gray-brown young, and other swallows join them along the way.

The bank swallow (*Riparia riparia*) has a brown back like the immature tree swallow, but a distinct dark band crosses the white breast. It breeds in colonies across Canada and the northern states, excavating nest burrows in steep banks of streams, road cuts and gravel pits. It nests locally in Texas and joins other swallows in migrations across the state.

The northern rough-winged swallow bears the imposing scientific name of *Stelgidopteryx serripennis*, which means "scraper-winged" and "saw-winged," referring to the stiff bristle hooks along the leading edges of the wings. It, too, is brown above and lighter below, but with a dingy gray-brown wash on the throat and breast. The rough-wing also nests in burrows in dirt banks, but it is solitary rather than colonial like the bank swallow. It breeds throughout most of the United States and locally across Texas.

It can be difficult to identify individual species among the darting, milling throngs of swallows. That is much easier as they perch to rest, lining the telephone wires and fences, row after row. But the enjoyment comes in watching the aerial ballet as the tree swallows and their relatives dance across the land.

Tree swallows nest in an old woodpecker hole.

Cliff Swallow

Hirundo pyrrhonota

With quivering wings, a young cliff swallow begs for food.

They are perhaps most famous as the swallows that return to Capistrano every spring, but cliff swallows also rank among the world's premier architects. They construct their gourd-shaped mud nests with small pellets carried in their beaks from a patch of wet clay and packed into place, creating solid fortresses attached to a vertical wall. Cliff swallows are highly social, and hundreds, even thousands, of nests are packed together in the larger colonies. Preferred sites include cliff faces beneath sheltering overhangs and in open canyons, usually near running water.

Modern-day swallows, however, have also adapted to sites beneath bridges and culverts, under the eaves of barns and sheds, and even on the walls of office buildings. This practice has enabled the cliff swallow to spread across the plains and to establish new territories in the southeastern states. It has also occasioned a few territorial squabbles between guest and host. "No matter if he fills the evening sky with 'poems of motion,' " writes Roy Bedichek in *Adventures with a Texas Naturalist,* "—no matter: he has habits which make him impossible as a guest lodged above the entrance to a public building."

The graceful six-inch birds sweep in and out of the colony, hawking flying insects. At nest-building time they congregate on stream banks and at mud puddles, rolling in their beaks the balls of mud they methodically add to their growing structures or use to refurbish older nests. Unlike most other birds, they do not add grass or straw to their adobe mix, preferring to use only clay. The entrance frequently arches like a short spout from the enclosed nest, and the chamber inside is lined with grass and feathers to hold the four or five spotted eggs. Construction usually requires about five days, but some pairs may spend up to two weeks.

Recent studies have revealed a previously unsuspected high rate of "intraspecific brood parasitism"; many of the swallows lay eggs in nests other than their own. Biologists discovered that more than two new eggs often appeared in a nest within a 24-hour period, yet no bird is known to lay more than one egg a day. Banded swallows were subsequently seen entering other nests to lay eggs, the process usually requiring less than a minute while the host was otherwise distracted. Some also tossed out an egg, presumably to replace it with one of their own. The study estimated that one-fourth of all cliff swallow nests in the colony were parasitized.

Birds inclined toward such practices thereby increase the number of their offspring, producing not only their own brood but those raised by other swallows as well. However, the differences remain unexplained. Are such habits passed on genetically? Or does the behavior result from environmental factors? Even more surprising was a discovery by Charles and Mary Brown published in a 1988 issue of *Nature.* They observed swallows actually carrying eggs in their beaks to deposit them in other nests, a totally unknown form of brood parasitism.

Cliff swallows have square tails and buffy rumps, distinguishing them from all other North American swallows except the cave swallow. The latter has a buffy throat and a dark forehead; the cliff swallow has a dark chestnut throat and a pale forehead. One southwestern race of the cliff swallow, which might be encountered in West Texas, has a dark forehead, but its throat is also dark.

The cliff swallow breeds across North America, from Alaska and Canada southward into Mexico, and winters in South America. It migrates throughout Texas and remains to nest locally except in East Texas. However, small colonies are slowly moving north and east, nesting under highway bridges and culverts, and will probably increase in that area of the state as well. In spite of these range expansions, the cliff swallow has declined in some historic locations and is the subject of some concern.

CAVE SWALLOW   *Hirundo fulva*

The cave swallow is a Central American and Caribbean species that reaches its northern limit in central Texas and at Carlsbad in New Mexico. It breeds in limestone caves and sinkholes, building its nest in the twilight zone where the young are protected from sunlight but receive enough light to feed. Unlike the juglike nest of the cliff swallow, the cave swallow's nest is an open cup of mud stuck to the cavern wall. Both parents apparently incubate the two to four speckled eggs and feed the young. Like most other swallows, they consume primarily insects.

The cave swallow closely resembles the more common and widely distributed cliff swallow. A squarish tail and buff-colored rump characterize both species, but the cave swallow also has a light buffy throat and a dark chestnut forehead. Those colors are reversed on the cliff swallow. A southwestern race of the latter with a dark forehead might be encountered in West Texas, but all cliff swallows have dark throats.

According to Oberholser, the cave swallow was not known to breed anywhere in the United States prior to 1915. It was later discovered in Kerr County, Texas, and subsequent investigations found other nest sites. Roger Tory Peterson noted in *A Field Guide to the Birds of Texas* in 1960 that it was a summer resident on the southern edge of the Edwards Plateau and was known to nest in about 16 limestone caves.

In 1973, however, cave swallows were discovered nesting in culverts with colonies of barn swallows. Others were then found with both barn and cliff swallows beneath a highway bridge. These adopted nesting sites allowed the cave swallow to spread more widely across the state. In 1989, at least two pairs nested with barn swallows and a few cliff swallows under the eaves of a boat stall at Sea Rim State Park in Jefferson County. In an amazing range extension, the cave swallow had crossed the state to reach the upper coast.

Although much like cliff swallows, cave swallows have pale throats and dark foreheads.

BARN SWALLOW

Hirundo rustica

Few birds epitomize more completely the traits we admire in the avian world than does the barn swallow. Colorful, sleek and graceful, it is truly a master of the skies. Along lakeshores and riverbanks, over open fields and farms, swallows wheel and dart, catching flying insects in midair. So adept are they at flight that they skim low to drink on the wing and even dip breast-deep to bathe, later landing on a limb or wire to preen.

Ruffling its plumage, the barn swallow uses its beak to rehook the tiny barbs and smooth each feather back in place. The attentive care provides protection from rain and cold and makes precision flying possible. It is done out of necessity, rather than from any vanity or pride.

Glossy, iridescent blue-black above and rich cinnamon below, the barn swallow has a long, streaming, deeply forked tail that distinguishes it from other swallow species. The tail, when spread in flight or preening, displays a band of white spots. The sexes are similar, although the male has a darker breast and throat. Juvenile birds have pale buffy breasts and shorter tails.

The barn swallow is the most widely distributed of the world's 75 swallow species. It nests virtually throughout the Northern Hemisphere and then migrates southward after the breeding season. In winter, it inhabits South America, Africa and southern Asia.

Migrating barn swallows can be seen across Texas in both spring and fall. Many remain to breed in the western portions of the state; they are less frequent nesters in the North and East. The nests were once tucked into caves or sheltered by rocky cliffs, but such natural sites are now virtually unknown. The friendly birds have adopted human architecture and build their open, cuplike nests of mud and straw beneath the eaves of barns and other buildings, under bridges,

The sleek, graceful barn swallow has a deeply forked tail.

and in culverts. Lined with feathers and grasses, the nests cradle four or five white eggs speckled with brown. Both adults share in the incubation and feeding of the young and are sometimes aided by non-nesting, year-old swallows or by immatures from the parents' earlier brood.

Visiting Big Bend National Park one spring, I watched a typical pair of barn swallows nesting over the front door of the Chisos Mountains Lodge.

The tame birds scarcely moved as visitors streamed in and out. Barn swallows frequently return to the same sites year after year, sometimes seeking solitude in isolated pairs, sometimes joining a larger colony. When not on their nests, the active little birds are almost constantly on the wing. Alexander Wilson once estimated that a barn swallow might travel more than two million miles in a ten-year life span.

SWIFTS (Family Apodidae)

The chimney swift has a small beak but an enormous, gaping mouth.

Swifts presently share the scientific order Apodiformes with the hummingbirds and precede them in taxonomic lists, although the full extent of that relationship has yet to be established. In the field, however, they are far more likely to be confused with the swallows, which they resemble in appearance and behavior. As the name implies, swifts are among the fastest of all birds, darting across the sky on slender wings in pursuit of insects, spending most of the day aloft.

The swifts have slender bodies with short tails and long, bowed wings. They have frequently been called "flying cigars." The "upper arm" and "forearm" bones are extremely short and thick, while the "hand" is greatly elongated. Thus the wings bend much closer to the body than do those of the swallows and are made up mostly of long, stiff primary flight feathers. The flickering wingbeats are almost too rapid to see except as a blur, and they allow amazing bursts of speed.

In contrast to their prowess on the wing, swifts are poorly adapted for life on the ground. Their feet are small and weak; the family name, Apodidae, stems from a Greek word for "footless." In addition, all four toes point forward, allowing swifts to cling to vertical walls but not to perch on branches or wires like the swallows.

Swifts possess highly developed salivary glands that produce secretions used as glue in building nests. Small twigs are literally glued together and attached to the wall of the nesting cavity. In one Oriental species the entire nest is made of this congealed saliva, the source of the famous and expensive bird's nest soup.

CHIMNEY SWIFT *Chaetura pelagica*

What the sooty gray chimney swift lacks in colorful plumage, it more than makes up for in scintillating aerobatic skill. This drab little five-inch bird darts across the sky on flickering, scythelike wings that bend so close to the body that they appear virtually unjointed. Its short tail functions poorly as a rudder, and the swift steers by changing the angle of its slender wings, at times appearing almost to beat them alternately, al-though such is not the case. The beak is tiny, but a swift's mouth has a very wide gape and proves an effective insect trap, wielded with considerable dexterity.

The chimney swift ranges across the eastern half of North America, from southern Canada to the Gulf States, and migrates throughout Texas except for the Trans-Pecos, where it is replaced by the white-throated swift. It nests in the eastern two-thirds of the state but is less common south of about Corpus Christi and Beeville. The winter home of the chimney swift remained a mystery until 1943, when Peruvian Indians found leg bands of birds that had been banded as far away as Connecticut and Ontario. Most of the population is now believed to winter in the Upper Amazon Basin.

The range in Texas expanded dramatically during the mid-1900s because of the increasing availability of man-made nest sites. Swifts formerly utilized hollow trees and rocky crevices, but they now have adopted tall chimneys, silos, old wells and abandoned buildings as nesting and roosting places. They attach their stick nests to the vertical walls, gluing them together with secretions from their salivary glands.

I recently had a chance to examine closely a chimney-swift nest and three little hatchlings that had fallen down a chimney after heavy rains. One description I have read of the nest calls it a "frail, thin, half-saucer of twigs," and that is true. But the description conveys little of the patience and skill required in construction. I was reminded, instead, of wooden models we built as youths, models whose many pieces were held together with a liberal coating of glue. The nest contained 130 twigs, each of them one and one-half to two inches long and the thickness of a toothpick or matchstick. All were laid parallel along the longer axis of the nest, forming a half-saucer about four inches across and two inches deep. That bowed shelf had been glued along one edge to the inside wall of the chimney.

Reliable observers report that the swifts break twigs from the ends of dead branches with their feet while in flight. They then transfer the miniature building beams to their beaks and carry them back to the nest site. Once inside the darkened chimney, the swifts fit them into place and glue them with saliva. Both sexes work on nest construction over several days, and both incubate the three to five white eggs, sometimes sitting together on the wooden platform. The eggs hatch in 19 to 21 days, and the young fledge in about four weeks. At about three weeks of age they outgrow the nest and cling to the walls of their shelter, using their tiny feet with four forward-pointing toes and their stiff tail feathers that end in sharp spine-like projections. The genus name of the chimney swift, *Chaetura*, comes from the Greek for "spine-tailed."

The white-throated swift (*Aeronautes saxatalis*) replaces the chimney swift in the mountains of West Texas. It displays the typical long, narrow, stiff wings but is more flashily plumaged in black and white. Seen from below in its twinkling flight, it has white underparts with black side-patches, wings and tail. It can easily be mistaken for the violet-green swallow, but the shapes and flight patterns of the two are distinctive. A bird of the western U.S., the white-throated swift is a summer resident among the rocky crags and canyons of the Guadalupe, Davis and Chisos mountains. The genus name *Aeronautes* means "sailor of the air" in Greek, while *saxatalis* is Latin for "rock-inhabiting."

Young chimney swifts outgrow their twig nest and cling to the vertical walls of the nest chamber with sharp claws and spiny tails.

JAYS AND CROWS (Family Corvidae)

Young common ravens beg for food.

The corvids are the largest of all the perching birds. Their size, harsh voices, and aggressive manner make them particularly noticeable, and most are relatively easy to identify. Except for the several species of all-black crows and ravens, each has its own distinctive plumage that is essentially the same regardless of sex, age or season of the year. Most people recognize the generic "crow" or "jay-bird," but few realize how many different species there really are. Roughly 100 are found throughout the world, and 14 of them occur at least occasionally in Texas. Seven jay species range into Texas, and there are five black crows and ravens. In addition, the Clark's nutcracker *(Nucifraga columbiana)* and the black-billed magpie *(Pica pica)* occupy "accidental" listings on the state checklist.

The large, powerful, all-purpose beaks of the corvids enable them to consume almost anything edible. Seeds, insects, fruit and carrion are all taken readily. A crow might dine on corn left in a field and then capture and eat a mouse that attempts to share the bounty. Their innate curiosity and seemingly acute intelligence allow them to adapt well to human intrusions, and they obtain food in ingenious ways. Although strong fliers, most corvids are relatively sedentary. They are extremely hardy and "inclined to stay put" regardless of the weather. The common raven is one of the few birds to endure the Arctic winter, while the Chihuahuan raven braves the sweltering summer sun of the Desert Southwest.

BLUE JAY *Cyanocitta cristata*

Most regions of the country have their resident "blue jay," but *cristata* is the species officially designated by that name. It ranges through Canada and the United States east of the Rocky Mountains and is the only jay species in much of that area. Several other blue-colored jays occur in the West, but only one, Steller's jay, shares the blue jay's handsome crest.

In Texas, the blue jay ranges through the northern and eastern portions of the state and the Panhandle, occurring westward to the Edwards Plateau and south to about Victoria. It may also wander farther south and west in the winter. Huge migrating flocks are sometimes encountered in the fall, when the blue jay withdraws from the northern edge of its range.

Other individuals, however, seem to remain sedentary throughout the year.

White patches and black-and-white barring ornament the blue jay's blue wings and tail, while a black necklace crosses the whitish breast. Washington Irving described it as "That noisy coxcomb, in his gay light blue coat and white underclothes," while 19th-century ornithologist Charles Bendire was more fascinated by its ever-changing personality: "Cunning, inquisitive, an admirable mimic, full of mischief; in some localities extremely shy, in others exactly the reverse, it is difficult to paint him in his true colors."

Most common in its vocal repertoire is a piercing *jay jay jay*, often hurled at interlopers. Nothing rouses the ire of a blue jay more than a perching owl, but hawks, cats and humans are all suitable targets of the tirade. Thoreau calls it the "unrelenting steel-cold scream of a jay, unmelted, that never flows into a song, a sort of wintry trumpet . . . ." Yet the jay also communicates with softer tones, including a musical *weedle-eedle* and an almost bell-like *tull-ull*. Other calls mimic the screams of the red-shouldered hawk.

Blue jays roam woodlands, parks and towns in search of a variety of foods. One study found their summer diet to contain 30 percent insects and other invertebrates, as well as some small vertebrates; the other 70 percent was made up of acorns, fruit and seeds. Audubon wrote of the blue jay, "It robs every nest it can find, sucks the eggs like the Crow, or tears to pieces and devours the young birds." His painting of the species shows several jays eating stolen eggs. Jays are, indeed, notorious nest-robbers in the spring. In midwinter, acorns and pine seeds constitute nearly the entire menu.

Jays are also famous as hoarders of surplus food, and experiments clearly indicate that they can recall where they cached acorns and other seeds. They apparently remember the sites in relation to certain landmarks.

The blue jay's nest is a bowl of twigs and dry leaves high in a tree; the three to five eggs are blue or greenish spotted with brown. They hatch after 16 to 18 days of incubation by the female, and the young fledge in 17 to 21 days more. Although the parents are not above eating the eggs or young of other species, they are fiercely defensive of their own. An intruder in their territory is likely to face a flashing beak and the "unrelenting steel-cold scream," *jay jay jay*.

The blue jay is the only jay species seen regularly in East Texas and across the eastern portion of the country. It is replaced by several others in the West.

STELLER'S JAY   *Cyanocitta stelleri*

Steller's jay, the western counterpart of the blue jay, is a resident of the coniferous forests and pine-oak woodlands from southern Alaska south through the higher elevations of the United States and Mexico to Nicaragua. In Texas, it breeds in the Guadalupe and Davis mountains, mainly above 6,000 feet. It wanders more widely in winter, descending from the peaks to forage at lower elevations and occasionally turning up on the Edwards Plateau or in the Panhandle.

Like the eastern blue jay, Steller's jay has an erect crest, but its overall color is a deeper blue, and it lacks the white markings on the wings and tail. The crest, throat and upper breast are black. Where the two species overlap on the eastern slopes of the Rocky Mountains, hybrids sometimes occur. This interbreeding will probably in-

crease, for the blue jay continues to expand its range into the Northwest.

Named for German naturalist Georg Wilhelm Steller, who accompanied Vitus Bering on his 1740 expedition to Alaska, Steller's jay is a raucous, aggressive bird. Its most common call is a harsh *shaack shaack shaack*. An excellent mimic, it frequently screams like the red-tailed hawk.

The nesting and feeding habits of Steller's jay are much like those of the blue jay. A frequent scavenger around campgrounds and picnic areas, it consumes insects, acorns, fruits and seeds, relying primarily on acorns and conifer seeds in the winter. It occasionally catches small vertebrates and is not above pilfering an egg or two.

The blue color of jays is not produced by pigment as is, for example, the red of a cardinal's feathers. It is a

Scrub Jay

Aphelocoma coerulescens

Steller's jay is the only western jay species with a crest.

The scrub jay represents the corvid family throughout the West. It inhabits scrub oak and pinyon-juniper woodlands and wanders widely into towns and suburbs. Unlike the eastern blue jay and the Steller's jay of the higher western mountains, it does not have a crest. In fact the genus name *Aphelocoma* was coined from Greek words meaning "smooth hair."

Blue above and pale gray below, the scrub jay has a gray-brown patch on the back. A faint necklace of darker gray streaking separates the white throat from the dingy underparts. The scrub jay is a year-round resident of western Texas, ranging from the Guadalupe and Davis mountains across much of the Edwards Plateau. It is generally absent, however, from the Chisos Mountains of Big Bend, where it is replaced by the gray-breasted jay.

Like its relatives, the scrub jay tends to wander more widely in winter and occasionally turns up along the eastern edge of the Edwards Plateau and in the Panhandle. It flies in an undulating, swooping manner and has a wide variety of vocalizations. Some of the most common have been described as a raspy *shreeep* and a repeated *check-check-check*.

The scrub jay builds a nest of twigs in a low tree or shrub, and the three to six greenish eggs are beautifully marked with reddish brown. Incubation by the female requires 15 to 17 days; the young fledge 18 or 19 days later. Like its relatives, the scrub jay consumes a varied diet. Until the 1930s, large numbers were shot in California because of their raids on crops.

A disjunct race of the scrub jay also occurs in central Florida. Unlike the western scrub jays, which nest in normal fashion, Florida birds are cooperative breeders. Groups normally consist of a mated pair and from one to six helpers, which assist with the nest duties and defend the group ter-

"structural color," produced by tiny particles in the feathers that are smaller than the wavelength of red light. The particles influence only the shorter wavelengths at the blue end of the visible spectrum and scatter them in all directions. Thus the blue color is consistent when viewed at different angles, unlike the iridescent colors reflected by the hummingbirds.

ritory. Studies have shown the helpers to be mainly unmated offspring from prior breeding seasons.

The pinyon jay (*Gymnorhinus cyanocephalus*) also ranges into West Texas. Slightly smaller than the foot-long scrub jay, it is more like a miniature crow in form and habits, with a short tail and a long spikelike beak. Its plumage is entirely blue, although immatures are paler and grayer beneath. Pinyon jays inhabit the western U.S. and occur in the Guadalupe Mountains. The gregarious birds wander in large flocks in winter, sometimes reaching other portions of the Trans-Pecos, the Panhandle, and the western edge of the Edwards Plateau.

Gray-breasted Jay
Aphelocoma ultramarina

Formerly called the Mexican jay, *A. ultramarina* inhabits the Chisos Mountains of Texas' Big Bend National Park, replacing the scrub jay found elsewhere in the Trans-Pecos. It also occurs in southeastern Arizona and ranges southward to central Mexico. Although the two species look much alike, the gray-breasted jay is more uniformly colored beneath and lacks the contrasting white throat and darker necklace of the scrub jay. Its range is extremely limited in Texas, but it is common in the Chisos Basin and on the Chisos mountain trails. Any jay occurring there is almost certain to be this species.

The loud, ringing call of the gray-breasted jay has been described by various authors as *week, drenk, jenk, jink,* and a number of other one-syllable approximations. These jays forage mainly in the oak forests on the mountain slopes and include insects, fruits and seeds in their diets. They depend heavily on acorns, especially during the winter months, and are major agents of acorn dispersal. Many oak seedlings sprout from their unused caches.

Found throughout much of western and central Texas, the scrub jay (above) lacks the crest of the blue and Steller's jays. The gray-breasted jay (left) replaces the scrub jay in the Chisos Mountains of Big Bend National Park.

Gray-breasted jays band together in communal flocks of up to 20 birds and defend permanent group territories. They also carry cooperative breeding even further than does the Florida race of the scrub jay. Two or three monogamous pairs usually breed each year, while the others in the flock assist with nest-building and other chores. The mated females incubate their eggs, but the helpers feed them and their hatchling young.

GREEN JAY *Cyanocorax yncas*

No bird epitomizes the exotic tropical wildlife of the lower Rio Grande Valley more thoroughly than the beautiful green jay. It reaches its northern limit in south Texas and occurs nowhere else in the United States. From there it ranges south to Honduras and also inhabits northern South America. Its specific name, *yncas*, is an alternate form of "Inca," for the first descriptions of this species were based on birds taken in Peru.

Yncas is our only green-colored jay. It is a darker olive-green above and yellowish green below, with yellow outer tail feathers. The bright blue head contrasts with black facial markings and a large black throat patch. As colorful as the plumage is, it blends remarkably well with the dappled sunlight and shade of the brushy thickets and remnant woodlands along the Rio Grande. The green jay ranges upriver sparingly to Laredo and northward to Alice, Kingsville and the Corpus Christi area, but it is most commonly sought in such parks and refuges as Bentsen–Rio Grande State Park and Santa Ana National Wildlife Refuge.

Green jays troop through the trees in small groups, and though sometimes secretive, also tend to be inquisitive. Ornithologist Olin Sewall Pettingill notes that "Any human intrusion into their haunts quickly brings them out of the dense cover to investigate. They scream and caw and toot for a while, then melt silently into the bush." One of their most common calls is a raspy *cheh-cheh-cheh*, but they converse in a variety of sounds including a dry rattle like the song of a cricket frog.

Assorted insects, small vertebrates, fruits and seeds make up the omnivorous diet of the green jays. Like other jays, they sometimes descend on picnic tables to search for scraps, and they are not above stealing eggs or small nestlings of other birds. Some years ago, a well-known wildlife photographer set up his blind in a Valley woodland to photograph a pauraque on her nest, only to watch as a green jay snatched the eggs.

Small family flocks, usually of four to nine birds, set up and defend permanent group territories. Each group contains only one breeding pair. The female incubates the three to five spotted eggs, while her mate feeds her on the nest. The eggs hatch in 17 or 18 days, and both sexes then brood and feed the young. The helpers, usually offspring from a previous nesting, take no part in these nest chores, but they aid in territorial defense. Such cooperation undoubtedly increases the survival rate of the eggs and young.

An even bigger prize for birders in the Rio Grande Valley is the 17-inch brown jay *(Cyanocorax morio)*. A tropical species that ranges from Mexico to Panama, it was first seen in the U.S. just below Falcon Dam in 1969. Since then it has become a rare but regular resident of Texas along the river between Falcon Dam and Roma. This huge jay is dark sooty brown with a white belly and a long, broad tail. Adults have black bills; those of the juveniles are yellow. The noisy birds travel in family groups and are more easily heard than seen. Their harsh screams mimic those of the red-shouldered hawk, while another common call sounds like a loud hiccup.

Green jays.

AMERICAN CROW

Corvus brachyrhynchos

According to the legends of several Native American cultures, Crow was a good planter and reaper. He brought corn and many other useful seeds from the south for the people to plant. Later-day farmers, however, regarded the American crow more as a plunderer than a planter. Its fondness for corn and other seeds and fruits, and for the eggs and nestlings of birds, occasioned organized crow hunts and mass poisonings. Roosts were the targets of bombs and grenades. Through it all, the crow survived—audacious, inventive, among the most intelligent of birds, alert to potential dangers, and seemingly aware of the limited range of guns. Henry Ward Beecher, the 19th-century preacher, asserted that if people wore feathers and wings, very few of them would be clever enough to be crows.

The common crow ranges from central Canada to the Gulf States. It inhabits the woods and farmlands of northern and eastern Texas, west to the Panhandle and the Edwards Plateau and south to about San Antonio and Victoria. It tends to range more widely in winter, occasionally reaching into western Texas and along the central coast. Two smaller crows and two species of ravens replace the American crow in portions of the state. To the uninitiated, all of these are collectively called "crows."

The all-black, 18-inch American crow has a long, heavy bill, but it is still noticeably smaller than the massive bills of the ravens. The tail is fan-shaped in flight, in contrast to the ravens' wedge-shaped tails. The basic call of the American crow is a loud *caw,* although it uses many variations and inflections to convey information to other crows.

The nest of twigs high in a tree is lined with shredded bark, leaves, grasses and other soft materials and holds a normal clutch of four to six greenish eggs spotted with brown. In-

The American crow has a smaller beak than those of the ravens.

cubation requires 18 days, and the fledglings leave the nest about five weeks later. The omnivorous crows consume insects and other invertebrates, small vertebrates, seeds, fruits and carrion—almost anything that doesn't eat them first.

Partially migratory, American crows withdraw from the more northern portions of their range in winter and assemble in large, raucous flocks. They forage widely across the countryside by day and return at night to the communal roost. As sunset approaches they fly with powerful, rowing wingbeats, heading directly for the roost, "as the crow flies."

The fish crow (*Corvus ossifragus*) inhabits tidal marshes and river valleys along the eastern and Gulf coasts. It occurs along the Texas coast from the Sabine to Galveston. Although it is slightly smaller than the American crow, the sizes overlap and are not useful field characteristics. Most reliable are the short, nasal *car* or *ca* notes of the fish crow, in contrast to the American crow's lusty *caw,* but the distinction is not always an easy one.

The Mexican crow (*C. imparatus*) was unknown in the United States until 1968. It is now relatively common in winter in the lower Rio Grande Valley. Birders normally search for it at the landfill near the Port of Brownsville, a celebrated birding hotspot. Scarcely larger than a great-tailed grackle, the Mexican crow is much smaller than the Chihuahuan raven, which shares its range. Its call is a distinctive froglike croak.

COMMON RAVEN *Corvus corax*

The raven has been the object of countless myths and legends around the world. Odin, the supreme deity of Norse mythology, sent out a pair of ravens at sunrise every day, and at noon they would return to perch on his shoulders and tell him what they had learned. Ravens were sent to sustain the prophet Elijah in the desert, and Native American peoples in the Pacific Northwest considered Raven to be the god who brought life and order. To such tribes as the Haida and the Tlingit, Raven was not only the creator of the land and waters, he brought human life as well. He was also a trickster and succeeded in stealing light from the power who wanted to keep the world in darkness.

While I cannot attest to the common raven's creative role, I have seen its trickery firsthand. On several raft trips through the Grand Canyon, ravens joined us every day. Each sandbar campsite had its resident pair, and they brazenly wandered through the camp, watching intently for any scrap of food or a bright trinket to adorn their cliff-top ledge. One hungry raven pulled a tube of shampoo from a pack and cut it open to eat the contents; its mate consumed a stock of granola bars and part of the box, then washed that down with half a bar of soap. Later, one of them snatched a watch from a riverside rock while its owner was bathing and flew with it down the canyon, fortunately dropping it in the sand before crossing the water.

This is the common raven. Voracious, belligerent, amazingly intelligent. An artist in the air and a comedian on the ground. The stuff of Indian legends, Shakespeare's plays and Edgar Allan Poe's most famous poem. It ranges around the globe in the Northern Hemisphere and few, if any, birds are less influenced by climate and altitude. Ravens occur from the Arctic tundra to Central America and from the tops of the highest mountains to parched deserts and rocky shores. Largely nonmigratory, they stand their ground under the most forbidding conditions. On an Audubon Christmas Bird Count at Yellowknife in Canada's Northwest Territories, birders braved minus 31-degree temperatures and two feet of new snow to record 762 individual birds of only five different species; 488 of them were common ravens.

The common raven is a year-round resident of Trans-Pecos Texas and the western edge of the Edwards Plateau. In the Chisos Mountains, it builds its large stick nest on the rocky crags and forages through the canyons and across the desert scrub. The raven feeds heavily on carrion but also takes insects, small vertebrates, eggs and nestlings, seeds and fruits. I

Common raven.

have watched ravens tear at a road-killed deer and then flock to a meadow after a plague of grasshoppers. The sight of scores of the huge black birds leaping and whirling in pursuit of the insects was an indelibly comic spectacle.

At more than two feet in length, the common raven is much larger and bulkier than the crow and has a longer, heavier bill. The neck feathers are loose and shaggy, contributing to the impression of a tough, disheveled street thug as the raven swaggers across the ground. In the air, however, it is a consummate artist, sometimes tumbling and diving along the ridges in an awesome display of aerial gymnastics. Its powered flight alternates flapping with flat-winged soaring, much like that of the larger hawks, and its wedge-shaped tail distinguishes it as a raven.

A low-pitched, drawn-out croak is the most common vocalization, a raspy *cr-r-rock* or *prruk,* quite unlike the *caw* of a crow. The Chihuahuan raven, which shares much of the common raven's range in the Trans-Pecos and occurs deeper into the southern portion of the state, is smaller and has a slightly higher pitched call.

CHIHUAHUAN RAVEN

Corvus cryptoleucus

The Chihuahuan raven was formerly known as the white-necked raven; however, that earlier name was misleading to the novice birder. The white is located at the base of the neck feathers and is visible only when the feathers are ruffled, a characteristic reflected in the species name *cryptoleucus,* from the Greek for "hidden white."

The Chihuahuan raven inhabits the arid Southwest and ranges southward to central Mexico. In Texas it is a resident of the western half of the state, ranging eastward onto the Edwards Plateau and southward along the Rio Grande to Brownsville. It

Chihuahuan ravens replace the crow in the Desert Southwest.

withdraws from much of the Panhandle during the winter and becomes more common in the brush country of South Texas and the lower coast and through the Rio Grande Valley.

Slightly larger than the American crow, which it replaces in southern and western Texas, it is easily recognized as a raven by its wedge-shaped tail and the heavier bill that gives it a pronounced "Roman nose." The call is a harsh *kraak,* higher pitched and less resonant than the croak of the common raven.

In West Texas where both ravens occur, the common raven tends to remain in the mountains and rugged canyons, while the Chihuahuan raven prefers the mesquite flats and desert scrub. Roland Wauer notes in *Birds of Big Bend National Park and Vicinity,* however, that although the Chihuahuan raven is common in the northern part of Brewster County, it is only a rare summer visitor and migrant in the more southerly park. Instead, the common raven occupies

the entire range of elevations in Big Bend.

The bulky nest of the Chihuahuan raven consists of a platform of thorny twigs lined with wool, rabbit fur and other soft materials. It might be placed in a tree, on an old windmill or building, or on a utility pole. The five to seven pretty greenish eggs are spotted with brown and lilac and hatch in about 21 days. Both adults apparently incubate and feed their young, and the breeding season is timed for late in the season when summer rains increase the available food supply. The nestlings consume only animal food and fledge in about 30 days. They will later share the typical omnivorous raven diet of carrion, insects, small animals, seeds and fruits.

After breeding, Chihuahuan ravens assemble in large flocks for the fall and winter, ranging more widely in search of food. Their plumage may be dark and somber, but their flight is filled with the rollicking, tumbling antics that make both raven species such a delight to watch.

CHICKADEES AND TITMICE (Family Paridae)

Black-crested form of the tufted titmouse.

The plump little chickadees and titmice are among the friendliest of birds, chattering cheerfully throughout the year and visiting backyard feeders for seeds, suet and other fare. They frequently become quite tame and, with patience, may even be induced to accept food from a person's hand. Ten species occur in North America.

The Paridae have short little beaks, short wings, and generally drab plumage. They are essentially nonmigratory, and even those that inhabit the Far North and the higher mountain zones remain in their breeding range throughout the year. Seeds and berries sustain them through the winter when insects are difficult to find. During that season, both chickadees and titmice roam the woodlands in small mixed flocks with other species. They are active and agile, frequently hanging upside-down to feed. Most species nest in tree cavities, some chipping the holes themselves in rotting wood, others utilizing old woodpecker holes.

Two other groups of small birds were formerly classified with the Paridae. The verdins and their relatives (family Remizidae) and the bushtits (family Aegithalidae) have recently been assigned to families of their own. The sixth edition (1983) of the AOU *Check-list of North American Birds* notes that "their true relationships are uncertain, so they are placed after the Paridae pending new evidence."

The verdin (*Auriparus flaviceps*) inhabits the Desert Southwest and is a resident from Trans-Pecos Texas east locally to Abilene and Austin and south to the Rio Grande and the lower coast. Scarcely four inches long, it is a tiny gray bird with a yellowish head. A rusty patch at the bend of the wing is sometimes concealed. Unlike the members of the Paridae, it constructs a nest consisting of a round ball of twigs in a tree or shrub.

The bushtit (*Psaltriparus minimus*) occurs widely in the western states, from the Pacific Northwest into Mexico. It inhabits the Trans-Pecos and ranges eastward through the Edwards Plateau. Bushtits move about in small flocks, twittering constantly in high-pitched tones. Like feathered mice, they forage through the trees or desert scrub and are off again, constantly on the move. Their tails are relatively long, but the tiny birds still measure little more than four inches in length. The nest is a pendant bag suspended in a tree.

Neither the verdin nor the bushtit is uncommon, but both are overlooked because of their small size and drab plumage. Few people except the birders ever notice them, and they do not enjoy the popularity and recognition of the chickadees and titmice.

CAROLINA CHICKADEE *Parus carolinensis*

The tiny, acrobatic bird flits quickly from tree to tree, often hanging upside-down to probe for beetles or caterpillars concealed in the bark. It drops lightly to the backyard bird feeder and carefully selects a sunflower seed, but instead of perching there to eat with the finches, it flies up to a branch. There it holds the seed beneath its foot and hammers it open with its short, stubby bill. Only when the tender kernel has been consumed does the bird return for more. Its small size and the black cap and bib framing white cheeks clearly mark it as a chickadee. As if that were not enough, it cheerfully calls its name, *chick-a-dee-dee-dee.*

The black-capped chickadee *(Parus atricapillus)* is perhaps best known throughout the nation, but Texas' common resident is the Carolina chickadee. Its range extends from Kansas to New Jersey and south to Texas and Florida. It is confined primarily to the eastern, northern and central portions of our state, west to the edge of the Panhandle and the central Edwards Plateau and southward to the central coast. In winter it may wander more widely, although it is essentially nonmigratory.

At about four and one-half inches in length, the Carolina chickadee is slightly smaller than its northern counterpart and lacks the white feather edgings on the wings that give the black-cap its "frosty" appearance. The lower edge of the black bib is also less "ragged" and more sharply marked. These distinctions are subjective, however, and their voices provide the best aid to identification where the two species overlap. The familiar *chick-a-dee-dee-dee* call of the Carolina chickadee is faster and higher in pitch, and the song, a whistled *fee-bee fee-bay,* has four notes rather than the typical two-note *fee-bee* song of the black-capped. Hybrids occur in the zone of overlap, and these birds respond vigorously to the territorial songs of both species.

The chickadee nests in a hole in a tree or stump and will also adopt birdhouses, lining the cavity with grasses, feathers, fur and thistledown. The six to eight eggs are speckled with reddish brown. The identically plumaged parents share in the incubation, and the eggs hatch in 11 or 12 days. Within two weeks the young are ready to leave the nest, already clearly marked as chickadees.

Pairs remain together throughout the year and often join small feeding flocks of other birds, moving through the treetops with titmice, woodpeckers, brown creepers, gnatcatchers, kinglets and wintering warblers and vireos. These mixed flocks carefully examine every trunk and limb, seeking concealed insects and their eggs and pupae. While this collective feeding strategy may seem at first to be counter-productive, it is probably the most efficient. It enables the group to take advantage of newly discovered feeding places, and it prevents birds from searching areas that others have recently covered. The Carolina chickadee eats primarily insects and spiders but also consumes small berries and seeds.

The black-capped chickadee ranges across North America from Alaska to Newfoundland and south to the central states. Although Peterson's Texas field guide describes it as a "casual winter visitor to w. Texas and Panhandle," and records are imbedded in the literature, no confirming specimens or photographs exist.

Five other chickadee species can be found in North America, but only one, the mountain chickadee *(Parus gambeli),* occurs in Texas. It has a distinctive white eyebrow stripe through the black cap above each eye, and its call is huskier and hoarser than that of the Carolina chickadee. A resident of western Canada and the U.S., it inhabits Texas' Guadalupe and Davis mountains.

Carolina chickadee.

TUFTED TITMOUSE *Parus bicolor*

The boisterous, friendly tufted titmouse is usually heard before it is seen. Sometimes called "tomtit" in the South, this saucy little bundle of nervous energy bounces through the treetops, scolding *peter peter peter* at any intruder to his territory. Although titmice lack the distinctive black caps and bibs of their compatriots, the chickadees, they are easily recognizable as the only small gray birds with pronounced crests. Both belong to the genus *Parus.*

The word titmouse, according to Edward Gruson in *Words for Birds,* "is derived from the Old Icelandic *titr,* meaning 'something small,' and *mouse,* a corruption of the Old English *mase,* 'small bird.' " *Parus* is the Latin for "titmouse," and in England all members of the genus are simply called "tits."

Two forms of the tufted titmouse occur in Texas, and they were formerly considered separate species. The typical form, the "tufted titmouse" of older field guides, ranges across most of the eastern United States, from the Canadian border to Florida and the Gulf States. It occurs in the eastern half of Texas, westward to about Fort Worth and Austin and south to the Rockport area on the central coast. About six inches long, it is gray above and pale gray or whitish below, with rusty patches on the flanks. Most distinctive are the short gray crest and a small black patch on the forehead above the beak.

The "black-crested titmouse" occurs south and west of the other's range, inhabiting West Texas from the middle of the Panhandle and the Davis Mountains south to the Rio Grande Valley. It has a black crest and a light forehead, just the reverse of the typical eastern form. Where these two former "species" meet in central Texas, however, they freely interbreed, and a variety of intermediate plumages might be seen.

Both forms inhabit woodlands, parks and towns, feeding on a mixed diet of insects, spiders, seeds and small berries and foraging in mixed-species flocks through the winter months. Tufted titmice nest in tree cavities and old woodpecker holes, packing the cavity with leaves, mosses, shreds of bark, grasses and animal hair. They form long-term pair bonds, and the male feeds his mate through courtship and while she incubates her five or six speckled eggs.

The increasing popularity of winter bird-feeding has enabled the tufted titmouse to expand its range northward across the country in recent years. Along with the cardinal and several other species, it has become more numerous in the Upper Midwest and in New England, where it subsists on generous handouts when natural foods are scarce.

Another southwestern species, the plain titmouse *(P. inornatus),* occurs in the Guadalupe Mountains. Smaller and drabber than the tufted titmouse, it has a shorter crest and lacks the black forehead and the rufous on the flanks. Frequent reports from the Edwards Plateau, however, are probably of young "black-crested titmice," for immatures of that form have short gray crests as well.

Tufted titmouse in pink flowering dogwood.

WRENS (Family Troglodytidae)

Cactus wren nest.

The wrens are characteristically small, chunky brown birds with slender, slightly curved bills. Many cock their tails up over their backs. While shy at times, they are inordinately curious and can usually be coaxed into view by the variety of squeaking and kissing sounds that birders employ. Wrens are also aggressive in defense of their territories, and their loud songs belie their size. Some must be included among the premier singers in the bird world. According to Cherokee legend, the wren was a busybody that slipped about to discover everyone else's business and report it to the birds' council.

More than 60 species of wrens make up the family Troglodytidae, and most are concentrated in Central and South America. Nine of those occur in the United States and in Texas. Surprisingly, only one species inhabits Eurasia. Known in this country as the winter wren, it is simply "the wren" in England or, in homey tales, "Jenny wren."

The family name stems from the Greek *troglodytes,* for "cave dweller." That word has carried into English as denoting a reclusive and brutish cave man. Wrens do at times seek shelter and nesting spots in hidden nooks and crannies, but with their sprightly behavior and charming voices they can hardly be considered troglodytes.

HOUSE WREN *Troglodytes aedon*

The jaunty, belligerent little house wren is a backyard favorite in the northern states. It readily accepts birdhouses and sings what the National Geographic Society *Field Guide to the Birds of North America* calls an "exuberant song, a cascade of bubbling whistled notes." The Chippewa Indians of the northern woodlands called it *O-du-na-mis-sug-ud-da-we'-shi,* "a big noise for its size."

The house wren ranges from southern Canada into Mexico in the West and as far south as the central states in the East. It is a spring and fall migrant throughout most of Texas and remains through the winter in all but the Panhandle and the extreme northern edge of the state. It must move south far enough to satisfy its appetite for insects, spiders and other small invertebrates during the colder months. House wrens also nest in the Guadalupe Mountains and, more rarely, in the Panhandle.

This five-inch wren is brown, with only a faint eyebrow stripe, and the lack of prominent facial stripes distinguishes it from most other wren species. Its short tail is often cocked up over its back. The house wren inhabits woodlands, thickets, parks and gardens during its winter stay in Texas and can often be located by its harsh, scolding calls. It leaves Texas again in March or April to return to its breeding grounds farther north.

The aggressive male establishes his territory and scouts prospective nesting sites. Tree cavities and old woodpecker holes once sheltered most wren nests, but people have now attracted many of the birds to fancy houses. Others might seek out less traditional hidden niches, building in an old boot or hat in an open garage, a flower box, or a clothespin bag hanging on the line.

Selecting several places he thinks

CAROLINA WREN
Thryothorus ludovicianus

It is just getting light on a damp, dreary morning, the dawn no more than a faint glow in the eastern sky. Blackened tree limbs drip from an all-night rain, and more rain is forecast throughout the day. In spite of the gloom, a song begins just outside our patio door, *teakettle teakettle teakettle.* I open the drapes to see a little bird perched on the rim of a potted fern. Head back, tail cocked, he continues to sing. The song is absurdly loud for so small a bird and seems out of place in the dripping darkness. Absurd, perhaps; but typical, too. For Carolina wrens are among the most irrepressible of birds, singing their lively songs throughout the year, come rain or shine.

The bird forages through the patio plants in search of breakfast, gleaning small insects and spiders from the leaves, poking and probing with his long and slightly decurved bill. Occasionally he stops long enough to repeat a version of his explosive song and then resumes his darting, curious explorations. As it grows lighter, I can see the rusty back, rich buff underparts, and prominent white eye-stripe that mark him as a Carolina wren.

The five-and-one-half- to six-inch Carolina wren ranges from southern New England through the southeastern states to Florida and Texas. It does not migrate, and pairs of wrens remain together throughout the year on permanent territories. After the breeding season, however, immature birds tend to wander, and the population slowly expands northward. During mild years such adventurers become well established, but severe winters take their toll. A long period of cold weather may kill all of the new colonists, and the gradual northern advance must start anew.

Carolina wrens reside year-round in the eastern two-thirds of Texas, occurring west to the Edwards Plateau and Del Rio and south all the way to the lower Rio Grande Valley. They inhabit woodlands, swamps and tree-

appropriate, the male fills the entrances with twigs and then courts his mate with bubbling song, escorting her on a tour of the apartment sites. Once she has chosen, however, she cleans out the twigs and builds a better cushion for her six to eight speckled eggs. She normally decorates with twigs, grasses and feathers, but other objects frequently turn up in house-wren nests. One account describes a nest containing "52 hairpins, 188 nails, 4 tacks, 13 staples, 10 pins, 11 safety pins, 6 paper clips, 2 hooks, 3 garter fasteners, and a buckle."

The genus of the house wren, *Troglodytes,* is Greek for "cave dweller." *Aedon* was the mythical queen of Thebes. Jealous of her sister-in-law, who had many children, she plotted to kill her oldest nephew but slew her own son by mistake. Zeus relieved her grief by turning her into a bird with a beautiful voice.

Even smaller than the house wren is the four-inch winter wren *(T. troglodytes).* It has an extremely short, stubby tail and more pronounced

dark barring on the belly and flanks. A breeding resident of Canada and the northern states, it winters throughout much of Texas, especially in the northern parts. Shy and secretive, the winter wren inhabits dense thickets and woodland underbrush.

Also small and secretive are the marsh wren *(Cistothorus palustris)* and the sedge wren *(C. platensis),* formerly known as the long-billed marsh wren and the short-billed marsh wren, respectively. The former breeds locally among the tall rushes or cattails of Texas marshes and winters throughout much of the state. The latter, the sedge wren, winters mainly along the coast and prefers grassy marshes and cordgrass flats. The marsh wren has a bold white eye-line, while that of the sedge wren is less distinct. Both have streaked backs.

A popular nesting bird across much of the country, the house wren is primarily a migrant and winter resident in Texas.

This Carolina wren raised her brood in the author's backyard barbecue.

BEWICK'S WREN

Thryomanes bewickii

Bewick's wren (pronounced *Buick's*) is the western counterpart of the Carolina wren. It occurs throughout the western states, where it is the most common and widespread of the wrens, and has traditionally ranged through the midsection of the country. However, it has declined severely east of the Mississippi River. Bewick's wren inhabits most of the state except for East Texas and the upper coast, where it turns up occasionally as a winter vagrant.

Brown above and whitish below, Bewick's wren has a long white eyebrow stripe and a long, white-edged tail, which it often wags from side to side. The light underparts and white tail edges distinguish it from the Carolina wren, with which it shares a portion of its range in central and southern Texas. The song is a sweet, complex warble with a number of geographical dialects. When irritated,

Bewick's wren poses with tail cocked.

lined suburbs, where they nest in tree cavities, brush piles and other sheltered niches. Bird lovers who are newly arrived from the North often try to attract wrens with backyard birdhouses, and the efforts sometimes succeed; however, the Carolina wren is larger than the well-known house wren and requires a larger entrance hole. It also exhibits an independent streak and prefers to select its own nest site, usually choosing a hanging basket of flowers or an unused barbecue grill and leaving the birdhouse vacant.

The female lays her four to six spotted eggs in a nest of grasses and plant fibers and incubates them alone. The altricial, helpless babies hatch in 12 to 14 days and grow rapidly to leave the nest within two weeks. Because pairs may raise two or three broods a year, the male often takes over the feeding of the young while his mate begins her next clutch.

Biologists have reported that male Carolina wrens sing as many as 40 different versions of their song, repeating one several times and then switching to something new. Neighboring males may match that song from the boundaries of their territories, and courting pairs often sing duets. *Teakettle teakettle teakettle* and *cheery cheery cheery* are the phonetic phrases most often used to describe the wren's repertoire, but other listeners hear such phrases as *wheat eater, giddyap, tea-party* and *it's raining.* All are immediately recognizable, however, as the loud rain-or-shine lyrics of the Carolina wren.

the wren has a buzzy call someone once likened to an "old-fashioned Bronx cheer."

Bewick's wren inhabits brushlands, open woods, ranches and farm lands, where it seeks out tree cavities and other crevices in which to build its nest. A friendly, rather tame bird, it might also nest in old buildings, beneath a tractor seat, or in an unused mailbox. West Texas ranchers sometimes call it the "house wren" because of its close approach to human habitation, but it is very different from the smaller all-brown species that officially bears that name. Soft grasses and feathers line the nest of twigs and plant fibers. The five to seven whitish eggs, flecked with brown, hatch after 14 days of incubation by the female alone. Fed a typical wren diet of in-

sects, spiders and other invertebrates by both parents, the young fledge two weeks later, and the pair may soon begin preparation for a second brood.

Bewick's wren was named by Audubon for English engraver Thomas Bewick (1753?–1828), who restored the art of lifelike nature engravings. His works remain classics in that genre. One critic wrote of Bewick, "Besides being an engraver, he was, in his own way, an artist of remarkable capacity as a faithful interpreter of animal life."

Bobbing excitedly on his perch, a rock wren serenades the Chisos Mountain campground.

ROCK WREN
Salpinctes obsoletus

The spry little wren perches on top of a boulder and bobs excitedly up and down. Wagging its long tail, it throws back its head and sings in an amazingly loud voice, *tew tew tew tew, cher-wee cher-wee cher-wee.* The song is somewhat harsh and mechanical, but the tinkling mixture of buzzes and trills is nonetheless appealing for its sheer exuberance. Some have likened it to the repetitious phrases of the mockingbird, but without the element of mimicry. More than 100 versions of the varied repertoire have been documented.

Flying from its perch with quick, jerky wingbeats, the six-inch wren lands on the steep slope and probes into a crevice with its long, slender bill. It finds an insect and gulps it down, then hops onto another rock to sing again, leaving no doubt as to who lays claim to this section of the canyon wall. His back is a duller grayish brown than most other wrens, and the pale underparts are lightly streaked with gray. A black band and buffy corners on the long tail confirm his identity as a rock wren, an appropriate name for this bird that inhabits the arid talus slopes, washes and scrubby brushlands of the American West.

The rock wren is a year-round resident of western Texas, ranging across the Trans-Pecos, the Panhandle and the Edwards Plateau. Its range extends eastward to Austin and south to Eagle Pass and San Antonio. Winter wanderers may turn up in the Rio Grande Valley on occasion. The rock wren can be distinguished from Bewick's wren, which shares its range, by its pale grayish (instead of brown) upperparts; and from the canyon wren by its pale underparts (instead of dark chestnut belly and white breast and throat).

Nesting in rocky crevices, the rock wren paves the floor of its chamber with pebbles and stone chips and usually constructs a pathway leading to it. The reason for this patient masonry

work is not known, but the effort is substantial. One observer discovered a nest cavity paved with 1,600 bits of stone, metal and bone, each laid precisely in place. Inside, a nest of grasses and other soft materials contains five to eight white eggs lightly dotted with brown. The female apparently incubates them alone, but the breeding biology and the incubation and fledging periods have not been fully investigated.

The scientific name of the rock wren comes from the Greek *salpinktes,* or "trumpeter," and the Latin *obsoletus,* for "effaced" or "dull." True, the rock wren is not a brightly colored bird, but its loud voice and lively antics make it a welcome addition to the birdlife of West Texas.

CANYON WREN

Catherpes mexicanus

It is, to my musically untrained ear, one of the most beautiful of all birdsongs. The clear, ringing song of the canyon wren descends through a series of liquid notes in a silvery glissando, *te-you te-you te-you tew tew tew tew*. Reflected by the rock walls of the canyon habitat, it may be audible a half mile away. It is impossible to be objective about such a song, however, for the singer performs on some of the most beautiful stages in the world. I have awakened to the song of the canyon wren in the bottom of the Grand Canyon and heard it serenade the coming of spring along the Virgin River in Utah's Zion National Park. Its clear whistles echo from the walls of Santa Elena Canyon in Big Bend and complement the crystal waters of a Hill Country stream as it trickles down a limestone ledge. Steep, rocky walls and running water prove most attractive to this charming and lively wren, and its song takes on the qualities of its home.

Rich, rusty hues adorn the canyon wren.

There is a comic ending to the canyon wren's bubbling cascade, but it is audible only at close range. Following the clear notes is an absurd *bzz bzz,* as if the artist refuses to take his concert too seriously.

Ranging through the western United States and Mexico, the canyon wren inhabits the Trans-Pecos, Edwards Plateau and Panhandle regions of Texas. More often heard than seen, it creeps mouselike over the rocky walls of its territory, probing with its long bill for insects, spiders and other invertebrates. When discovered on its perch, it is easily recognized by its rusty upperparts, chestnut belly and contrasting, biblike white throat and breast. *Catherpes* comes from the Greek for "a creeper" and refers to its habits. *Mexicanus* is for the type locality in Hidalgo, Mexico, from which Swainson first described the canyon wren in 1829.

The canyon wren usually tucks its nest into a crevice in the rocks, although it sometimes uses abandoned buildings. The female lays four to six speckled eggs in a cup of moss, grasses, spider webs and other soft materials, but biologists know very little about the breeding habits. Many of our common birds still hide intimate secrets of their life histories, and ornithology is a science where observant amateurs can still make an enormous contribution to the existing body of knowledge.

CACTUS WREN   *Campylorhynchus brunneicapillus*

Perched atop a thorny bush, he breaks the sweltering stillness of a summer afternoon with his harsh, scolding notes. The noisy, aggressive cactus wren can be heard throughout the day, even when most other desert dwellers seek seclusion in some shady niche. Its morning song serves as a wake-up call for Big Bend campers. One park ranger compared it to the sound of a reluctant '52 Chevy pickup trying to start.

More than eight inches long, the cactus wren is much larger than any other North American wren and seems almost like a thrasher in its proportions. Indeed, its heavily spotted breast might also cause confusion with the larger thrashers, but the cactus wren has a distinctive white eyebrow stripe, a streaked brown back, and striking black-and-white barring on its wings and tail.

The state bird of Arizona, the cactus wren inhabits the deserts and arid brushlands of the southwestern states and Mexico and occurs as a common year-round resident in West Texas and the southern Staked Plains. It ranges eastward locally to San Antonio, Beeville and the central coast and south into the Rio Grande Valley. The imposing scientific name seems almost as long as the bird itself, but it merely describes the species. *Campylorhynchus* is from the Greek for "curved beak"; *brunneicapillus* is from the Latin for "brown crown."

Nests of the cactus wren conspicuously mark its range, for they are large football-shaped masses in the tops of cacti and spiny shrubs. The entrance is on the side of the woven-grass nest and leads through a narrow passage into a central chamber lined with feathers. The female alone incubates her three or four pinkish, speckled eggs, but both parents feed the babies that hatch in 16 days. Fledglings leave the nest at about three weeks of age. During the latter stages of incubation, the male often wanders off to build another nest that can be used either for a second brood or as a roosting place. The cactus wren is one of the few species of perching birds that refurbishes old nests or builds new ones to use as roosting sites throughout the year.

Insects and spiders make up the bulk of the cactus wren's diet, but its size also allows this largest of the wrens to take occasional lizards and other small vertebrates as well. In some studies, fruits and seeds have comprised 15 to 20 percent of the diet, particularly during the winter months when insects are scarce.

Cactus wrens on an ocotillo stalk provide the perfect vignette of the Desert Southwest.

THRUSHES AND THEIR ALLIES (Family Muscicapidae)

Eastern bluebird nest and eggs.

In the sixth edition (1983) of its *Check-list of North American Birds,* the American Ornithologists' Union made sweeping changes in bird taxonomy at the family level. The family Muscicapidae now contains several subfamilies that were formerly considered separate families. These include two groups common in Texas: the kinglets and gnatcatchers (subfamily Sylviinae) and the thrushes (subfamily Turdinae). Other subfamilies include the Old World flycatchers and the monarch flycatchers (which are not related to our tyrant flycatchers), the babblers and the wrentit.

"The Committee feels that this arrangement expresses probable relationships much better than the traditional system and that the changes are necessary and desirable, although we recognize that new evidence will surely require modification of it. Other proposed changes will doubtless be validated in the future," notes the preface to the AOU checklist.

Not all authors agree. Terence Shortt, in his *Wild Birds of the Americas,* takes issue with the creation of so large and unwieldy a family unit that lumps together more than 1,400 species. It renders passé long-established divisions and a century of literature on what Shortt calls "no more than a heads-or-tails choice."

Most birders would sympathize with Shortt's point of view, for they prefer to group birds in more manageable categories. That can still be done, however, on the subfamily level, the approach taken in this book.

American robin.

KINGLETS AND GNATCATCHERS (Muscicapidae: Subfamily Sylviinae)

Our kinglets and gnatcatchers are tiny, active birds with small, slender bills. They inhabit woodlands and thickets and consume primarily insects, along with their larvae and eggs. Only a few of the Sylviinae occur in North America, but more than 300 species occupy the forested areas of the world. They include the tropical gnatwrens and the large and complex group of Old World warblers. The latter have generally drab plumages and are not related to the American warblers, or wood warblers, that are abundant in Texas.

GOLDEN-CROWNED KINGLET *Regulus satrapa*

The plump little golden-crowned kinglet, at four inches, is one of the smallest of Texas birds. It breeds in the coniferous forests of Canada and the northern states, ranging southward in the mountains as far as Mexico and Guatemala in the West and North Carolina in the East. It moves south to the Gulf states in winter and occurs throughout Texas from late October until March or early April. The charming, active kinglet forages through woodlands and thickets for the insects that make up the major portion of its diet, and it often travels in mixed-species flocks with other small birds.

Grayish green above and whitish below, the golden-crowned kinglet has two pale wing-bars and a broad white eyebrow stripe. The black-bordered crown patch is orange on the male and yellow on the female. This distinctive head pattern separates the golden-crowned kinglet from the ruby-crowned, which has no strong eyebrow stripe and no black-bordered crown patch. The red cap of the male ruby-crowned kinglet is usually concealed. The call of the golden-crowned is a high-pitched *see-see* or *see-seep*.

The golden-crowned kinglet builds a globular nest of mosses, lichens and spider webs and hangs it from the branches of an evergreen tree. The normal clutch of eight or nine eggs is so large that the eggs are often crowded two-deep in the nest, and many pairs raise a second brood as large as the first. Such productivity illustrates clearly the many hazards young birds must face, for each pair need only reproduce itself to achieve a stable population. Even with such large broods, few survive their first year, and the golden-crowned kinglet showed signs of declining during the 1980s.

Its bright head stripes and wing-bars characterize the tiny golden-crowned kinglet.

RUBY-CROWNED KINGLET

Regulus calendula

Scarcely four inches long, the ruby-crowned kinglet ranks with the hummingbirds, the smallest wrens and the golden-crowned kinglet as the tiniest of our birds. It is grayish olive above and pale dusky gray below, with a yellowish wash on the underparts and two prominent white wing-bars. A broken white eye-ring gives it a startled, wide-eyed look. The ruby crown of the male is usually concealed, and only in courtship or territorial defense does the agitated kinglet flare his crown feathers to reveal the small red patch.

Ruby-crowned kinglets nest in the forests of Alaska and Canada and along the northern border of the contiguous states. They also range southward in the western mountains to California and New Mexico. Because they feed primarily on insects, they must move south for the winter months, and it is then that they invade Texas in large numbers. Migrating throughout the state, they remain through the winter in all but the northern Panhandle. Christmas Bird Counts in Texas tally hundreds, even thousands, of ruby-crowned kinglets, making them one of the most common of all our small perching birds during that season. They flit through the woodlands and thickets and visit backyard gardens and shade trees, often in company with several other species that troop along together in search of food.

Because of their small size and drab plumage, kinglets attract little attention. Yet they are delightful bundles of nervous energy, bouncing through the trees and flicking their wings repeatedly as they chatter loudly in scolding voices, *ji-dit ji-dit ji-dit*. Frequently mistaken for warblers, ruby-crowned kinglets are smaller and have shorter, stubbier tails.

The ruby-crowned kinglet is one of the smallest of all Texas birds.

BLUE-GRAY GNATCATCHER   *Polioptila caerulea*

An icy blast made me shiver as I opened the front door to check our outdoor faucets and covered plants. It was midnight on the day before Christmas, and we were once again feeling the fury of the Arctic Express. As I was retreating back inside, I noticed a tiny bit of fluff pressed tightly into a corner of the brick wall beside the door. It was about the size of a golf ball, and at first glance it seemed to be a mouse. Then I saw a thin black tail feather sticking out. Picking it up, I held in my hand a sleepy blue-gray gnatcatcher no larger than my thumb. Curled up, with its feathers ruffled, it was lethargic with the cold.

I brought the little bird indoors and bedded it down in a warm cardboard box, turning out the lights to keep it quiet. The next morning it was peering back at me as I peeped into its temporary refuge, and in a few minutes it hopped onto a proffered finger and drank water from my cupped hand. Released outside, it flew to the top of a cedar elm and began foraging through the remaining leaves.

Blue-gray above and white below, the aptly named blue-gray gnatcatcher is a little more than four inches long. A good portion of that length is the black tail, which has white outer feathers. Peterson refers to it as a "very tiny, slender mite, even smaller than a chickadee." He and several other authors describe it as similar to a miniature mockingbird, although without the white patches in the wings.

The blue-gray gnatcatcher ranges across the continent from northern California to Minnesota and Maine and southward as far as Guatemala. In Texas, it breeds across most of the state except for the southern counties. It withdraws from much of its range in winter and occupies the southern half of Texas and the Gulf Coast. There it is one of the most abundant of our woodland birds.

The closely related black-tailed gnatcatcher *(Polioptila melanura)* of the Desert Southwest is similar; however, it has less white on the sides of the tail, which is mostly black below. In contrast, the white outer tail feathers of the blue-gray gnatcatcher cause most of the folded tail to appear white when viewed from below. The male black-tail also has a black cap in breeding plumage, but that distinctive mark is absent in the winter. It is a permanent resident of the desert washes and dry brushlands of the Trans-Pecos and occurs occasionally along the lower portions of the Rio Grande.

Gnatcatchers feed on insects and spiders, which they pursue through the foliage and pry from cracks and crevices with their slender beaks. They are continually on the move, flitting back and forth, long tails ruddering their twisting flight as they dart after gnats and flies.

A habitat generalist, the blue-gray gnatcatcher inhabits woods, swamps and desert scrub. The nest is a tiny, compact cup saddled on a limb or in a fork, constructed of plant down and spider silk and covered with bits of lichen. The four or five pale blue eggs, usually flecked with brown, are incubated by both parents and hatch in 13 days. The tiny young grow quickly and fledge in only 10 or 11 days.

An hour after I released my little blue-gray gnatcatcher, I noticed it hopping along on the ground in the flower bed. I walked slowly toward it and sat down on the frozen grass about three feet away. It paid little attention to me and went on hunting, occasionally finding a tasty tidbit. Its foraging was confined to a small sunlit area, for the morning was still bitterly cold, and it apparently preferred dining in my presence to retreating to the shade. It was tempting to believe this tiny bird had befriended me during our brief encounter, but I knew its need for food and warmth was simply more pressing than any innate fear.

After nearly half an hour, I was the first to succumb to the cold, leaving the gnatcatcher to go on alone. It will always be one of my favorite Christmas memories, a gift wrapped in blue-gray feathers and delivered to my door on Christmas Eve.

The long black tail of the blue-gray gnatcatcher is edged with white.

Formerly placed in a family of their own, the Turdidae, the thrushes are medium-sized birds with rather long legs and slender bills. The ones we actually call "thrush" are brownish in color and have spotted breasts; however, the bluebirds, solitaires and robins are closely related. The young of these latter groups also have spotted breasts but lose their markings in adult plumage. Among the more than 300 members of this worldwide subfamily are some of the finest of all avian singers, including the celebrated nightingale. They consume insects, worms and fruits, and most lay "robin's-egg blue" eggs.

EASTERN BLUEBIRD

Sialia sialis

The lovely seven-inch eastern bluebird must certainly rank among the most popular of all our common birds, and it has become the state bird of both New York and Missouri. Thoreau describes it as "carrying the sky on its back." The male is an intense, shiny blue above, with a rich chestnut-red throat and breast and a contrasting white belly. Although grayer and paler than her mate, the female is readily recognizable.

The eastern bluebird occurs east of the Rocky Mountains, from southern Canada to the Gulf States and south through Mexico to Honduras. It breeds across the eastern two-thirds of Texas, from the northeastern Panhandle to the lower coast and west to the Edwards Plateau. It is most common as a nesting species, however, in the open woodlands and farmyards of East Texas. Partially migratory, the eastern bluebird withdraws from the northern portions of its range in winter and is then fairly common throughout the state except for the Trans-Pecos, where it is replaced by the western and mountain bluebirds. It depends heavily on berries and other fruits to supplement its insect diet during the colder months.

The eastern bluebird has suffered a drastic population decline during the last few decades, in some areas decreasing by as much as 90 percent. The clearing of dead trees and the

Birdhouses have aided greatly in the return of the eastern bluebird.

heavy use of agricultural pesticides have undoubtedly contributed to the decline, but most authors cite competition with the introduced house sparrow and European starling as the primary cause.

Bluebirds prefer open farmland with scattered trees, established orchards, cutover woodlands, and even suburban yards and parks. They utilize cavities and old woodpecker holes in trees and posts as nesting sites and, although they often defend their chosen locations against house sparrows and tree swallows, they cannot repel the larger and more aggressive starlings. Recent interest in putting up bluebird boxes has helped to turn the tide in many areas across the country, including Texas. Conservation groups, scout troops and interested individuals have even created "bluebird trails" with series of birdhouses to reestablish the birds in their former range.

The bluebird nest is a loose cup of grasses, plant stems and rootlets in the cavity or nest box and is usually built over a period of about ten days. The female incubates her three to six sky-blue eggs, and they hatch in 12 to 14 days. Fed by both parents on a diet of insects, the babies remain in the nest for 15 to 20 days more. Fledglings are grayish with speckled breasts, revealing their family ties to the thrushes; however, they have enough blue in the wings and tail to mark them as bluebirds at any age. Because pairs begin nesting early in the season, they may easily raise two or three broods each year. Studies show that young from a previous brood sometimes help with subse-

quent nesting chores. Some broods have also involved more than one male or female, indicating less than total fidelity by both sexes.

It is their early return to the northern portions of their range, even while snow remains on the ground, that has helped make bluebirds so popular across the country. In the Northeast, they are truly harbingers of spring. "In New York and New England the sap starts up the sugar maple the very day the bluebird arrives, and sugar-making begins forthwith," writes famed naturalist John Burroughs.

The call note of the eastern bluebird is a musical *chur-lee,* or *chur-wi,* that when repeated serves as the song throughout the seasons, *chur chur-lee chur-lee.* Romantics assign to it such words as *pur-ity* and *tru-ly* and coin phrases like "the bluebird of happiness." "Few sounds in all Nature," writes Robert Lemmon, "are so pleasantly rich and yet so simple." The same might be said for the bluebird's elegant plumage.

WESTERN BLUEBIRD
Sialia mexicana

The western bluebird replaces its eastern counterpart in the region from the Rocky Mountains to the Pacific Coast. It breeds from southwestern Canada through the mountains as far south as central Mexico, moving southward and to lower elevations for the winter. Western bluebirds breed in Texas in the Guadalupe Mountains and less frequently in the Davis Mountains. In winter they range throughout the open woodlands, ranches and mesquite scrub of the Trans-Pecos, occurring irregularly in the Panhandle and across the Edwards Plateau.

The male resembles the eastern bluebird but has darker, almost purplish blue upperparts and throat. Most birds also have a chestnut patch on the shoulders and upper back, but a few are entirely blue above. The blue throat, however, remains diagnostic, since male eastern bluebirds have rusty throats. The female plumage is duller and grayer.

Bluebirds feed heavily on insects during the summer months but rely on berries through the winter when insects are scarce. Juniper and mistletoe are favorites, and the birds apparently spread the sticky mistletoe seeds to other trees. Ironically, this spreading of the parasitic plant probably serves to create new rotting limbs and nest cavities for future bluebird generations.

As is the case with the eastern bluebird, competition with house sparrows and starlings has led to a decrease in available nest sites and a severe decline in the western bluebird population. The breeding biology has not been studied fully, but the nesting habits and the incubation and fledging times are probably much like those of the eastern species.

The western bluebird replaces its eastern counterpart in Trans-Pecos Texas.

MOUNTAIN BLUEBIRD
Sialia currucoides

A glow in the eastern sky hints at the approaching dawn, but the birds of the high mountain meadow still doze in silence. Then, from the top of a small pine, comes the first voice of the dawn chorus. It is a sweet song, composed of short phrases and sung in a soft, clear warble, the matins of the mountain bluebird. As the first rays light the meadow, other birds join in, but the initial voice is quickly stilled. The mountain bluebird seldom sings for long. It is, the Navajos say, the herald of the rising sun.

This bluebird lacks the rusty breast of the other two members of its genus. The male is clear turquoise-blue above and a slightly lighter blue beneath, while the female is a drabber brownish gray with bluish shading in the wings and tail. The state bird of Nevada and Idaho, the mountain bluebird inhabits the higher elevations from Alaska and western Canada southward to California and Arizona. It prefers meadows and open rangelands with scattered trees, usually above 6,000 feet.

A highly migratory species, the mountain bluebird descends to the lowlands and moves southward to winter along the U.S. border and into northern Mexico. It can be found from September until early May in the western two-thirds of Texas, ranging eastward occasionally to Dallas, Austin and San Antonio. Hovering in the air or darting out from its perch, it hawks insects on the wing, but it also supplements its diet with berries and fruit during the colder months.

Like its close relatives, the mountain bluebird nests in tree cavities and old woodpecker holes, and like them it suffers from competition with alien house sparrows, starlings and other cavity-nesting birds. The population has declined severely over the past century.

Sharing much of the mountain bluebird's range is a more unusual and less familiar member of the

thrush family, the Townsend's solitaire (*Myadestes townsendi*). It nests in western mountains from Alaska to the southwestern states and moves to warmer climates for the winter. It then ranges through the canyons of the Texas Panhandle and occurs sparingly in the Trans-Pecos and on the Edwards Plateau. Larger than the bluebirds, the nine-inch solitaire is slim and gray, with buffy patches on the wings and white outer tail feathers. It somewhat resembles the common mockingbird but has a darker gray breast and a pronounced white ring around the eye.

Unlike the eastern and western bluebirds, the male mountain bluebird is entirely blue.

Swainson's thrush drinks from a pond.

SWAINSON'S THRUSH   *Catharus ustulatus*

Swainson's thrush has also been called the "olive-backed thrush" for its uniformly olive-brown upperparts that contain no hint of warmer reddish hues. Bright buffy cheeks and lores (the area between the bill and eye) and bold buffy eye-rings distinguish Swainson's thrush from the other three *Catharus* thrushes. The buffy breast is speckled with brown spots.

Swainson's thrush nests across Alaska and Canada, ranging southward in the western mountains to California and Colorado and in the East to West Virginia. It passes through Texas in late September and October on its way to its wintering grounds in Central and South America and returns again in April and May. Although it can be found throughout the state, it is most common in the eastern portions, particularly among the waves of spring migrants along the coast. Swainson's thrush forages widely on the ground in woodlands and thickets, seeking the insects, worms and fruits that make up its varied diet. However, it is the least terrestrial of the thrushes and also gleans insects and plucks berries from the trees.

Named for English-born naturalist William Swainson (1789–1855), this common buffy-faced thrush is one of three North American birds to bear his name. Swainson's hawk and Swainson's warbler also occur in Texas.

The genus name *Catharus* comes from the Greek *katharos*, meaning "pure," and alludes to the flutelike songs of the thrushes, some of the most pleasing and melodious in the world. Gruson notes that the specific name *ustulatus* stems from the Latin for "having been singed," referring to the ash-colored plumage.

The gray-cheeked thrush (*C. minimus*) most closely resembles Swainson's thrush, with its olive-brown plumage and spotted underparts. However, it lacks the buffy lores and distinct eye-ring of the latter and has a grayer face. It, too, nests in the far North and crosses most of Texas on its way to and from South America, although it is less frequent in the western portions of the state.

The veery (*C. fuscescens*) is similar to its relatives in form and habits, but it is a richer reddish brown above, with fainter speckling on its pale buffy breast. A shy denizen of moist woodlands and thickets, it migrates through the eastern portions of Texas and is most frequently seen along the coast on its way to Canada and the northern states.

HERMIT THRUSH

Catharus guttatus

The lovely voice of the hermit thrush has been praised by authors ranging from John Burroughs to Walt Whitman. Oberholser writes that the clear, flutelike song is considered by most naturalists to be the finest of any U.S. bird. The three or four phrases are on different pitches, each prefaced by a long introductory note. The song, Oberholser notes, "sounds deliberate, serene, relaxed." Unfortunately, the hermit thrush seldom sings outside its nesting territory, and it nests in Texas only in the high Guadalupe Mountains, the southernmost limit of a range that extends through Alaska, Canada and the western mountains.

The hermit thrush does remain in Texas, however, when the other spotted *Catharus* thrushes migrate to the tropics. It spends the winter throughout the southern states and Mexico, migrating across most of Texas and vacating only the colder sections of the Panhandle and the West. During those cold months, it depends heavily on fruits and berries to supplement its summer diet of insects, spiders and worms.

Olive-brown above and spotted below, the hermit thrush has a contrasting reddish tail that distinguishes it from the others of its genus. Its actions, too, are diagnostic, for it constantly jerks its tail upward and then lowers it slowly, a habit the others do not have. Such unique mannerisms frequently provide clues to bird identification that are as useful in the field as plumage differences. The hermit thrush also flicks its wings repeatedly as it forages through fallen leaves, sometimes uttering its low *chuck* or *tuck-tuck-tuck* calls. Named for its shy and reclusive manner, the hermit thrush inhabits woodlands and thickets, but it may also wander into suburban yards and gardens during its winter sojourn in our state.

WOOD THRUSH

Hylocichla mustelina

It has been a hot, humid summer day in the river-bottom forest of East Texas. The slanting rays of the descending sun dapple the forest floor, and the only sound is the low drone of mosquitoes and the occasional chatter of a squirrel. Then from somewhere in the shadows come the clear liquid notes of a flute, bar after bar of magical music, *ee-o-lay ee-o-lay,* each phrase ending with a complex trill. It is the song of the wood thrush, providing a perfect ending for the day.

At eight inches long, the wood thrush is larger and plumper than the other spotted thrushes. Some authors have suggested combining them in the same genus, but current practice places it in another, *Hylocichla*. The AOU checklist notes that the wood thrush may be more closely related to the larger robins and thrushes of the genus *Turdus* than to the smaller *Catharus* thrushes.

The wood thrush is reddish brown above, with the brightest rusty hues on the head and neck. *Mustelina* comes from the Latin for "weasel-like" and refers to this rufous color. White underparts are marked with large, round spots, and a streaked cheek patch and bold white eye-ring ornament the face.

The rusty tail of the hermit thrush matches autumn hues of Virginia creeper.

The wood thrush inhabits wooded swamps and moist forests throughout the eastern half of the United States, from the southern edge of Canada to the Gulf of Mexico. That breeding range includes East Texas and extends westward to Dallas and Houston. The three or four blue-green eggs are laid in a bulky cup of leaves, mud, grasses and rootlets and are incubated by the female. Hatching in about two weeks, the young are fed by both parents and fledge at 12 or 13 days of age. Insects and other invertebrates constitute the diet of the young, but fruits and berries are added as they grow, making up as much as one-third of the thrush's normal fare.

The wood thrush is typical of a large and diverse array of birds called neotropical migrants, which include many of the thrushes, vireos, warblers, orioles and tanagers. Nesting in the forests of North America, they make long migration flights to winter in Latin America and the Caribbean Islands. They are particularly vulnerable to deforestation in their winter range, where they must compete with the resident species, but they are also affected by fragmentation of the woodlands in this country. In some states, more than 70 percent of the neotropical species experienced severe population declines during the last decade. International efforts will be necessary to stem the tide. "We simply are not going to have these birds in the future unless we make a serious effort to conserve their habitats throughout our hemisphere," said John Turner, director of the U.S. Fish and Wildlife Service, in 1991.

Large, dark spots dot the breast of the wood thrush.

AMERICAN ROBIN
Turdus migratorius

This largest of our thrushes needs little introduction, for few other birds are as widely recognized. It ranges across the length and breadth of the continent and serves as the state bird of three states—Connecticut, Michigan and Wisconsin. The American robin nests from the treeline in Alaska and northern Canada south to the Gulf Coast and the mountains of Mexico. While many bird species occupy either the eastern or the western states, the robin is equally at home on both the Atlantic and Pacific coasts. It withdraws from the northern portion of its range in winter and migrates southward to seek more abundant food supplies. Its return to the North is widely heralded as the first sign of spring, although other less popular birds may actually precede it on the migration flyways. For many people, winter is not over until the robin sings.

American robins winter throughout Texas but remain to breed primarily in the northern and eastern portions of the state and locally in the mountains of the West. In *The Bird Life of Texas,* Oberholser notes that in historic times the robin was only a local breeder in Texas, except in the forested eastern quarter. Most of the state was too hot, dry and bare to provide suitable habitat. Between 1925 and 1940, however, there was an increase in tree planting and lawn sprinkling in Texas communities, resulting in well-spaced trees, increased humidity, and mud for nest construction. Breeding robins thus increased in North Texas and spread south to Waco, Austin and San Antonio, reaching Corpus Christi by 1967.

On their southern wintering grounds robins congregate in huge flocks, feeding together on insects, worms and berries and massing in the trees to roost at night. In spring the hormonal drive sends the males northward first to establish territories in which they will woo their prospective mates. It is then that the robin emerges in its true glory, a colorful songbird with brilliant plumage and a rich, caroling song of lilting phrases.

The nest is a solid fortress of grass and mud, which the female shapes with her breast and wings by turning round and round in it. A lining of softer fibers cushions the three to five eggs of clear "robin's-egg blue." One of the robin's endearing traits is its penchant for nesting near human habitation. Seemingly unafraid, it may select a backyard apple tree or a sheltered window ledge as readily as a pine tree on the forest's edge. I have seen nests in city stoplights, on the newly hung rafters of a barn under construction, and under the raised cowling of a farmer's tractor.

Hatching after 12 to 14 days of incubation by the female, the young leave the nest at 14 to 16 days of age. Their speckled breasts betray their relationship to the thrushes. Adults are gray-brown above, with brick-red breasts, white bellies, and black-streaked white throats. Older males often have black heads, contrasting strongly with the white eye-ring and yellow bill, but there is a great deal of individual color variation, and the sexes cannot be safely separated by plumage alone.

Although to most of us this familiar bird is simply "the robin," its proper name is American robin. Other robin species occur through Latin American and the Caribbean,

and three of them have been reported as vagrants along the Rio Grande. One, the clay-colored robin *(Turdus grayi)*, is seen regularly in the lower Valley at places like Bentsen–Rio Grande State Park and Santa Ana National Wildlife Refuge. The American robin was named by homesick colonists for the robin that occurs commonly across Europe. The two are only distantly related, but both have red breasts.

Most American robins come to Texas only as winter residents.

MOCKINGBIRDS AND THRASHERS (Family Mimidae)

The family Mimidae consists of a group of remarkable vocalists noted for the variety and volume of their songs. Their talent for mimicry is legendary, and they are often called "mimic thrushes." Most Texans know the ubiquitous northern mockingbird as the official state bird, but there are a number of other mockingbird species in Latin America. The family also includes the catbird and several thrashers that range widely across the continent. The brown thrasher occurs through the eastern U.S., while seven other thrashers inhabit the western states. Texas hosts five of the thrasher species.

The Mimidae is an exclusively New World family of about 30 species. They have long tails and relatively long, slightly decurved bills. Most have rather drab plumage in shades of gray or brown, but they make up for their lack of bright colors and command attention with their vocal ability. Thrashers might be confused with the spotted thrushes but for their much longer tails and bills.

NORTHERN MOCKINGBIRD *Mimus polyglottos*

The 50,000-member Texas Federation of Women's Clubs nominated the northern mockingbird as the state bird of Texas in November 1926, according to Robin Doughty in his delightful book *The Mockingbird*. On January 31, 1927, the legislature adopted the resolution unanimously, noting that the mockingbird "is found in all parts of the State, in winter and in summer, in the city and in the country, on the prairie and in the woods and hills, and is a singer of distinctive type, a fighter for the protection of his home, falling, if need be, in its defense, like any true Texan . . . ." Other states apparently shared Texans' enthusiasm for *Mimus polyglottos*, the "many-tongued mimic," for Florida, Arkansas, Tennessee and Mississippi subsequently made it their state bird as well.

The northern mockingbird does, indeed, live year-round across the entire state. It also ranges widely over the continent, from southern Canada to Mexico and the West Indies, withdrawing from only the northern states in winter. Over the years, it has also expanded its range slowly northward, undoubtedly with some help from bountiful feeders. Several other mockingbird species occur in Latin America, necessitating the full name of "northern mockingbird" for *polyglottos*.

Mockingbirds form long-term pair bonds and show unusual fidelity to their mates. They may, however, establish separate feeding territories during the winter months, when insects and berries are harder to find. The male begins to build the twiggy, cuplike nest, and the female lines it with softer grasses and plant fibers, laying three to five bluish green eggs spotted with brown. She incubates them for about 12 days, and both parents feed the young that leave the nest some 12 days after hatching. The male may take over the care and feeding of the fledglings while his mate renests, for most raise at least two broods a year and sometimes three or four. Fiercely aggressive and territorial, mockingbirds do not hesitate to attack in defense of their eggs and young. Audubon's famous mockingbird painting depicts four birds mobbing a rattlesnake that threatens a clutch of eggs.

Dull gray above, with white outer tail feathers and white patches in the wings that flash brightly in flight, the ten-inch northern mockingbird is not particularly colorful, but it makes up for that with its amazing vocal talents. John Burroughs called it "the lark and the nightingale in one," and colonial naturalist Mark Catesby reported that "The Indians, by way of eminence or admiration, call it *Cencontlatolly*, or four hundred tongues."

The mockingbird imitates other birds so expertly that sound spectrographs show the renditions to be exact duplicates, even to the high-pitched overtones inaudible to human ears. A famous mockingbird at Boston's Arnold Arboretum was heard to reproduce "39 bird songs, 50 bird calls, and the sounds of a frog and a cricket." The literature contains countless stories of notable imitations. One New York City bird reproduced perfectly the *beep-beep-beep* of a backhoe in reverse, while another threw a high school football game into confusion by mimicking the referee's whistle. Yet another "joined the National Symphony Orchestra during an outdoor concert in Washington, D.C.," according to writer Alden Miller. "He imitated the flute which

The northern mockingbird (opposite) occurs throughout Texas, from the Piney Woods to the cactus-covered western deserts.

imitated the bird calls in 'Peter and the Wolf ' ! "

Unlike the catbird, which sings each phrase but once, the mockingbird repeats each phrase two or three times before moving on to the next. In the springtime, it may sing for hours, both day and night. Researchers have found these nocturnal vocalists to be primarily unmated males, but both sexes sing in the fall when they are claiming feeding territories.

The exact purpose of the mockingbird's mimicry continues to engender arguments among biologists. Mimicry normally connotes some deception by the mimic, either as a defense against predators or in competition with another. However, most of the mockingbird's vocalizations are unlikely to deceive anyone, particularly in combination with all of the other complex and unrelated phrases. Several studies suggest that natural selection favors a large and varied repertoire, which aids the male in attracting and stimulating a mate and intimidating rivals. The mockingbird simply adopts new sounds that he hears to add variety to his song, even sounds that do not normally belong to his own species.

the mockingbird and the brown thrasher, however, it does not repeat each element of its song. Scattered through the repertoire are the mewing, catlike cries that give the species its name. The distinctive *mee-ew* also serves as an alarm call.

Known simply as the catbird in older publications, the U.S. species is now properly called the gray catbird to distinguish it from the black catbird (*Melanoptila glabrirostris*) of Mexico. It ranges throughout the northern and eastern states, from southern Canada to the Gulf of Mexico, and winters from the Gulf States to Panama and the West Indies. It migrates across the eastern two-thirds of Texas, where it can be quite common, and remains along the coast in smaller numbers through the winter. The gray catbird nests only along the northern edge of the state and into the northeastern counties.

Plain, dark slaty gray above, and slightly smaller than the mockingbird, the gray catbird has a jaunty black cap and a long black tail that it flips about as it skulks through the dense thickets it prefers. Its undertail coverts are a rich chestnut-red. The genus name *Dumetella* comes from the Latin for "little shrub," or "brambles," in which the catbird stays safely hidden. *Carolinensis* refers to the type locality from which the species was described.

The catbird builds a nest of twigs and lines it with softer grasses and rootlets. Usually placed in a thick bush or tangle of vines, it contains four to six blue-green eggs that are incubated by the female. The eggs hatch in 12 or 13 days, and both parents feed their hatchlings almost exclusively on insects. The young leave the nest after only 10 to 12 days. Adult catbirds consume as much as 50 percent fruits and berries to supplement their insect diet and are partial to mulberries and pokeberries as they move across eastern and central Texas in migration.

GRAY CATBIRD *Dumetella carolinensis*

The catbird takes a back seat only to the mockingbird in its talent for mimicry. It appropriates the phrases of other birds and incorporates them into its rambling mixture of melodious notes, combining them with a strange assortment of whistles, squeaks and cackling sounds. Unlike

A gray catbird picks a ripe mulberry.

Brown Thrasher

Toxostoma rufum

A flurry of leaves catches my eye, and I look out the patio door to see a large rusty brown bird at the center of a miniature whirlwind. Hopping about with quick, jerky movements, it uses wide sweeps of its head to toss the fallen oak leaves in all directions. Suddenly it stops, cocks a bright yellow eye at the ground, and grabs a beetle in its long, slightly downcurved bill. It bashes the unlucky insect against the edge of the patio and then gulps it down, returning quickly to the relentless hunt. Another bird drops from a tree limb to the ground, and there is an immediate chase, twisting and turning through the trees until both disappear over the back fence. Soon the brown thrashers return, however, their differences settled for a time, and both begin pitching leaves out of the flower bed.

Some believe the thrashers got their name from this thrashing, or threshing, of fallen leaves in search of food. Others indicate it is derived from a Middle English word for "thrush." Although the thrashers and thrushes are members of separate families, their plumages and habits are much alike. However, thrashers have much longer bills and tails.

The brown thrasher represents its genus east of the Rocky Mountains and is the common species in the northern and eastern portions of Texas. It is a year-round resident from the Panhandle south to Waco and Houston, although it does not nest on the coastal prairie. In the winter it occurs commonly throughout much of the state, except for the Trans-Pecos and the region south of Corpus Christi. Other thrashers replace the brown thrasher in the latter areas.

The foot-long brown thrasher has rufous upperparts and a heavily streaked whitish breast. Its beady yellow eyes give it a fierce look of defiance and determination. Like many others of the family Mimidae, it is an excellent vocalist. Ehrlich, Dobkin and Wheye note that more than 1,100 song types have been documented, the largest repertoire of all North American birds. The brown thrasher sings from an exposed perch, throwing back its head and giving vent to long series of melodious phrases. It occasionally appropriates sounds from other species, but unlike the mockingbird, it seldom resorts to extensive mimicry. The thrasher usually sings each phrase twice; the mockingbird, three times or more. Reserving its lovely song for the nesting grounds, it challenges intruders with harsh *chack chack* calls through the remainder of the year.

Both sexes incubate the four or five spotted eggs in a nest of twigs, leaves and grasses well hidden in a bush or on the ground. The eggs hatch in 11 to 14 days, and the young depart some 10 to 13 days later. Each pair normally raises two or even three broods, especially in the southern portion of their range. Insects and other invertebrates, occasional small vertebrates, and a variety of fruits and berries make up the brown thrasher's varied diet.

The long-billed thrasher (*Toxostoma longirostre*) replaces the brown thrasher in the lower Rio Grande Valley and northward to Beeville and Corpus Christi. The two species normally overlap only during the winter months, when the latter species moves sparingly southward into the long-bill's territory. Similar in appearance and habits, the long-billed thrasher has darker, less rusty upperparts, grayer cheeks, and blackish breast streaks rather than brown.

A brown thrasher slips quietly onto her twiggy nest in a boxelder thicket.

CURVE-BILLED THRASHER *Toxostoma curvirostre*

The tough, belligerent look of the robin-sized curve-billed thrasher belies its rich, melodic song. Its formidable, strongly curved beak and orange eyes make it appear, as one author noted, somewhat crazed from life in the harsh desert sun. Indeed, this most common and widespread of our western thrashers inhabits an exacting environment in the deserts, canyons and arid brushlands of the Southwest, where it builds its nest of spiny twigs in a clump of cactus or thorny shrub and forages through the prickly underbrush. It stakes its claim to the territory surrounding its favorite cactus or sharp-leaved yucca with distinctive calls of *whit!* and *whit-wheet!* that Peterson describes as "like a human whistle of attention," and flies out quickly to repel intruders. The elaborate song filled with warbles and trills resembles that of the mockingbird, but with less repetition.

The curve-billed thrasher is dull grayish brown above, its pale grayish breast faintly mottled with darker gray spots. Narrow wing-bars and white tips on the outer tail feathers are conspicuous in flight. The curve-bill occurs throughout the year in the western half of Texas, from the southern Panhandle to the lower Rio Grande Valley and eastward to San Antonio, Beeville and Rockport.

Both sexes incubate the three to five blue-green eggs speckled with brown, but only the female sits at night. The eggs hatch in 12 to 15 days, and the young fledge from 11 to 18 days later. When the open nest is exposed to the blazing sun, the female broods for nearly two weeks to shelter her altricial babies from the heat. The adults remain paired on their territory after the breeding season, which runs from March through August in Texas, and consume a varied diet of insects, spiders and other invertebrates, fruits and berries, and the nectar and blooms of desert flowers.

Two other thrasher species occur in West Texas. The sage thrasher (*Oreoscoptes montanus*) winters in the western half of the state and breeds occasionally in the Panhandle. Smaller than the other thrashers, it has a gray back, a heavily streaked breast, and a shorter bill. The crissal thrasher (*Toxostoma dorsale*) inhabits the dry brush and streamside thickets of the Trans-Pecos. It is a large brownish gray bird with a long tail and reddish undertail coverts (the crissum, for which the bird was named). The long, deeply curved bill and unmarked underparts distinguish it from other Texas thrashers.

When Henry described the crissal thrasher in 1858 from a specimen collected in New Mexico, he named it *Toxostoma dorsalis*, later amended to *dorsale*. However, the AOU checklist notes that other evidence illustrates clearly that a mistake was made, and that Henry intended it to be named *T. crissalis*. Current field guides and checklists use both *dorsale* and *crissale*, and a final ruling by the International Commission on Zoological Nomenclature is still pending.

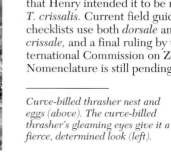

Curve-billed thrasher nest and eggs (above). The curve-billed thrasher's gleaming eyes give it a fierce, determined look (left).

PIPITS (Family Motacillidae)

The pipits and the wagtails compose a worldwide family of some 50 species, but only two, the American and Sprague's pipits, occur regularly in the lower 48 states. Several others range into Alaska from Asia and wander occasionally down the Pacific Coast. The sparrow-sized birds inhabit open fields and grasslands, where they walk and run rather than hop, and they constantly wag their tails up and down as they search for the insects and spiders that make up their diet. Anatomically, the Motacillidae have only nine primary flight feathers instead of the usual ten, and they have slender bills and very long hind claws.

According to Gruson and Choate, "pipit" comes from the French name for the bird and ultimately from the Latin *pipio,* meaning "to peep" or "to chirp." It imitates the calls, which in the case of the American pipit could be interpreted as *jee-eet* or *pi-pit.*

AMERICAN PIPIT

Anthus rubescens

The American pipit still appears in most bird books as the water pipit (*Anthus spinoletta*), a race of a widespread species that also occurs in Eurasia. In 1989, however, the American Ornithologists' Union granted the American race full species status, because both forms were found nesting together in southern Siberia without apparent interbreeding.

Grayish brown and faintly streaked above, this six-inch pipit has buffy underparts streaked with brown. In flight it flashes white outer tail feathers, while on the ground it wags its tail as it walks along. This tail wagging, the slim profile, and the slender, warblerlike beak serve to distinguish the pipit from several sparrows of similar size and color.

The American pipit breeds on the Arctic tundra of Alaska and Canada and on the alpine tundra of the Rocky Mountains. It migrates in flocks throughout Texas and remains through the winter except in the Panhandle. The small brown birds walk about in the open fields and marshes and seldom perch up off the ground. They fly with an up-and-down,

The American pipit is a ground dweller, rarely perching in bushes or trees.

rollercoaster flight and call repeatedly in the air, *pi-pit pi-pit.*

Sprague's pipit (*A. spragueii*) resembles the American pipit but has more streaking on the back. Its legs are pale pinkish rather than black.

More solitary and much harder to find than the American pipit, it migrates across most of Texas and winters mainly south of the Panhandle and east of the Pecos River. It, too, prefers grassy plains and prairies.

Sleek crests and smooth, silky plumage characterize the charming waxwings. The name comes from the unusual red tips of the inner secondary wing feathers that have the texture of sealing wax. Black masks and yellow-tipped tails also mark the North American species. Only three species make up the family Bombycillidae. One is found in Asia and a second, the Bohemian waxwing *(Bombycilla garrulus)*, reaches northern Texas only rarely as a winter visitor. The third, the cedar waxwing *(B. cedrorum)*, appears in flocks throughout Texas during fall migration and remains until late spring before heading northward to its breeding grounds in Canada and the more northern states.

CEDAR WAXWING

Bombycilla cedrorum

If a prize were awarded for the best-mannered, most courteous bird, it would probably go to the cedar waxwing. Highly gregarious, except during the breeding season farther north, waxwings congregate in large flocks that move into Texas in the fall and range across the entire state. They feed voraciously on berries and small fruits but seldom bicker with their fellow diners as many other birds are prone to do. Instead, they keep up what seems to be a pleasant table conversation in their soft, high-pitched trills and whistles. A group of birds might sit side-by-side on a branch, all facing the same direction, and pass a choice morsel down the line until one bird decides to eat it. If the berry reaches the end of the line unclaimed, it is passed back again.

Waxwings obtain some food by hawking insects like the flycatchers or gleaning caterpillars from the trees; however, fruits and berries make up a major portion of their diet. Even tiny nestlings consume them, an unusual trait among birds, for most seed-eating and fruit-eating species still feed high-protein insects to their young. For this reason, waxwings nest late in the season, when there is an ample crop of ripening fruit.

The cedar waxwing is a dapper

Cedar waxwings (opposite and left) are sleek, dapper little birds that come to Texas for the winter, often congregating in large, social flocks.

seven- to eight-inch bird with a slender crest. Somewhat smaller than a cardinal, and with a slimmer shape and silky plumage, it is brown above and lighter yellowish buff below. A black mask above the beak and through the eyes adds to the rakish, debonair look, as does the yellow band on the tip of the tail.

So social are these lovely birds that when I once reported a single cedar waxwing on a Freeport Christmas Bird Count, another birder asserted loudly, "There's no such thing!"

A flock might sweep into your backyard to dine at a pyracantha, yaupon or juniper laden with berries.

There they will sit, whispering to each other, calmly eating until they loll on the branches, so full they can scarcely fly. When they depart, not a berry will remain.

Having arrived in Texas with the first "blue norther," they will stay well into spring to feed on mulberries as they ripen. They are in no hurry to head north until the crops are ready there. Sometimes waxwings gorge on fruit that is overripe and has started to ferment, and then the effect is pure comic relief. The inebriated birds cling to the limbs, trying desperately to maintain their balance and their dignity.

SHRIKES (Family Laniidae)

The family name Laniidae and the genus *Lanius* owe their origins to the Latin word for "butcher," an allusion to the shrikes' habit of hanging their prey from sharp thorns. Indeed, many people across the country still call them "butcher birds."

Widespread in the Old World, the family contains about 70 species, but only two occur regularly in North America. Their gray plumage, with black-and-white wings and tail, is not unlike that of the mockingbird; however, the shrikes have shorter tails and distinctive black masks across their faces.

LOGGERHEAD SHRIKE *Lanius ludovicianus*

A lizard hangs from a cactus spine, slowly drying in the desert sun. Nearby, a yucca bears several large beetles and grasshoppers, each impaled on the tip of a leaf. On a roadside fence, the torn and headless body of a sparrow dangles from the barbed wire, while a black-masked assassin sits watchfully beside it. The surrealistic scene marks the feeding territory of the "butcher bird," a Texas loggerhead shrike.

Although taxonomically a songbird, the shrike has the inclinations of a hawk. Its diet consists of insects, reptiles, amphibians, and small birds and mammals, which it kills with a razor-sharp, viciously hooked bill. Diving on a sparrow or mouse, it batters its prey into submission with blows from its beak and then severs the vertebrae with a bite to the neck. Lacking the talons of the larger raptors, the shrike carries its prey laboriously in its beak to a convenient thorny branch or barbed-wire fence and hangs it there. It may sit down to dine immediately if hungry, or it may not return for several days. According to Ehrlich, Dobkin and Wheye, "Shrikes show an amazing memory for the placement of their victims: In Texas, shrikes were reported returning to mummified frogs they had stored eight months before." Superior eyesight, too, aids in the hunt,

A loggerhead shrike has stored a ground skink for future use.

and experiments have shown that shrikes can spot a moving insect at 70 yards.

Gray above and white below, the nine-inch loggerhead shrike has black wings with white patches and a white-tipped black tail. It presents a big-headed, bull-necked appearance as it perches, and it seldom descends to the ground except after prey. Launching into flight from a lookout point, it

drops low and flies with rapidly beating wings, then rises to its new perch. The black mask and short, bulky profile readily distinguish it from the lanky, longer-tailed mockingbird. Its song is a strange medley of musical tones and harsh, squeaky notes, alternating with raspy *shack shack* calls. "Shrike" is related through Old English forms to "shriek."

The loggerhead shrike winters throughout Texas, from the humid coastal plain to the arid Trans-Pecos, and remains to breed in the eastern, northern and western portions of the state. According to Oberholser and Peterson, it is much less common as a nesting bird on the southern Edwards Plateau and in the brush country south of Beeville and the central coast. The shrike prefers open country with scattered trees or the West Texas desert scrub and builds its twiggy nest in a bush or tree. The female incubates her four to six spotted eggs while the male feeds her, often from his cache of prey. That cache may also be used for feeding young when food is scarce. Each of the pair establishes its own feeding territory after the breeding season.

The loggerhead shrike ranges from southern Canada to Mexico, but it has declined dramatically in the Northeast and in the Midwest. It has occupied a place on the Audubon Society's Blue List throughout the 1970s and 1980s as deserving special concern. Both habitat loss and pesticides have been implicated in the decline. One

Canadian study determined that a pair requires at least 25 acres for successful nesting, and human interference is not tolerated.

The northern shrike (*Lanius excubitor*) visits North Texas only rarely in the winter and is never to be expected. Slightly larger than the loggerhead shrike, and with a lightly barred breast, it also has a longer bill with a more distinct hook at the tip.

The mask is narrower and does not extend above the eyes. Although a few authors have suggested the two are conspecific, separated only by the northern shrike's more remote breeding range in Alaska and northern Canada, that view is not widely held. The AOU considers the two North American shrikes and a similar Asian species to be members of a larger "superspecies."

Lacking strong talons to grasp its prey, a loggerhead shrike impales a mouse and sits beside it to feed.

STARLINGS (Family Sturnidae)

The family Sturnidae contains more than 100 species of starlings and mynas that inhabit Africa and Eurasia. None is native to the Americas. Unfortunately, however, the European starling was introduced in the United States a century ago and rapidly spread across the continent, much to the detriment of native species. It is now one of our most abundant birds. Although frequently lumped with the collective "blackbirds," the starling is not closely related to our native blackbirds and grackles.

Many of the African starlings are brilliantly colored, while the Asian mynas have become popular cage birds because of their ability to mimic human speech. One, the crested myna (*Acridotheres cristatellus*), was introduced in Vancouver, British Columbia, in the 1890s and has become established in that region.

EUROPEAN STARLING   *Sturnus vulgaris*

In Shakespeare's *Henry IV*, young Henry Percy, known as Hotspur, says: "Nay, I'll have a starling shall be taught to speak / Nothing but 'Mortimer,' and give it him." Because of these lines, *Sturnus vulgaris* invaded America.

The man responsible was Eugene Schieffelin, an eccentric figure in New York society. As part of a scheme to introduce all of the birds mentioned by Shakespeare, he released 60 starlings in Central Park in March 1890. Forty more were liberated the following year. They might as well have flown from Pandora's box. Within a few weeks of the initial release, a pair of starlings was nesting under the eaves of the American Museum of Natural History.

They appeared in Connecticut and New Jersey in 1904 and crossed the Allegheny Mountains in 1916. By 1925 they reached Illinois; in 1942, California. Their ranks swelling by several broods every year, the prolific starlings had covered the continent and penetrated Alaska by 1952. From Schieffelin's ill-advised tribute to William Shakespeare has come an estimated population of 200 million starlings in a single century.

European starling.

According to Oberholser, the first European starling recorded in Texas was a bird found dead at Cove in Chambers County in 1925. Others appeared in Beaumont the following year. Winter flocks began sweeping across the state, with a great surge in the winter of 1933-34. By 1936 starlings had reached Port Isabel at the southern tip of Texas; in 1939 they invaded El Paso. Another enormous starling wave appeared during the winter of 1952-53, and Oberholser wrote that "during this season, huge coalesced flocks of *S. vulgaris* hung over the city of San Antonio like a thick pall of black oil smoke." Winter flocks now envelop all of Texas, and starlings breed in almost all regions of the state.

Shorter tailed than the true blackbirds, and with a more triangular, delta-winged shape in flight, the European starling varies a great deal in seasonal attire. The black breeding plumage of spring and summer is glossed with green and purple iridescence, and the bill is a bright, gleaming yellow. With the fall molt, however, the bill turns dark, and the new body feathers are tipped with spots of white and buff. Those light feather tips wear away as winter progresses, leaving the simple basic-black dress.

The European starling possesses jaw muscles that work in the opposite manner from those of most birds. Instead of clamping the bill shut, they spring it open, enabling starlings to pry apart plant stems and thick turf to expose hidden prey. As the bill opens, the eyes move forward in the head, giving the bird focused binocular vision capable of spotting both moving and dormant insects. According to William Beecher, who discovered this unique adaptation, it opens new avenues of foraging behavior and may be a key to the high winter survival rate of starlings.

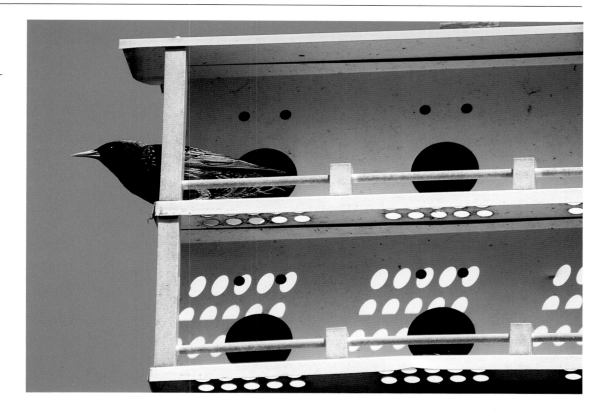

An unwelcome European starling sets up housekeeping in a home intended for purple martins.

The aggressive starling competes for nest space with bluebirds, tree swallows, purple martins and other cavity-nesting birds, one of the major problems with its successful invasion. It has been a major cause of the decline of bluebird species. Laying claim to a natural cavity, an old woodpecker hole, or a birdhouse intended for a more welcome species, the starling moves right in, filling its new home with a slovenly mass of grasses, twigs and straw. It may even lurk around while a flicker or red-headed woodpecker patiently chisels out its residence and then evict the builder.

The female incubates her four to six speckled, pale blue eggs with only a little help from her mate, and the voracious young hatch in 12 to 14 days. Fed by both parents, the grayish brown juveniles leave the nest 18 to 21 days later. Starlings have some redeeming value, for they consume large quantities of insects harmful to food crops. Fruits and seeds make up the remainder of their diet.

The European starling's kinship with the mynas is evidenced by its amazing skill at mimicry. While the inherent song of the species consists of an assemblage of squeaks, rattles, wheezes and whistles, it can also produce mechanical sounds and imitate other birds and human voices. One starling mentioned in an *American Scientist* article repeated verbatim, a day after hearing it, "Does Hammacher Schlemmer have a toll-free number?" Another routinely cried "DEE-fence!" whenever the television was tuned to sporting events, and a bird living with a Japanese family not only learned Japanese phrases but spoke English with that accent.

Starlings appear to like human music, report Meredith West and Andrew King, a husband-and-wife research team at Indiana University, but they "tend to sing off-key and fracture the phrasing at unexpected points." One Indiana starling persisted in whistling the first line of "Dixie," but interjected notes from "The Star-Spangled Banner."

Mozart's "The Musical Joke" has long confounded musicologists, but some now suspect that the piece's fractured structure may have been a simple transcription of his pet starling's musical flights. Another famous theme from one of his piano concertos bears remarkable resemblance to a tune the starling already knew when purchased by the famed composer. So fond was Mozart of his pet that when it died, he buried it at a funeral attended by mourners who sang hymns and listened to a graveside poem composed in the starling's honor.

VIREOS (Family Vireonidae)

The name vireo comes from the Latin *virere*, "to be green." Indeed, most of these small songbirds and their tropical relatives, the greenlets, wear shades of olive-green, gray and yellow. They resemble warblers in size, ranging from about four to six inches in length, but they have chunkier profiles and heavier bills with slightly hooked tips. Less active than warblers, which flit quickly through the tree-tops, vireos feed by methodically gleaning insects from the undersides of the leaves. They sing incessantly through the day, even at noon when most other birds lapse into quiet lethargy. Their songs are typically composed of repeated short, slightly harsh phrases with intervening pauses.

About 40 species of the Vireonidae range through the Americas from Canada to Argentina. The Texas checklist contains 13 species, all in the genus *Vireo*, but three of those are listed as "accidental" and seldom cross our borders. Some, like the white-eyed and red-eyed vireos, occur widely across eastern Texas, while such species as Hutton's vireo and the gray vireo are confined to small areas of the Trans-Pecos. One group of vireo species has prominent light wing-bars and bright eye-rings linked by stripes through the lores to form "spectacles." The others lack the wing-bars and have pronounced eyebrow stripes.

Red-eyed vireo.

RED-EYED VIREO   *Vireo olivaceus*

Country people have long called the red-eyed vireo "preacher." Arriving from its winter home in the Amazon Basin of South America, it sets up housekeeping in the streamside woodlands of eastern Texas and proclaims ownership with persistent song from dawn until dark. The short phrases, separated by deliberate pauses, have a robinlike quality. One common interpretation of the preacher's "sermon," according to Oberholser, is: *You see it—you know it—do you hear me?—do you believe it?* He may sing as many as 40 different phrases in a minute, and one diligent field observer reported 22,000 individual songs a day. "To some the song seems monotonous, to others cheerful," Oklahoma ornithologist and artist George Miksch Sutton once wrote. "Everyone agrees the sermon is long-winded."

Olive-green above and whitish below, the red-eyed vireo lacks the wing-bars of many of its relatives. It has a gray crown and prominent white eyebrows bordered above and below with black. The gleaming ruby eyes are visible only in good light and at close range.

The red-eyed vireo breeds from Canada to the Gulf States and inhabits the eastern half of Texas, south to the upper coast and San Antonio. In migration, however, it moves across most of the state east of the Pecos.

It constructs a finely woven, basketlike nest of grasses, strips of bark, and the silk of spider webs and moth cocoons. Usually hung from a forked twig, the nest holds three or four white eggs dotted with brown or black. Incubation by the female requires 11 to 14 days, and the young fledge about 12 days later. As immatures, they have brown eyes and a pale yellow wash on the sides. Small fruits supplement the red-eyed vireo's insect diet.

Once one of the most abundant birds in the eastern forests, the red-eye has declined in the last few decades. The proliferation of the brown-headed cowbird has certainly contributed to that decline, for the vireo is one of the primary hosts of that notorious brood parasite. Pesticides have also played a major role, as has the fragmentation of the forest in both its summer and winter homes. The red-eyed vireo is one of the neotropical migrants whose fate depends on habitat preservation at both ends of its lengthy migrations.

The yellow-green vireo (*Vireo flavoviridis*) occurs as a rare visitor along the Rio Grande in deep South Texas. Yellower above than the red-eyed vireo, it is a bright yellow on the sides and undertail coverts, and its head stripes are less pronounced. The yellow-green vireo shares a love-hate relationship with taxonomists. Once considered a valid species, it was later "lumped" with the red-eyed vireo. More recently, the AOU again granted full species status to this tropical bird.

The warbling vireo (*V. gilvus*) shares much of the red-eyed vireo's eastern range and occurs in the West as well. Paler and more uniformly gray above, it lacks the black borders on the white eyebrow stripes. A migrant throughout Texas, the warbling vireo breeds in scattered locations in the northern and eastern counties, in the northern Panhandle, and in the mountains of the Trans-Pecos.

WHITE-EYED VIREO   *Vireo griseus*

Grayish olive above and whitish below, this five-inch vireo sports bright yellow spectacles around its distinctive white eyes. It also has two white wing-bars and a pale yellow wash along its sides. A resident of dense woodlands and streamside thickets, the white-eyed vireo makes its presence known with a loud, scolding song. Peterson describes the syncopated rhythm as *chick-a-perweeoo-chick,* but Houston naturalist Carl Aiken asserts its message is *Come to the woods with me!* It also whistles and mews and employs a host of vocal fragments that resemble the call notes of other birds.

The white-eyed vireo seems virtually fearless, especially near its nest, and bounces out to confront an intruder at close range, scolding constantly. It hangs its carefully woven nest from a forked twig, as most vireos do, and usually raises two broods a year in Texas. The four white eggs are dotted with black or brown. Incubated by both parents,

they hatch in 12 to 15 days. Like the red-eyed vireo, the white-eye may be heavily parasitized by the brown-headed cowbird, and the parents end up feeding babies larger than themselves. Juvenile vireos have duller plumage than the adults, and their eyes remain dark until the following spring.

These charming, noisy little vireos range from Nebraska to New England and south to the Gulf States and Mexico. In Texas they breed in the eastern portions of the state, westward to Fort Worth, Austin, San Antonio and Del Rio. Migrating across the eastern two-thirds of Texas, they remain to winter in the South.

Bell's vireo (*Vireo bellii*) is grayer than the white-eyed vireo and has dark eyes and indistinct white spectacles. Its characteristic song, many birders note, asks a question and then

White-eyed vireo.

answers it. Peterson's oft-quoted rendition is *cheedle cheedle chee?—cheedle cheedle chew!* Bell's vireo nests in most of western and central Texas and migrates throughout much of the state, although it is very rare along the upper coast. John Graham

Bell was a taxidermist and collector for a number of better-known naturalists in the mid–19th century. Bell accompanied Audubon on the artist's Missouri River expedition in 1843 and collected the vireo that Audubon named for him.

BLACK-CAPPED VIREO
Vireo atricapillus

In October 1987 the U.S. Fish and Wildlife Service placed the black-capped vireo on its endangered species list. This smallest and most distinctively marked of all North American vireos faces possible extinction because of severe habitat loss and nest parasitism by the brown-headed cowbird. Studies have documented such parasitism in up to 90 percent of the vireo nests in some areas of Texas, and those birds succeed in raising fewer than one chick for every two adult pairs.

The female cowbird frequently removes the hosts' eggs before depositing her own in untended nests. Even when both are incubated by the unwitting "foster parents," the odds are stacked heavily in favor of the young cowbirds. They hatch in 10 to 12 days, while the baby vireos require 14 to 17 days. If the adults persist until their own eggs hatch, the nearly helpless vireo chicks are poorly matched in competition with the older and larger interlopers for nest space and food.

An extensive cowbird-eradication program may be required to save the black-capped vireo and the golden-cheeked warbler, another endangered songbird with which the vireo shares much of its range in the Texas Hill Country. "There doesn't seem to be any other way," says Bob Short of the Fish and Wildlife Service. "The cowbird is such a problem for reproduction that the vireo just wouldn't have a chance." The Service also cites "habitat loss due to urbanization, range management, overbrowsing by animals, and the changing of the succession of the vegetation of the vireo's habitat into a type less preferred by the bird" as critical factors in its decline.

A male black-capped vireo (left) takes its turn in the nest. Prominent white spectacles adorn the solitary vireo (opposite).

The breeding range of the black-capped vireo formerly extended from central Kansas through Oklahoma and Texas into Mexico. It winters in the Pacific foothills and flatlands of western Mexico, from southern Sonora to Guerrero. Throughout its range, the vireo utilizes scrub-oak habitats where thickets of low trees combine with heavy ground cover. It prefers rocky canyons and low ridges with bright sunlight, locations that one ornithologist describes as "the hottest places imaginable." There the male sings throughout the season, even during the midday heat. The song is somewhat harsh and hurried, and remarkably varied, with a "restless, almost angry quality." That song, however, has been stilled in portions of the vireo's former range. The black-capped vireo was last reported in Kansas in 1953, and recent census work in Oklahoma showed there may be no more than 30 to 50 breeding pairs in that state.

Once locally common in the oak-juniper thickets of Central and West Texas, with the major population on the Edwards Plateau, the vireo has also vanished from much of that range. The largest known concentration occurs near Austin, where increasing real-estate development threatens to crowd out the tiny birds. The black-cap arrives in March and leaves by September, hanging its compact, cuplike nest of plant fibers and bark strips in a scrub oak or other dense tree or bush and laying from three to five white eggs. The young consume insects and spiders, with some berries supplementing the diet of the older birds.

Scarcely larger than a kinglet, the black-capped vireo flits about more quickly than the other, more lethargic, members of its genus. It gleans caterpillars and beetles from the foliage, often hanging head downward in a characteristic pose before fluttering down to a lower branch. Olive above and white below, with yellowish flanks and wing-bars, the male is strikingly marked with a black cap and conspicuous white spectacles. The drabber female has a slate-gray head and whitish wing-bars.

SOLITARY VIREO *Vireo solitarius*

Prominent white "spectacles" adorn the blue-gray head of the solitary vireo, while the wings bear two light bars. In the eastern race, which migrates across much of Texas and remains through the winter in the southern and coastal regions of the state, the head color contrasts strongly with a greenish back. White underparts are marked with greenish yellow on the sides and flanks. A Rocky Mountain race also breeds in the Guadalupe, Davis and Chisos mountains of Trans-Pecos Texas. Called the "plumbeous form," it is more uniformly lead gray above, without the contrast between head and back. It has, at most, only a tinge of yellow on the sides.

Many authorities consider this latter western form to be a distinct species, but that stand has not yet been adopted by the AOU. Current field guides describe it as *Vireo solitarius plumbeus*. Collectively, the forms range across Canada and southward at higher elevations through the U.S. to El Salvador.

The solitary vireo prefers mixed woodlands, where it forages slowly and deliberately through the treetops. Its diet consists almost entirely of insects during the warmer months, although berries and other fleshy fruits are added in midwinter. Something of a loner, as its name implies, this five- to six-inch vireo travels with mixed flocks of other small birds less frequently than do its relatives. It sings a rich, variable song of separated phrases sometimes described as *chu-wee cheerio*. More musical than the vocalizations of many vireos, the song is most often heard in Texas during April and May; however, nesting birds in the West Texas mountains sing through the summer.

The yellow-throated vireo (*Vireo flavifrons*) migrates across the eastern two-thirds of the state and remains to breed locally in the woodlands of East Texas. Olive-green above, with two white wing-bars, it has a bright yellow breast, throat and spectacles. It, too, suffers from cowbird predation and habitat loss.

Warblers, Sparrows and Their Allies (Family Emberizidae)

The emberizids form a huge and complex family that contains such diverse subfamilies as the warblers; tanagers; grosbeaks and buntings; sparrows; and blackbirds and orioles. This combination of several groups formerly considered to be separate families was published in the sixth edition of the American Ornithologists' Union *Check-list of North American Birds* in 1983. While such a consolidation may seem at first absurd, the varied groups do appear to be closely related. All of the emberizids are linked by genetic similarities that are not always reflected in such outward manifestations as size, shape and color.

The AOU decision constitutes the "official" nomenclature and taxonomy used by most groups and individual authors who produce checklists and books on the birds of North America. Not all agree with the reorganization, however. The newly created family of the Emberizidae has been called an "already bulging conglomerate" and a "catch-all." While it may more closely approach the genetic "truth," it constitutes an unwieldy classification for the amateur birder, who prefers to list birds in convenient groupings of reasonable size. For that reason, the emberizids are here divided further into their respective subfamilies.

At the same time, it is important to remember that some of the AOU's divisions are arbitrary, and some species or groups of species bridge the lines of distinction in classical taxonomy. "It is not nature's way to conform to a rigid system which places blocks of species in neatly circumscribed compartments," writes Canadian ornithologist Terence Shortt in *Wild Birds of the Americas,* "and no linear system that can possibly be devised will ever adequately demonstrate the complexities of avian interrelationships."

WARBLERS (Emberizidae: Subfamily Parulinae)

A male northern parula shows the slender bill typical of most warblers.

Leonardo da Vinci wrote in *Madrid Codex I,* " . . . come men, to see the wonders which may be discovered in Nature . . . ." The Florentine master could not have seen the New World warblers when he penned those lines, but he would certainly have ranked them high on the list of Nature's wonders. Few birds are more delightfully active and colorful than these "butterflies of the bird world." As Charles Maynard wrote nearly a century ago, "Throughout the world we find no finer group of birds, thus they may well be considered the pride of the American ornithologist."

Actually, these feathered jewels are more properly called "wood warblers," but most U.S. birders quickly shorten it to "warblers" as a matter of convenience. Exclusively residents of the New World, the wood warblers occur throughout North, Central and South America and the West Indies. Early American naturalists apparently mistook these tiny birds for the familiar Old World warblers, a family that includes our kinglets and gnatcatchers. Later it became clear that the two families were not closely related, but the name was firmly entrenched.

About 110 species of wood warblers inhabit the Americas from Alaska to Argentina. Some are abundant and widespread; others are extremely rare. The endangered Kirtland's warbler *(Dendroica kirtlandii)* nests only in the jack-pine stands of Michigan, while the equally endangered golden-cheeked warbler *(D. chrysoparia)* depends on Ashe junipers in central Texas. One Texas prize, the Colima warbler *(Vermivora crissalis),* nests in the U.S. only in the higher elevations of Big Bend's Chisos Mountains. Because of their reliance on insects to fuel their active little bodies, northern species fly thousands of miles to winter in tropical America. The blackpoll warbler *(D. striata),* for example, migrates from the northernmost forests of Alaska and Canada to central South America, one of the longest journeys of any songbird.

A male yellow warbler returns to its nest with food.

Although several species of warblers may occupy the same woodland habitat, they partition the food resources by feeding in separate niches. Some hawk insects from the outer branches of the tree, while others feed primarily through the interior of the crown. Still others forage through the understory or among fallen leaves upon the ground.

More than 50 warbler species occur in North America, and most are seen at least occasionally in Texas. Some range into the Trans-Pecos from the Rocky Mountains or the Desert Southwest, while others are typically eastern birds that migrate along the coast or nest in the forests of deep East Texas. A few species enter our state from Mexico as rare strays along the Rio Grande. Some do not have the word "warbler" in their names. The ovenbird, waterthrushes, redstarts, yellowthroats and chat are all classified as wood warblers, although they differ slightly in appearance and habits.

It is during spring migration along the Texas coast that the warblers create the greatest excitement among birders. Flying in loose flocks across the Gulf of Mexico, they stream across our shores on the way to their northern breeding grounds. If they have flown through azure skies and with following winds, they may pass the coast unseen, scattering far inland before they stop to rest and feed. If, however, they encounter chilling rains or strong head winds, they reach the shore exhausted and drop from the sky by the thousands in what birders term a "fallout." They seek shelter in the limited woodlands and mottes near the Gulf, filling every tree with rainbow hues. Places like High Island, Galveston and Rockport have become famous as "migrant traps," and birders frequently see 25 to 30 species of warblers in a single day.

This spring migration spans a period of several weeks. In general, those species that nest in the southern states arrive first, assured of finding warm weather and abundant food, while those that will continue on to the northern states and Canada delay their migration until later. The former arrive on the Texas coast in late March and early April, but the latter may not come until late April or May. Most birders hope to be on the Texas coast during the last two weeks of April, where a sudden rain storm or advancing "norther" can produce a deluge of birds as well. "The fields, bushes, and trees may be flooded with tanagers, orioles, buntings, kingbirds, thrushes, flycatchers, vireos, and warblers, warblers, warblers," wrote the late James Lane in *A Birder's Guide to the Texas Coast.* "On these spectacular occasions, it is possible to see more birds in an hour than in a couple of years of normal birding."

Identification of spring warblers poses few problems even for beginning birders, for most are distinctively marked in courtship plumage. Autumn, however, brings a confusing array of dingy olive-yellow species that all look much alike, their ranks swelled even more by nondescript young birds in immature plumages. They can be "so difficult to identify," noted Jim Lane, "that with a little imagination you can make them into anything you need for your list." Roger Tory Peterson wrote in *A Field Guide to the Birds of Texas*, "Master the spring warblers first. If at the end of ten years you can say you really know the fall warblers you are doing very well."

The consideration of all Texas warblers in all of their plumages goes far beyond the scope of this book. Several of the field guides illustrate the variations with sex, age and season and are essential companions in the field.

The drab orange-crowned warbler lacks obvious field marks.

ORANGE-CROWNED WARBLER   *Vermivora celata*

The hyperactive little orange-crowned warbler forages restlessly through the brushy woodlands and thickets, darting out with quick, jerky movements to pick insects from the foliage or snatch them in midflight. The dingiest of all our warblers, it lacks the wing-bars and facial pattern that characterize many of the others. Even the orange crown is concealed by overlapping greenish feather tips, a trait noted in the scientific name *celata,* which is Latin for "hidden" or "concealed." The genus, *Vermivora,* means "worm-eating" in Latin.

Olive-green above and paler yellowish green below, the orange-crowned warbler has faint, blurred streaks along its sides. Its thin, sharply pointed bill distinguishes it from the vireos; the faint streaking and yellow under-tail coverts, from the Tennessee warbler.

The orange-crowned warbler breeds from Alaska and Canada southward throughout the western states. While most of the warblers move south into tropical America, the orange-crowned remains in the southern states and Mexico. It migrates throughout Texas and is a common winter resident in the southern half of the state. It usually feeds low in the trees and brush, supplementing its insect diet with fruits and the nectar of flowers. This five-inch warbler sometimes visits hummingbird feeders and eats tree sap from holes drilled by sapsuckers.

The orange-crown is a welcome addition to Texas woodlands and yards on chill wintry days. Its constant activity and sharp *chip* notes make it easier to find than its small size and drab plumage would suggest, and it is one of the few warblers that remain through the season. In the spring most will depart for their northern breeding grounds, but some remain to nest at high elevations in the Guadalupe Mountains.

Northern Parula

Parula americana

The tiny northern parula measures only four and one-half inches long and weighs but a quarter of an ounce. Four of the charming birds could be mailed along their cross-country migration route with a single first-class postage stamp. Gray-blue above, the parula has a bright yellow throat and breast and a white belly. Two prominent white wing-bars, a broken white eye-ring, and a green patch on the upper back provide additional distinctive field marks. The male sports a rusty band across his chest, a mark that is indistinct or lacking on the female.

Ranging across eastern North America from Canada to the Gulf States, the northern parula nests in the woodlands and groves of East Texas, occurring westward to Fort Worth, Austin and Kerrville and south along the upper coast. It arrives in March from its wintering grounds in Mexico and Central America and sings from the treetops before the mainstream warbler migration has begun. Its song is a rising trill that can be easily distinguished over the spring medleys of other birds. Peterson describes it as a "buzzy trill or rattle that climbs the scale and snaps over at the top, *zeeeeeeeee-up*."

The parula nests where Spanish moss is abundant, weaving its purse-like cup into a hanging clump of that common southeastern bromeliad. In the North, beyond the range of Spanish moss, it utilizes *Usnea* lichens, sometimes known as "old-man's beard." The female apparently incubates her four or five spotted eggs alone, and they hatch in 12 to 14 days, but the breeding biology is not fully known.

The name parula is the Latin diminutive of *parus*, hence a "little titmouse." The agile northern parula does indeed flit actively about, sometimes clinging upside-down like a chickadee or titmouse to search for the insects on which it feeds exclusively.

The tropical parula *(Parula pitiayumi)* is a rare birding prize that strays occasionally into Texas along the Rio Grande. Formerly called the olive-backed warbler, it lacks the white eye-ring and distinct breast-band of its northern counterpart, and the male has a black mask across his face.

A northern parula gathers cattail fluff to line its nest.

YELLOW WARBLER   *Dendroica petechia*

The yellow warbler is an active, all-yellow bird that has been described as a "capricious sunbeam." It seems particularly at home in streamside willow and alder thickets but also spreads its sunshine through open woodlands, gardens and orchards across the continent. It is the most widely distributed of all the warblers, ranging from northern Alaska and Canada to the West Indies and central Peru. The good news is that the yellow warbler remains a common migrant throughout virtually all of Texas; the bad news is that it has become rare as a nesting resident. Oberholser notes that "The Yellow Warbler seems to be almost out of the breeding business in the state."

Never a common nesting bird around the Gulf of Mexico, the yellow warbler recently occupied a place on the Blue List as declining over significant portions of its range. Pesticides, pollution, droughts, and the destruction of streamside vegetation have all been blamed for the decline, and the eruption of the brown-headed cowbird has certainly played an important role. One of the most frequent of all cowbird hosts, the five-inch warbler is dwarfed by the young cowbirds it attempts to raise. A study in Michigan found that one female cowbird apparently laid 18 eggs in a single season, all of them in yellow-warbler nests.

When parasitized early in its nesting cycle, however, the yellow warbler has developed a defensive strategy. It simply adds a new bottom to its nest, covering the alien egg so that it is not incubated. Three- or four-layer nests are not uncommon, each layer containing a rejected cowbird egg, and the reputed champion was a nest six stories high.

The yellow warbler is yellow both above and below, the only warbler so uniformly colored. Yellow feather edgings on the greenish yellow wings and yellow spots in the tail also provide distinctive field marks. Prominent reddish streaks mark the breast of the adult male, resulting in the scientific name *petechia,* from the Latin term for a red rash on the skin. *Dendroica,* a large genus containing many of our warblers, means "tree-dweller" in Greek.

Several tropical races found in Mexico, including the "golden warbler" and the "mangrove warbler," have varying amounts of red on the head as well. Some authorities consider them valid species, but the AOU checklist treats them all as forms of the yellow warbler.

Foraging through the thickets or proclaiming its territory from a tree-top perch, this charming warbler serenades listeners with its rapid, clear song. Some books describe it as *tsee-tsee-tsee-ti-ti-wee,* while a more anthropomorphic version is *sweet sweet sweet, I'm so sweet.* Whatever the translation, the "capricious sunbeam" is a welcome visitor during its seasonal wanderings through Texas.

Female yellow warbler.

YELLOW-RUMPED WARBLER

Dendroica coronata

The yellow-rumped warbler comprises two forms that were previously considered separate species, the "myrtle warbler" of the eastern states and "Audubon's warbler" of the West. Although the two have distinctive plumages and can be distinguished in the field, they interbreed where their nesting ranges overlap in western Canada. This promiscuity cost them their individual status in the eyes of ornithologists.

Adult males in spring plumage are blue-gray above and white below, with a broad black band crossing the breast and trailing in black streaks down the sides. Bright butter-yellow patches adorn the sides, crown and rump. The small crown patch accounts for the scientific name, *coronata,* while the yellow rump gives rise to the common name of the newly combined forms. The "myrtle warbler" has a white throat in all plumages, however, while "Audubon's warbler" has a yellow throat.

Females, immature birds, and males in fall and winter plumage are dingy grayish brown above and lightly streaked below. All display the yellow rump and side patches that make the yellow-rumped warbler recognizable at any season of the year. The winter plumage is the one most often seen in Texas, for this common warbler is one of the last to leave its northern breeding grounds in autumn and one of the first to return in spring. Most leave Texas before attaining their full breeding plumage.

The "myrtle warbler" migrates across the state, although it is less common in the Trans-Pecos, and remains in most regions throughout the winter, when most other warblers continue to the tropics. One of the most gregarious of warblers, it bands together in small flocks to forage through open woodlands, thickets and suburban yards. The little troops swirl through the treetops, feeding on caterpillars and other insects, and then sweep off again, often in company with chickadees, titmice, kinglets and other winter residents.

The "myrtle warbler" breeds from Alaska to the northeastern edge of the United States and is the most abundant warbler in Canada. It winters from southern New England southward to Panama, remaining farther north in the U.S. than any of its warbler relatives. This hardiness arises from its opportunistic feeding habits. Although usually an insectivore, the "myrtle warbler" survives for long periods on berries and seeds and has a particular fondness for the berries of wax myrtle, from which it took its name. In East Texas it also scrapes the wax from seeds of the alien Chinese tallow trees.

Ehrlich, Dobkin and Wheye note

in *The Birder's Handbook* that waxes are "a chemical grab-bag of waterproof organic materials" that few animals can digest. Yellow-rumped warblers, however, have evolved the appropriate enzymes to digest wax and can thus gain energy from berries other birds cannot utilize. "This ability," suggest the authors, "is probably why Yellow-rumped Warblers can overwinter farther north than most wood warblers."

"Audubon's warbler" breeds through western Canada and the U.S. to Mexico. Nests have been found in the Guadalupe Mountains. It migrates and winters through the western half of Texas, with an occasional individual wandering eastward even to the coast, where it can be separated from the abundant "myrtle warblers" by its yellow throat.

One of the first birds I banded after receiving my state and federal permits was a yellow-rumped—nee myrtle—warbler. Caught in a mistnet on February 27, 1974, it was released again with aluminum band #1330-58507 clamped securely around its left leg. Three years later, on February 14, 1977, that same bird reappeared. It had apparently made three round trips of at least 2500 miles each, only to return to the very same tree in my backyard in Texas.

A "myrtle warbler" in winter plumage flashes its trademark yellow rump. This and "Audubon's warbler" are now known collectively as the yellow-rumped warbler.

Black-throated gray warbler.

BLACK-THROATED GRAY WARBLER   *Dendroica nigrescens*

When Texas birders talk excitedly about the warbler migration, they usually refer to the movement of eastern species along the coast. Some warblers maintain an exclusively western breeding range, however, and occur as migrants in the Trans-Pecos and other portions of West Texas. One of these is the black-throated gray warbler, a five-inch black-and-white bird that breeds in the woodlands and on the dry, brushy slopes from southwestern Canada to Arizona and New Mexico and spends the winter across the border in Mexico. It moves through the western half of Texas from September through November and again on the return trip in March and April. Nesting has also been confirmed in the Guadalupe Mountains, but the extent of the black-throated gray warbler's breeding range in Texas requires further study.

Unlike some warbler species that molt into an obscure, drab plumage after the nesting season, the black-throated gray maintains the same pattern through the year. Gray above and white below, the male has a black crown, cheek and throat. A tiny patch of yellow ornaments the lores (the area between the eyes and bill). The female is slightly dingier, with some dark streaking on her white throat. The black-throated gray warbler might be confused with the black-and-white warbler, but the latter species has a white stripe down the center of the crown.

Although primarily a western bird, the black-throated gray warbler wanders occasionally to the Gulf Coast and even turns up in the eastern states. Ever alert for such rare vagrants, birders are fond of noting that "birds have wings, and they don't read the books."

GOLDEN-CHEEKED WARBLER
Dendroica chrysoparia

Of the hundreds of bird species that occur in Texas, only one breeds entirely within the boundaries of our state. Every golden-cheeked warbler in the world fledged from a nest in central Texas, one of the most restricted nesting ranges of any North American bird. In the mid-1970s, an estimated 7,500 pairs of warblers inhabited the Edwards Plateau and adjacent counties to the north. Now there may be no more than 1,500 pairs, and this native Texan faces serious problems. On May 4, 1990, the U.S. Fish and Wildlife Service added the golden-cheeked warbler to its endangered species list on an emergency basis because of habitat loss. That temporary classification was made permanent under the Endangered Species Act and published in the *Federal Register* on December 27, 1990.

The male golden-cheeked warbler, as both the common and scientific names imply, has a bright yellow face framed by a black crown, bib and back. A prominent black line extends through the eye. The underparts are white with black streaks along the sides. Females and immature males are duller and olive-green above, with dark streaking on their backs. They resemble the widespread black-throated green warbler *(Dendroica virens)*, but the latter species is uncommon on the Edwards Plateau and has a greenish cheek patch on the yellow face rather than a black eye-line.

The tiny golden-cheeks begin arriving in central Texas in early March from their wintering grounds in Central America, flying across the Sierra Madre Oriental in Mexico. Males arrive first, to be followed in a few days by the females. The males' buzzy courtship songs, described by Edgar Kincaid as *bzzzz layzee dayzee,* echo through the Hill Country, and the mated females soon select their nesting sites and begin to build.

As Warren Pulich notes in his book *The Golden-cheeked Warbler*, somewhere along its evolutionary path the golden-cheek acquired the compulsive need to construct her nest of strips of bark from mature Ashe juniper trees. She pulls the long strips from the tree and weaves them into a little cup, binding them with spider webs. She then lines the nest with grasses, feathers and fur, providing a soft bed for her four speckled eggs. Neither the bark from young trees nor that from any other species of juniper, locally called "cedar," seems to be acceptable, and the birds are thus confined to habitats in which Ashe juniper predominates. It represents an amazing dependence on a single environmental niche.

Stands of Ashe juniper alone, however, do not constitute prime warbler habitat. Because the birds are totally insectivorous, they depend on a diversity of trees, shrubs, grasses and wildflowers to provide the numerous caterpillars and other insects they require for themselves and for their young. It is only in the Texas Hill Country that Ashe juniper grows with several species of oaks, redbud, bumelia, cedar elm, pecan, river walnut and other such trees that support the requisite insect population. Nesting golden-cheeks have been observed in Pedernales Falls, Guadalupe River, Lost Maples, Garner, Kerrville and Meridian state parks, as well as on private land in the surrounding countryside.

Urban expansion and the clearing of land threaten a large portion of the golden-cheek's habitat. A recent survey reported a loss of up to 45 percent of the suitable habitat over a ten-year period. Satellite imagery also indicates that of approximately 57,000 acres remaining, 70 percent is in fragments too small for the birds to use. At present rates, according to the Fish and Wildlife Service, the carrying capacity of the warblers' domain will be reduced by more than 50 percent by the year 2000, with the most immediate threat coming from commercial development.

Brood parasitism by the brown-headed cowbird also plays a role in the decline of the golden-cheeked warbler, as it does with the similarly endangered black-capped vireo. However, habitat preservation constitutes the single most important concern in the fight to preserve the only bird we can consider a pure-bred Texan. In saving that environment, of course, we provide not only for the warbler but for a host of other Texas plants and animals as well.

A male golden-cheeked warbler approaches its nest with food.

PINE WARBLER *Dendroica pinus*

While many bird names seem to be of obscure origin, that of the pine warbler could not be more appropriate. This little green-and-yellow warbler inhabits pine woodlands throughout its range in the eastern United States, from the jack pines and Norway pines of Minnesota and Michigan to the loblolly and longleaf stands of eastern Texas. It builds its shallow cuplike nest of pine needles, twigs and shreds of pine bark and binds it together with the silk of spiders and caterpillars. The nest is often placed far out on a limb, hidden among the tufts of needles or in a cluster of cones. Only during migration, or when foraging with small mixed-species flocks in winter, does the pine warbler leave its beloved pine forest for deciduous woodlands and thickets.

Olive-green above, the male pine warbler has a bright yellow throat and breast and white belly and undertail coverts. Dingy streaks on the sides of the breast and two prominent white bars on each wing provide the only distinctive marks. The female is duller in color, and immature birds are brownish above with little or no yellow on the underparts. Peterson suggests the pine warbler is best identified by the "boiling-down" system of eliminating all other possibilities. The similarly colored yellow-throated vireo lacks the breast streaks and has a thicker vireo bill. Most of the other autumn warblers with whitish wing-bars also have streaked backs. "No other *bright* yellow-breasted warbler, lacking other conspicuous marks, has *white wing-bars*," notes Peterson in *A Field Guide to the Birds of Texas*.

The pine warbler breeds in coniferous forests from the Canadian border to the Gulf Coast and winters in the southeastern states, Mexico and the West Indies. In Texas it nests in the eastern portions of the state and along the upper coast. Its twittering, musical trill, all on one pitch, can also be heard as far west as Bastrop and Buescher state parks, where it somehow finds the "lost pines" of that region. Migrating throughout the eastern half of Texas, the pine warbler may also remain there through the winter. It forages for insects and spiders as well as berries and selected seeds of pines, grasses and other plants. Its sharp *chip* notes and sunny color brighten winter days when most warblers, other than the yellow-rumped and orange-crowned, have moved south to the tropics.

BLACK-AND-WHITE WARBLER

Mniotilta varia

The little bird creeps up and down the trunk of the tree like a nuthatch or brown creeper, exploring each limb in turn and frequently hanging upside-down to probe a crevice in the bark. Finding a tasty caterpillar or spider, it grabs the squirming morsel in its slender, pointed beak and thrashes it against the tree before gulping it down. Then it resumes its methodical, persistent search for more.

The five-inch bird is boldly striped lengthwise with black and white, marking it as the well-named black-and-white warbler. The male has a black throat; the female and immatures, white. This species might be mistaken for the male blackpoll warbler (*Dendroica striata*), a rare spring migrant along the Texas coast, but the latter species has a solid black cap and contrasting white cheeks. The crown of the black-and-white warbler has a central white stripe.

The black-and-white warbler ranges across eastern North America, from Canada to the Gulf States, and winters from the Gulf southward through Mexico and the West Indies to northern South America. It nests in the woodlands of eastern Texas, south sparingly to Bryan and Houston, and on the Edwards Plateau. It migrates throughout most of the state, especially in the eastern half, and a few remain along the coast in winter.

The little "black-and-white creeper," as it was once called, is one of the first warblers to return from the tropics in the spring. Because it forages on the bark of trees, it has no need to wait until those trees leaf out. Its springtime song, a thin, repeated *weesee weesee weesee,* can be heard through the East Texas forests and groves as it claims its territory and searches for a nesting site. The black-and-white warbler makes its abode on the ground, as do several of its relatives. The well-lined cup of leaves and grasses is concealed under fallen leaves or branches at the base of a shrub and can be almost impossible to detect. The four or five spotted eggs hatch after ten days of incubation by the female. Both parents then feed their young, which leave the nest in 8 to 12 days and take to the trees.

A frequent cowbird host, the black-and-white warbler is also very sensitive to fragmentation of the forests within its breeding range. Those factors, as well as habitat loss on the wintering grounds in tropical America, have contributed to a dramatic population decline in portions of the eastern states.

The pine warbler (opposite) is well-named for its habitat. A female black-and-white warbler (above right) feeds her young concealed on the forest floor.

AMERICAN REDSTART   *Setophaga ruticilla*

Settlers to the New World named the American redstart for their familiar redstart of England, a member of an entirely different avian family. The word originated as a corruption of the Old German *rothstert,* or "red-tail," according to Gruson. Spanish speaking people of the West Indies call it *candelita,* the "little torch." That is a perfect name for what Roger Tory Peterson called "one of the most butterfly-like of birds, constantly flitting about . . ." Indeed, the hyperactive little redstart persistently flicks its wings and fans its tail to flash patches of bright color, like a flickering torch in the forest.

The male American redstart is glossy black, with a white belly and undertail coverts. Bright orange patches ornament the sides, wings and tail. The female is olive-gray above and white below, with yellow patches to match her mate's flaming garb. Immatures resemble females, and the young males develop their color gradually, reaching full plumage by their second fall season.

Redstarts are common in migration throughout the eastern half of Texas and are somewhat less abundant in the West. According to Oberholser, they once nested commonly in the northeastern corner of the state, but more recent records are widely scattered. Definition of the American redstart's full breeding range in Texas awaits the breeding-bird atlas now being prepared by volunteers across the state.

On a continent-wide basis, it breeds from southeastern Alaska and Canada across the northern and eastern states to the Gulf. Primarily an eastern species, it wanders occasionally into the Southwest. Like most neotropical migrants that winter in Central and South America and the Caribbean, the redstart has suffered from habitat losses and urbanization at both ends of its long migration route.

An inhabitant of second-growth woodlands and groves, the American redstart feeds primarily on insects, many of which it darts out to catch in flight. To that end, it is equipped with long rictal bristles around its mouth in the manner of the flycatchers. It builds its neat cuplike nest in the crotch of a tree or sapling and defends its territory aggressively. When parasitized by cowbirds, it sometimes destroys their eggs by burying them in the bottom of the nest, thereby preventing incubation.

The painted redstart (*Myioborus pictus*) is only distantly related to the American redstart in spite of its name. Taxonomists have placed it in a separate genus with ties to more tropical redstart species. Largely black, the painted redstart has a bright red lower breast and belly and white wing-patches and outer tail feathers. A flashy, colorful bird, it ranges northward from Mexico into the Chisos Mountains of Big Bend and appears to breed there sporadically.

PROTHONOTARY WARBLER   *Protonotaria citrea*

The deep recesses of the cypress swamp seem at first a dark and forbidding place. Then the eye discovers hidden beauty in the sunlight filtering through the leafy canopy overhead. Large white swamp lilies bloom in the shallow water, and a shiny red-eared turtle suns itself on a floating log. From the mossy darkness flits a plump little bird that shines as golden-yellow as the sun. It perches on a cypress stump and sings a loud, ringing song, *tweet tweet tweet tweet,* with all of the notes on a single pitch. A male prothonotary warbler has returned to the Texas Big Thicket to claim its spring and summer home.

This short-tailed warbler with the long bill took its name from the color-ful ceremonial robes worn by clerical officials of the Roman Catholic Church. Members of the College of Prothonotaries Apostolic are charged with keeping the registry of important pontifical proceedings. Few, perhaps, realized their colors also graced the hood and robes of a small bird in the wooded swamps and river bottoms of the eastern United States.

The male prothonotary warbler has a bright orange-yellow head and underparts and an olive back. The blue-gray wings have no light bars, but the blue-gray tail bears large white spots that flash in flight. His mate is duller and less golden. They breed from the Great Lakes area to the Gulf States and inhabit East Texas

westward at least to Denton, Fort Worth and Houston. In migration, the prothonotary warbler ranges throughout the eastern third of the state but is most often seen along the coast.

The prothonotary warbler is the only eastern warbler to nest in tree cavities, preferring a site over the water or very close to it. An old woodpecker hole will do, as will a natural cavity in an old stub or some other sheltered niche. One author of the Reader's Digest *Book of North American Birds* noted nest sites in "a bridge support, a cigar box, a tin cup, a glass jar—and a coat pocket." Presumably the coat was not being worn at the time.

While the male may construct dummy nests around his territory, the female builds the real one. She stuffs the cavity nearly full of moss, leaves, twigs and bits of bark and lines the mass with softer materials. She alone incubates her four to six spotted eggs, but both parents feed the young that hatch in 12 to 14 days. Insects, spiders and occasional snails constitute the major portion of their diet. Brown-headed cowbirds frequently parasitize prothonotary warblers, and one recorded nest contained seven cowbird eggs and not a single warbler egg.

By September, these colorful warblers are on their way south again to winter from Mexico through Central America to Venezuela. Like so many other warblers and small neotropical migrants, they are affected by the loss of tropical forests across their winter range. The prothonotary warbler may also be declining due to loss of the wetland habitats in which it insists on nesting.

The male American redstart (opposite) is unmistakable in his bright plumage. A prothonotary warbler (above right) is successful in the hunt.

COMMON YELLOWTHROAT   *Geothlypis trichas*

From deep in the cattail marsh comes the loud, distinctive song, *wichity wichity wichity wich*. The singer remains well hidden, but I purse my lips and make the sharp kissing sounds birders often use to attract curious birds. He answers, this time at closer range, and I squeak again. Finally I see a tiny bird creeping through the reeds, tail cocked alertly, almost like a wren. He hops up on an exposed stalk, throws back his head, and again loudly proclaims ownership of his territory. His bright yellow underparts and dashing black domino mask mark him immediately as a common yellowthroat.

Somewhere in the marsh his mate incubates her three to five spotted eggs in a nest well hidden on or near the ground. When the eggs hatch in 12 days, both parents will feed their young on insects until they can leave the nest some eight to ten days later. The female's furtiveness and the camouflaged nest, however, do not pro-

tect the family from the watchful brown-headed cowbird. The yellowthroat is one of the most common hosts for that invasive brood parasite.

Perhaps the most abundant of all North American warblers, the common yellowthroat is not a woodland bird as are most of its relatives, nor does it often perch high in trees. Instead, it prefers freshwater and saline marshes, grassy fields and wet thickets, usually remaining near the ground. It can be surprisingly difficult to see in spite of its wide distribution and its absurdly loud voice for a bird just five inches long.

The male is olive-green above and yellow below, his broad black mask bordered above with white. His mate and their young lack the mask entirely and are much more difficult to identify. The yellow throat and breast combined with a whitish belly and the lack of distinctive face pattern or wing-bars rule out most other warblers, and the habitat provides a helpful clue. Several races occur across the United States, with the western ones having much brighter yellow underparts than those in the East.

The common yellowthroat was once known as the Maryland yellowthroat, after the type locality, and then simply as the yellowthroat. Several related species inhabit the American tropics, and one, the gray-crowned yellowthroat (*Geothlypis poliocephala*), occasionally wanders into the lower Rio Grande Valley at places like Santa Ana Refuge or the Sabal Palm Grove Sanctuary. Lacking the black mask, it was formerly called the ground-chat before being placed in the genus with the masked yellowthroats.

Breeding from southeastern Alaska and Canada through virtually all of the U.S. to Mexico, the common yellowthroat winters in the southern states and Central America. It migrates throughout Texas and remains through the winter in all but the colder portions of the North and West. Nesting birds are abundant in the eastern portions of the state, but races that formerly bred in South Texas, the Panhandle and the Trans-Pecos seem to be less common and are apparently on the decline. Nevertheless, the common yellowthroat turns up in marshy and streamside habitats in most portions of the state to delight birders with its dapper good looks and cheerful voice.

HOODED WARBLER

Wilsonia citrina

There can be no mistaking the male hooded warbler. Olive-green above and bright yellow below, he sports an extensive black hood that frames his golden face and forehead. So intense is the contrast that the face seems to glow with an inner light, even in the dense shade of the forest floor. The hooded warbler has no wing-bars, but white webs of the outer tail feathers appear as large white spots as the bird flits actively about or flies up to catch an insect in midair.

The female lacks the complete black hood, although she sometimes shows traces of it on her olive crown or on the sides of her neck and upper breast. In her nondescript olive-and-yellow plumage, she resembles several of the other female warblers, but the white spots in the tail prove diagnostic.

A breeding resident of the timbered swamps and wet woodlands of deep East Texas, the hooded warbler usually stays well hidden in the low undergrowth. Its loud, whistled song has several variations described as *ta-wit ta-wit tee-yo* or *weeta wee-tee-yo*, but the final slurred *tee-yo* provides a clue to the identity of the singer. A flat, metallic *chink* call note is also heard frequently.

The hooded warbler constructs its cuplike nest in the upright fork of a shrub, often no more than two or three feet above the ground. Both sexes share in the 12-day incubation of the three or four spotted eggs and feed the young that fledge in less than ten days. Most pairs apparently raise a second brood when the first is complete, but like many of the other warblers, they suffer from severe cowbird parasitism.

Hooded warblers feed almost en-

The black-masked male common yellowthroat is a loud, boisterous singer.

tirely on insects, and the sexes partition the resources by foraging in different niches. The female hunts through fallen leaves and gleans insects from the lower tree branches, while her mate moves higher and often flies out to hawk insects in the air.

Nesting across the eastern U.S., from the Great Lakes and southern New England to the Gulf Coast, hooded warblers spend the winter in Mexico and Central America. During migration, from late August through September and again from late March until early May, they occur commonly through eastern Texas and along the coast.

Also breeding in East Texas and occupying much the same woodland undergrowth is the slightly larger Kentucky warbler (*Oporornis formosus*). It is also olive above and bright yellow below, but it has prominent black "sideburns" extending from the eyes down the sides of the neck. The sideburns are more distinct on the male than on the female. Like the hooded warbler, the Kentucky warbler nests throughout the eastern states and winters in tropical America. During migration, it moves through the eastern half of Texas.

Wilson's warbler (*Wilsonia pusilla*) is closely related to the hooded warbler. It, too, has olive-green upperparts and yellow underparts, but the male wears a neat little black skullcap. The female may lack all traces of the black cap, but she also lacks the white tail-spots of the female hooded warbler. Wilson's warbler nests across Alaska and Canada and south through the western states. It migrates throughout Texas on its way to and from Central America and remains sparingly in winter along the coast and in the Rio Grande Valley.

Wilson's warbler and the genus were named for early ornithologist Alexander Wilson. Born in Scotland in 1766, Wilson followed his father's trade as a weaver and then became an itinerant poet. Perpetually in trouble and arrested in 1794 for political conspiracy, he emigrated to the United States. Here he conceived the idea of illustrating and producing a series of volumes on the birds of the eastern

states. Self-taught as an artist, Wilson finally received financial support and published the first volume in 1808. At the time of his death in 1813, the eighth volume was completed. The ninth and final one was written by Wilson's friend, George Ord. Although now outdated for the average birder, they were classics in the early age of American ornithology.

A male hooded warbler feeds young brown-headed cowbirds already larger than himself. Cowbird parasitism is a major problem for many warblers and other small perching birds.

Yellow-breasted Chat   *Icteria virens*

At more than seven inches in length, the yellow-breasted chat is the largest of all our warblers. Its long tail and heavy bill do not fit the family mold. The chat is dark olive above with a yellow throat and breast and a white belly. Conspicuous white "spectacles" surround the eyes. The lores of the male are black; those of the female, dingy gray. "Except for its color," writes Peterson, "the Chat seems more like a Catbird or a Mockingbird than a warbler." Indeed, its size and long tail, as well as its preferred brushland habitat and loud, raucous voice, all suggest one of the mimic thrushes. So, too, does its habit of singing frequently at night. Recent DNA studies have shown that in spite of its unusual appearance and habits, the affinities of the yellow-breasted chat do, indeed, lie with the wood warblers.

The yellow-breasted chat ranges across virtually all of the United States, from the Canadian border southward into Mexico, and it winters from Mexico to Panama. It nests from the woodlands of East Texas to the streamside thickets of the Trans-Pecos; however, it rarely spends summer on the coastal prairie or on the Staked Plains. Oberholser also notes that the chat "has virtually ceased nesting in the south Texas brush country since 1900; from 1933 it has declined somewhat on the Edwards Plateau. Climatic warming plus excessive bulldozing and overgoating of thickets seem to be the chief chat inhibitors."

Although locally common, the chat can be shy and solitary. It frequents dense thickets and tangles and is more often heard than seen. One writer calls it the "buffoon of the brier patch." An accomplished ventriloquist, the chat sings an unmusical medley of squawks, whistles, clucks, rattles, chuckles and pops. The song suggests that of the mockingbird but is less repetitive. Peterson notes that "Single notes, such as *whoit* or *kook*, are distinctive." During the spring, however, the reclusive chat may sing from an exposed perch or launch into an aerial display in which it sings in flight above its perch, legs dangling, and then drops back again.

The yellow-breasted chat builds a large, bulky nest of grasses and plant fibers and ornaments it with lichens, bark and feathers. Located in the fork of a low tree, it is well hidden in spite of its size. The female incubates her three or four spotted eggs that hatch in 11 days, but both adults feed their altricial babies. Fledging in about eight days, the young receive a diet of insects; later they will consume fruits and berries as well. Brown-headed cowbirds present a constant hazard to the success of the clutch.

The raucous yellow-breasted chat is much larger than the other warblers, but it is more often heard than seen.

TANAGERS (Emberizidae: Subfamily Thraupinae)

No other group of birds outshines the tanagers in the sheer brilliance and variability of their plumage. Exclusively New World birds, most of the 200 species inhabit the hot, humid forests of Central and South America. There they ornament the treetops with all the colors of the rainbow. The names of tropical tanagers describe their exotic plumages: glistening-green, beryl-spangled, opal-crowned, green-and-gold, golden-hooded, flame-faced and purple-mantled, to mention just a few.

The name tanager comes from the Tupi Indians of the Amazon region, who call these colorful birds *tangara.* The word also serves as the name for one of the several genera.

Most tanagers tend to be medium-sized, rather chunky birds with moderately heavy beaks. The four species that breed in North America have a notch on the cutting edge of the upper mandible, a feature that is not present in all tanagers. In fact, there are no clear-cut familial characteristics, and taxonomic lines are the subject of great ornithological debate. Some species exhibit similarities to the finches, the wood warblers and even the honeycreepers, and modern taxonomy places them in a large and complex family. In practice, however, it is convenient for the birder to consider the typical tanagers as a distinct group, whatever their genetic affinities.

Female summer tanager.

Because they feed on insects and berries, North American tanagers must normally retreat in winter to their ancestral home in the tropics. While we tend to think of them as northern birds that migrate southward in search of winter food, the reverse is quite clearly the case: The tanagers trace their origins to tropical America, and an adventuresome few have extended their breeding range northward to take advantage of an unoccupied niche with a longer period of daylight. Abundant food and longer days for feeding young more than make up for the dangers of migration.

Although many tropical tanagers have similar male and female plumages, North American species show a high degree of sexual dimorphism. Males in breeding plumage are brightly colored, while females remain dull greenish above and yellowish below. The latter might be mistaken for female orioles but for their heavier bills and lack of wing-bars. Only the western tanager has the pronounced wing-bars more characteristic of the slender-billed orioles.

and wasps that some people call them "red beebirds," and they are unwelcome guests around beehives. Raiding the nests of paper wasps, they gleefully catch the adults in their beaks and batter them against a branch to break off the sharp stingers before gulping them down. They then pick the tasty white larvae and pupae from the unprotected comb.

The similar hepatic tanager *(Piranga flava)* occurs as a migrant in Trans-Pecos Texas and less frequently in the Hill Country and along the lower coast. It breeds in the highland forests of the Chisos, Davis and Guadalupe mountains. The male, a duller red than the bright rose-red summer tanager, has a dark gray cheek patch and a blackish bill. The darker bill also distinguishes the dusky greenish and yellow female.

SUMMER TANAGER   *Piranga rubra*

The most widespread and abundant tanager in Texas, the summer tanager migrates throughout the state and remains to breed in all but the treeless plains and much of the Panhandle. Ranging widely across the southern United States, it spends the winters in tropical America, from Mexico to the Amazon Basin of Brazil.

Sometimes called the "summer redbird," the all-red male might at first glance be taken for a cardinal, but it lacks the prominent crest and black face of that familiar year-round resident. The fairly heavy bill is yellowish or horn-colored. The female remains a drabber greenish above and mustard yellow or gold below, often with an orange cast. During their first spring, immature males begin to take

on the red adult plumage, and they exhibit blotchy patterns of red and greenish yellow. Because the molt often begins on the head, these young birds are frequently mistaken for western tanagers; however, they lack the dark wings and tail and the prominent light wing-bars of the western.

Nesting summer tanagers inhabit the mixed pine-hardwood forests of East Texas and the streamside cottonwood and willow thickets of the West, building their loose, cuplike nests on horizontal branches. The three or four bluish eggs speckled with brown hatch in about 12 days, and the young are fed primarily on insects. Mature birds also consume quantities of fruits and berries.

So fond are these tanagers of bees

SCARLET TANAGER

Piranga olivacea

The scarlet tanager arrives on the Texas coast from its winter home in South America when spring migration is in full swing. Hordes of colorful warblers, buntings, orioles and grosbeaks forage through the trees, but none surpasses the male scarlet tanager in its vernal finery. A brilliant, almost fluorescent, red contrasting with jet-black wings and tail, it seems to glow from within as if lit by some internal flame. As a child, pioneering American ornithologist Elliott Coues was deeply moved by the sight of the scarlet tanager: "I hold this bird in particular, almost superstitious, recollection, as the very first of all the feathered tribe to stir within me those emotions that have never ceased to stimulate and gratify my love for birds."

It ranges through East Texas and along the coast during migration and then continues northward to nest in the East and Midwest, from Oklahoma, Tennessee and Georgia to southern Canada. After the breeding season, however, the male molts its colorful courtship plumage. Unlike the male summer tanager, which keeps its red color year-round after once attaining it in its second year, the scarlet tanager reverts each fall to the basic femalelike plumage. Both sexes are then greenish above and yellow below, with darker wings and tails, a plumage that gave rise to the scientific name *olivacea.*

Where their breeding ranges overlap, scarlet and summer tanagers display an unusual interspecific aggression. Each responds to the songs of the other and countersings its challenge in an effort to establish territorial boundaries and apportion the resources.

Although they also eat fruits and berries, scarlet tanagers subsist primarily on vast quantities of insects. Observers have documented consumption of hundreds of the harmful larvae of gypsy moths and tent caterpillars, a trait of enormous benefit to deciduous woodlands and orchards. This champion long-distance migrant, however, is subject to severe cowbird predation and suffers the hazards shared by other neotropical migrants that must cope with habitat loss in both their summer and winter homes. The scarlet tanager has sadly declined over much of the eastern United States.

The male summer tanager (opposite) is sometimes called the "summer redbird" in Texas. It lacks the crest and black face of the cardinal. Black wings and tail set off the flaming plumage of the male scarlet tanager (above right).

WESTERN TANAGER *Piranga ludoviciana*

The charming, brightly colored western tanager is the only North American tanager with distinct wing-bars. The female—grayish green above and yellow below, with darker wings and tail—resembles the female orioles, but her chunkier body and heavier tanager bill are distinctive. The male has a bright yellow body and black wings, tail and upper back. The upper wing-bar is yellow; the narrow lower one, paler yellow or white. In breeding plumage the male displays a flame-red head, but most of that color is lost in fall and winter plumage. The

more widely distributed summer tanager may also appear red-headed as the immature male begins its molt to adult plumage, and it might be mistaken for its western relative.

The scientific name of the western tanager, *ludoviciana,* comes from the Latin form of "Louisiana." The species was first discovered in the early 19th century in what is now Idaho by the famed Lewis and Clark Expedition. The Louisiana Territory then included the land between the Mississippi River and the Rocky Mountains. In fact, the western tanager inhabits the high country from southeastern Alaska to California and West Texas, ranging up to elevations of 10,000 feet. Only as a rare straggler does it reach the eastern half of the country. It winters from Mexico to Costa Rica.

The western tanager occurs throughout the western half of Texas during migration, although it is most abundant in the Trans-Pecos. A few also remain there to breed in the higher mountain ranges. A loose cup of grasses, twigs and mosses on a horizontal limb of a conifer cradles the three or four bluish, brown-spotted eggs that hatch in about 13 days. The female incubates alone, while her mate rarely visits the nest site, but both parents join in bringing insects to the hungry young. Insects make up the major portion of the adult diet as well, but berries and fruits supplement the menu. Western tanagers can be a nuisance in cherry orchards, but they consume vast quantities of harmful caterpillars, stinkbugs and grasshoppers.

Male western tanager.

BLACKBIRDS, ORIOLES AND MEADOWLARKS

(Emberizidae: Subfamily Icterinae)

This heterogeneous group of nearly 100 species ranges throughout the New World, from Alaska to Tierra del Fuego, with most of its members occurring in the tropics and subtropics. It includes the blackbirds, grackles, cowbirds, orioles, meadowlarks and bobolink. So diverse are they, in fact, that it is difficult to select a convenient and comprehensive title for them. Ornithologists call them simply "icterids."

The icterids range from medium- to large-sized birds and have conical, sharply pointed bills and large, strong feet. There is a high degree of sexual dimorphism, and males of most North American species are considerably larger and more colorful than their

A female red-winged blackbird (left) feeds her hungry fledgling.

mates. Some, like the orioles and bobolink, are excellent singers, while the grackles produce a vocal repertoire more befitting a rusty gate. Orioles and their tropical relatives, the oropendolas and caciques, build elaborately woven hanging nests, but the meadowlarks and bobolink hide their structures on the ground. The cowbirds build no nests at all, preferring to slip their eggs into the clutches of other birds and let the unwitting foster parents raise their young.

Icterids also vary widely in their chosen habitats, but the blackbirds, grackles and cowbirds frequently band together in large communal flocks, particularly after the nesting season. Most people know them simply as "blackbirds," without attempting to sort them out by size, shape and color pattern. The introduced European starling may also join these icterid flocks, but it is not closely related to the others.

The flocks prove highly unpopular within the cities. With an apparent population boom in recent years, hundreds of thousands of mixed blackbird species may occupy a single roost. The noise is deafening, the residue messy. Blackbird and grackle control efforts have been the subject of some controversy in many portions of the South, for the species are protected by migratory-bird laws. Yet these huge flocks present an awesome spectacle as they swirl like clouds of smoke across the sky, wheeling and banking in perfect unison.

A male bronzed cowbird erects his ruff to impress a mate.

BOBOLINK   *Dolichonyx oryzivorus*

William Cullen Bryant, in his poem "Robert of Lincoln," described the bobolink as "wearing a bright black wedding coat; / White are his shoulders and white his crest." The male bobolink does indeed cut a fine figure in his nuptial finery. His black plumage contrasts with white scapulars and rump; his nape is buff-colored, fading to whitish in the summer. After the breeding season, however, the male undergoes a complete fall molt to acquire more modest buffy plumage with dark streaks on the back and sides and brown stripes on the head. He then looks much like his somber, sparrow-drab mate. Hers is a plumage more suited for incubating eggs hidden among the grasses, while her mate proclaims ownership of their territory.

The name bobolink is onomatopoeic in origin and mimics the rollicking, bubbling song that is often sung in flight. The lovely, lyrical bobolink, however, does not nest in Texas. The champion long-distance migrant among the blackbirds and their relatives, it wanders irregularly through the eastern and northern portions of the state on its way from its winter home in South America to its breeding grounds in southern Canada and the northern states. It occurs only casually along the coast, but when present in its spring courtship plumage, it is readily seen and recognized.

Bobolinks prefer to nest in hayfields and weedy meadows but suffer heavy losses when the fields are cut before the young have fledged. In the fall they mass in flocks and migrate through the Southeast, where they once wreaked havoc with the rice fields of South Carolina. Its scientific name, *Dolichonyx oryzivorus*, in fact, means "long-clawed rice eater." People there called them "rice-birds" or "butter-birds," for bobolinks became "fat as butter" on the banquet of rice and were shot by the tens of thousands for shipment to markets in the East.

Loss of tall-grass breeding habitat and the onslaught by hunters in the 19th century severely depleted the bobolink population. More recently, the conversion of land to agriculture on the wintering ground 5,000 miles away in southern Brazil and northern Argentina has had a marked effect. The huge flocks of sparrowlike "rice-birds" are gone, but smaller numbers of bobolinks still make their twice yearly flights between the American continents.

Perched in a meadow, a male bobolink sings his name.

RED-WINGED BLACKBIRD
Agelaius phoeniceus

Nearly everyone recognizes the male red-winged blackbird. Glossy black, he sports vivid scarlet epaulettes edged in buffy yellow. In Texas, he can be confused with no other North American species.

The female, however, is much less distinctive and less frequently recognized. Significantly smaller than the nine-inch male, she is dark brown above and heavily streaked below. There may be a hint of red on the shoulder, but that becomes visible only at close range. The female redwing resembles a large and strongly marked sparrow with a sharply pointed bill.

Ranging across the continent, from Alaska to Nova Scotia and southward to Costa Rica, Cuba and the Bahamas, the red-winged blackbird withdraws from the northern edge of its range in winter. Huge flocks then descend on Texas, often in company with other blackbirds, grackles, cowbirds and starlings. They haunt the open fields and pastures, eating prodigious quantities of grain. One estimate places crop losses of rice, corn and sorghum at $20 to $30 million a year across the country; however, at least part of the destruction is compensated by the large numbers of harmful insects and weed seeds that the birds also consume.

The red-wing sexes often remain segregated through the winter, an unusual behavior among birds. Many flocks that arrive at backyard feeders contain only females, with no males present to facilitate identification of their less distinctive mates. Once spring arrives, however, the instinctive breeding urge replaces such flocking behavior. Red-winged blackbirds fan out across the countryside in distinct waves: older males first, followed by the females and then the immature bachelor males. In Texas, they nest throughout the state, although red-wings are less abundant in the arid Trans-Pecos.

Breeding males stake out their territories in marshes and in wet fields

The male red-winged blackbird sings from a perch to claim territory occupied by his harem.

and thickets around ponds and flood-plains. Disputes over territorial boundaries are resolved in stylized "fights" involving elaborate display of the red shoulder patches and shrill songs of *konk-la-reee*. Field experiments have shown the importance of these rituals, for males whose epaulettes were dyed black had great difficulty holding their territories. In two separate tests, more than 60 percent of the blackened males lost their territories, while less than 10 percent of untreated control males were evicted by others.

When the females arrive, they choose their nest sites within the territory of a selected polygynous male. If a female's amorous attentions are rejected, the male drives her off. If accepted, she joins his harem and begins to weave a nest of reeds or grasses, usually near or over the wa-ter. Her three to five bluish eggs ornamented with darker scrawls hatch in 10 to 12 days; the young leave the nest in 11 to 14 days more.

The male takes no part in the nest-building or incubation of the eggs. His function is territorial defense, loudly proclaimed from the top of a bush or cattail stalk. The bright plumage of the male is tailored for that task; the drab plumage of the female, for camouflage on the nest.

Numerous predators of the marsh—raccoons, foxes, weasels, water snakes, crows and grackles—keep the prolific red-wings in check. Parasitic cowbirds also lay their eggs in untended nests, sometimes removing an egg of the host. Despite severe predation, however, the ubiquitous red-winged blackbird more than holds its own. It may well be the most numerous land bird in North America.

YELLOW-HEADED BLACKBIRD
Xanthocephalus xanthocephalus

Some bird names seem at first obscure and poorly chosen, but few are more descriptive of the species than "yellow-headed blackbird." Both halves of the scientific name also reflect the same feature, for *xanthocephalus* means "yellow-headed" in Greek. The ten-inch adult male does indeed have a bright yellow head and breast, contrasting strongly with his black plumage. A white wing-patch shows primarily in flight. The smaller, dusky brown female lacks the wing-patch, and the yellow or buffy yellow color is confined largely to the eyebrow, lower cheek and throat.

The yellow-headed blackbird inhabits freshwater marshes and reed-bordered lakes from the Canadian prairies southward through the West and Midwest to California and New Mexico. It winters in the southwestern U.S. and Mexico and occurs commonly in the western two-thirds of Texas during migration. It also wanders eastward occasionally to the coast, where birders delight in its showy plumage. A few remain along the Rio Grande in winter, and yellow-headed blackbirds can frequently be found through the summer in the northern Panhandle and the Trans-Pecos, although substantiated records of breeding activity are scarce.

On their nesting grounds, yellow-heads congregate in colonies, sometimes in large numbers, attaching their woven nests to stalks of emergent vegetation over the water. Where they share a habitat with the smaller red-winged blackbirds, yellow-heads normally utilize deeper water, thereby deriving added protection from predators. They defend their territory fiercely, rising in screaming groups to chase off coursing hawks and crows. Females build their nests and incubate alone, receiving only a

Male yellow-headed blackbird.

little help from their mates in the care and feeding of the young.

The male spends his time posturing and loudly proclaiming ownership of his little patch of reeds. Ruffling his golden neck feathers and drooping his wings to reveal the white patches, he throws back his head at an awkward, contorted angle and emits a song with all the musical quality of a rusty hinge. Oberholser describes the hoarse, rasping notes as "like a buzz saw biting into a hard log," while W.L. Dawson calls it "a wail of despairing agony which would do credit to a dying catamount."

In migration and through the winter, yellow-headed blackbirds congregate in flocks, frequently joining other blackbird species to forage in open farmlands and fields as well as in the marshes. Seeds make up about two-thirds of their overall diet, particularly in the winter. During the warmer months these large, showy blackbirds consume quantities of caterpillars, beetles and grasshoppers, with occasional snails and tadpoles.

BREWER'S BLACKBIRD

Euphagus cyanocephalus

Brewer's blackbirds depend much less on wetland environments than do most of the other blackbird and grackle species. They prefer open fields, farms and ranches and inhabit the central Great Plains and the western states. The tamest of all the blackbirds, they have also adapted to city parks and yards and appear to be expanding their range slowly eastward. Nesting in colonies of only a few to as many as a hundred pairs, they build their twiggy, grass-lined nests in trees or shrubs or even on the ground.

Brewer's blackbirds nest occasionally in the Panhandle and in Trans-Pecos Texas but are much more common as winter residents, when they move into the southern U.S. and Mexico. After the breeding season, they join the huge foraging flocks of other blackbird species and drift across the countryside, massing at communal roosts for the night. Most abundant in West Texas, they nevertheless range across the entire state.

As with many of the other icterids, the sexes differ in size and color. The nine-inch male is glossy black with a purplish iridescence on the head, the reason for the name *cyanocephalus*, Greek for "blue-headed." Its eyes are a bright, pale yellow. In contrast, the smaller female is a dingy, sooty gray with dark brown eyes. Brewer's blackbird differs from the much larger grackles in having a rounder head, a shorter bill and a shorter, rounded tail. Small flocks usually contain both males and females, and their dimorphism in plumage and eye color facilitates identification.

According to Gruson, Thomas Mayo Brewer was born to a Brahmin family of Boston in 1814. He graduated from Harvard Medical School but practiced for only a couple of years before taking up political journalism. A friend of Nuttall and Audubon, he later published several volumes on birds and collected extensively for his friends. In gratitude, Audubon named several species in his honor, including Brewer's blackbird.

The rusty blackbird (*Euphagus carolinus*) resembles Brewer's blackbird in size and shape, but both male and female are heavily marked with rusty brown in fall and winter plumage. Both sexes also have light eyes. The less common rusty blackbird nests in Alaska and Canada and winters in the eastern half of Texas, where it prefers wet woodlands and thickets rather than open fields and farmlands.

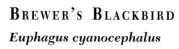

Male Brewer's blackbird.

COMMON GRACKLE *Quiscalus quiscula*

In a popular vote, grackles would probably win election as the bullies of the neighborhood. They swagger brazenly across the lawn, posing and posturing haughtily, and descend on backyard bird feeders to dominate the smaller, more timid patrons. The foot-long common grackle is the smallest of the grackle genus, but its long, wedge-shaped tail and large bill separate it from the still smaller Brewer's blackbird. The tail is often creased down the center and raised at the edges, giving it a keeled look.

The male common grackle appears entirely black at a distance or in poor light, but it glows with a rainbow spectrum of iridescent color in the sunshine. The head is glossed with purple; the body, with shimmering bronze. The female averages slightly smaller and duller in plumage, but the distinction is not as dramatic as with the other grackles. Both sexes have fierce yellow eyes as adults, while juvenile birds are brownish and have dark eyes. In older literature, the race found commonly in Texas was called the "bronzed grackle," while a race with purple iridescence east of the Appalachians was called the "purple grackle." The two have been regarded as a single species for many years.

The common grackle ranges from Canada to the Gulf of Mexico east of the Rocky Mountains and is partially migratory, withdrawing from the northern states in winter. It resides year-round in the northern and eastern portions of Texas, west to Fort Worth and south to Austin and the upper coast. In winter, however, grackles assemble in huge flocks that descend on the state and roam farther west and south as well.

Common grackles breed in loose colonies in the fields, parks and towns of East Texas, building their deep, bulky nests among the trees and shrubs. The female lays four or five greenish or light brown eggs beautifully blotched and scrawled with dark brown and purple. She incubates them alone, but her mate shares in caring for the young and fiercely protects them from intruders. Incubation requires about two weeks, and the young fledge 16 to 20 days later after being fed primarily an insect diet. Adult grackles feed voraciously on insects and other invertebrates, seeds and grain, fruits, acorns and nuts, and small vertebrates. They sometimes invade the nests of other birds to break and consume the eggs.

Classed technically as "songbirds" because of their anatomy, grackles do not thrill human ears with their musical abilities. The short, creaking-gate "song" was described by one author as a "wheelbarrow chorus," and the call notes are loud, harsh *chack* or *chuck* cries. As unmusical as the offerings may be, the arrogant singers seem inordinately proud of their efforts. Drooping their wings and spreading their long, graduated tails to exhibit every iridescent feather, they throw back their heads as their throats swell with sound. Their prospective mates apparently regard it as the most beautiful music in the world, for the common grackle has been extremely successful in maintaining its jaunty, dominating presence among North American birds.

The common grackle (above left) gleams with iridescent colors in the sunlight. A male great-tailed grackle (opposite) postures to intimidate his rivals.

GREAT-TAILED GRACKLE   *Quiscalus mexicanus*

The largest of the grackles, this resident of the southwestern states does not appear by name in some of the older books still in use among Texas birders. It was long regarded as a subspecies of the boat-tailed grackle found along the Atlantic and Gulf coasts. Where the two forms overlap in the coastal marshes of southwestern Louisiana and southeastern Texas, however, interbreeding "has never occurred with sufficient frequency to produce a hybrid population," according to George Lowery in *Louisiana Birds.* Consequently, the two are now treated as separate species. Ornithologist and wildlife artist H. Douglas Pratt made an extensive study of the two forms in Louisiana and documented their vocal repertoires. Although the two are similar in appearance, they apparently achieve reproductive isolation by virtue of their different songs.

An iridescent, glossy black, the 18-inch male great-tailed grackle displays a purple sheen in good light, and its enormous tail is keel-shaped. The smaller, shorter-tailed female is brown in color, with a buffy breast. Both sexes have bright yellow eyes as adults, the easiest feature to use in separating them from the boat-tailed grackle. The latter is slightly smaller, has a more rounded head, and has brown eyes. The boat-tail is also restricted in its Texas range to the marshes of the upper coast.

The great-tailed grackle ranges through the Southwest from Louisiana and Texas to southeastern California and south through Mexico and Central America to Ecuador and Peru. "The breeding range has expanded greatly in the last century, and is apparently continuing to do so," says the AOU *Check-list of North American Birds.*

Oberholser notes that the great-tailed grackle was largely confined to the South Texas brush country and the coastal prairie in the early 20th century. It reached Austin in the 1920s and Waco about 1938. A statewide survey of Texas Ornithological Society members revealed it was well established in Dallas and Fort Worth in the 1950s. By that time, it was also nesting in El Paso and at numerous places along the Pecos River.

Sometimes called the "jackdaw" and the "crow-blackbird" by Texans, the great-tailed grackle prefers open flatlands with scattered groves of

trees or marshes and river bottoms. Consequently, it remains less common in forested parts of East Texas and the Edwards Plateau and in the mountains and deserts of the Trans-Pecos. But it has moved into towns and city suburbs across the state and may be crowding out the common grackle from portions of its range.

Males in the spring stage a fascinating courtship display as they strut with drooping wings and spread tails, their bills pointed skyward in a "stargazing" pose. They then vibrate their wings to produce strange rattling, crashing sounds and "sing" an unmusical assortment of piercing whistles, squeals and shrieks befitting unoiled machinery.

Gathering in colonies to nest, the promiscuous males match their poses and voices against one another but seldom appear to have serious disputes. Females, however, squabble constantly over their nest sites and building materials. They, alone, construct the bulky, grass-lined nests in trees and shrubs or in the reeds and incubate their three or four bluish eggs ornamented with darker scrawls. Unlike many male icterids that assume a portion of the feeding chores, male great-tails appear to show little interest in their young.

Insects and other invertebrates, small vertebrates, grain, seeds, fruit, and the eggs and nestlings of other birds make up the great-tail's diet. The huge grackles frequently nest on the fringes of heron colonies or among white-winged doves, and their raids on untended nests can be a serious problem for the conservation of those species.

BOAT-TAILED GRACKLE
Quiscalus major

Unlike the great-tailed grackle, which ranges inland across the state, the boat-tailed grackle is confined to the marshes of the upper Texas coast and occurs sparingly southward along the shore. Oberholser notes that it is seldom found more than 30 miles from the Gulf of Mexico. It can most easily be seen in the marshes and wet fields around Sabine, High Island, Bolivar and the Anahuac National Wildlife Refuge.

Slightly smaller than the great-tail, with which it was formerly lumped as a single species, the male boat-tail is also an iridescent, glossy blue-black with a long, keel-shaped tail. The female is tawny brown. Both sexes of Texas' boat-tailed grackle have brown eyes, while the eyes of the great-tail are bright yellow.

Pratt noted that the calls of the boat-tailed grackle are harsher than those of the great-tail but never as mechanical. The different vocalizations apparently prevent the two species from interbreeding in the coastal marshes where their ranges overlap.

Boat-tailed grackles are promiscuous, according to Ehrlich, Dobkin and Wheye, and both adult and nestling sex ratios average a surprising two females to one male. Males do not breed until their second year, but females breed as yearlings, contributing greatly to the fecundity of the colony. Within a selected male's territory, the females build their nests and care for their eggs and young alone.

Like the omnivorous great-tailed grackle, the boat-tail consumes a wide variety of animal and vegetable foods. Grain, weed seeds, fruits, caterpillars, wasps, grasshoppers, beetles, crayfish, crabs, snails and small fish all fuel these handsome but raucous dwellers of the marsh. They may even wade in shallow water to fish or steal food from unwary ibises and herons.

Dark eyes distinguish the male (above) and female (right) boat-tailed grackles from the similar great-tailed grackle.

BROWN-HEADED COWBIRD

Molothrus ater

In order to save the endangered black-capped vireo and golden-cheeked warbler in the Texas Hill Country, says the U.S. Fish and Wildlife Service in its recovery plan, a "broad-based reduction" of cowbirds will be necessary. A similar eradication of the brown-headed cowbird has already been employed in Michigan to benefit the endangered Kirtland's warbler. Few other birds are so thoroughly despised, yet few have a more fascinating biology.

The object of this ornithological offensive is the most innocuous looking of the blackbirds, a chunky little bird scarcely seven inches long with a short, conical, sparrowlike bill. The glossy black male wears a chocolate brown hood; the female is entirely dusky brownish-gray. These gregarious cowbirds roam year-round through open woodlands, farms, ranches and suburbs throughout Texas. In winter they join the mixed flocks of other icterids, among which they can be recognized by their small size and their habit of holding their tails lifted high as they walk about in search of food.

It is their breeding habits that have brought brown-headed cowbirds into disfavor, for they are obligate brood parasites. Rather than building their own nests and caring for their own young, females simply lay their eggs in the nests of other species. Brown-headed cowbirds once lived primarily on the Great Plains, where they followed herds of American bison. With the clearing of the forests, they expanded both eastward and westward, and cowbirds now occupy most of the continent south of the Arctic, from Canada through northern Mexico. The name is a contraction of "cowpen-bird," applied by Mark Catesby. "They delight much to feed in the pens of cattle, which has given them their name," wrote the early 18th-century naturalist. Their breeding habits facilitate a vagabond

A *male brown-headed cowbird stakes his claim to a feeder.*

life style, for they have no household chores to tie them down.

Brown-headed cowbirds parasitize a wide range of species but prey most heavily on flycatchers, vireos, warblers and sparrows. Not all birds are appropriate hosts, for some recognize and reject the foreign egg by either destroying it, rebuilding the nest to cover it, or abandoning the nest entirely. Cowbird eggs have been found in the nests of at least 220 different species, but not all successfully raised the chicks.

Only three percent of cowbird eggs result in adults, according to Ehrlich, Dobkin and Wheye. Yet in spite of those tremendous losses, cowbirds continue to expand their range and numbers. The secret lies in the unusual breeding behavior and physiology. Female brown-headed cowbirds have long reproductive periods with short intervals between clutches. Indeed, the laying cycles may be almost continuous over a two-month period, leading ornithologists to refer to female cowbirds as "passerine

chickens." According to field studies, an average female lays 40 eggs per year for two years. If three percent of those 80 offspring survive, each female will generate 2.4 adults. Thus each pair replaces itself with an average of 1.2 pairs, thereby doubling a cowbird population in eight years.

The mating system also shows a remarkable degree of flexibility. If potential host nests are abundant, the female cowbird maintains a small home breeding range. This allows the male to guard his mate (or mates) in a monogamous or polygynous relationship. If host nests are widely dispersed, on the other hand, the female ranges over a greater area and mates promiscuously with several males.

The female often locates a potential nest during its construction and visits it regularly until its owner begins her clutch. She then drops in to deposit an egg of her own, frequently removing one from the host. She generally lays but one egg per nest, but another cowbird may also lay an egg in the same nest when her range overlaps that of the first. About one-third of all parasitized nests hold more than one cowbird egg, apparently from different females.

Because cowbird eggs have a short incubation period of only 10 to 13 days, they usually hatch a day or two before the others. In addition, the young cowbirds are larger and tend to grow more rapidly than most of their nest mates. They therefore receive most of the food and may even crowd the others from the nest. It is not uncommon to find a tiny warbler patiently stuffing caterpillars into the gaping mouth of a much larger cowbird fledgling. How that cowbird then establishes its own identity and recognizes others of its species, however, remains a mystery.

BRONZED COWBIRD
Molothrus aeneus

Slightly larger than the more widely distributed brown-headed cowbird, the bronzed cowbird of South Texas has black plumage and a larger bill. The body of the male is glossed with a greenish bronze iridescence; the wings and tail, with purple. A thick feathered ruff on the nape and upper back gives it a distinctively bulky, hunchbacked appearance. Bright red eyes are responsible for the alternate name "red-eyed cowbird," but they become visible only at close range. The smaller female is dull black with a smaller, inconspicuous ruff.

In the springtime the male bronzed cowbird stages a fascinating courtship show. Throwing back his head and erecting his large ruff like a devilish cape, he walks stiffly around the female, quivering his wings. He then bounces up and down while singing his high-pitched, creaky song and jumps up to hover in the air like a tiny black helicopter just above his intended mate.

While this mating performance de-

Male bronzed cowbird in courtship display.

lights South Texas birders, the outcome does not, for bronzed cowbirds are brood parasites that lay their eggs in other nests. Piercing an egg of the host and removing it, the female replaces it with one of her own greenish blue eggs and leaves the rearing of her young to the unsuspecting foster parents. At least 77 species of birds have been documented as hosts of the bronzed cowbird throughout its range from southern Texas and Arizona to Panama, but orioles appear to be the most frequent victims in Texas.

Bronzed cowbirds occur from the lower Rio Grande Valley northward to Eagle Pass, San Antonio and the central coast and wander as far as Houston and Galveston on rare occasions. The gregarious birds forage in small flocks through open farmlands and thickets for the insects and seeds that make up their diet, and they frequently prowl the lawns of suburban neighborhoods. In winter, they may join the mixed blackbird flocks that swirl across the prairies like clouds of windblown smoke.

The genus name of the cowbirds, *Molothrus*, was apparently a misspelling by Swainson of the Greek *molobros*, meaning "a parasite or greedy vagabond." By the rules of taxonomy, the error is perpetuated. *Aeneus* comes from the Latin for "brassy," an appropriate allusion to both the metallic gloss of the bird's plumage and its character.

ORCHARD ORIOLE

Icterus spurius

The tall *Tabebuia* tree stands alone on a cleared hillside in the western highlands of Guatemala. Local people call it *"roble,"* or "savanna oak." Covered with large, trumpet-shaped pinkish blooms, it also hosts a flock of small birds of various plumages. Some are deep chestnut or mahogany in color with black heads, wings and

Male orchard oriole.

tails, while others appear olive-green above and yellowish below with two narrow white bars across each wing. A few of the latter also sport dapper black bibs on their throats and upper breasts. They forage through the tree for both insects and nectar, picking flowers with their thin, sharply pointed beaks and dropping them to the ground like swirling pink snowflakes after nibbling at them for a moment.

The colorful birds and blossoms lend an exotic air to the pastoral scene, but these birds are not rare species exclusive to the tropics. They are orchard orioles seeking winter refuge, and soon they will stream across the Rio Grande and the Gulf to Texas and the other states east of the Rocky Mountains. They are the smallest of North American orioles at scarcely seven inches in length, and the males are also our only dark chestnut-colored orioles. The yellowish females can be distinguished by their size and by the lack of warm orange tones in

their plumage. Black bibs ornament immature males in their first spring, a transition from femalelike immature plumage to adulthood that puzzles many beginning birders.

The genus name of this and all our orioles, *Icterus*, comes from the Greek *ikteros*, or "jaundice," referring to the yellowish color. An old myth asserted that the sight of an oriole would cure jaundice, but it seems far more likely to cause severe spring fever among ardent birders as the orioles and other colorful migrants stream northward across Texas.

The other portion of the scientific name, *spurius*, stems from the Latin for "illegitimate," or "spurious." According to Alexander Wilson, the name resulted from an erroneous belief that the female Baltimore oriole was the male orchard oriole. Mark Catesby then called it "the bastard Baltimore," a name that stuck through the early days of American ornithology.

In Texas, the orchard oriole ranges

from the wetlands along the Louisiana border to the thickets of the Trans-Pecos and from the streamside groves of the Panhandle to the mesquite woodlands along the Rio Grande. It builds a shallow pouchlike nest woven of grasses and hung from a branch to support its four to six pale bluish white eggs marked with brown and purple. The eggs hatch in about 12 days, and both sexes feed the chicks. Once the young leave the nest in 11 to 14 days, however, the parents often divide the fledglings between them and care for each group separately until ready for their fall migration.

A frequent host of the parasitic cowbirds, orchard orioles face the threats shared by other neotropical migrants as they range southward in winter to Central and South America. Not only are they dependent on mesquite thickets and orchards in the United States, but they rely on that *Tabebuia* tree in Guatemala.

NORTHERN ORIOLE   *Icterus galbula*

George Calvert, Lord Baltimore, rose to prominence in the Court of James I and was granted land to found a colony north of the Potomac River after a similar venture in Newfoundland failed dismally. The 17th-century colonists noted that a beautiful orange-and-black bird they first called the "fiery hang-nest" wore the family colors of the lords Baltimore, and they named it "Baltimore-bird." Described scientifically by Linnaeus in 1758, the Baltimore oriole *(Icterus galbula)* later became the state bird of Maryland. It ranged across the country east of the Great Plains, from southern Canada to Texas and Georgia.

Another orange-and-black oriole was described by Swainson in 1827. Bullock's oriole *(I. bullockii)* owed its name to William Bullock (1775-1840), an English entrepreneur and naturalist who traveled widely in Mexico to collect archeological and natural-history specimens, including a number of birds new to science. Bullock's oriole nested in the western portions of the United States and Mexico and, like the Baltimore, wintered in tropical America.

Both Baltimore and Bullock's orioles disappeared from the lists of North American species in the mid-1980s, not through any natural disaster but because of an ornithological decision. The two were merged into a single species now called the northern oriole. Because the Baltimore form was named first, *Icterus galbula* remained the scientific name of the new composite species.

The two forms differ markedly in their plumage. The male "Baltimore oriole" has an entirely black hood covering its head, neck and upper back, while the "Bullock's oriole" has a black crown and throat and an orange face with a black eyeline. Large white patches adorn its wings. The female "Baltimore" is olive above and dull orange below, often with black markings on the head. Its western counterpart is grayer on the upperparts and has a yellow breast and whitish belly.

These two denizens of open woodlands and riverside groves remained on opposite sides of the treeless Great Plains, reproductively isolated by a lack of suitable habitat. As settlers planted farm groves and shelterbelts, however, the two forms expanded into overlapping territories and began to interbreed. For the most part, there seems to be little preferential mating with birds of the same form, and hybrids with varying combinations of the two typical patterns occur frequently in the areas of overlap. Thus the recent literature considers them to be a single species.

The eastern form, the "Baltimore oriole," migrates through the eastern half of Texas and remains to nest sparingly along the eastern edge and

This male northern ("Baltimore") oriole is just attaining full breeding plumage.

through North Texas to the Panhandle. "Bullock's oriole" breeds in the western half of the state and occurs as an uncommon migrant farther east. Warren Pulich, in *The Birds of North Central Texas*, documents the nesting of both forms in that region as well as a number of hybrids in Dallas, Parker and Tarrant counties. The presence of mesquite favors the distribution of the western "Bullock's oriole," Pulich notes, while cottonwoods favor the eastern "Baltimore oriole."

The colorful northern oriole is considered one of the most accomplished of our avian architects. It constructs an elaborately woven hanging pouch and suspends it from the tip of a high branch, where it swings freely in the breeze. The female does the major portion of the building and incubates her four or five eggs, but the male joins in the care and feeding of their young. Proclaiming his territory from the treetops, the male sings a highly variable but musical array of rich, piping notes which ornithologist Alexander Wilson thought had "the pleasing tranquility of a careless ploughboy, whistling merely for his own amusement." Modern field guides note the frequent inclusion of the phrase *hew-li*, but Henry Thoreau heard in the oriole's whistle, *Eat it, Potter, eat it!*

An Altamira oriole samples a cup of sugar water.

ALTAMIRA ORIOLE

Icterus gularis

At ten inches in length, this beautiful orange-and-black bird is the largest of the Texas orioles. Formerly known as Lichtenstein's oriole, it ranges from the lower Rio Grande Valley southward to Nicaragua. Although it occupies only the southern tip of the state, it can readily be found in such birding "hot spots" as Santa Ana National Wildlife Refuge and Bentsen–Rio Grande State Park. It remains one of the prizes that birders come from across the continent to see, for it can be found nowhere else north of Mexico.

Unlike most other orioles and their blackbird relatives, the sexes of the Altamira oriole look alike. A bright fiery orange, they have black throats, upper backs, wings and tails. The upper wing-bar forms a distinct orange shoulder patch, while the lower bar is whitish. Immature birds of both sexes appear yellower than the adults. Cavorting through the remnant woodlands along the Rio Grande, these flame-colored birds complement the green jays, great kiskadees and other tropical exotics that make the Valley so exciting. Their loud calls have been described as a raspy *ike-ike-ike*, while both sexes sing a medley of clear, whistled notes.

The female constructs a conspicuous hanging stocking of grasses, plant fibers and Spanish moss up to two feet long, suspending it from the high branch of a tree or even from an overhead wire. Oberholser notes that the Altamira oriole in Texas seems to prefer tepeguaje trees for nesting, although it also utilizes mesquites, willows and other species with slender, flexible terminal twigs. It usually avoids the large Texas ebony trees, whose branches are strong and stiff, because rats and other mammals can more easily reach the nest. In this secure pouch the female incubates her three or four bluish-white eggs marked with purples and browns. The male, however, frequently takes over the feeding of the young while his mate begins construction of another nest for her second brood. Much of the breeding biology of the Altamira oriole remains to be studied.

Although a frequent host of the bronzed cowbird, the Altamira oriole does not seem to have suffered as severely from the parasitism as many other species. Indeed, its numbers increased significantly in the Rio Grande Valley from the 1950s into the 1970s, according to Oberholser. It was a rare resident in 1951, when the first active nest was discovered, but it increased steadily over the next decades. Perhaps, Oberholser suggested, this big and aggressive oriole is more capable of defending itself against the cowbird than such smaller birds as the orchard, northern and hooded orioles.

The hooded oriole (*Icterus cucullatus*) resembles the Altamira but is smaller, at eight inches in length, and lacks the distinct orange shoulder patches. It also occurs through the Rio Grande Valley but ranges farther upriver to breed locally in Trans-Pecos Texas. It conceals its pouchlike nest in a yucca or mass of Spanish moss or under old palm fronds.

Two other Texas orioles wear yellow-and-black rather than orange-and-black plumage as adults. Audubon's oriole (*I. graduacauda*), formerly called the black-headed oriole, is an uncommon resident of deep South Texas. Its yellow body (including the diagnostic yellow back) contrasts with its black head, wings and tail. Scott's oriole (*I. parisorum*) is a smaller, lemon-yellow bird with a black head, back, wings and tail. A summer resident of the southwestern states, it nests locally in Trans-Pecos Texas and wanders occasionally eastward.

EASTERN MEADOWLARK   *Sturnella magna*
WESTERN MEADOWLARK   *Sturnella neglecta*

Alexander Wilson wrote of the meadowlark in his *American Ornithology* in 1828, "Though this well-known species cannot boast the powers of song which distinguish that 'harbinger of day,' the Sky Lark of Europe, yet in richness of plumage, as well as in sweetness of voice (as far as his few notes extend), he stands eminently its superior."

Certainly most people recognize the lovely meadowlark and delight in its crystal notes, but the distinction between the two species that inhabit our continent is not a simple one. Wilson's praise was directed solely at the eastern meadowlark; its western counterpart was not described until 1844. In addition, several races of the eastern meadowlark vary significantly among themselves. Most field guides note that the two species cannot be safely distinguished in the field except by song.

The clear, whistled song of the eastern meadowlark is a simple *see-you see-yeeer*, sometimes written as *tee-yah tee-yair* or *spring is here*. The high-pitched, buzzy call note, *drzzt*, is also distinctive. The western meadowlark sings a more complex and variable series of five to ten bubbling, flutelike notes, and its call note is a low, emphatic *chuck*. Both songs can be heard across much of Texas, and once learned, they prove the key to meadowlark identification.

The generic meadowlark has a black V-shaped breast band against yellow underparts. That band is sharply defined in breeding plumage but duller and more diffuse in the fall and winter. The dark brown feathers of the upperparts are lighter along the edges to give a streaked appearance. Prominent stripes adorn the head. In flight, white outer feathers flash in the short, stubby tail.

The eastern meadowlark, as its name implies, ranges from southeastern Canada through the eastern half of the country and on through the tropics to Brazil. It is a year-round resident in the eastern half of Texas, westward to the Panhandle and Austin, while another race of the species inhabits the Trans-Pecos. In winter, when they withdraw from the northern portions of their range, flocks of eastern meadowlarks roam across most of the state.

The western meadowlark breeds through the western portions of the continent from Canada to Mexico, a range that includes the Panhandle, the Staked Plains and Trans-Pecos Texas. It, too, wanders in winter across the state, although it is rare along the eastern edge.

Both meadowlark species appear to be expanding their ranges, and the area of overlap is large and confusing. While newer publications summarize plumage differences and offer tips for identification, the songs remain the greatest help in the field. Those vocal clues apparently aid the birds as well, for the number of hybrids is small.

An inhabitant of fields and open prairies, the meadowlark conceals its nest on the ground among the long grasses and weeds. The saucer of grass is partially covered by a woven dome, with the entrance on the side. So perfect is the camouflage of the nest and its three to five brown-spotted eggs, and of the incubating bird, that they are almost impossible to find. The female incubates alone and feeds her hatchling young; however, as they grow, she begins preparations for a second brood. When she is ready to incubate again in another nest, the male may take over the care of the half-grown chicks. Farmers welcome these "field larks" for the insects and weed seeds they destroy, but the mowing of hayfields during the nesting season takes a heavy toll.

In 1844 Audubon wrote of the "curious notes" uttered by meadowlarks along the upper Missouri River. Members of the Lewis and Clark Expedition had discovered the difference, but no one had paid the "least notice" since that time. Consequently, Audubon named the western meadowlark *Sturnella neglecta*. The species is neglected no longer, for Kansas, Montana, Nebraska, North Dakota, Oregon and Wyoming all claim the colorful, cheerful western meadowlark as their official state bird.

A western meadowlark welcomes spring.

GROSBEAKS AND BUNTINGS (Emberizidae: Subfamily Cardinalinae)

The heavy-billed grosbeaks and the buntings now constitute a strictly New World branch of the very large and complex emberizine family. They were formerly combined with the sparrows and the finches in the family Fringillidae, but those groups have recently been rearranged to reflect new hypotheses about avian origins and relationships. All have the stout, conical bills suitable for cracking seeds. Most of the grosbeaks and buntings are colorful species, the males of which are more brightly plumaged than the females.

NORTHERN CARDINAL
Cardinalis cardinalis

A strange noise awakened me at day-break one spring morning in my campsite at Lake Corpus Christi State Park. I listened for a moment and heard it again, a little flutter and then a "thump" against the side of my van, repeated over and over again. Rousing myself to peer out, I discovered a male cardinal fighting an imagined opponent in the rearview mirror. Perching on the window sill, he would look in the mirror and then attack, hitting his reflected image and landing atop the mirror. Hoping for a few more moments of sleep, I reached out and pulled a canvas bag over the offending mirror, but the noise soon resumed. The cardinal had found another rival on the opposite side of the van.

Few birds defend their territories more vigorously than does the northern cardinal. The female was probably ensconced nearby, quietly incubating as her mate attempted to drive off the persistent intruders. That goal achieved, he took up his post in the top of a tree, whistling his loud, liquid song, *what-cheer cheer cheer.*

The monogamous cardinals remain together throughout the year, and both sexes sing forcefully, especially as they establish their territory and before the female begins to nest. She does most of the incubating of her three or four spotted eggs, while the male brings her tasty tidbits as he did during their ritual courtship feed-

ing. The eggs hatch in 12 or 13 days, and both sexes then feed the young that fledge about 10 or 11 days later. The male may also take over the care of the brood while his mate incubates a second clutch. The young consume primarily high-protein insects; adults eat seeds and berries as well.

Cardinals in Texas nest two or even three times a year, and captive birds have lived as long as 22 years. The present longevity record in the wild, established from banding records, is more than 15 years, an unusually old age for so small a bird.

The familiar "redbird" occurs as a year-round resident throughout the state, although it is less abundant and more local in West Texas and the Panhandle. It also ranges throughout the eastern half of the country, from southern Ontario to the Gulf of Mexico, and through the Southwest and Mexico. Once rare in the northern states, it has expanded its range during the 20th century, perhaps because of abundant food supplies at winter feeders.

The male northern cardinal is red with a heavy, conical reddish bill and a black face. No other all-red bird has a conspicuous crest. The female also displays the crest but is buffy brown with tinges of red on the head, wings and tail. The name, of course, comes from the color worn by the cardinals of the Roman Catholic Church. They, in turn, took their title from the Latin *cardinalis* meaning "important," or "that on which something depends," from *cardo*, or "hinge."

Audubon wrote of the colorful cardinal: "In richness of plumage, elegance of motion, and strength of song, this species surpasses all its kindred in the United States." Few would argue his selection, and seven states—Illinois, Indiana, Kentucky, North Carolina, Ohio, Virginia and West Virginia—have chosen the northern cardinal as their official state bird.

This male northern cardinal (opposite) repeatedly attacked his image in the mirror. Slender crest and yellow bill help distinguish the pyrrhuloxia (above right).

PYRRHULOXIA   *Cardinalis sinuatus*

The clear, whistled call, *what-cheer what-cheer,* is much like that of a cardinal, yet it seems slightly thinner and reedier in tone. It provides an excuse to stop again and rest on the uphill climb from the "Window" in West Texas' Big Bend National Park. Beneath our feet the spectacular scenery falls away in a series of giant stone steps to the desert below. Ahead loom rugged peaks cloaked in gnarled pines and oaks. The whistle begins again, and we purse our lips and squeak in response. A rather drab little bird pops from a thorny thicket and flies to the very top of a tree, where it erects its tall, slender crest and peers quizzically down at the intruders to its territory.

In the sunlight, it is anything but drab. The soft gray plumage of this alert, handsome bird is suffused with red on the crest and around the eyes and beak. The red continues as a blaze down the breast and onto the thighs, a rich rose-red, seemingly splashed haphazardly without regard for plan or pattern. The key to identification lies in the bright yellow bill,

heavy and sharply hooked. The curious bird is a pyrrhuloxia, the cardinal "cousin" with the strange name, a special treat of the Desert Southwest.

First described in 1837 by Bonaparte, the ornithologist nephew of Emperor Napoleon, from a type specimen collected in western Mexico, it was given its present scientific name. Later placed in a genus of its own as *Pyrrhuloxia sinuata*, it reverted more recently to the genus *Cardinalis*, confirming its close ties to the more familiar northern cardinal. The common name has been retained, however, in spite of such other suggestions as "gray cardinal" and "bullfinch cardinal." The name, according to Gruson, comes from the Greek *pyrhinos*, or "red," and *loxos*, "crooked"—the red bird with the crooked bill.

The pyrrhuloxia occurs as a fairly common resident from south-central Arizona to western and southern Texas, ranging eastward in our state to San Antonio and south along the coast from Rockport to the Rio Grande. An inhabitant of thorny brushlands and mesquite thickets as well as desert creekbeds and woodland edges, it is essentially nonmigratory but may wander erratically in winter in search of food.

More buffy gray than the male, the female wears little or no red except for hints of color on the thighs and in the wing linings. The bill is usually a duller yellow but never pink or reddish. The yellow color and the abruptly curved mandible, often described as "parrotlike," are diagnostic, as is the tall, thin crest. When fully erected, that crest appears longer and spikier than the shaggy topknot of the cardinal.

The breeding behavior of the pyrrhuloxia resembles that of the northern cardinal, although the female apparently plays a larger role in establishing and defending a territory. A compact nest of twigs and weed stalks is lined with softer grasses and hidden in a thorny bush. The three or four grayish white eggs are heavily speckled with grays and browns. The male feeds his mate during courtship and while she sits incubating; both will then care for and feed their young.

ROSE-BREASTED GROSBEAK
Pheucticus ludovicianus

Few scenes typify April migration along the Texas coast better than a group of rose-breasted grosbeaks gorging themselves in a mulberry tree. The flashy black-and-white males sit quietly among the glossy green leaves, picking fruits with their huge bills and wolfing them down. Mulberry juice stains their faces and pale bills, matching the triangular rose-red patches on their breasts. The females are less conspicuous amidst the foliage as they, too, eat their fill. Their brown backs and lighter breasts are heavily streaked, but their massive bills and broad white eyelines mark them as grosbeaks.

The flock may remain for only a few hours or for a day or two, but then the colorful grosbeaks are off again on their journey to Canada or the northern states east of the Rocky Mountains. They do not remain to nest in Texas, for their breeding range extends southward only to Kansas, Missouri and Georgia. Their brief stop along the coast is a vital one, however, for these migrants must refuel along the route from their winter home in Mexico and Central America. These birds may well have flown nonstop across the Gulf of Mexico from the Yucatán, landing in the first grove of trees they saw to rest and feed. The scene repeats all along the coast and through East Texas in the spring and, to a lesser extent, during the autumn reversal of the migration process.

This colorful resident of the East is regarded as a member of a superspecies with the black-headed grosbeak of the West. The two form another pair of species once separated by the treeless Great Plains, but where their ranges overlap along the Platte River in central Nebraska, hybrids frequently occur. A few orni-

Male rose-breasted grosbeak.

thologists have argued for considering the two grosbeaks as forms of a single species, but that view has not been widely adopted.

Rose-breasted grosbeaks inhabit open woodlands and thickets along lakes and streams, where they feed on a variety of insects, seeds, fruits and buds. Females often feed higher in the trees than males and hover to pick insects from the foliage, thereby apportioning the food resources. Unlike most male birds adorned in bright, colorful plumage, male grosbeaks assist with the nest building and share in the incubation of the eggs. They even sing loudly while sitting on the nest, making no attempt to keep the nest site hidden.

A common cowbird host, the rose-breasted grosbeak also faces hazards on its long migration flights and in the depletion of suitable habitat at both ends of the route. It is a popular cage bird in its winter range in tropical America because of its colorful plumage and melodious, robinlike song. Fortunately, such practices are illegal in the United States, where all native wild birds are protected by law.

A male black-headed grosbeak accepts a handout of bread crumbs in the Davis Mountains.

BLACK-HEADED GROSBEAK

Pheucticus melanocephalus

The melody drifts down from a gnarled Emory oak in my campsite at Davis Mountains State Park in far West Texas. Startled by the unexpected dinner music, I look up from the picnic table to discover a male black-headed grosbeak sitting on a nest of twigs. He seems unperturbed by my presence and continues to sing. It is a lilting, robinlike song, but more fluid and mellow in its phrasing.

I am surprised by the song, for it seems unusual for a bird to sing while incubating, thus revealing the position of the nest to potential predators. More often the female sits quietly alone, especially when her mate wears brightly colored plumage less suitable as camouflage. Male and female black-headed grosbeaks, however, share equally in the incubation chores, and both sing frequently on the nest.

The male has bright rusty underparts and an all-black head; his black-and-white wings are boldly marked. His mate is brown above and rich cinnamon-buff below, with less streaking on the breast than the similar female rose-breasted grosbeak. Her prominent wing-bars and facial stripes and her massive, seed-cracking bill identify her as a grosbeak.

A summer resident of the American West, from southwestern Canada through Mexico, the black-headed grosbeak migrates through western Texas and the Panhandle and remains to breed in the mountain woodlands of the Trans-Pecos. There it builds its twiggy saucer-shaped nest in a tree or bush and lines it with finer grasses and plant fibers. The three or four pale greenish or bluish eggs are marked with brown and purple. They hatch in about 13 days, and the young leave the nest some 12 days later. The adults feed their nestlings primarily on insects but include seeds and fruit in their own diets.

The term grosbeak enters our vocabulary from the French *gros bec,* or "large beak." However, the scientific name of the genus that contains both the black-headed and rose-breasted grosbeaks presents a tougher problem in etymology. Edward Gruson, in his *Words for Birds,* writes that *Pheucticus* stems from the Greek for "shy or evasive" and notes that the choice was "not especially illuminating." Ernest Choate in *The Dictionary of American Bird Names,* however, suggests the name was probably coined from the Greek *phycticos,* "painted with cosmetics," as if the male's breast were rouged. *Melanocephalus* is simpler; it means "black-headed" in Greek.

Blue Grosbeak   *Guiraca caerulea*

Although smaller than the other grosbeaks, the seven-inch blue grosbeak is larger than the buntings with which it often associates in migration. The breeding male is deep blue with two prominent rusty wing-bars, while the brown female has a tinge of blue on the rump and also displays two buffy bars on its darker wings. Those wing-bars, their larger size, and their more massive bills separate both sexes of the blue grosbeak from the similarly colored indigo bunting.

As with other blue birds, the color is produced not by pigments, as are reds or yellows, but by the scattering of the light by small particles in the feathers. Unlike the iridescent structural colors that are dependent on the angle of the light, however, the shorter wavelengths of the blue light are reflected in all directions and appear blue at any angle.

Blue grosbeaks occur as migrants and nesting summer residents throughout virtually all of Texas. They breed across the U.S. from California to New Jersey and southward as far as Costa Rica. The northern portion of the population retreats into Mexico and Central America for the winter.

Reaching Texas borders in April, blue grosbeaks fan out across the state, seeking their preferred habitats of tangled brush and brambles in overgrown fields, brushy roadsides and streamside woodlands. Although they can be secretive while nesting, the males often sing from high wires or exposed limbs. The warbling song is a rich series of rising and falling phrases, and the loud *chink* call note is also distinctive.

The nest is a loose and flimsy cup of twigs, bark and stems lined with grasses, hair and finer plant fibers. Placed in a bush or low tree, it often includes snakeskins, paper or dried leaves woven into the outer structure. The three to five pale bluish white eggs hatch after about 12 days of incubation by the female alone, and both parents feed the young that are ready to leave the nest within 10 or 11 days. The helpless, altricial babies consume primarily insects; seeds and fruits are added to the diet later.

Both sexes undergo a complete postnuptial molt after the nesting season. The autumn male is then tinged with brown on the head and back. It attains full breeding plumage in the spring not by another molt but by the gradual wearing away of the brown feather tips to reveal the blue bases underneath.

A young male blue grosbeak begins to get his first nuptial plumage.

INDIGO BUNTING

Passerina cyanea

The irrepressible male indigo bunting sings throughout the summer.

The weedy field seems at first to be filled with bright blue flowers gently moving in the breeze. Then some of those flowers take flight to perch on a nearby fence, while others climb the stems of tall grasses and weeds to eat the seeds still hanging there. A flock of indigo buntings has moved in off the Gulf in spring migration and settled into a coastal field to rest and feed. A closer view reveals the less striking brown females too, and a few painted buntings and orchard orioles have joined the group. Together they provide a moving rainbow tapestry across the bright green field.

In its spring finery the male indigo bunting is a deep, almost electric blue, while the female is dull brown above and buffy below, her breast faintly and diffusely streaked. Young males just achieving adult plumage wear patchwork brown and blue. Scarcely more than five inches long, both sexes' smaller size and lack of prominent wing-bars distinguish them from blue grosbeaks. Their sparrow-like bills are also smaller and more delicate.

Indigo buntings migrate across most of Texas, although they are most abundant along the coast and casual in the Trans-Pecos. They then fan out across the eastern portions of the country, from the Gulf States to the Canadian border. Some remain to breed in northern and eastern Texas, westward to the Panhandle, Fort Worth and Kerrville and southward to San Antonio and the upper coast.

Mated pairs seek out brushy pastures and woodland edges in which to nest. While the female builds her cup of dried grasses, leaves and stems in the crotch of a bush, sometimes ornamenting it with a cast-off snakeskin, the male defends his territory with song. Each individual has his own signature score, but the melody is usually a varied series of high-pitched phrases, most of them paired. Oberholser describes it as: *sweet-sweet, swee-swee, here-here, see it-see it.* Long after most birds have ceased singing for the season, the indigo bunting continues, frequently well into August.

Her clutch of three or four pale blue eggs completed, the quiet, more somber female settles down to incubate in secrecy. A frequent victim of parasitic cowbirds, she sometimes constructs a new floor in the nest to bury the intruder's eggs and prevent them from hatching. The naked, altricial bunting babies hatch in 12 or 13 days. Growing rapidly on a diet of insects, they leave the nest about ten days later. The female then prepares for a second brood. The role of the male varies greatly, but most take only a minor part in feeding the young. As fall approaches, seeds and berries become major items in their diet, and the adults undergo a complete postnuptial molt. Brown and buff feather edgings then obscure the male's bright blue plumage, but hints of color usually remain in the wings and tail.

In recent years, the indigo bunting has expanded its range westward across Nebraska and Kansas and into the southwestern states. There it shares its territory with the lazuli bunting *(Passerina amoena),* a western sibling species. In those areas of contact, according to Ehrlich, Dobkin and Wheye, an estimated one-third of indigo and lazuli buntings hybridize. However, the hybrids appear to have reduced vitality, and the two are thus considered sufficiently distinct to be regarded as separate species.

The male lazuli bunting has a turquoise-blue head and upperparts, a broad cinnamon band across the breast and down the sides, and a white belly and wing-bars. The female is brownish with more pronounced light wing-bars than the female indigo. Lazuli buntings migrate through western Texas and remain to nest occasionally in the Panhandle.

PAINTED BUNTING   *Passerina ciris*

If indeed, as Emerson writes in *The Rhodora,* "Beauty is its own excuse for being," the painted bunting requires no further justification for its existence. Roger Tory Peterson calls the tiny gem "the most gaudily colored American bird." To Spanish-speaking settlers, this resident of the southeastern states and adjacent Mexico was the *mariposa pintada,* the "painted butterfly." French colonists called it *nonpareil,* "without equal."

There are few who do not gasp in surprise and delight on seeing their first male painted bunting. Its head is a deep indigo blue; its back, a bright lime green. The underparts, the rump, and a distinct eye-ring are flaming red. Unlike many other colorful birds that molt to drabber plumage in the fall, the *nonpareil* retains his courtship attire throughout the year, as if too proud to give it up. The female adopts a more subtle plumage befitting her shy demeanor. She is green above and paler yellowish green below, without any wing-bars or streaking, the only green finch within our area.

The painted bunting arrives in Texas in April and nests across most of the state except for the northern Panhandle. It departs again in October or November for its winter home in Mexico and Central America. Males select their territories in brushy thickets and streamside woodlands and claim them with their rapid, warbling songs. They are pugnacious, animated little birds, and they defend their territories fervently, sometimes to the point of fierce and bloody fights with rivals.

Females, meanwhile, incubate their three or four speckled eggs in well-woven cups of grasses and plant stems, usually from three to six feet above the ground in sheltering bushes. The babies hatch in 11 or 12 days and leave the nest two weeks later. Once they have fledged, they subsist primarily on a diet of seeds.

Because of its great beauty, cheery song and easily satisfied food requirements, the painted bunting was once a popular cage bird in the South. Capturing or possessing native birds is now illegal in the United States, but such practices continue south of the border. This unfortunate trade in wild birds presents a major threat to species already suffering from habitat destruction.

Another colorful bunting ranges from southern Texas and Arizona southward through Mexico. The varied bunting (*Passerina versicolor*) spends the summer in Trans-Pecos Texas and along the Rio Grande, occasionally reaching the lower Valley and the coast. Most frequently sighted in the Big Bend region, the male has a purple body, a blue head and rump, and a bright red patch on the nape. At a distance or in poor light, however, it appears almost black. The female resembles others of its genus, but its plain brown plumage has no trace of wing-bars or streaking on the breast.

Few birds can match the colorful plumage of the male painted bunting.

DICKCISSEL

Spiza americana

Perched upright on a fence post, black bib outlined against his bright yellow breast, the little bird resembles a meadowlark. He is much smaller, however, no larger than a house sparrow, and bears distinctive chestnut shoulder patches and yellow eyebrows on a grayish head. Then, as if to aid the bewildered birder, he throws back his head and begins loudly to sing his name, *dick-dick-ciss-ciss-cissel*, over and over again. Identity suitably established, the charming dickcissel flies up with a comical "electric-buzzer" call, *bzrrrrt*, and drops back into the prairie grass.

Nearby, his mate incubates her four blue eggs in a well-hidden cup of grasses on the ground or in a low bush. She lacks the black bib of the male and strongly resembles a female house sparrow; however, the yellowish breast and bolder light stripe above the eye confirm her identity. She incubates her eggs alone and will receive no help with her hungry young. Male dickcissels are polygynous and pay little heed to their nesting mates, except to defend their territories.

Dickcissels nest throughout the eastern two-thirds of Texas and in the northern Panhandle, arriving in April from their winter homes in the tropics and remaining until October. They are birds of the open prairies, occupying weedy meadows and grainfields across the midsection of the country, from western Montana and southern Ontario to Texas and Louisiana. Extremely gregarious, especially during migration, they wander in large flocks and frequently turn up far from their normal range. Local populations may vary greatly from year to year.

The dickcissel's erratic movements make it difficult to assess its numbers, but the species has been on the Audubon Society's Blue List as needing special concern. The increasing cowbird population poses a threat, for the dickcissel is a frequent host of that unpopular brood parasite. Suitable habitat is steadily declining over its wintering range from Mexico to northern South America, and mowers and farm machinery take a heavy toll of eggs and young on the summer nesting grounds.

While his mate nests in the grass nearby, a male dickcissel lays vocal claim to the surrounding territory.

SPARROWS AND THEIR ALLIES (Emberizidae: Subfamily Emberizinae)

The emberizines occur primarily in the Americas, although a number of Old World buntings are also included in the subfamily. The term bunting is not a precise one and is used not only for the colorful birds of the genus *Passerina*, which have been treated previously in this book, but for such species as the lark bunting, snow bunting, and several European birds that are closely related to our sparrows. Other members of the Emberizinae include the towhees, juncos, longspurs, seedeaters, grassquits and a variety of disparate "finches." Most are ground-dwelling birds with strong legs and feet. Their bills are cone-shaped, combining the sturdiness for cracking seeds with the dexterity for grasping insects and other small items. Older references included all of these in the Fringillidae, a family now reserved for the Old World finches and a few of their relatives that have infiltrated America.

On hearing the term "sparrow," most nonbirders think of the ubiquitous house sparrow, a species introduced to this continent from Europe. However, it belongs to a group of Old World sparrows now placed in the family Passeridae. Our true native sparrows are delightful songbirds of the fields and forests. Some are colorful and distinctively marked, while others appear almost identical to one another. Identification of the smaller, more secretive sparrows presents one of the most difficult problems in birding.

The Texas checklist contains more than 40 species of sparrows and other emberizines. Those presented here include representative examples of the group and those most frequently encountered in the field.

Rusty cap and black "whiskers" distinguish the rufous-crowned sparrow (above). A male rufous-sided towhee (right) forages through fallen leaves.

RUFOUS-SIDED TOWHEE

Pipilo erythrophthalmus

From deep in the thicket comes a loud rustling and thrashing of dry leaves as if from some large animal. The sound continues and draws slowly closer, engendering a vague uneasiness at its approach. Then, from beneath a bush, a small bird emerges. About the size of a cardinal, it has a black head and back, white underparts, and bright chestnut sides. Rummaging through the litter, it scratches with both feet together, moving forward with short hops and kicking leaves furiously in all directions. Occasionally it stops and cocks its head to focus on an insect or spider thus exposed. Its beady red eyes seek out every edible invertebrate, seed and berry on the forest floor. Appetite sated, it darts off through the brush with a flash of white in its wings and tail. Its departing call is a sharp, rising *tow-whee, tow-whee.*

This form of the rufous-sided towhee breeds across the eastern half of the United States, east of the Great Plains. The male has a solid black head and back; his mate is dusky brown above. West of the Great Plains, the towhee is spotted with white on its dark back and has two white wing-bars. It was once regarded as a separate species, but mixed forms occur frequently where the two ranges overlap. Since 1957 the "red-eyed towhee" of the East and the "spotted towhee" of the West have been regarded as a single species now called the rufous-sided towhee.

Both forms are common in Texas in the winter, when they withdraw from the northern portions of their ranges. As might be expected, the plain-backed towhee occurs most frequently in the eastern half of the state; the spotted form, in the West. However, they tend to wander widely, and some overlap occurs. The latter also remains through the summer to nest in the higher mountains of Trans-Pecos Texas. It can be heard along rocky forest trails, singing its whining, buzzy trill, *chee-eeee.* It conceals its cuplike nest on the ground in dense undergrowth or in a low, sheltering shrub.

The eastern form normally occurs in Texas only as a winter resident. Oberholser reported one nest with eggs in the northeastern corner of the state, but the full extent of its presence as a nesting bird must await conclusion of the five-year project leading to a comprehensive breeding-bird atlas for Texas. Vocalizations by the eastern birds include a distinctive song usually described as *drink-your-tea-ee-ee* and calls of *tow-whee* or *chee-wink.* Many easterners, in fact, have long called the towhee "chewink."

The name *Pipilo,* the genus of the towhees, stems from the Latin *pipo,* "to chirp." *Erythrophthalmus,* while an imposing construction, simply means "red-eyed" in Greek. The eyes of the rufous-sided towhee are indeed bright ruby red, except for an isolated race in Florida that has white eyes.

CANYON TOWHEE   *Pipilo fuscus*

Until 1989, the canyon towhee was known as the brown towhee. Many authors noted differences in plumage, voice and behavior between a form of the brown towhee found through the Desert Southwest and one occurring on the Pacific Coast. Oberholser's *The Bird Life of Texas,* as edited by Edgar Kincaid, noted in 1974 that birds from Arizona to western Texas were distinctive and should more appropriately be called canyon towhees. Committees move with glacial slowness, however, and it was not until the 37th supplement to the AOU's *Check-list of North American Birds* that the two were officially separated. Because the canyon form was described by Swainson in 1827 as *Pipilo fuscus,* a dozen years before a description of the Pacific form, the canyon towhee retained the scientific name already in use for the brown towhee. The newly named California towhee became *P. crissalis.*

The canyon towhee is grayish brown above and slightly paler below.

Canyon towhees.

The crown and undertail coverts display a rusty hue, while the buffy throat is lightly bordered with diffuse dark streaks. Some individuals show a dark spot in the center of the breast. This rather drab bird, notes Peterson, "suggests a very plain overgrown sparrow."

It inhabits rocky, brushy hillsides and wooded canyons in Trans-Pecos Texas and across the western portions of the Edwards Plateau. A common year-round resident of those regions, the canyon towhee visits campsites and picnic areas in Big Bend, the Davis Mountains and some of the other western parks, perching trustingly on the tables and searching for crumbs underfoot. What it lacks in colorful plumage, it makes up for with tameness and charm. Its song is a mellow, chipping trill; its sharp call note, a metallic *chink*.

The female incubates her three or four brown-spotted eggs in a bulky nest of grasses and plant stems located in a thorny bush or low tree. They hatch in about 11 days, and the young leave the nest eight days later. Fed by both parents, they may be driven from the territory when the adults are ready to start a second brood. They then disperse across the arid hillsides, consuming a varied diet of seeds, insects and berries and drinking the morning dew from the grasses when no other water is available.

The green-tailed towhee (*P. chlorurus*) shares portions of the canyon towhee's habitat during the winter months. It breeds on the mountains and high plateaus of the western states and wanders through the western half of Texas, even reaching the coast on rare occasions. Somewhat smaller and slimmer than the canyon towhee, it has olive-green upperparts and a gray breast highlighted by a rusty cap and white throat.

LARK BUNTING
Calamospiza melanocorys

A large flock of sparrowlike birds rolls across a grassy pasture near Marathon in far West Texas on an early November afternoon. It moves like a giant wheel, those at the rear of the flock rising to fly ahead and drop down again, then yielding their temporary leadership to others as they stop to forage. Scores of the small birds line the fences; others perch on scattered yuccas and acacias that dot the fields. They are grayish brown above and white below, heavily streaked with brown. Their heavy bills suggest they are sparrows or finches, but many flash white or buffy patches in their wings as they mill about. The wing-patches identify them as lark buntings, although they otherwise resemble several species of sparrows that share their winter habitat.

Later in the season, as spring approaches, some of the birds begin to change. The males become mottled and blotched with black as they molt from their femalelike winter plumage. Eventually they will be entirely black, marked only with large white patches on the wings and beneath the tip of the tail. By then the gregarious lark buntings will be moving northward toward their breeding grounds on the Great Plains. Some eventually reach the prairie provinces of southern Canada; others will stop in Montana, the Dakotas, Nebraska or Kansas. Many inhabit the plains of eastern Colorado, where *melanocorys*, the "black lark," was chosen as the state bird. And a few will fly no farther than the Texas Panhandle or high plains, remaining there to nest on the dry grasslands.

Males establish their territories and begin their skylarking courtship flights, rising high into the air and fluttering down on beating wings,

In his formal breeding plumage, the male lark bunting is unmistakable.

singing their rich and varied melodies filled with whistles and trills. They perch on the fence posts to display their striking black-and-white garb, enticing arriving females to join them for the season.

The nest is a grassy cup in a shallow depression on the ground, sheltered and camouflaged by overhanging grass. The four or five pale blue eggs hatch in 11 or 12 days, and both parents feed the ravenous young that grow rapidly and leave the nest nine days later. Females arriving late on the breeding grounds sometimes mate polygynously with males already involved, but they must then incubate their eggs and feed their young alone. Insects, especially grasshoppers, make up as much as 80 percent of the lark buntings' diet during the breeding season. Later the birds will shift to seeds of the abundant weeds and grasses.

In autumn the flocks assemble and drift southward once again, reaching the southwestern states and Mexico. Many will remain to winter across the western half of Texas and in the fields along the Rio Grande.

Four species of longspurs also assemble in large flocks and invade the fields and prairies of our state in winter. The chestnut-collared (*Calcarius ornatus*) and McCown's (*C. mccownii*) longspurs breed on the northern Great Plains; Smith's (*C. pictus*) and Lapland (*C. lapponicus*) longspurs nest on the tundra of Alaska and Canada. All are erratic in their movements but occur sporadically across northern Texas. Drab and sparrowlike in winter plumage, they can be identified by characteristic white tail patterns. Longspurs, which are members of the subfamily Emberizinae along with the lark bunting and the sparrows, take their name from extremely long claws on their hind toes.

A rufous-crowned sparrow (above right) adds a lively accent to a dramatic West Texas scene.

RUFOUS-CROWNED SPARROW *Aimophila ruficeps*

The steep, rocky hillsides and canyons of Trans-Pecos Texas and the Edwards Plateau provide ideal habitat for the rufous-crowned sparrow, which ranges through the Southwest and Mexico. Within our state, it occurs eastward as far as Fort Worth and Austin. Less elusive than many of the other sparrows, it is inquisitive and often responds to the squeaks and chips used by birders to lure their quarry into view. Its own call is a series of sharp, distinctive *dear, dear, dear* notes, and its rapid, bubbling song is described by Oberholser as *chipity-chipity-chipity*, "which stutters into a jumble."

The rufous-crowned sparrow is the most frequently seen of four *Aimophila* sparrows in Texas. Others include Bachman's sparrow (*A. aestivalis*) of the East Texas Piney Woods; Botteri's sparrow (*A. botterii*), found in the extreme southern tip of the state; and Cassin's sparrow (*A. cassinii*), of the arid grasslands in western and southern Texas. A brown, long-tailed sparrow with an unstreaked breast and no wing-bars, the rufous-crowned has a rusty cap and a dark "whisker mark" extending downward from the corner of the bill and bordering the throat.

The rufous-crowned sparrow forages on the ground and around boulders and thorny brush for the insects, seeds and young plant shoots that constitute its diet. It remains in West Texas throughout the year and builds its nest in a depression on the ground, with the rim of the grass-lined cup flush with the surface. The female lays three or four white or pale bluish white eggs, but the incubation and fledging periods and the remainder of the breeding biology have not been thoroughly investigated. Family groups often remain together after the breeding season; however, they do not congregate in winter flocks as do many of the other sparrows.

CHIPPING SPARROW *Spizella passerina*

The charming little chipping sparrow is easily identified in breeding plumage. Both sexes are brown above and clear gray below, with gray napes and bright chestnut crowns. A thin black line passes through the eye and borders a broad white eyebrow stripe. In fall and winter plumage, however, the facial marks become less distinct, and the crown bears faint dark stripes. Juvenile birds have prominent streaking on their breasts until late fall and then become more buffy underneath than the adults. The resulting winter flocks that wander throughout most of the state may thus seem a confusing blend of forms.

The chipping sparrow ranges across most of North America. It breeds from the tree line in Canada to Nicaragua, withdrawing from the northern portion of that range to winter across the southern states. Migrants occur commonly throughout Texas and remain through the winter in all but the northern Panhandle. Spring finds them breeding in the mountains of West Texas and on the Edwards Plateau, while others nest locally in the farmlands and open woodlands of East Texas.

From mid-March or April into July the males sing from their perches in the trees. The song from which the chipping sparrow takes its name is a rapid, dry chipping trill on a single pitch. Field guides usually describe the call note as a high-pitched *chip* or *seep*. Courtship complete, the female builds her nest in a bush or low tree, preferably lining the small cup of grasses and plant fibers with hair, an instinct so strong that sparrows have been seen pulling hair from horses' tails. If hair is unavailable, fine grasses and rootlets serve to cushion the three to five bluish green eggs speckled with brown. The female incubates alone, although her mate may feed her on the nest. When the eggs hatch some 11 to 14 days later, both work to feed the helpless, altricial chicks. Fledglings leave the nest in about ten days, and the pair soon begins another brood.

In some field studies, males mated with a second female as well. They began to advertise during the first days of incubation by their mates, when they had little else to do. Very few females were still unattached, however, and only about five percent of the males succeeded in establishing a second family.

The chipping sparrow is the most abundant and widespread of the small *Spizella* sparrows, a name coined as a Latinized diminutive of the Greek *spiza*, or "finch." Five other species—the clay-colored *(S. pallida)*, Brewer's *(S. breweri)*, field *(S. pusilla)*, black-chinned *(S. atrogularis)* and American tree *(S. arborea)* sparrows —occur in portions of Texas either as winter visitors or as less common breeding residents.

VESPER SPARROW

Pooecetes gramineus

Many writers and ornithologists, including John Burroughs and George Sutton, have praised the musical abilities of the vesper sparrow. Although it may sing throughout the day, it seems particularly vocal on quiet evenings, a trait for which it earned its name. The song is rich and melodious, beginning with two clear whistled notes and ending in a series of descending trills.

Unfortunately for Texans, the vesper sparrow seldom sings outside the breeding season. It nests in Canada and the northern states and migrates across most of Texas, where it remains throughout the winter in all but the northern Panhandle. Thus, Texans hear it singing only on rare occasions in the spring, before it departs for its northern nesting grounds. Oberholser lists only one definite breeding record for the state, a nest with eggs collected near San Angelo in 1885.

A fairly large sparrow at more than six inches in length, it is streaked below and has a narrow whitish eye-ring and a dark cheek patch bordered by white. Western birds that move into

A chipping sparrow has several hungry mouths to feed.

Texas tend to be paler and grayer than the brown-striped races of the East. A small chestnut patch on the shoulder is diagnostic but not always visible. In flight the vesper sparrow reveals white outer feathers in its notched tail, the most useful clue to its identity. A few other sparrows and their relatives have white in the tail, but they can easily be distinguished by facial markings and other characteristics.

The scientific name of the vesper sparrow reflects its choice of habitat. *Pooecetes* is Greek for "grass dweller," while the redundant *gramineus* means "grass-loving" in Latin. The little singer of the evening prefers dry, open grasslands and fields, where it dust-bathes on the ground and forages for its mixed diet of insects and seeds. Because it often raises its broods in cultivated croplands, however, many eggs and young are destroyed by agricultural machinery. Cowbirds, too, take their toll, for the ground-nesting sparrows are some of their favorite victims.

Lark Sparrow

Chondestes grammacus

Anyone who thinks all sparrows are drab, retiring little birds has never met a lark sparrow face to face. With its harlequin head pattern and jaunty manner, this large, plump bird is one of the most striking of its tribe. Males waste no opportunity to show off their plumage for the ladies. They swagger and strut about, fluttering their wings and spreading their white-tipped tails in courtship ardor, even when they have already mated in monogamous relationships. Occasionally they do attract and mate with a second female.

The sexes look alike, for pronounced sexual dimorphism is unusual among the sparrows. Bright chestnut ear-patches and chestnut crown-stripes ornament the black-and-white face of the adult. Brown upperparts are heavily streaked; clean

White outer tail feathers of the vesper sparrow (above) are often concealed except in flight. The handsome lark sparrow (left) is one of the largest and most colorful of the sparrows.

white underparts are marked only with a black central breast spot. In flight, the long tail shows conspicuous white corners. Juvenile lark sparrows appear duller than the adults, with streaked breasts and sides; however their white-cornered tails remain distinctive.

Lark sparrows are highly gregarious and often feed in small flocks, even during the breeding season. They seem to lose their territorial instincts once incubation begins, and males may sit side by side on a fence or bush, each singing his own rich, melodious song. The melody begins with two clear notes and then breaks into a series of trills and whistles interspersed with peculiar buzzes and punctuated with brief pauses. This virtuoso performance and the habit of flying up to sing, larklike, on the wing accounts for this handsome sparrow's common name.

Relatively common west of the Mississippi River, the lark sparrow breeds from the prairies of southern Canada to Mexico. It withdraws from much of that range in winter, migrating into the southwestern states and as far south as El Salvador. Although common throughout most of Texas, lark sparrows prefer open prairies, farmlands and roadsides with scattered trees and bushes. They are infrequently found, therefore, in heavily wooded East Texas and along the upper coast. They can also be difficult to find in the treeless portions of the northern Panhandle.

The female builds her nest either on the ground or in a bush or low tree and lays four or five spotted eggs. She incubates alone for about 12 days but receives help from her mate in feeding the young. He often brings in food, while she accepts the morsels and stuffs them into gaping mouths. The young leave the nest at about ten days of age, and the family groups soon merge into larger flocks. Most common in winter in the southern portions of Texas, they nevertheless roam widely across the state. They forage on the ground for insects and seeds and line the roadside fences, showing the world just how striking and colorful sparrows can be.

BLACK-THROATED SPARROW
Amphispiza bilineata

Dawn brings a special music to the arid South Texas brush country and the harsh, parched deserts of the West. A small gray bird with a striking black-and-white face pattern flies up to the top of a cactus or yucca to herald the coming day. Throwing back his head, he begins reveille with two clear notes followed by a high-pitched, rapid trill, *cheet cheet cheeeeeeee!* It is not as melodious a song as some, but it seems to hold a special, irrepressible challenge. The rugged terrain and blazing summer heat present no threats to the black-throated sparrow. This is his preferred environment.

This handsome emberizine was once called the desert sparrow, a most appropriate appellation. It seems a shame that many of these older names are being lost in favor of what some consider more descriptive terms. Modern nomenclature is filled with assorted colors and body parts, combined in all possible permutations and combinations. We have a black-throated sparrow and a black-chinned sparrow, a white-throated sparrow and a white-crowned sparrow. The combinations continue across family lines. There are black-throated gray, black-throated green and black-throated blue

A black-throated sparrow serenades the desert dawn from an ocotillo.

warblers; black-tailed gnatcatchers, black-capped chickadees, black-chinned hummingbirds and black-billed cuckoos and magpies. Each, in itself, is descriptive, but the array of color-coordinated bits and pieces can also be confusing, especially to the beginner. True, other sparrows inhabit the arid lands, but the black-throated is most of all a desert sparrow.

As with most of the sparrows, the sexes are similar. Gray above and white below, the black-throated sparrow has a blackish, white-edged tail. A triangular black patch adorns the throat and upper breast, contrasting vividly with white eyebrow and whisker stripes. Juvenile sparrows always present problems in identification, and this is no exception. Young birds lack the adults' black throat and are finely streaked on the back and breast; however, the white eyebrow is always conspicuous. Because fall and winter sparrows frequently travel in small flocks, the association with well-marked adults also provides a useful clue.

The "desert sparrow" ranges from California and Wyoming through the Southwest to Mexico. It is a year-round resident in the western and southern portions of Texas, eastward to Austin, Beeville, Kingsville and the lower coast. It also occurs irregularly in the Panhandle and along the central coast.

Desert scrub and rocky slopes provide suitable nesting habitat, and the female builds her nest of grasses and plant fibers in a clump of cactus or a thorny bush. She lays three or four unmarked whitish eggs, but the incubation and fledging periods have not been fully studied. Most pairs probably raise two broods a year. The Texas breeding season extends from March through September, although nesting times may vary from year to year, depending on the amount of rainfall and the abundance of food. Drinking water becomes important during the hot summer months, but for much of the year this hardy desert sparrow can make do with moisture extracted from the insects, seeds and tender plant shoots it consumes.

SAVANNAH SPARROW *Passerculus sandwichensis*

The little Savannah sparrow spends the winter on the open prairies and in the marshes across virtually all of Texas. It appears from the North in late September or October and remains until April or May, one of the most abundant of the sparrows found in the fields and along the roadsides. Although it has no strong markings to separate it from all others, it can usually be identified by a combination of plumage, habitat and behavior. Several of the rarer species with which it could be confused are far more shy and secretive.

The Savannah sparrow exhibits streaked brown upperparts and pronounced dark streaking on the whitish sides and breast, sometimes with a central breast spot. The tail is short and notched; the legs are pink. Light eyebrow streaks are usually yellowish, particularly on the lores, the regions between the bill and eyes. A pale crown stripe and dark whisker marks complete the markings on the head.

Its common and scientific names illustrate the broad range of the Savannah sparrow. *Sandwichensis* comes from the species' type location at Sandwich Bay on Unalaska in the Aleutian Islands. Gmelin described it from there in 1789 as the "Sandwich bunting." Alexander Wilson discovered the same species in Savannah, Georgia, in 1811. Indeed, the Savannah sparrow breeds from the tundra of Alaska, northern Canada and Labrador southward across the northern half of the United States, withdrawing for the winter from the coldest parts

A Savannah sparrow pauses to stretch.

of that range. Other populations occur locally in the West, as far south as Mexico and Guatemala. As might be expected for a bird with such an enormously wide and fragmented range, numerous subspecies have also been described. They vary greatly in size and color from region to region. One, the "Ipswich sparrow," breeds only on Sable Island off Nova Scotia and occurs in winter along the Atlantic Coast. Larger and paler than most other forms, it was long regarded as a distinct species.

Savannah sparrows are less gregarious than most others on their wintering grounds in Texas. Although they may occur in large numbers in a field, they remain scattered, wandering through the grass in search of seeds and insects or perching on the fences alone or in small, isolated groups. Their calls are versions of a soft *tsip*, while their song has been translated by several authors as a lispy *tsit-tsit-tsit, tseeee-tsaaay*. Texans hear the song infrequently, however, for Savannah sparrows depart for the northern latitudes before they begin to sing in earnest in the spring.

SONG SPARROW
Melospiza melodia

The large, heavily streaked song sparrow ranges throughout Texas from October until April. Unfortunately, however, it does not stay to breed within the state, and Texas residents seldom hear the songs of what one writer called the "unchallenged virtuoso of the sparrow clan." Named *melodia* for its voice, the song sparrow begins with three or four clear, whistled notes and follows with a rapid trill and other buzzy phrases. Thoreau claimed to hear, *Maids! Maids! Maids! Hang up your tea-kettle-ettle-ettle!* Whatever the avian translation, the male usually launches into several different versions of the basic melody within a few minutes and may try hundreds of them in a single day. Even young fledglings learn songs from the adults and soon begin improvising on the theme.

The song sparrow has a long, rounded tail, and its grayish brown upperparts are streaked with black. Heavy streaking on the light sides and breast merges into a prominent central breast spot. Broad grayish eyebrows and dark whisker marks bordering the white throat also aid identification.

Ornithologists have described at least 31 subspecies of *Melospiza melodia,* making it the most variable of all U.S. birds. The species breeds from Alaska and Canada through the western states to Mexico and through the eastern states to the mountains of Georgia. Partially migratory, it ranges in winter from the Canadian border to the Gulf of Mexico and into tropical America. The subspecies vary geographically in size, bill shape, coloration and the amount of streaking on both breast and back. Those inhabiting the Desert Southwest are much smaller and paler than the dark forms nesting in Alaska. Some of the former barely reach five inches in

A central spot ornaments the streaked breast of most song sparrows.

length, while the latter may exceed seven inches. Many other birds and mammals exhibit similar trends with latitude.

Song sparrows prefer streamside thickets and brushy woodland edges, where they hunt for the insects, seeds and berries that compose their varied diet. Along coastal marshes, they also take small crustaceans and mollusks.

The song sparrow is perhaps the most frequent host of the brown-headed cowbird, a dubious honor it shares with the yellow warbler. There are indications that it may recognize the threat from this brood parasite, for song sparrows have been seen attacking cowbirds and driving them away.

LINCOLN'S SPARROW

Melospiza lincolnii

On a summer morning in 1833, near the mouth of the Natashquan River in Quebec, John James Audubon heard a sweet, liquid birdsong he did not recognize. One of his companions on the sailing trip along the Canadian coast, 21-year-old Thomas Lincoln of Maine, succeeded in finding the bird and collecting it. It proved to be a new species, the only one collected on the expedition, and Audubon named it in the young man's honor. Thus did the bird we now know as *Melospiza lincolnii* get its name, literally "Lincoln's song finch."

Breeding across Alaska and Canada and southward in the mountains of the western states, Lincoln's sparrow winters from the southern states to Guatemala. It migrates throughout Texas and remains as a very common winter resident in all but the northern Panhandle. The timid little bird has been described as a skulker "afraid of its shadow," and it seldom ventures far from the protection of brushy thickets or tangles of briars and weeds.

More numerous in Texas than the song sparrow, Lincoln's sparrow has a

distinctive buffy wash across the breast and is finely streaked on the breast and sides. The reddish brown crown bears a central gray stripe, and there is a broad gray eyebrow stripe as well. It is a smaller, slimmer bird than the song sparrow, with a grayer face and more finely streaked breast. Lincoln's sparrow also lacks that bird's prominent central breast spot.

The closely related swamp sparrow *(M. georgiana)* also winters in Texas as a migrant from Canada and the Northeast. It occurs most abundantly along the upper coast and in the eastern third of the state but wanders in smaller numbers as far as the Rio Grande and the Trans-Pecos. A dark, rust-colored sparrow, it has a reddish crown that develops a gray central stripe in winter plumage.

A bird of the thickets, Lincoln's sparrow ranges across most of Texas in the winter.

WHITE-THROATED SPARROW

Zonotrichia albicollis

Conspicuous black and white stripes on the head and a white throat make the typical adult white-throated sparrow almost unmistakable. The streaked upperparts are rusty brown; the underparts, pale gray. The portion of the white eyebrow stripe between the bill and eye is usually yellow. Immature birds have brown-and-buff-striped heads, but the basic pattern remains the same. The genus name of the white-throated sparrow and its relatives, *Zonotrichia,* comes from the Greek for "bird with bands," referring to the head stripes. *Albicollis* means "white-necked" in Latin, although only the throat is white, rather than the entire neck.

In addition to the black-and-white striped form illustrated in most books, a black-and-tan form also occurs. Recent field studies surprisingly indicate that each tends to mate with the form

WHITE-CROWNED SPARROW
Zonotrichia leucophrys

Like its white-throated relative, the adult white-crowned sparrow displays a flashy black-and-white striped head; however, it lacks the contrasting white throat and the yellow spot between the bill and eye. The bill of the white-crown is pinkish; that of the white-throat is dark. The white-crowned sparrow also appears to be a grayer brown than the rusty-backed white-throat, while its underparts are pale gray. Immatures have reddish brown and buffy stripes, but they are nevertheless recognizable by the characteristic pattern and by their large size. All of the *Zonotrichia* seem large-headed, with "puffy crowns," the feathers of which are sometimes raised to give a shaggy, semi-crested effect.

White-crowned sparrows nest across Alaska and Canada and southward through the western states to California and New Mexico. They desert the northern portions of that range in winter and migrate to the southern U.S. and Mexico. They then move into virtually all of Texas, becoming abundant in the western and central portions of the state, where they prefer open woodlands and brushy fields. White-crowns seem partial to mesquite brushlands and other arid terrain and are less common in the eastern quarter of Texas, where the white-throated sparrow is the dominant *Zonotrichia*.

Forming stable winter flocks, white-crowns show remarkable fidelity to their winter feeding territories and may return year after year. In a now-famous experiment, biologists trapped 574 white-crowned sparrows in their winter home near San Jose, California, and shipped them to the Patuxent Wildlife Research Center in Maryland. The banded birds were released in October 1962, thousands of miles from their normal migration path. The next fall, however, at least eight of the sparrows returned to San Jose.

of the opposite color. White-striped males are more aggressive than tan-striped ones, while among the females, only the white-striped ones sing. Territorial, singing white-striped males thus tend to drive off not only rival males but the white-striped females as well, and they consequently mate with the silent and submissive tan-striped females.

The pensive, leisurely whistles of the white-throated sparrow constitute one of the loveliest and most ethereal of songs. Two slow, single notes are followed by three triplet notes. New Englanders hear it as *old Sam Peabody, Peabody, Peabody,* while others might hear *pure sweet Canada, Canada, Canada.* Since the white-throat breeds across both Canada and the northeastern states, either seems appropriate.

During the winter months, white-throated sparrows descend on Texas. Some remain as far north as New England, but others migrate to the Gulf States and even into northeastern Mexico. Immature birds tend to move farther south, while adult males remain closest to their home territories. The Texas population thus contains a disproportionate number of young birds, but gaudily striped adults also occur.

These large sparrows are particularly abundant from October through April in the eastern third of the state, becoming less common farther west. Some, however, range as far as the Panhandle and Trans-Pecos. They inhabit woodland undergrowth, thickets and brushy, overgrown fields, seldom straying far from cover. They feed primarily on the ground, often scratching like towhees through fallen leaves for seeds and insects. They also consume more fruits and berries than most other sparrow species. Curious birds, they respond well to the squeaks and kissing sounds birders use to coax them into view.

At day's end, the white-throats gather in bushes and vine tangles for the night, and the thickets ring with a chorus of sharp *chink* calls until dusk. Unlike many other sparrows, white-throats also sing on their wintering grounds, particularly as spring draws near. Sometimes their efforts are tentative and halting; sometimes they break into full song. Even as darkness falls, the pure, whistled tones ring from the thickets, *old Sam Peabody, Peabody, Peabody.*

The white-throated sparrow has a distinctive facial pattern.

Similarly, white-crowned sparrows return to the thickets and brushy roadsides of Texas year after year to spend the winter. Among the most beautiful of the sparrows, they also delight us with their plaintive songs. Unlike most songbirds, they sing virtually throughout the year. The melody consists of one to three whistles followed by a buzzy trill of three notes. It is a song reminiscent of the white-throated sparrow's.

Even larger than the white-crown or white-throat is Harris' sparrow (*Z. querula*). It also arrives from northern Canada to spend the winter in north-central Texas. Common from the Oklahoma border to the Austin area, according to Oberholser, it becomes less numerous both east and west of

that region. However, it does occur sporadically in brushy thickets and fencerows even near the coast and west of the Pecos River. The adult has a striking black face and bib, while immatures show bibs of heavy black streaks across the upper breast. The seven-inch size and large pink bill also aid in identifying this biggest of the sparrows.

Although its head is striped like that of the white-throated sparrow, the white-crowned sparrow lacks the former's namesake white throat.

DARK-EYED JUNCO

Junco hyemalis

Birders' life-lists suffered greatly when the dark-eyed junco was "created" by the AOU in the 1973 supplement to its checklist. Until that time, several forms of this variable bird traveled under separate names. The "slate-colored junco" of the East, the "Oregon junco" of the West, the "gray-headed junco" of the southern Rocky Mountains, the "white-winged junco" of the Black Hills of South Dakota, and the "Guadalupe junco" from Guadalupe Island off Baja California were all regarded as separate species and were treated as such in the older books still in use by many people. Even within those former "species," various color forms had been described by Ridgway and other authors. Now all have been merged into a single species, the dark-eyed junco, distinct only from the yellow-eyed junco (*J. phaeonotus*) of Mexico and the extreme southern edge of Arizona and New Mexico.

Not all ornithologists agree with that decision, of course. Yet while the plumages differ markedly, the voices and habits of the various forms seem much alike. Intergrades also appear in the areas of breeding overlap.

Whether or not these distinctive forms deserve separate recognition constitutes an enormously complex problem. Only centuries of continued evolution will indicate the direction in which the forms are heading. Even if they cannot be listed separately in the game of ornithological golf that birders play, however, these charming birds deserve attention as fascinating entities.

The collective juncos are slightly smaller than house sparrows and display conspicuous white outer tail feathers in flight. Most have a gray head and breast contrasting sharply with a white belly. Females tend to be duller than males, and sparrowlike immatures are brownish and heavily streaked below. Peterson noted in *A Field Guide to the Birds of Texas* in 1960, when they were still considered separate species, that the forms could best be separated by consideration of the head (whether black or gray), sides (pinkish or gray), and back (rusty or gray).

Three of these forms are common winter residents in various portions of Texas. Breeding across Alaska and Canada and through the mountains of both the East and West, they shift southward in the fall. They forage in small flocks through open woodlands and thickets and become popular feeder birds in backyards across the country.

The male "slate-colored junco" has a dark gray hood and upperparts and a white belly, while the female is a duller brownish gray above. It winters virtually throughout Texas but is rare in the Trans-Pecos and in the southern tip of the state. Catesby called the slate-colored form "the snow-bird," a term still used in the East, and its plumage was said to mirror the winter season: "leaden skies above, snow below."

The male "Oregon junco" has a black hood, brown back and pinkish sides, while the hood of the female is a deep grayish brown. A less common "pink-sided" form has a paler gray head and more extensive pinkish cinnamon on the sides and underparts. The "Oregon junco" occurs in winter across the western half of Texas, ranging only rarely into East Texas and southward toward the lower Rio Grande.

The "gray-headed junco" migrates to Texas from the southern Rockies and winters in the Panhandle and Trans-Pecos, turning up only occasionally farther east. It has a pale gray head, barely darker than its grayish underparts, and a bright rufous patch on the back. A form Oberholser called the "red-backed junco" breeds sparingly in the Guadalupe Mountains, the only junco to nest in Texas.

A hardy dark-eyed junco visits an ice-covered winter rose.

OLD WORLD SPARROWS (Family Passeridae)

The well-known house sparrow found throughout the state is not related to our native sparrows. Instead, it belongs to a family of Old World birds that have shorter legs and thicker bills. The group was formerly placed in the family Ploceidae with the Old World weaver finches, but the two have now been separated.

Two species of the Passeridae have been introduced into the United States. One, the house sparrow *(Passer domesticus)*, has spread uncontrollably across the country to become a nuisance species, overrunning our towns and cities and displacing several native birds. The other, the Eurasian tree sparrow *(P. montanus)*, was introduced at St. Louis, Missouri, in 1870. Although it became established in that area and has spread locally into east-central Missouri and western Illinois, it has not proliferated like the house sparrow.

HOUSE SPARROW   *Passer domesticus*

Most of our birds are creatures of the wild, preferring to live and raise their young in undisturbed fields, forests and marshes. House sparrows, however, seldom venture far from human habitation, earning the name *domesticus.* They have developed into the street urchins of the bird world, brawling in the gutters and depending largely on human activities for food and shelter.

Also called "English sparrows," house sparrows are native to Europe, parts of Asia, and northern Africa. Ehrlich, Dobkin and Wheye speculate in *The Birder's Handbook* that they probably formed a close attachment to *Homo sapiens* shortly after people in the Middle East first settled down and began to farm. Gradually losing their migratory instincts over many generations, sparrows remained to overwinter near settlements where food was plentiful. Populations grew especially large in cities when horses and their grain-rich droppings were common in the streets.

Most sources agree that the first house sparrows were brought to America in 1850. Because the species consumed caterpillars in England, eight pairs were released in Brooklyn in an attempt to combat canker-worms. The first birds failed to survive and multiply, but 100 more were imported in 1852, the first successful introduction. Within five years, they had spread over a 25-mile radius. In 15 years, there were colonies 100 miles away.

More than a hundred cities in the United States and Canada released house sparrows in the next few years, both for insect control and for aesthetic reasons. European immigrants wanted birds to remind them of home and to rid the city's shade trees of harmful insects. According to Robin Doughty's *Wildlife and Man in Texas*, James M. Brown, a public figure in Galveston, decided the "City of Oleanders" also deserved the sparrows and imported some in the late 1860s. By 1880, their nests had clogged Galveston's water system, and the sparrows had driven away many of the native songbirds, including the aggressive mockingbird.

It was a lesson learned time and time again across the country, from Portland, Maine, and Iowa City, Iowa, to Salt Lake City, Utah. Civic authorities in Philadelphia released a thousand house sparrows from Europe in 1869; in 1883 they passed a law to encourage killing them. Many were trapped and shipped to gun clubs for live shooting contests, but the survivors only spread the species farther. Sparrow pot-pie became a favored item on many menus. By the turn of the century, there was scarcely a town or farmyard without an abundance of the six-inch tyrants. In the early 1900s, the house sparrow was perhaps the most abundant bird species in the country, although it subsequently declined slightly as automobiles replaced grain-eating horses.

The male house sparrow is easily recognized in breeding plumage by his gray crown, chestnut nape and extensive black bib. A fall molt obscures the bib with gray feather edgings that wear away through the winter to produce the next season's courtship plumage. The female is less distinctive with her brown-streaked back and light underparts. A buffy eyebrow stripe provides the best field mark. Males sing a variety of chirping, twittering notes, but they normally converse in choruses of loud *cheep* notes.

House sparrows inhabit cities, towns, farms and ranches throughout Texas. They build bulky, untidy nests of grass or hay and line them with feathers, cloth and other debris. The eaves of buildings, industrial towers, block walls and even traffic lights serve as homesites, and the sparrows also appropriate nests of other species, sometimes destroying their eggs or nestlings. Competition with such desirable species as bluebirds, purple martins and tree swallows earn them no plaudits from bird lovers across the country.

Both sexes work to construct the nest, but the female incubates her four to six speckled eggs alone. Hatching in 10 to 13 days, the help- less babies are fed by both attentive parents and leave the nest 14 to 17 days later.

House sparrows must certainly rank among the most successful colo- nizers in the world, and few inhabited corners of the globe have escaped the aggressive flocks. These street urchins are prolific, tough and smart, and they are obviously here to stay. Since their introduction to North America, they have even become differentiated geo- graphically to suit conditions, with populations varying in color and body size across their range.

House sparrows.

FINCHES (Family Fringillidae)

Purple finches and American goldfinches flock to sunflower-seed feeders.

Some books label the Fringillidae as the "Old World finches" because of the group's apparent origins. About 25 species have colonized America, but some of those also occur in Europe or have close counterparts in that region. They are colorful, seed-eating birds with a peculiar undulating flight.

In addition to the species we call finches, the family includes the siskins, crossbills, redpolls and the evening and pine grosbeaks. In spite of their name, the latter two differ in anatomy and behavior from the other grosbeaks of the family Emberizidae, sharing only the large seed-cracking bill.

Many of the fringillids nest in the conifer forests of the far North or at high altitudes in the mountains of the West, and some of those do not reach Texas regularly. Flocks of the "winter finches" move southward erratically in the fall in response to dwindling food supplies rather than to cold weather. Their range thus changes from year to year. One winter they may be abundant in northern or eastern Texas, for example; the next year they may not appear at all. When present, they readily visit backyard feeders, sometimes remaining there throughout the season.

PURPLE FINCH *Carpodacus purpureus*

In spite of its name, the adult male purple finch is more wine-red than purple, "like a sparrow dipped in raspberry juice," as one author describes it. The color appears brightest on the head, upper breast and rump. The back is streaked, while the tail is strongly notched. The female resembles a chunky, heavily streaked sparrow, but her large, stout bill shows her to be a finch. She has a whitish breast with brown streaks and a prominent light eyebrow stripe above a dark cheek patch. Immature birds resemble the female, and young males do not gain adult plumage until their second fall.

The purple finch breeds in coniferous forests across Canada and the northeastern states and along the Pacific Coast. The Pacific form migrates altitudinally, moving down from the mountains to lower elevations in the fall. The northern population moves southward across the entire eastern half of the United States, reaching as far south as Texas and Florida. Like most of the "winter finches," however, the purple finch is erratic in its movements. Some years it occurs abundantly in the eastern half of Texas, ranging southward in lesser numbers to Corpus Christi and San Antonio. In other years, it remains farther north, putting in a token appearance only in the northeastern corner of the state.

The purple finch's diet varies with the season. In spring it consumes insects, buds and even flowers, while in summer it adds large quantities of ripening fruits and berries. It turns to seeds for sustenance in fall and winter, gathering in small flocks to prowl woodlands and thickets, moving southward until sufficient food is found. Seeds of elms, sycamores, sweetgums and pines prove popular, and sunflower seeds provide a special treat. Finding a well-provisioned feeder, these handsome finches may stay for weeks.

Cassin's finch (*Carpodacus cassinii*) replaces the purple finch in Rocky Mountain forests and other regions in the West. Its bright red cap contrasts strongly with its browner neck and back. The sparrowlike female has narrower streaks on her breast, and her face pattern appears less pronounced than that of the purple finch; however, the distinction is not an easy one. Cassin's finch oc- curs as a winter visitor in the El Paso region and ranges less frequently through the Trans-Pecos to Big Bend and onto the Staked Plains and the western edge of the Edwards Plateau.

Male purple finch.

HOUSE FINCH

Carpodacus mexicanus

Unlike most of its northern relatives, the house finch prefers desert areas and canyon slopes in western North America, where it ranges from the Pacific Coast eastward to Nebraska and Texas and south through Mexico. At home around farms and ranches, it even inhabits busy cities and shares space with resident house sparrows.

Like the others of its genus, the purple and Cassin's finches, the sparrow-sized house finch has a sturdy, seed-eating bill. Its back is brown; its underparts are lighter and heavily streaked with brown. Adult males show bright red feathers on the forehead and along the sides of the head over the eyes, contrasting sharply with a brown cap. The breast and rump are also red. Occasional aberrant males have buffy orange or yellow replacing the red plumage. The female is heavily streaked both above and below, without the pronounced light face pattern of the other two *Carpodacus* finches. The latter two species appear only as winter wanderers in Texas, while the house finch remains as a common year-round resident in the arid western half of the state.

House finches build rough cuplike nests of twigs, grasses, hair and other debris in tree cavities or buildings or in thickets of dense foliage. Females lay four or five pale bluish eggs speckled with brown and black and incubate for 12 to 14 days. The young fledge 11 to 19 days later. Adults consume very few insects, preferring seeds, fruits and buds. They even feed their nestlings on seeds, an unusual habit among birds but an adaptation that probably offers advantages in arid environments where insect populations are ephemeral.

In Texas, house finches have been moving steadily eastward from their original range in the arid Trans-Pecos. Since 1930, they have colonized the Edwards Plateau as far east as Austin and San Antonio. Occasional stragglers also reach the southern coast. The winter of 1990-91, however, saw one of the major ornithological developments in eastern Texas in recent years. Hundreds of house finches invaded bird feeders in the Houston-Galveston area, where previously there had been but a single record for the species. They probably moved in from the West, but their origin remains uncertain.

In about 1940, cage-bird dealers were illegally trapping house finches in the West and shipping them to New York as "Hollywood finches," popular for their bright plumage and cheery, highly variable song. Prompted by the National Audubon Society, government agents stopped the illegal practice, for all native North American species are protected by the Migratory Bird Treaty that bans their capture and sale. To avoid prosecution, dealers apparently released their finches on Long Island, where they not only survived but proliferated. Within two decades the new eastern population had reached as far as the Carolinas. House finches now breed in the East from southern Canada to Alabama.

Although largely nonmigratory, house finches tend to gather in small flocks after the breeding season and wander in search of food. As they expand their range from both sides of the continent, they are now well on the way to occupying all of Texas and closing the gap between western natives and eastern immigrants.

Male house finch.

PINE SISKIN

Carduelis pinus

One of the smallest of the winter finches, the pine siskin shares the genus *Carduelis* with the goldfinches and redpolls. Brown above and pale grayish or buffy below, it is heavily streaked with darker brown. The streaked breast and rather slender, sharply pointed bill distinguish it from the goldfinches with which it often associates in Texas. Characteristic, too, are yellow patches on the flight feathers of the wings and at the base of the deeply notched tail; however, the patches vary in extent and often remain concealed except in flight. Some individuals have bright, flashy yellow markings, while others show smaller creamy yellow bands. The sexes look alike, and variations in pattern cannot be safely correlated with either sex or age. Distinctive call notes include a rising *wee-zee* and a buzzy *shreeee.*

Siskins breed in coniferous and mixed forests across Canada and the northern United States and southward in the western mountains to Mexico. In winter they wander southward to the Gulf Coast and occur irregularly throughout most of Texas. They appear most frequently in the northern two-thirds of the state and are rarer along the southern border. Siskins also nest in the high country of the Trans-Pecos, particularly in the Guadalupe Mountains.

Pine siskins wander erratically throughout their range, even altering their breeding sites from year to year. Highly social and gregarious birds, they are irruptive migrants throughout the South, appearing in large numbers one year and failing to appear at all the next. During the winter of 1977-78, for example, siskins roamed southward in unprecedented numbers, swarming through Texas woodlands and thickets and mobbing backyard bird feeders across the state. No one could remember seeing these tame finches in greater numbers, nor was the invasion limited to Texas. Similar flocks occurred from California and Arizona to the Florida Keys, and siskins even turned up in Guatemala.

I banded more than 600 siskins in my own backyard that winter, a total limited only by frequent trips away

AMERICAN GOLDFINCH
Carduelis tristis

Most Texans know the American goldfinch only as a winter resident. Flocks of the plump, five-inch "wild canaries" mob backyard feeders and troop through the fields and open woodlands across the state. They fly in an undulating, up-and-down fashion, filling the air with their twittering calls of *per-chic-o-ree* or *Just-look-at-me!* Lured to sunflower or thistle-seed feeders, they methodically gorge themselves on the tasty kernels, occasionally jockeying for position with a flurry of wings, but usually without major squabbles. Goldfinches seem to be amiable and social birds.

Its selection as the state bird of three states illustrates the widespread popularity of the American goldfinch. New Jersey on the eastern seaboard, Washington in the West, and Iowa in the nation's heartland have all honored this pretty finch. It breeds across southern Canada and in all but the most southerly portions of the United States and spends the winter months from the northern tier of states to Mexico. Although a common winter resident throughout most of Texas, the goldfinch remains to breed only sparingly in the northeastern corner of the state.

In breeding plumage the male is a bright, glowing yellow with a small black cap, wings and tail. White wing-bars and white feather edgings on the tail contrast sharply with the black background. He is the only small yellow bird with black wings. The female wears less striking garb. Olive-green above and paler yellow below, she lacks the black cap and the bright yellow shoulder patches on her brownish black wings. Winter adults and immatures resemble females but are duller and more grayish, sometimes with only traces of the characteristic golden plumage. Their conical finch bills, however, separate them from the olive or yellowish warblers with which they might be confused.

Appearing in Texas in October, goldfinches sometimes linger until

from home. Since that time, I have banded but a handful more. Unlike many other long-distance migrants, however, none of that huge flock ever returned. Birds as varied as yellow-rumped warblers and white-throated sparrows have been recaptured in subsequent years at the same location. So, too, the goldfinches, which might return year after year. But not so the pine siskins. They roam in a seemingly random pattern across the land.

The unpredictable irruptions of these five-inch-long finches occur, at least in part, because of food shortages farther north. Siskins can withstand the winter chill, but they must have sufficient food to stoke their internal fires against the cold. During my banding studies, siskins lost an average of ten percent of their body weight overnight and gained it back by feeding voraciously through the day. Even a single day without food can spell disaster to a bird weighing no more than half an ounce.

Successive years of abundant pine, spruce and fir cones lead to an increasing bird population. Then, if the cone crop fails over a broad area, the siskins must move southward in search of a substitute for their favorite winter seeds. Thus they are abundant in Texas in some years, far less common in others. Small flocks can usually be found from late October through April, however, particularly in the northern portions of the state.

Pine siskins relish sweetgum seeds.

late May or early June, for they move northward to nest later in the season than most other birds. By that time they have achieved full breeding plumage. Only when the thistles and other wildflowers go to seed do they pair off and begin their household chores, thereby assuring a plentiful supply of food for their growing young. Goldfinches normally change mates between breeding seasons, and it is the female that shows nest-site fidelity, often returning to her old territory each year.

She places her compact cuplike nest in the fork of a shrub or tree, usually near water. Carefully woven of plant fibers and lined with thistledown, it is so well constructed that it may fill with water and drown the young unless sheltered by one of the parents during rainy weather. The female builds the nest and incubates her four to six pale bluish white eggs, but her attentive mate collects nesting material for her and feeds her as she sits. Both then feed the young on a mash of regurgitated thistle and other seeds, an unusual diet for baby birds. Adults, too, are primarily seed eaters, consuming only occasional insects and berries.

Female American goldfinch (right). Young male lesser goldfinch (below).

Lesser Goldfinch

Carduelis psaltria

While the better known American goldfinch occurs only as a common winter visitor to most of Texas, the lesser goldfinch is a year-round resident of the arid Trans-Pecos and the Edwards Plateau, ranging east to Austin and Beeville and southward locally to the Rio Grande Valley. Its range also includes most of the southwestern United States, Mexico and Central America.

The eastern "black-backed" form of the adult male that occurs in Texas is glossy black above and yellow below, with contrasting white patches in the wings and tail. The female resembles the female American goldfinch with her greenish back and yellow underparts, but she lacks the whitish rump of the latter species. The immature male has a black cap but retains the green back, a plumage resembling the "green-backed" adult form from the western portion of the country. Although individual males vary in back color and in the intensity of the yellow on the breast, they do not molt into a drab winter plumage. Once they achieve adulthood, they

maintain their colors throughout the year.

Lesser goldfinches inhabit dry, brushy country and open woodlands, where they build their cuplike nests in bushes or trees. Nests with eggs have been found in Texas from mid-March until late June and range from near sea level in the southern tip of the state to 7,000 feet in the Trans-Pecos mountains. Pairs may stay together through the winter, and the male feeds his mate as she incubates her four or five pale bluish eggs. The complete breeding biology, however, requires a more thorough investigation.

Like most of their relatives, lesser goldfinches assemble in large winter flocks to forage through the fields and thickets. Their plaintive calls, *tee-yee tee-yer,* sound across the Texas hills as they flock to bird feeders and bird-baths. Water is important, apparently because goldfinches consume mainly seeds, and its availability affects the birds' distribution and abundance during dry seasons and through periods of prolonged drought.

EVENING GROSBEAK   *Coccothraustes vespertinus*

Few Texans welcome the "blue northers" that sweep across the state with bone-chilling winds and flurries of ice and snow. With those fronts, however, may come a more welcome sign of winter, the handsome evening grosbeaks of the northern forests. Like many other winter finches, these flashy eight-inch birds stage erratic invasions of Texas and the southern states. Most frequent in West Texas and the Panhandle, they wander occasionally into the East Texas Piney Woods and have appeared as far south as San Antonio and Brazoria County during their sporadic irruptions. While not a common species in Texas, they are hard to overlook when present, for they descend on bird feeders to consume enormous quantities of sunflower seeds. Their large size, colorful plumage and loud, strident cries of *clee-ip* or *cleeer* make identification simple.

The adult male is yellow with a brownish head and a prominent yellow forehead and eyebrow stripe. Black wings bear prominent white patches, and the tail is also black. The huge seed-cracking bill is whitish. The more somber female and immatures are silvery gray, but yellowish hues in their body plumage, their boldly marked black-and-white wings and tails, and their powerful bills serve as identifying marks.

Evening grosbeaks breed in the coniferous and mixed forests across Canada and through the western mountains into Mexico. Since about 1900, they have expanded their range into the northeastern states, where they were once extremely rare. This eastward expansion was probably aided by winter bird feeders, and some of the wanderers then remained to nest. Ornithologists speculate that continued expansion may result in a breeding population in the Appalachians as well.

Although evening grosbeaks can endure the snow and cold of northern forests, they depend on the seeds of various trees and shrubs. When those crops fail, the birds move southward in search of food. Their movements are unpredictable, and numbers vary greatly from year to year. When they do appear in Texas, however, the large, relatively tame grosbeaks attract a great deal of attention as they drift in on the wings of winter.

Though more subtly colored than her golden mate, the female evening grosbeak still lights the winter woods.

The following checklist is based on the official list of the Texas Bird Records Committee (TBRC) of the Texas Ornithological Society. It includes all fully documented records for the state through February 1993.

For recognition of a species, the TBRC requires documentation by means of a specimen, photographs or tape recordings that clearly demonstrate definitive characteristics. Some other lists include "hypothetical" species substantiated by sight records alone. This list follows the former policy, excluding the hypothetical records and those from historic, unsubstantiated reports. An exception has been made in the case of the parrots, where several species are unquestionably present in Texas but their origin remains in question. Species appearing in boldface type receive major treatment in the text.

GUIDE TO SYMBOLS:

A = Accidental (one or more records, but not expected yearly)

E = Extirpated (no longer occurs in Texas)

I = Introduced

X = Extinct (no longer exists)

? = Status uncertain (present, but origin in question)

FAMILY GAVIIDAE

Red-throated Loon (*Gavia stellata*) A

Pacific Loon (*G. pacifica*) A

Common Loon (*G. immer*)

Yellow-billed Loon (*G. adamsii*) A

FAMILY PODICIPEDIDAE

Least Grebe (*Tachybaptus dominicus*)

Pied-billed Grebe (*Podilymbus podiceps*)

Horned Grebe (*Podiceps auritus*)

Red-necked Grebe (*P. grisegena*) A

Eared Grebe (*P. nigricollis*)

Western Grebe (*Aechmophorus occidentalis*)

Clark's Grebe (*A. clarkii*)

FAMILY DIOMEDEIDAE

Yellow-nosed Albatross (*Diomedea chlororhynchos*) A

FAMILY PROCELLARIIDAE

White-chinned Petrel (*Procellaria aequinoctialis*) A

Cory's Shearwater (*Calonectris diomedea*)

Greater Shearwater (*Puffinus gravis*) A

Sooty Shearwater (*P. griseus*) A

Manx Shearwater (*P. puffinus*) A

Audubon's Shearwater (*P. lherminieri*) A

FAMILY HYDROBATIDAE

Wilson's Storm-Petrel (*Oceanites oceanicus*) A

Leach's Storm-Petrel (*Oceanodroma leucorhoa*) A

Band-rumped Storm-Petrel (*O. castro*) A

FAMILY PHAETHONTIDAE

Red-billed Tropicbird (*Phaethon aethereus*) A

FAMILY SULIDAE

Masked Booby (*Sula dactylatra*)

Blue-footed Booby (*S. nebouxii*) A

Brown Booby (*S. leucogaster*) A

Red-footed Booby (*S. sula*) A

Northern Gannet (*Morus bassanus*)

FAMILY PELECANIDAE

American White Pelican (*Pelecanus erythrorhynchos*)

Brown Pelican (*P. occidentalis*)

FAMILY PHALACROCORACIDAE

Double-crested Cormorant (*Phalacrocorax auritus*)

Neotropic Cormorant (*P. brasilianus*)

FAMILY ANHINGIDAE

Anhinga (*Anhinga anhinga*)

FAMILY FREGATIDAE

Magnificent Frigatebird (*Fregata magnificens*)

FAMILY ARDEIDAE

American Bittern (*Botaurus lentiginosus*)

Least Bittern (*Ixobrychus exilis*)

Great Blue Heron (*Ardea herodias*)

Great Egret (*Casmerodius albus*)

Snowy Egret (*Egretta thula*)

Little Blue Heron (*E. caerulea*)

Tricolored Heron (*E. tricolor*)

Reddish Egret (*E. rufescens*)

Cattle Egret (*Bubulcus ibis*)

Green-backed Heron (*Butorides striatus*)

Black-crowned Night-Heron (*Nycticorax nycticorax*)

Yellow-crowned Night-Heron (*Nyctanassa violacea*)

FAMILY THRESKIORNITHIDAE

SUBFAMILY THRESKIORNITHINAE

White Ibis (*Eudocimus albus*)

Glossy Ibis (*Plegadis falcinellus*) A

White-faced Ibis (*P. chihi*)

SUBFAMILY PLATALEINAE

Roseate Spoonbill (*Ajaia ajaja*)

FAMILY CICONIIDAE

Jabiru (*Jabiru mycteria*) A

Wood Stork (*Mycteria americana*)

FAMILY PHOENICOPTERIDAE

Greater Flamingo (*Phoenicopterus ruber*) A

FAMILY ANATIDAE

SUBFAMILY ANSERINAE

Fulvous Whistling-Duck (*Dendrocygna bicolor*)

Black-bellied Whistling-Duck (*D. autumnalis*)

Tundra Swan (*Cygnus columbianus*)

Trumpeter Swan (*C. buccinator*) A

Greater White-fronted Goose (*Anser albifrons*)

Snow Goose (*Chen caerulescens*)

Ross' Goose (*C. rossii*)

Brant (*Branta bernicla*) A

Canada Goose (*B. canadensis*)

SUBFAMILY ANATINAE

Muscovy Duck (*Cairina moschata*)

Wood Duck (*Aix sponsa*)

Green-winged Teal (*Anas crecca*)

American Black Duck (*A. rubripes*) A

Mottled Duck (*A. fulvigula*)

Mallard (*A. platyrhynchos*)

White-cheeked Pintail (*A. bahamensis*) A

Northern Pintail (*A. acuta*)

Garganey (*A. querquedula*) A

Blue-winged Teal (*A. discors*)

Cinnamon Teal (*A. cyanoptera*)

Northern Shoveler (*A. clypeata*)

Gadwall (*A. strepera*)

Eurasian Wigeon (*A. penelope*)   A

American Wigeon (*A. americana*)

Canvasback (*Aythya valisineria*)

Redhead (*A. americana*)

Ring-necked Duck (*A. collaris*)

Greater Scaup (*A. marila*)

Lesser Scaup (*A. affinis*)

Harlequin Duck (*Histrionicus histrionicus*)   A

Oldsquaw (*Clangula hyemalis*)

Black Scoter (*Melanitta nigra*)

Surf Scoter (*M. perspicillata*)

White-winged Scoter (*M. fusca*)

Common Goldeneye (*Bucephala clangula*)

Barrow's Goldeneye (*B. islandica*)   A

Bufflehead (*B. albeola*)

Hooded Merganser (*Lophodytes cucullatus*)

Common Merganser (*Mergus merganser*)

Red-breasted Merganser (*M. serrator*)

Ruddy Duck (*Oxyura jamaicensis*)

Masked Duck (*O. dominica*)   A

FAMILY CATHARTIDAE

Black Vulture (*Coragyps atratus*)

Turkey Vulture (*Cathartes aura*)

FAMILY ACCIPITRIDAE

SUBFAMILY PANDIONINAE

Osprey (*Pandion haliaetus*)

SUBFAMILY ACCIPITRINAE

Hook-billed Kite (*Chondrohierax uncinatus*)

American Swallow-tailed Kite (*Elanoides forficatus*)

Black-shouldered Kite (*Elanus caeruleus*)

Snail Kite (*Rostrhamus sociabilis*)   A

Mississippi Kite (*Ictinia mississippiensis*)

Bald Eagle (*Haliaeetus leucocephalus*)

Northern Harrier (*Circus cyaneus*)

Sharp-shinned Hawk (*Accipiter striatus*)

Cooper's Hawk (*A. cooperii*)

Northern Goshawk (*A. gentilis*)   A

Crane Hawk (*Geranospiza caerulescens*)   A

Common Black-Hawk (*Buteogallus anthracinus*)

Harris' Hawk (*Parabuteo unicinctus*)

Gray Hawk (*Buteo nitidus*)

Roadside Hawk (*B. magnirostris*)   A

Red-shouldered Hawk (*B. lineatus*)

Broad-winged Hawk (*B. platypterus*)

Short-tailed Hawk (*B. brachyurus*)   A

Swainson's Hawk (*B. swainsoni*)

White-tailed Hawk (*B. albicaudatus*)

Zone-tailed Hawk (*B. albonotatus*)

Red-tailed Hawk (*B. jamaicensis*)

Ferruginous Hawk (*B. regalis*)

Rough-legged Hawk (*B. lagopus*)

Golden Eagle (*Aquila chrysaetos*)

FAMILY FALCONIDAE

Crested Caracara (*Polyborus plancus*)

American Kestrel (*Falco sparverius*)

Merlin (*F. columbarius*)

Aplomado Falcon (*F. femoralis*)   A

Prairie Falcon (*F. mexicanus*)

Peregrine Falcon (*F. peregrinus*)

FAMILY CRACIDAE

Plain Chachalaca (*Ortalis vetula*)

FAMILY PHASIANIDAE

SUBFAMILY PHASIANINAE

Ring-necked Pheasant (*Phasianus colchicus*)   I

SUBFAMILY TETRAONINAE

Greater Prairie-Chicken (*Tympanuchus cupido*)

Lesser Prairie-Chicken (*T. pallidicinctus*)

SUBFAMILY MELEAGRIDINAE

Wild Turkey (*Meleagris gallopavo*)

SUBFAMILY ODONTOPHORINAE

Montezuma Quail (*Cyrtonyx montezumae*)

Northern Bobwhite (*Colinus virginianus*)

Scaled Quail (*Callipepla squamata*)

Gambel's Quail (*C. gambelii*)

FAMILY RALLIDAE

SUBFAMILY RALLINAE

Yellow Rail (*Coturnicops noveboracensis*)

Black Rail (*Laterallus jamaicensis*)

Clapper Rail (*Rallus longirostris*)

King Rail (*R. elegans*)

Virginia Rail (*R. limicola*)

Sora (*Porzana carolina*)

Paint-billed Crake (*Neocrex erythrops*)   A

Spotted Rail (*Pardirallus maculatus*)   A

Purple Gallinule (*Porphyrula martinica*)

Common Moorhen (*Gallinula chloropus*)

American Coot (*Fulica americana*)

FAMILY GRUIDAE

SUBFAMILY GRUINAE

Sandhill Crane (*Grus canadensis*)

Whooping Crane (*G. americana*)

FAMILY BURHINIDAE

Double-striped Thick-knee (*Burhinus bistriatus*)   A

FAMILY CHARADRIIDAE

SUBFAMILY CHARADRIINAE

Black-bellied Plover (*Pluvialis squatarola*)

Lesser Golden-Plover (*P. dominica*)

Collared Plover (*Charadrius collaris*)   A

Snowy Plover (*C. alexandrinus*)

Wilson's Plover (*C. wilsonia*)

Semipalmated Plover (*C. semipalmatus*)

Piping Plover (*C. melodus*)

Killdeer (*C. vociferus*)

Mountain Plover (*C. montanus*)

FAMILY HAEMATOPODIDAE

American Oystercatcher (*Haematopus palliatus*)

FAMILY RECURVIROSTRIDAE

Black-necked Stilt (*Himantopus mexicanus*)

American Avocet (*Recurvirostra americana*)

FAMILY JACANIDAE

Northern Jacana (*Jacana spinosa*)   A

FAMILY SCOLOPACIDAE

SUBFAMILY SCOLOPACINAE

Greater Yellowlegs (*Tringa melanoleuca*)

Lesser Yellowlegs (*T. flavipes*)

Solitary Sandpiper (*T. solitaria*)

Willet (*Catoptrophorus semipalmatus*)

Wandering Tattler (*Heteroscelus incanus*)   A

Spotted Sandpiper (*Actitis macularia*)

Upland Sandpiper (*Bartramia longicauda*)

Eskimo Curlew (*Numenius borealis*)   A

Whimbrel (*N. phaeopus*)

Long-billed Curlew (*N. americanus*)

Hudsonian Godwit (*Limosa haemastica*)
Marbled Godwit (*L. fedoa*)
Ruddy Turnstone (*Arenaria interpres*)
Surfbird (*Aphriza virgata*) A
Red Knot (*Calidris canutus*)
Sanderling (*C. alba*)
Semipalmated Sandpiper (*C. pusilla*)
Western Sandpiper (*C. mauri*)
Least Sandpiper (*C. minutilla*)
White-rumped Sandpiper (*C. fuscicollis*)
Baird's Sandpiper (*C. bairdii*)
Pectoral Sandpiper (*C. melanotos*)
Sharp-tailed Sandpiper
  (*C. acuminata*) A
Purple Sandpiper (*C. maritima*) A
Dunlin (*C. alpina*)
Curlew Sandpiper (*C. ferruginea*) A
Stilt Sandpiper (*C. himantopus*)
Buff-breasted Sandpiper (*Tryngites subruficollis*)
Ruff (*Philomachus pugnax*) A
Short-billed Dowitcher (*Limnodromus griseus*)
Long-billed Dowitcher
  (*L. scolopaceus*)
Common Snipe (*Gallinago gallinago*)
American Woodcock (*Scolopax minor*)

SUBFAMILY PHALAROPODINAE
Wilson's Phalarope (*Phalaropus tricolor*)
Red-necked Phalarope (*P. lobatus*)
Red Phalarope (*P. fulicaria*) A

FAMILY LARIDAE

SUBFAMILY STERCORARIINAE
Pomarine Jaeger (*Stercorarius pomarinus*)
Parasitic Jaeger (*S. parasiticus*)
Long-tailed Jaeger (*S. longicaudus*) A

SUBFAMILY LARINAE
Laughing Gull (*Larus atricilla*)
Franklin's Gull (*L. pipixcan*)
Little Gull (*L. minutus*) A
Common Black-headed Gull
  (*L. ridibundus*) A
Bonaparte's Gull (*L. philadelphia*)
Heermann's Gull (*L. heermanni*) A
Mew Gull (*L. canus*) A
Ring-billed Gull (*L. delawarensis*)
California Gull (*L. californicus*) A
Herring Gull (*L. argentatus*)
Thayer's Gull (*L. thayeri*) A
Iceland Gull (*L. glaucoides*) A
Lesser Black-backed Gull (*L. fuscus*) A

Slaty-backed Gull (*L. schistisagus*) A
Western Gull (*L. occidentalis*) A
Glaucous Gull (*L. hyperboreus*) A
Great Black-backed Gull
  (*L. marinus*) A
Black-legged Kittiwake (*Rissa tridactyla*) A
Sabine's Gull (*Xema sabini*) A

SUBFAMILY STERNINAE
Gull-billed Tern (*Sterna nilotica*)
Caspian Tern (*S. caspia*)
Royal Tern (*S. maxima*)
Elegant Tern (*S. elegans*) A
Sandwich Tern (*S. sandvicensis*)
Common Tern (*S. hirundo*)
Forster's Tern (*S. forsteri*)
Least Tern (*S. antillarum*)
Bridled Tern (*S. anaethetus*) A
Sooty Tern (*S. fuscata*) A
Black Tern (*Chlidonias niger*)
Brown Noddy (*Anous stolidus*) A
Black Noddy (*A. minutus*) A

SUBFAMILY RYNCHOPINAE
Black Skimmer (*Rynchops niger*)

FAMILY COLUMBIDAE
Rock Dove (*Columba livia*) I
White-crowned Pigeon
  (*C. leucocephala*) A
Red-billed Pigeon (*C. flavirostris*)
Band-tailed Pigeon (*C. fasciata*)
Ringed Turtle-Dove (*Streptopelia risoria*) I
White-winged Dove (*Zenaida asiatica*)
Mourning Dove (*Z. macroura*)
Passenger Pigeon (*Ectopistes migratorius*) X
Inca Dove (*Columbina inca*)
Common Ground-Dove (*C. passerina*)
Ruddy Ground-Dove (*C. talpacoti*) A
White-tipped Dove (*Leptotila verreauxi*)

FAMILY PSITTACIDAE

SUBFAMILY ARINAE
Monk Parakeet (*Myiopsitta monachus*) I
Carolina Parakeet (*Conuropsis carolinensis*) X
Green Parakeet (*Aratinga holochlora*) ?
Red-crowned Parrot (*Amazona viridigenalis*) ?
Red-lored Parrot (*A. autumnalis*) I
Yellow-headed Parrot (*A. oratrix*) ?

FAMILY CUCULIDAE

SUBFAMILY COCCYZINAE
Black-billed Cuckoo (*Coccyzus erythropthalmus*)
Yellow-billed Cuckoo (*C. americanus*)
Mangrove Cuckoo (*C. minor*) A

SUBFAMILY NEOMORPHINAE
Greater Roadrunner (*Geococcyx californianus*)

SUBFAMILY CROTOPHAGINAE
Groove-billed Ani (*Crotophaga sulcirostris*)

FAMILY TYTONIDAE
Barn Owl (*Tyto alba*)

FAMILY STRIGIDAE
Flammulated Owl (*Otus flammeolus*)
Eastern Screech-Owl (*O. asio*)
Western Screech-Owl (*O. kennicottii*)
Great Horned Owl (*Bubo virginianus*)
Snowy Owl (*Nyctea scandiaca*) A
Northern Pygmy-Owl (*Glaucidium gnoma*) A
Ferruginous Pygmy-Owl
  (*G. brasilianum*)
Elf Owl (*Micrathene whitneyi*)
Burrowing Owl (*Speotyto cunicularia*)
Mottled Owl (*Ciccaba virgata*) A
Spotted Owl (*Strix occidentalis*)
Barred Owl (*S. varia*)
Long-eared Owl (*Asio otus*)
Short-eared Owl (*A. flammeus*)
Northern Saw-whet Owl (*Aegolius acadicus*)

FAMILY CAPRIMULGIDAE

SUBFAMILY CHORDEILINAE
Lesser Nighthawk (*Chordeiles acutipennis*)
Common Nighthawk (*C. minor*)

SUBFAMILY CAPRIMULGINAE
Pauraque (*Nyctidromus albicollis*)
Common Poorwill (*Phalaenoptilus nuttallii*)
Chuck-will's-widow (*Caprimulgus carolinensis*)
Whip-poor-will (*C. vociferus*)

FAMILY APODIDAE

SUBFAMILY CYPSELOIDINAE
White-collared Swift (*Streptoprocne zonaris*) A

SUBFAMILY CHAETURINAE
Chimney Swift (*Chaetura pelagica*)

SUBFAMILY APODINAE

White-throated Swift (*Aeronautes saxatalis*)

FAMILY TROCHILIDAE

Green Violet-ear (*Colibri thalassinus*)   A

Green-breasted Mango (*Anthracothorax prevostii*)   A

Broad-billed Hummingbird (*Cynanthus latirostris*)   A

White-eared Hummingbird (*Hylocharis leucotis*)   A

Berylline Hummingbird (*Amazilia beryllina*)   A

Buff-bellied Hummingbird (*A. yucatanensis*)

Violet-crowned Hummingbird (*A. violiceps*)   A

Blue-throated Hummingbird (*Lampornis clemenciae*)

Magnificent Hummingbird (*Eugenes fulgens*)

Lucifer Hummingbird (*Calothorax lucifer*)

Ruby-throated Hummingbird (*Archilochus colubris*)

Black-chinned Hummingbird (*A. alexandri*)

Anna's Hummingbird (*Calypte anna*)   A

Costa's Hummingbird (*C. costae*)   A

Calliope Hummingbird (*Stellula calliope*)

Broad-tailed Hummingbird (*Selasphorus platycercus*)

Rufous Hummingbird (*S. rufus*)

Allen's Hummingbird (*S. sasin*)   A

FAMILY TROGONIDAE

Elegant Trogon (*Trogon elegans*)   A

FAMILY ALCEDINIDAE

SUBFAMILY CERYLINAE

Ringed Kingfisher (*Ceryle torquata*)

Belted Kingfisher (*C. alcyon*)

Green Kingfisher (*Chloroceryle americana*)

FAMILY PICIDAE

SUBFAMILY PICINAE

Lewis' Woodpecker (*Melanerpes lewis*)   A

Red-headed Woodpecker (*M. erythrocephalus*)

Acorn Woodpecker (*M. formicivorus*)

Golden-fronted Woodpecker (*M. aurifrons*)

Red-bellied Woodpecker (*M. carolinus*)

Yellow-bellied Sapsucker (*Sphyrapicus varius*)

Red-naped Sapsucker (*S. nuchalis*)

Williamson's Sapsucker (*S. thyroideus*)

Ladder-backed Woodpecker (*Picoides scalaris*)

Downy Woodpecker (*P. pubescens*)

Hairy Woodpecker (*P. villosus*)

Red-cockaded Woodpecker (*P. borealis*)

Northern Flicker (*Colaptes auratus*)

Pileated Woodpecker (*Dryocopus pileatus*)

Ivory-billed Woodpecker (*Campephilus principalis*)   E

FAMILY TYRANNIDAE

SUBFAMILY ELAENIINAE

Northern Beardless-Tyrannulet (*Camptostoma imberbe*)

Greenish Elaenia (*Myiopagis viridicata*)   A

SUBFAMILY FLUVICOLINAE

Tufted Flycatcher (*Mitrephanes phaeocercus*)   A

Olive-sided Flycatcher (*Contopus borealis*)

Greater Pewee (*C. pertinax*)   A

Western Wood-Pewee (*C. sordidulus*)

Eastern Wood-Pewee (*C. virens*)

Yellow-bellied Flycatcher (*Empidonax flaviventris*)

Acadian Flycatcher (*E. virescens*)

Alder Flycatcher (*E. alnorum*)

Willow Flycatcher (*E. traillii*)

Least Flycatcher (*E. minimus*)

Hammond's Flycatcher (*E. hammondii*)

Dusky Flycatcher (*E. oberholseri*)

Gray Flycatcher (*E. wrightii*)

Cordilleran Flycatcher (*E. occidentalis*)

Black Phoebe (*Sayornis nigricans*)

Eastern Phoebe (*S. phoebe*)

Say's Phoebe (*S. saya*)

Vermilion Flycatcher (*Pyrocephalus rubinus*)

SUBFAMILY TYRANNINAE

Dusky-capped Flycatcher (*Myiarchus tuberculifer*)   A

Ash-throated Flycatcher (*M. cinerascens*)

Great Crested Flycatcher (*M. crinitus*)

Brown-crested Flycatcher (*M. tyrannulus*)

Great Kiskadee (*Pitangus sulphuratus*)

Sulphur-bellied Flycatcher (*Myiodynastes luteiventris*)   A

Tropical Kingbird (*Tyrannus melancholicus*)   A

Couch's Kingbird (*T. couchii*)

Cassin's Kingbird (*T. vociferans*)

Thick-billed Kingbird (*T. crassirostris*)   A

Western Kingbird (*T. verticalis*)

Eastern Kingbird (*T. tyrannus*)

Gray Kingbird (*T. dominicensis*)   A

Scissor-tailed Flycatcher (*T. forficatus*)

Fork-tailed Flycatcher (*T. savana*)   A

SUBFAMILY TITYRINAE

Rose-throated Becard (*Pachyramphus aglaiae*)   A

Masked Tityra (*Tityra semifasciata*)   A

FAMILY ALAUDIDAE

Horned Lark (*Eremophila alpestris*)

FAMILY HIRUNDINIDAE

SUBFAMILY HIRUNDININAE

Purple Martin (*Progne subis*)

Gray-breasted Martin (*P. chalybea*)   A

Tree Swallow (*Tachycineta bicolor*)

Violet-green Swallow (*T. thalassina*)

Northern Rough-winged Swallow (*Stelgidopteryx serripennis*)

Bank Swallow (*Riparia riparia*)

Cliff Swallow (*Hirundo pyrrhonota*)

Cave Swallow (*H. fulva*)

Barn Swallow (*H. rustica*)

FAMILY CORVIDAE

Steller's Jay (*Cyanocitta stelleri*)

Blue Jay (*C. cristata*)

Green Jay (*Cyanocorax yncas*)

Brown Jay (*C. morio*)

Scrub Jay (*Aphelocoma coerulescens*)

Gray-breasted Jay (*A. ultramarina*)

Pinyon Jay (*Gymnorhinus cyanocephalus*)

Clark's Nutcracker (*Nucifraga columbiana*)   A

Black-billed Magpie (*Pica pica*)   A

American Crow (*Corvus brachyrhynchos*)

Mexican Crow (*C. imparatus*)

Fish Crow (*C. ossifragus*)

Chihuahuan Raven (*C. cryptoleucus*)

Common Raven (*C. corax*)

FAMILY PARIDAE

Carolina Chickadee (*Parus carolinensis*)

Mountain Chickadee (*P. gambeli*)

Plain Titmouse (*P. inornatus*)

Tufted Titmouse (*P. bicolor*)

FAMILY REMIZIDAE

Verdin (*Auriparus flaviceps*)

FAMILY AEGITHALIDAE

Bushtit (*Psaltriparus minimus*)

FAMILY SITTIDAE

SUBFAMILY SITTINAE

Red-breasted Nuthatch (*Sitta canadensis*)

White-breasted Nuthatch (*S. carolinensis*)

Pygmy Nuthatch (*S. pygmaea*)

Brown-headed Nuthatch (*S. pusilla*)

FAMILY CERTHIIDAE

SUBFAMILY CERTHIINAE

Brown Creeper (*Certhia americana*)

FAMILY TROGLODYTIDAE

Cactus Wren (*Campylorhynchus brunneicapillus*)

Rock Wren (*Salpinctes obsoletus*)

Canyon Wren (*Catherpes mexicanus*)

Carolina Wren (*Thryothorus ludovicianus*)

Bewick's Wren (*Thryomanes bewickii*)

House Wren (*Troglodytes aedon*)

Winter Wren (*T. troglodytes*)

Sedge Wren (*Cistothorus platensis*)

Marsh Wren (*C. palustris*)

FAMILY CINCLIDAE

American Dipper (*Cinclus mexicanus*)   A

FAMILY MUSCICAPIDAE

SUBFAMILY SYLVIINAE

Golden-crowned Kinglet (*Regulus satrapa*)

Ruby-crowned Kinglet (*R. calendula*)

Blue-gray Gnatcatcher (*Polioptila caerulea*)

Black-tailed Gnatcatcher (*P. melanura*)

SUBFAMILY TURDINAE

Eastern Bluebird (*Sialia sialis*)

Western Bluebird (*S. mexicana*)

Mountain Bluebird (*S. currucoides*)

Townsend's Solitaire (*Myadestes townsendi*)

Veery (*Catharus fuscescens*)

Gray-cheeked Thrush (*C. minimus*)

Swainson's Thrush (*C. ustulatus*)

Hermit Thrush (*C. guttatus*)

Wood Thrush (*Hylocichla mustelina*)

Clay-colored Robin (*Turdus grayi*)   A

White-throated Robin (*T. assimilis*)   A

Rufous-backed Robin (*T. rufopalliatus*)   A

American Robin (*T. migratorius*)

Varied Thrush (*Ixoreus naevius*)   A

Aztec Thrush (*Ridgewaya pinicola*)   A

FAMILY MIMIDAE

Gray Catbird (*Dumetella carolinensis*)

Black Catbird (*Melanoptila glabrirostris*)   A

Northern Mockingbird (*Mimus polyglottos*)

Sage Thrasher (*Oreoscoptes montanus*)

Brown Thrasher (*Toxostoma rufum*)

Long-billed Thrasher (*T. longirostre*)

Curve-billed Thrasher (*T. curvirostre*)

Crissal Thrasher (*T. dorsale*)

FAMILY MOTACILLIDAE

American Pipit (*Anthus rubescens*)

Sprague's Pipit (*A. spragueii*)

FAMILY BOMBYCILLIDAE

Bohemian Waxwing (*Bombycilla garrulus*)   A

Cedar Waxwing (*B. cedrorum*)

FAMILY PTILOGONATIDAE

Phainopepla (*Phainopepla nitens*)

Gray Silky-Flycatcher (*Ptilogonys cinereus*)   A

FAMILY LANIIDAE

SUBFAMILY LANIINAE

Northern Shrike (*Lanius excubitor*)

Loggerhead Shrike (*L. ludovicianus*)

FAMILY STURNIDAE

SUBFAMILY STURNINAE

European Starling (*Sturnus vulgaris*)   I

FAMILY VIREONIDAE

SUBFAMILY VIREONINAE

White-eyed Vireo (*Vireo griseus*)

Bell's Vireo (*V. bellii*)

Black-capped Vireo (*V. atricapillus*)

Gray Vireo (*V. vicinior*)

Solitary Vireo (*V. solitarius*)

Yellow-throated Vireo (*V. flavifrons*)

Hutton's Vireo (*V. huttoni*)

Warbling Vireo (*V. gilvus*)

Philadelphia Vireo (*V. philadelphicus*)

Red-eyed Vireo (*V. olivaceus*)

Yellow-green Vireo (*V. flavoviridis*)   A

Black-whiskered Vireo (*V. altiloquus*)   A

Yucatan Vireo (*V. magister*)   A

FAMILY EMBERIZIDAE

SUBFAMILY PARULINAE

Blue-winged Warbler (*Vermivora pinus*)

Golden-winged Warbler (*V. chrysoptera*)

Tennessee Warbler (*V. peregrina*)

Orange-crowned Warbler (*V. celata*)

Nashville Warbler (*V. ruficapilla*)

Virginia's Warbler (*V. virginiae*)

Colima Warbler (*V. crissalis*)

Lucy's Warbler (*V. luciae*)

Northern Parula (*Parula americana*)

Tropical Parula (*P. pitiayumi*)

Yellow Warbler (*Dendroica petechia*)

Chestnut-sided Warbler (*D. pensylvanica*)

Magnolia Warbler (*D. magnolia*)

Cape May Warbler (*D. tigrina*)

Black-throated Blue Warbler (*D. caerulescens*)

Yellow-rumped Warbler (*D. coronata*)

Black-throated Gray Warbler (*D. nigrescens*)

Townsend's Warbler (*D. townsendi*)

Hermit Warbler (*D. occidentalis*)

Black-throated Green Warbler (*D. virens*)

Golden-cheeked Warbler (*D. chrysoparia*)

Blackburnian Warbler (*D. fusca*)

Yellow-throated Warbler (*D. dominica*)

Grace's Warbler (*D. graciae*)

Pine Warbler (*D. pinus*)

Prairie Warbler (*D. discolor*)

Palm Warbler (*D. palmarum*)

Bay-breasted Warbler (*D. castanea*)

Blackpoll Warbler (*D. striata*)

Cerulean Warbler (*D. cerulea*)

Black-and-white Warbler (*Mniotilta varia*)

American Redstart (*Setophaga ruticilla*)

Prothonotary Warbler (*Protonotaria citrea*)

Worm-eating Warbler (*Helmitheros vermivorus*)

Swainson's Warbler (*Limnothlypis swainsonii*)

Ovenbird (*Seiurus aurocapillus*)

Northern Waterthrush (*S. noveboracensis*)

Louisiana Waterthrush (*S. motacilla*)

Kentucky Warbler (*Oporornis formosus*)

Connecticut Warbler (*O. agilis*) A

Mourning Warbler (*O. philadelphia*)

MacGillivray's Warbler (*O. tolmiei*)

Common Yellowthroat (*Geothlypis trichas*)

Gray-crowned Yellowthroat (*G. poliocephala*) A

Hooded Warbler (*Wilsonia citrina*)

Wilson's Warbler (*W. pusilla*)

Canada Warbler (*W. canadensis*)

Red-faced Warbler (*Cardellina rubrifrons*) A

Painted Redstart (*Myioborus pictus*)

Slate-throated Redstart (*M. miniatus*) A

Golden-crowned Warbler (*Basileuterus culicivorus*) A

Rufous-capped Warbler (*B. rufifrons*) A

Yellow-breasted Chat (*Icteria virens*)

Olive Warbler (*Peucedramus taeniatus*) A

SUBFAMILY THRAUPINAE

Hepatic Tanager (*Piranga flava*)

Summer Tanager (*P. rubra*)

Scarlet Tanager (*P. olivacea*)

Western Tanager (*P. ludoviciana*)

SUBFAMILY CARDINALINAE

Crimson-collared Grosbeak (*Rhodothraupis celaeno*) A

Northern Cardinal (*Cardinalis cardinalis*)

Pyrrhuloxia (*C. sinuatus*)

Rose-breasted Grosbeak (*Pheucticus ludovicianus*)

Black-headed Grosbeak (*P. melanocephalus*)

Blue Bunting (*Cyanocompsa parellina*) A

Blue Grosbeak (*Guiraca caerulea*)

Lazuli Bunting (*Passerina amoena*)

Indigo Bunting (*P. cyanea*)

Varied Bunting (*P. versicolor*)

Painted Bunting (*P. ciris*)

Dickcissel (*Spiza americana*)

SUBFAMILY EMBERIZINAE

Olive Sparrow (*Arremonops rufivirgatus*)

Green-tailed Towhee (*Pipilo chlorurus*)

Rufous-sided Towhee (*P. erythrophthalmus*)

Canyon Towhee (*P. fuscus*)

White-collared Seedeater (*Sporophila torqueola*)

Yellow-faced Grassquit (*Tiaris olivacea*) A

Bachman's Sparrow (*Aimophila aestivalis*)

Botteri's Sparrow (*A. botterii*)

Cassin's Sparrow (*A. cassinii*)

Rufous-crowned Sparrow (*A. ruficeps*)

American Tree Sparrow (*Spizella arborea*)

Chipping Sparrow (*S. passerina*)

Clay-colored Sparrow (*S. pallida*)

Brewer's Sparrow (*S. breweri*)

Field Sparrow (*S. pusilla*)

Black-chinned Sparrow (*S. atrogularis*)

Vesper Sparrow (*Pooecetes gramineus*)

Lark Sparrow (*Chondestes grammacus*)

Black-throated Sparrow (*Amphispiza bilineata*)

Sage Sparrow (*A. belli*)

Lark Bunting (*Calamospiza melanocorys*)

Savannah Sparrow (*Passerculus sandwichensis*)

Baird's Sparrow (*Ammodramus bairdii*)

Grasshopper Sparrow (*A. savannarum*)

Henslow's Sparrow (*A. henslowii*) A

Le Conte's Sparrow (*A. leconteii*)

Sharp-tailed Sparrow (*A. caudacutus*)

Seaside Sparrow (*A. maritimus*)

Fox Sparrow (*Passerella iliaca*)

Song Sparrow (*Melospiza melodia*)

Lincoln's Sparrow (*M. lincolnii*)

Swamp Sparrow (*M. georgiana*)

White-throated Sparrow (*Zonotrichia albicollis*)

Golden-crowned Sparrow (*Z. atricapilla*) A

White-crowned Sparrow (*Z. leucophrys*)

Harris' Sparrow (*Z. querula*)

Dark-eyed Junco (*Junco hyemalis*)

Yellow-eyed Junco (*J. phaeonotus*) A

McCown's Longspur (*Calcarius mccownii*)

Lapland Longspur (*C. lapponicus*)

Smith's Longspur (*C. pictus*)

Chestnut-collared Longspur (*C. ornatus*)

Snow Bunting (*Plectrophenax nivalis*) A

SUBFAMILY ICTERINAE

Bobolink (*Dolichonyx oryzivorus*)

Red-winged Blackbird (*Agelaius phoeniceus*)

Eastern Meadowlark (*Sturnella magna*)

Western Meadowlark (*S. neglecta*)

Yellow-headed Blackbird (*Xanthocephalus xanthocephalus*)

Rusty Blackbird (*Euphagus carolinus*)

Brewer's Blackbird (*E. cyanocephalus*)

Great-tailed Grackle (*Quiscalus mexicanus*)

Boat-tailed Grackle (*Q. major*)

Common Grackle (*Q. quiscula*)

Shiny Cowbird (*Molothrus bonariensis*) A

Bronzed Cowbird (*M. aeneus*)

Brown-headed Cowbird (*M. ater*)

Black-vented Oriole (*Icterus wagleri*) A

Orchard Oriole (*I. spurius*)

Hooded Oriole (*I. cucullatus*)

Altamira Oriole (*I. gularis*)

Audubon's Oriole (*I. graduacauda*)

Northern Oriole (*I. galbula*)

Scott's Oriole (*I. parisorum*)

FAMILY FRINGILLIDAE

SUBFAMILY CARDUELINAE

Pine Grosbeak (*Pinicola enucleator*) A

Purple Finch (*Carpodacus purpureus*)

Cassin's Finch (*C. cassinii*)

House Finch (*C. mexicanus*)

Red Crossbill (*Loxia curvirostra*)

White-winged Crossbill (*L. leucoptera*) A

Common Redpoll (*Carduelis flammea*) A

Pine Siskin (*C. pinus*)

Lesser Goldfinch (*C. psaltria*)

Lawrence's Goldfinch (*C. lawrencei*) A

American Goldfinch (*C. tristis*)

Evening Grosbeak (*Coccothraustes vespertinus*)

FAMILY PASSERIDAE

House Sparrow (*Passer domesticus*) I

Bird books number into the thousands and vary enormously in style and scope. During the writing of this book, the author had at his disposal several hundred volumes including identification guides, bird-finding guides, ornithology texts and references, and monographs on specific families and groups of birds. Some of the most useful are included here.

American Ornithologists' Union. 1983. *Check-list of North American birds.* 6th ed. Lawrence, KS: Allen Press.

_____. 1985. Thirty-fifth supplement to the American Ornithologists' Union check-list of North American birds. *The Auk* 102: 680-686.

_____. 1987. Thirty-sixth supplement to the American Ornithologists' Union check-list of North American birds. *The Auk* 104: 591-596.

_____. 1989. Thirty-seventh supplement to the American Ornithologists' Union check-list of North American birds. *The Auk* 106: 532-538.

_____. 1991. Thirty-eighth supplement to the American Ornithologists' Union check-list of North American birds. *The Auk* 108: 750-754.

Angell, Tony. 1978. *Ravens, crows, magpies, and jays.* Seattle: University of Washington Press.

Bedichek, Roy. 1961. *Adventures with a Texas naturalist.* rev. ed. Austin: University of Texas Press.

Bellrose, Frank C. 1980. *Ducks, geese and swans of North America.* 3rd ed. Harrisburg, PA: Stackpole Books.

Bent, Arthur Cleveland. 1961-1968. *Life histories of North American birds.* 26 vols. New York: Dover Publications.

Brooke, Michael, and Tim Birkhead. 1991. *The Cambridge encyclopedia of ornithology.* Cambridge: Cambridge University Press.

Brooks, Bruce. 1989. *On the wing: The life of birds from feathers to flight.* New York: Charles Scribner's Sons.

Bryan, Kelly, Tony Gallucci, Greg Lasley, and David H. Riskind. 1991. *A checklist of Texas birds.* Austin: Texas Parks & Wildlife Department.

Burton, John A., ed. 1973. *Owls of the world: Their evolution, structure and ecology.* New York: A&W Visual Library.

Burton, Robert. 1985. *Bird behavior.* New York: Alfred A. Knopf.

Chandler, Richard J. 1989. *The Facts on File field guide to North Atlantic shorebirds.* New York: Facts on File.

Choate, Ernest A. 1985. *The dictionary of American bird names.* rev. by Raymond A. Paynter, Jr. Harvard and Boston: The Harvard Common Press.

Clark, William S., and Brian K. Wheeler. 1987. *A field guide to hawks of North America.* Boston: Houghton Mifflin Co.

Cleave, Andrew. 1990. *Hummingbirds.* New York: Dorset Press.

Clements, James F. 1991. *Birds of the world: A check list.* 4th ed. Vista, CA: Ibis Publishing Co.

Dauphin, David T., A. Noel Pettingell, and Edward R. Rozenburg. 1989. *A birder's checklist of the upper Texas coast.* 7th ed. Houston: Ornithology Group, Houston Outdoor Nature Club.

Doughty, Robin W. 1983. *Wildlife and man in Texas: Environmental change and conservation.* College Station: Texas A&M University Press.

_____. 1988. *The mockingbird.* Austin: University of Texas Press.

_____. 1989. *Return of the whooping crane.* Austin: University of Texas Press.

Dunne, Pete, David Sibley, and Clay Sutton. 1988. *Hawks in flight.* Boston: Houghton Mifflin Co.

Eckert, Allan W., and Karl E. Karalus. 1987. *The owls of North America.* New York: Weathervane Books.

_____. 1987. *The wading birds of North America.* New York: Weathervane Books.

Ehrlich, Paul R., David S. Dobkin, and Darryl Wheye. 1988. *The birder's handbook: A field guide to the natural history of North American birds.* New York: Simon & Schuster.

_____. 1992. *Birds in jeopardy: The imperiled and extinct birds of the United States and Canada, including Hawaii and Puerto Rico.* Stanford, CA: Stanford University Press.

Farrand, John, Jr., ed. 1983. *The Audubon Society master guide to birding.* 3 vols. New York: Alfred A. Knopf.

Goodwin, Derek. 1976. *Crows of the world.* Ithaca, NY: Cornell University Press.

_____. 1983. *Pigeons and doves of the world.* 3rd ed. Ithaca, NY: Cornell University Press.

Grant, P. J. 1986. *Gulls: A guide to identification.* 2nd ed. Vermillion, SD: Buteo Books.

Gruson, Edward S. 1972. *Words for birds: A lexicon of North American birds with biographical notes.* New York: Quadrangle Books.

Halliday, Tim. 1978. *Vanishing birds: Their natural history and conservation.* New York: Holt, Rinehart & Winston.

Hancock, James, and Hugh Elliott. 1978. *The herons of the world.* New York: Harper & Row.

Harrison, Colin. 1978. *A field guide to the nests, eggs and nestlings of North American birds.* Cleveland and New York: Collins.

Harrison, Hal H. 1984. *Wood warblers' world.* New York: Simon & Schuster.

Harrison, Peter. 1983. *Seabirds: An identification guide.* Boston: Houghton Mifflin Co.

_____. 1987. *A field guide to seabirds of the world.* Lexington, MA: The Stephen Greene Press.

Hayman, Peter, John Marchant, and Tony Prater. 1986. *Shorebirds: An identification guide to the waders of the world.* Boston: Houghton Mifflin Co.

Holt, Harold R. 1992. *A birder's guide to the Rio Grande Valley of Texas.* Colorado Springs: American Birding Association.

Isler, Morton L., and Phyllis R. Isler. 1987. *The tanagers: Natural history, distribution, and identification.* Washington, D.C.: Smithsonian Institution Press.

Johnsgard, Paul A. 1975. *North American game birds of upland and shoreline.* Lincoln: University of Nebraska Press.

_____. 1981. *The plovers, sandpipers, and snipes of the world.* Lincoln: University of Nebraska Press.

Kaufman, Kenn. 1990. *A field*

guide to advanced birding. Boston: Houghton Mifflin Co.

Kilham, Lawrence. 1989. *The American crow and the common raven.* College Station: Texas A&M University Press.

Kress, Stephen W. 1981. *The Audubon Society handbook for birders.* New York: Charles Scribner's Sons.

_____. 1985. *The Audubon Society guide to attracting birds.* New York: Charles Scribner's Sons.

Krutch, Joseph Wood, and Paul S. Eriksson, eds. 1962. *A treasury of birdlore.* New York: Paul S. Eriksson.

Kutac, Edward A. 1989. *Birder's guide to Texas.* Houston: Lone Star Books.

Lane, James A., and John L. Tveten. 1984. *A birder's guide to the Texas coast.* Denver: L&P Press.

Leahy, Christopher. 1982. *The birdwatcher's companion: An encyclopedic handbook of North American birdlife.* New York: Hill & Wang.

Long, John L. 1981. *Introduced birds of the world: The worldwide history, distribution and influence of birds introduced to new environments.* London: David & Charles.

Lowery, George H., Jr. 1974. *Louisiana birds.* 3rd ed. Baton Rouge: Louisiana State University Press.

Mackenzie, John P. S. 1977. *Birds in peril: A guide to the endangered birds of the United States and Canada.* Boston: Houghton Mifflin Co.

Madge, Steve, and Hilary Burn. 1988. *Waterfowl: An identification guide to the ducks, geese and swans of the world.* Boston: Houghton Mifflin Co.

McClung, Robert M. 1979. *America's endangered birds: Programs and people working to save them.* New York: William Morrow & Co.

McFarlane, Robert W. 1992. *A stillness in the pines: The ecology of the red-cockaded woodpecker.* New York: W. W. Norton & Co.

National Geographic Society. 1987. *Field guide to the birds of North America.* 2nd ed. Washington, D.C.

Oberholser, Harry C. 1974. *The bird life of Texas.* 2 vols. Edited by Edgar B. Kincaid, Jr. Austin: University of Texas Press.

Page, Jake, and Eugene S. Morton. 1989. *Lords of the air: The Smithsonian book of birds.* New York: Orion Books.

Peterson, Roger Tory. 1960. *A field guide to the birds of Texas.* Boston: Houghton Mifflin Co.

_____. 1980. *A field guide to the birds.* 4th ed. Boston: Houghton Mifflin Co.

_____. 1990. *A field guide to western birds.* 3rd ed. Boston: Houghton Mifflin Co.

Peterson, Roger Tory, and Edward L. Chalif. 1973. *A field guide to Mexican birds.* Boston: Houghton Mifflin Co.

Pulich, Warren M. 1976. *The golden-cheeked warbler: A bioecological study.* Austin: Texas Parks & Wildlife Department.

_____. 1988. *The birds of north central Texas.* College Station: Texas A&M University Press.

Rappole, John H., and Gene W. Blacklock. 1985. *Birds of the Texas Coastal Bend: Abundance and distribution.* College Station: Texas A&M University Press.

Reader's Digest. 1990. *Book of North American Birds.* Pleasantville, NY: The Reader's Digest Association.

Reilly, Edgar M., Jr. 1968. *The Audubon illustrated handbook of American birds.* New York: McGraw-Hill Book Co.

Robbins, Chandler S., Bertel Bruun, and Herbert S. Zim. 1983. *Birds of North America: A guide to field identification.* rev. ed. New York: Golden Press.

Robison, B. C., and John L. Tveten. 1990. *Birds of Houston.* Houston: Rice University Press.

Shortt, Terence Michael. 1977. *Wild birds of the Americas.* Boston: Houghton Mifflin Co.

Skutch, Alexander F. 1976. *Parent birds and their young.* Austin: University of Texas Press.

_____. 1987. *Helpers at birds' nests: A worldwide survey of cooperative breeding and related behavior.* Iowa City: University of Iowa Press.

Sparks, John, and Tony Soper. 1970. *Owls: Their natural and unnatural history.* New York: Taplinger Publishing Co.

Stokes, Donald W., and Lillian Q. Stokes. 1989. *The hummingbird book: The complete guide to attracting, identifying, and enjoying hummingbirds.* Boston: Little, Brown & Co.

Terres, John K. 1980. *The Audubon Society encyclopedia of North American birds.* New York: Alfred A. Knopf.

Tyrrell, Esther Quesada, and Robert A. Tyrrell. 1985. *Hummingbirds: Their life and behavior.* New York: Crown Publishers.

Walker, Lewis Wayne. 1974. *The book of owls.* New York: Alfred A. Knopf.

Walkinshaw, Lawrence. 1973. *Cranes of the world.* New York: Winchester Press.

Wauer, Roland H. 1973. *Birds of Big Bend National Park and vicinity.* Austin: University of Texas Press.

Welty, Joel Carl. 1975. *The life of birds.* 2nd ed. Philadelphia: W. B. Saunders Co.

Wetmore, Alexander, et al. 1964. *Song and garden birds of North America.* Washington, D.C.: National Geographic Society.

_____. 1965. *Water, prey, and game birds of North America.* Washington, D.C.: National Geographic Society.

Zimmer, Kevin J. 1985. *The western bird watcher: An introduction to birding in the American West.* Englewood Cliffs, NJ: Prentice-Hall.

McCown's, 353
Smith's, 353
Loon
common, 51, 52-53
Pacific, 53
red-throated, 53

Mallard, 78
Martin, purple, 23, 256-57
Meadowlark, eastern, 327, 340-41
Meadowlark, western, 1, 327, 340-41
Melanerpes aurifrons, 217-18
Melanerpes carolinas, 214, 218-19
Melanerpes erythrocephalus, 215
Melanerpes formicivorus, 212-13, 216-17
Melanitta perspicillata, 88
Meleagris gallopavo, 178-79, 183-84
Melospiza lincolnii, 359
Melospiza melodia, 358-59
Merganser
common, 90
hooded, 90
red-breasted, 90-91
Mergus merganser, 90
Mergus serrator, 90-91
Mimidae, 292-96
Mimus polyglottos, 155, 292-94
Mniotilta varia, 316-17
Mockingbird, northern, 155, 292-94
Molothrus aeneus, 327, 336-37
Molothrus ater, 230-31, 321, 335-36
Moorhen, common, 62, 64
Morus bassanus, 94-95
Motacillidae, 297
Muleshoe National Wildlife Refuge, 49
Muscicapidae, 281-91
Mycteria americana, 45
Myiarchus crinitus, 247
Myiarchus cinerascens, 246-47
Myiopsitta monachus, 233-34

Names, 14-18
Nighthawk
common, 190-91
lesser, 191
Nightjars, 190-93
chuck-will's-widow, 192
common nighthawk, 190-91
common poorwill, 193
lesser nighthawk, 191
pauraque, 190, 192
whip-poor-will, 190, 192
Numenius americanus, 20, 133
Nuthatches, 212, 227
brown-headed, 227
pygmy, 227
red-breasted, 227-28
white-breasted, 228

Nyctanassa violacea, 40
Nycticorax nycticorax, 39-40

Orioles, 18, 308, 327
Altamira, 339-40
Audubon's, 340
hooded, 340
northern, 338-39
orchard, 337-38
Scott's, 340
Ortalis vetula, 187
Osprey, 142-43, 144-45, 146
Otus asio, 170-71
Otus kennicottii, 170-71
Owls, 169
barn, 176-77
barred, 174
burrowing, 173
eastern screech-, 170-71
great horned, 169, 171-72
long-eared, 175
short-eared, 175
snowy, 177
spotted, 174
western screech-, 170-71
Oxyura jamaicensis, 91
Oystercatcher, American, 117-19, 125-26

Padre Island, 7, 86
Pandion haliaetus, 142-43, 146
Pandionidae, 144
Parabuteo unicinctus, 144, 155
Parakeet
Carolina, 232
green, 232, 234-35
monk, 233-34
Parasitism
by cliff swallows, 259
by cowbirds, 306, 312, 315, 317, 321, 335, 338
by ducks, 85, 91
by starlings, 303
Paridae, 272-74
Parrots, 231, 232-35
red-crowned, 234
red-lored, 234
yellow-headed, 234
Parula, northern, 308, 311
Parula, tropical, 311
Parula americana, 308, 311
Parulinae, 308-22
Parus bicolor, 27, 272, 274
Parus carolinensis, 273
Passerculus sandwichensis, 357-58
Passer domesticus, 363-64
Passeridae, 363-64
Passerina ciris, 348
Passerina cyanea, 347

Pauraque, 190, 192
Pelecanidae, 96-99
Pelecanus erythrorhynchos, 97-98
Pelecanus occidentalis, 96, 98-99
Pelican, American white, 93, 96, 97-98
Pelican, brown, 93, 96, 98-99
Phalacrocoracidae, 57-59
Phalacrocorax auritus, 57-58
Phalacrocorax brasilianus, 57, 59
Phalaenoptilus nuttallii, 193
Phalarope
red, 141
red-necked, 141
Wilson's, 141
Phalaropus tricolor, 141
Phasianidae, 180-86
Phasianus colchicus, 180, 181
Pheasant, ring-necked, 180, 181
Pheucticus ludovicianus, 344-45
Pheucticus melanocephalus, 345
Phoebe
black, 251
eastern, 249-50
Say's, 250
Picidae, 214-26
Picoides borealis, 222-23
Picoides pubescens, 221-22
Picoides scalaris, 220-21
Picoides villosus, 222
Pigeons, 194-96. *See also* Doves
band-tailed, 198
passenger, 14, 30, 194
red-billed, 198
rock dove, 197-98
Pipilo erythrophthalmus, 25, 350-51
Pipilo fuscus, 351-52
Pipit, American, 297
Pipit, Sprague's, 297
Piranga ludoviciana, 325-26
Piranga olivacea, 324-25
Piranga rubra, 323-24
Pitangus sulphuratus, 246
Plegadis chihi, 42-43
Plovers, 117-20
black-bellied, 120-21
killdeer, 120, 124
lesser golden-, 121-22
mountain, 120
piping, 123
snowy, 123
Wilson's, 122-23
Plumage variation, 18-20, 69
Pluvialis dominica, 121-22
Pluvialis squatarola, 120-21
Podiceps nigricollis, 54, 56
Podicipedidae, 54-56
Podilymbus podiceps, 54-55
Polioptila caerulea, 283-84